90731

# DAILY LIFE IN

## TRADITIONAL
## CHINA

**The Greenwood Press "Daily Life Through History" Series**

# DAILY LIFE IN

## TRADITIONAL CHINA
## The Tang Dynasty

### CHARLES BENN

The Greenwood Press "Daily Life Through History" Series

**GREENWOOD PRESS**
Westport, Connecticut • London

**Library of Congress Cataloging-in-Publication Data**

Benn, Charles D., 1943–
  Daily life in traditional China : the Tang dynasty / by Charles Benn.
    p.  cm.—(The Greenwood Press "Daily life through history" series, ISSN 1080–4749)
  Includes bibliographical references and index.
  ISBN 0–313–30955–8 (alk. paper)
    1. China—Social life and customs.  2. China—History—Tang dynasty, 618–907.
  I. Title.  II. Greenwood Press "Daily life through history" series.
  DS721.B44  2002
  951'.017—dc21        2001023839

British Library Cataloguing in Publication Data is available.

Library of Congress Catalog Card Number: 2001023839
ISBN: 0–313–30955–8
ISSN: 1080–4749

First published in 2002

Greenwood Press, 88 Post Road West, Westport, CT 06881
An imprint of Greenwood Publishing Group, Inc.
www.greenwood.com

Printed in the United States of America

The paper used in this book complies with the
Permanent Paper Standard issued by the National
Information Standards Organization (Z39.48–1984).

10 9 8 7 6 5 4 3 2 1

This book is dedicated to Liana,
without whose support and encouragement
it would never have been completed

# Contents

# Preface

This text is the product of a college course titled "Daily Life in Traditional China" that I have taught half a dozen times. The objective of the course was to introduce students of history, philosophy, religion, literature, art, and other disciplines to the "nitty-gritty" of ancient China. Its content covered the physical and material aspects (from toilets to tombs), as well as the customs, of premodern times (from festivals to funerals), features that are sometimes overlooked in courses that concentrate on theoretical issues. The scope of the course, however, is far too large for a modest survey such as this since it covers 3,000 years. Consequently this work will cover the Tang dynasty (618–907) only, an epoch of some 300 years that is the period of my scholarly endeavors.

The Tang dynasty is worthy of special treatment because it was the golden age of Chinese culture, at least in the opinion of many later Chinese. They have esteemed two of its poets as the greatest in their history. An anthology of three hundred Tang poems compiled in the eighteenth century is still the primer for children when they begin their study of verse. It was a text treasured by intellectuals sent to prison camps during the Cultural Revolution. Tang writers devised a simplified and terse form of prose that subsequently became the dominant style until the twentieth century. One of its painters was regarded as the greatest of all time for centuries after his death, even though few of his works survived the fall of the dynasty. The Tang was also one of the greatest, if not the greatest, periods in the development of music, song, and dance during Chinese history. Its law code, promulgated in 637, remained in force until the Ming dynasty (1368–1644) revised it in 1397. Forty percent of it survived until the fall of the Qing dynasty (1644–1911). It also served as the basis for the law codes of premodern Japan, Korea, and Vietnam. Two new forms of historical compilations emerged during the Tang and became standard genres in later dynasties. The dynasty was the first to compile a national materia medica (compendium of medicinal substances), a text that was also the first to have illustrations. Both printing, as well as the first printed illustrations, and gunpowder—developments that profoundly affected the emergence of the modern world—were invented during the period. The Tang was the golden age of Buddhism. The religion attracted large numbers of adherents, amassed immense wealth, and exerted great influence at court. It also produced the only uniquely Chinese sect of the religion, Chan (Zen). Finally, tea became the national drink during the dynasty.

The history of the Tang dynasty is largely the story of its patricians (nobles and mandarins), intellectuals, and clergy (Taoist priests and Buddhist monks). Annals, biographies, documents, fiction, and other sources furnish a wealth of information about the daily lives of those elites. Historians and other writers, members of the upper classes themselves, paid little attention to merchants, artisans, peasants, and slaves. Those lower classes left no writings of their own. They appear occasionally in poetry, fiction, prose sketches, accounts of legal proceedings, and so forth. Most of what is known about them derives from laws, edicts, and official reports, where they are treated collectively. With some exceptions the nature of their daily existence is obscure. Women—mainly the mothers, wives, or daughters of the elite—fared somewhat better. At least imperial recorders and other authors compiled biographies and composed obituaries for them. However, they were in a distinct minority. Tang history is largely the story of men.

The Western reader will find much in this text that is unfamiliar, perhaps bizarre. Some of the strangeness derives from cultural differences. For much of history, Europe and China developed in relative isolation from one another. The ideas and customs of the two were, and are, distinct and unique. Some of it is due to time. Eleven centuries have passed since the demise of the Tang, and great changes have taken place since then. Modern Chinese will also find many aspects of the dynasty unusual.

To a large extent the contents of this text are my own translations or paraphrases done for this book or other works that I am writing. Since the original sources are in classical Chinese accessible only to sinologists trained in that language, I have omitted notes. I have, however, appended a list of suggested readings in Western languages that can be consulted for further information on the topics covered here.

Most of the materials in *Daily Life in Traditional China: The Tang Dynasty* derive from original Tang sources or secondary studies. The most notable exception to this rule is a work on agriculture written about ninety years before the founding of the dynasty. That book contains recipes for the preparation of food, rare formulas that can be found nowhere else for several centuries after the fall of the Tang. The fact that it survived when most other texts on farming and culinary arts did not, attests to its popularity and utility long after the time of its publication. For that reason I have translated some of its recipes for the chapter on food and feasts.

All of the illustrations in this book are my own. There are two categories. The first consists of those that I composed myself, some of which appear in other works I am writing. Except for the maps and certain illustrations of clothing, they are based on woodblock illustrations from books printed during the golden age of Chinese woodcuts (1600–1650). The second consists of illustrations based on figures in Chinese texts dating from 961 to 1905. Although they are faithful to the originals in general, I have redrawn most and altered the rest—pictures from ancient Chinese works are invariably in poor shape due to age. Ink faults and irrelevant background have been excised. Broken lines have been repaired. The objective was to enhance the clarity of the illustrations (Unfortunately, during the production of this text the illustrations were reduced and have lost their original definition and clarity). In one instance I made an addition to the original. "Carving Flesh to Feed an Ailing Elder" (actually a picture of bloodletting in the Ming dynasty) does not show the wound inflicted or the blood dripping from it.

Two previous works on daily life in ancient China are well worth reading: Michael Loewe's *Everyday Life in Early Imperial China* (New York, 1970), which covers the Han period (206 B.C.E.–C.E. 220), and Jacques Gernet's *Daily Life in China on the Eve of the Mongol Invasion, 1250–1276* (trans. by H. M. Wright; Stanford, 1962).

I am deeply grateful to Emily Birch, David Palmer and the rest of the staff at Greenwood Press for editing the manuscript of this text and overseeing its production. Any errors that remain in this book are my responsibility, not theirs.

# Tang China ca. 742

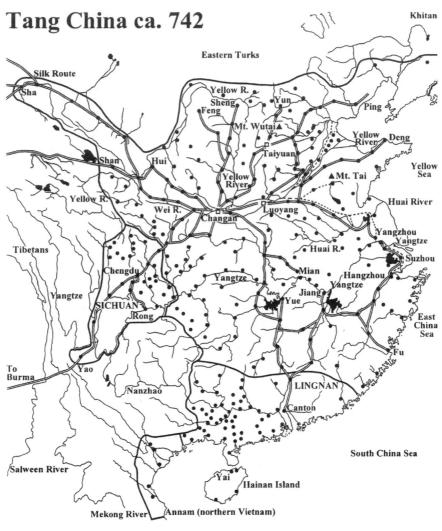

Legend

—— National or Provincial Boundaries of Tang China Proper

=== Post Road (Rapid Relay System)

- - - - Canals

• Cities and Towns

▲ Mountains

◢ Lakes

# Tang Changan

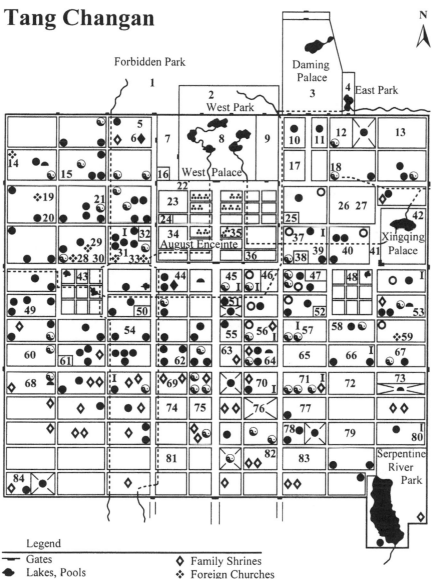

Forbidden Park

Daming Palace

West Park

East Park

West Palace

August Enceinte

Xingqing Palace

Serpentine River Park

Legend

—— Gates
🖤 Lakes, Pools
- - - - Canals
● Buddhist Monasteries
☯ Taoist Abbeys
◆ Official Temples

◇ Family Shrines
❖ Foreign Churches
⁂ Guard Units
○ Provincial Transmission Offices
I Inns, Rentals
▲ Graves

**Key to Diagram of Tang Changan**

1. Cherry orchard, pear grove, vineyard, football field, polo grounds.
2. Ice pits for refrigerating foods during the spring and summer.
3. Archery hall, bath hall, storehouse for musical instruments, drum tower, bell tower, football field, cockfighting arena, Pear Garden Troupe, Entertainment Ward.
4. A football field.
5. Barracks for the Divine Strategy Army.
6. A shrine for Lao Tzu's father.
7. The Flank Court, where women were incarcerated for the crimes that their menfolk committed. There was also a school for palace ladies here.
8. Archery hall, polo grounds, football field, drum tower, bell tower.
9. East Palace, the heir apparent's residence.
10. A branch of the Entertainment Ward that had the finest singers. A carriage park where mandarins attending court in the Daming Palace left their vehicles for the day. Empress Wu donated one of her dressing rooms to the monastery here. A family captured a "harvesting breath bag" by throwing it in a pot and pouring boiling water over it. By doing so, the kinsmen saved the life of a member who was about to die.
11. A eunuch who converted his mansion into a Buddhist monastery demanded that each guest at a feast that he held to celebrate the occasion strike the cloister's bell and donate 100,000 cash.
12. A branch of the Entertainment Ward that had the finest dancers. In 730 Emperor Illustrious August had four palace halls dismantled and reassembled as halls and gates for the Taoist abbey in the southwest corner. Formerly, the grounds of the temple were gardens for an agricultural bureau.
13. A residence for princes.
14. A Zoroastrian church.
15. In 828 a eunuch commanded fifty wrestlers to arrest 300 commoners over a land dispute here, and a riot between the grapplers and the citizens broke out in the roads of the ward.
16. Seat of the eunuch agency.
17. There was a tea shop here where palace troops captured the leaders of a failed coup against the eunuchs in 835.
18. The national Taoist abbey dedicated to the worship of Lao Tzu in this ward had statues of Illustrious August and later emperors.
19. A Persian (Nestorian) church.
20. The Inexhaustible Treasury.
21. Princess Anle's mansion.
22. This street was the site of a carnival held in 713.

23. Imperial factories.

24. Service for Supreme Justice.

25. Gold Bird Guard East. This ward had four provincial transmission offices. The home of an imperial flautist was located here. In the early ninth century an emperor spent 2 million cash to purchase the former mansion of a venerated chief minister so he could return the dwelling to the man's great-grandson.

26. Princess Tongchang's mansion. It had a well with a railing made of gold and silver.

27. A court for imperial musicians.

28. A Zoroastrian church.

29. The first site of the Persian (Nestorian) church (no. 19). The home of An Jinzang, who cut his belly open with a knife to defend Emperor Ruizong against charges of treason, was in this ward.

30. Princess Taiping's mansion.

31. A Zoroastrian church.

32. Gold Bird Guard West.

33. A Persian (Nestorian) church.

34. Imperial stables and hay fields for horses.

35. Halls for civil and military examinations.

36. The imperial ancestral shrine.

37. Twenty-five provincial transmission offices. There was a polo field in the western part of this ward.

38. At this former wedding hall for imperial princesses, An Lushan had eighty princesses, their husbands, and consorts of princes slaughtered in 756.

39. A workshop for a maker of musical instruments. By candlelight the Tang's most renowned painter, while drunk, in a single night executed a mural for a gate in the Buddhist monastery east of this ward's northern gate.

40. Three provincial transmission offices. Camel, a hunchbacked vendor of pastry, discovered a pot of gold under a pile of bricks in this ward. An angry army officer picked up a donkey mired in the mud and hurled it across a drainage ditch. Three girls played football under a tree beside a road here.

41. The street where Emperor Illustrious August convened public entertainments to celebrate his birthdays.

42. Illustrious August's aloeswood pavilion and an archery hall. A Buddhist monastery located in this area was converted into a palace in the early eighth century.

43. West Market. Lanes: Axes, Ready-Made Clothing, Bridles and Saddles, Weights and Measures, and Pongee. A Persian bazaar. Wineshops and taverns. Vendors of beverages, gruel, and cooked cereals. A safety deposit firm. The government offices for controlling commerce were located in the center block. There was a pond for releasing the living in the northwest corner.

The exact locations of the solitary willow under which most executions took place and the pool for storing wood are unknown.

44. A court for imperial musicians. The mansion of an eminent minister here had a "pavilion of automatic rain," that is, air conditioning. An academician who was injured on the forehead by a football in this ward drank twenty-five pints of ale that the emperor bestowed on him. The local school for citizens of the capital was located in the southeast corner.

45. In 720 the walls of this ward collapsed during a heavy rain. Here, Princess Taiping had a mansion, an emperor discovered that courtesans were living in a Taoist convent, and a dwarf illusionist changed herself into a bamboo stalk and a skull.

46. Capital schools: the Sons of State, Grand Learning, and Four Gates, as well as colleges for law, mathematics, and calligraphy. This ward had three provincial transmission offices.

47. North Hamlet (the Gay Quarters). The Alley of the Jingling Harness was located in the southwest. Seventeen provincial transmission offices. The mansion of a princess in the northwest corner of this ward had a polo field. The dwelling of a chief minister had a crescent-shaped hall for receiving officials. There was a portrait hall for a princess in one of the Taoist abbeys.

48. East Market. Ironmongers' Lane, a tavern, a pastry shop, and a seller of foreign musical instruments. The government offices for controlling commerce were located in the center block. In 775 a Uighur stabbed a man in broad daylight, and people in the market arrested him. There was a monastery in the market, and a pond for releasing the living in the northeast corner.

49. A Turkish prince had a mansion in this ward, as did Camel, the hunchbacked vendor of pastries (see 40).

50. The office of Changan's mayor. In the ninth century a mayor who had been forced to live in a private dwelling released prisoners to construct a residence for him in this compound.

51. The monastery occupying the entire southern half of this ward had a pond for releasing the living and the largest number of entertainment plazas in the capital. A mansion here was valued at 3 million coppers in the ninth century.

52. The offices of Wannian County, the eastern half of the city. The chieftain of the Uighurs broke into the county prison, freed the culprit who stabbed a man in East Market and wounded the wardens. In the seventh century Emperor Gaozong held the wedding feast for his daughter, Princess Taiping, in this office compound. This ward had six provincial transmission offices.

53. The brewery of Toad Tumulus Ale was located in this ward. In 788 a gang of four thieves killed their arresting officer here and then fled the city.

54. A bureau for managing the households of princes. In 613 a family threw their gold into the well of their mansion because they feared the government

would confiscate it. In 656 the throne converted the dwelling into the south-western monastery.

55. A chief minister's mansion here had a pavilion with walls that were covered with a plaster made from an aromatic plant that came from Central Asia. The Tang's Small Goose Pagoda in the northwest corner survives today.

56. A shop that sold fancy pastry. One of the monasteries here had a statue of Buddha carved out of jade from Central Asia.

57. One of the Taoist abbeys in this ward was originally a lavish mansion that Emperor Illustrious August bestowed on An Lushan. In the mid-eighth century the household of a general here numbered 3,000. A mandarin raised ducks and geese in a garden courtyard of his mansion. An official died at the inn in this ward.

58. A vendor peddled pastry here. After the son of a military governor returned his father's mansion to the throne, the emperor bestowed feasts on his mandarins at the garden there.

59. Zoroastrian church. Felt Alley. One provincial transmission office. There was a large polo field in the vacant land to the west that was attached to the mansion of a princess in the early eighth century.

60. There was a firm here that hired out square-faced exorcists and rented hearses and other equipment for funerals.

61. The offices for Changan County, the western half of the city.

62. Graduates of the Advanced Scholars examination held "cherry feasts" at the Pavilion of Buddha's Tooth in the southwestern monastery to commemorate their triumph. A mint for casting copper cash.

63. Illustrious August abolished the shrine for an imperial princess here and bestowed the property on a close aide for use as a polo field.

64. During construction of a chief minister's mansion, workmen dug a pit in the northeast corner of the property that disturbed the *fengshui* and destroyed the future of the mandarin's sons. In another dwelling a man, with the help of a ghost, dug up a pot containing forty-five pounds of gold. The monastery in the south had an entertainment plaza.

65. City archives, Directorate for Astronomy, and a garden that Illustrious August bestowed on An Lushan. After the death of a chief minister, a thief stole rare books and paintings hidden in a secret space between two walls at the mandarin's mansion, removed their gold and jade rollers, and discarded the books and paintings. The throne demoted an official when it discovered that he had assembled a large number of female entertainers in a dwelling here that was not his home. Three maidservants committed suicide by leaping into a well and drowning themselves when Huang Chao's men invaded their mistress's mansion.

66. An Entertainment Ward and the Board for Fife and Drum Music. Two fortune tellers lived here. An oil vendor bearing a vat on his back refused to

yield the road in an alley to an official during the night. The leader of the mandarin's entourage struck him on the head, knocking him down.

67. The assassins of Chief Minister Wu hid in the bamboo grove of a mansion here after committing the murder. In this ward crowds of people flocked to the home of a superb physiognomist, or face reader, to have their fortunes told. The Buddhist monastery here had an entertainment plaza.

68. The owner of a mansion here exhumed and reburied the remains of a long-dead general because the grave was too close to the dwelling's privy.

69. In 849 officials impeached an imperial son-in-law for erecting a building that encroached on the avenue outside this ward.

70. In 815 assassins murdered Chief Minister Wu as he was leaving the eastern gate of this ward in the predawn hours. An official died at the inn here.

71. A provincial official in town to attend an imperial audience died in the inn here. This ward had a pond for releasing the living.

72. A medicinal garden for the heir apparent was located in the northwest corner. A pastry shop stood beside the north gate. The ruins of an ancient shrine marked the highest point in the city. Citizens visited the spot to purify themselves on the third day of the third moon and ninth day of the ninth moon.

73. The southern half of this ward was entirely occupied by graves. It had no dwellings.

74. An Lushan's garden.

75. Graduates of the Advanced Scholars examination held "peony parties" at a pavilion in a garden here to celebrate their success. A mandarin built himself a studio in a secluded area of his garden so that he could get away from company to hum and whistle.

76. A field for training soldiers in the use of the crossbow occupied this entire ward. In the seventh century it had been a market for selling slaves, horses, cattle, and donkeys.

77. A haunted house. The monastery here had a room for making monk's robes. A mansion had a mural depicting the "Rainbow Skirt," a song and dance number that Illustrious August purportedly learned while on a voyage to the moon. A woman and her father sang songs in the streets to eke out a living until a general took her in as one of his entertainers.

78. The monastery on the right had more than ten courtyards and 1,897 bays. Its pagoda, the Large Goose, where graduates of the Advanced Scholars examination inscribed their names in the Tang, survives today. It also had a bathhouse and an entertainment plaza. The monastery on the lower left had a pond for releasing the living. A mansion in this ward had a bathhouse.

79. Graduates of the Advanced Scholars examination held peony parties to mark their achievements at two government pavilions in this ward.

80. The inn here was attached to a rapid relay post station.

81. A garden in this ward provided food for the heir apparent's household.

82. Among other things, the government garden here supplied pear blossom honey.

83. Apricot grove where graduates of the Advanced Scholars examination celebrated their success with feasts.

84. At the monastery on the right a 330-foot-tall pagoda was erected to counter the adverse yin forces of a lake west of the city. Its cloisters had one of Buddha's teeth, three inches long, that a pilgrim brought from India.

# Reigns of Tang Emperors

| | |
|---|---|
| Gaozu | 618–626 |
| Taizong | 626–649 |
| Gaozong | 649–683 |
| Zhongzong | 684 |
| Ruizong | 684–690 |

## ZHOU DYNASTY

| | |
|---|---|
| Empress Wu | 690–705 |
| Zhongzong | 705–710 |
| Shaodi | 710 |
| Ruizong | 710–712 |
| Xuanzong, Illustrious August | 712–756 |
| Suzong | 756–762 |
| Daizong | 762–779 |
| Dezong | 779–805 |
| Shunzong | 805 |
| Xianzong | 805–820 |
| Muzong | 820–824 |
| Jingzong | 824–827 |
| Wenzong | 827–840 |

# DAILY LIFE IN

## TRADITIONAL
## CHINA

# 1

# History

## REBELLION (617–618)

The Tang was the successor to the Sui (581–618), the dynasty that unified China after nearly four centuries of division. Despite that monumental achievement, the second ruler of the Sui squandered the state's resources, human and material, on three disastrous campaigns of conquest against northern Korea in 612, 613, and 614. Those debacles caused widespread disaffection and rebellions throughout northern China. In the face of mounting insurrections, the Sui court fled south to Yangzhou. After the emperor abandoned his capital Luoyang in the north, one of his commanders, Li Yuan—the Duke of Tang, known posthumously as Gaozu—rose in revolt. Li led his armies out of his base at Taiyuan and marched southwest to seize the western capital, a feat that he accomplished in late 617.

## RECONSTRUCTION (618–683)

On June 18, 618, Gaozu assumed the throne, adopted the name of his fief Tang as the title of his new dynasty, and changed the name of the western capital to Changan. His declaration of sovereignty was audacious and premature because he had not yet subjugated other anti-Sui contenders for power or conquered all of China. It was not until 624 that Tang forces defeated his last major rivals. However, Gaozu's troubles were not over. As soon as he established his dominion over China proper, the Eastern Turks north of his borders began making trouble by launching numerous incursions into China. Their depredations continued for six years before the armies of the second Tang emperor, Taizong, finally vanquished them. Thereafter the empire enjoyed more than half a century of peace and stability.

The rebellions against the Sui exacted a heavy toll on China's population. During the last years of the Sui, rebels impressed large numbers of able-bodied men to serve in their armies, and consequently the people were unable to sustain themselves through farming or other occupations. Military service at the time was so onerous that men took to breaking their limbs to escape forced conscription. They called their arms and legs "propitious paws" and "fortunate feet." The custom persisted well into the Tang dynasty. In 642 the emperor issued a decree increasing the punishment for deliberately inflicting wounds on oneself in an effort to eradicate the practice.

The Turkish invasions were equally devastating. According to a report written in 629, more than 1 million Chinese had surrendered to, fled to, or been abducted by the Eastern Turks in the last years of the Sui and the early years of the Tang. In 631, after the defeat of the Eastern Turks, the throne sent an envoy bearing gold and silk to redeem Chinese whom the Turks had enslaved. The emissary managed to save 80,000 men and women.

Soon after assuming the throne, Gaozu set to work restoring the imperial government that he had inherited from the Sui. At the apex of it were the chief ministers, the most powerful bureaucrats in the country.[1] They served on a council responsible for making policy decisions. Theoretically, they met with the emperor daily, but that was often not the case. The most powerful agencies in the government were three secretariats charged with composing and transmitting edicts as well as supplying advice. One of them also controlled the six departments—personnel, rites, war, households (revenue), justice, and public works—that implemented the decisions made by the throne. In addition there was an independent censorial agency that was responsible for maintaining surveillance over the conduct of officials to prevent corruption and misconduct. Another class of censors was in charge specifically of monitoring the behavior of the emperor and admonishing him for his faults and shortcomings. In fact, it was the custom that any official could reprove him for his mistakes and wrongdoings. Such censure might, however, cost him his head. Gaozu also reconstituted local government—the prefectures and beneath them the counties—as his armies conquered new territories. Furthermore, he reestablished the civil service examinations, reopened colleges in the capital, and established schools in all prefectures and counties to provide the government with qualified candidates for appointment to offices.

To provide security, the Tang established frontier garrisons containing large numbers of Eastern Turkish cavalry that had surrendered to the Tang in 630, instituted a number of regional commands that controlled military affairs in large areas, and restored the old militia system. As rationalized in 636, the militia, known as the Intrepid Militia, had 633 units. More than one-third of the troops were stationed in the immediate vicinity of Changan, and the rest around Luoyang and in the northeast. The soldiers, preferably from large and well-to-do families, served from the ages of twenty-one to sixty. They trained in the slack farming seasons (fall and winter), participated in formal battle exercises as well as a great hunt at the end of the winter, and enjoyed exemption from taxes and compulsory labor. The troops rotated into positions as members of the twelve guards of the emperor or the six guards of the heir apparent for short terms. As such they functioned as defenders of the capitals. The government supplied them with pack mules or horses, provisions, armor, weapons, and tents.

The most pressing problem for the Tang in the early seventh century was the restoration of fiscal solvency. The government's granaries and treasuries were virtually empty at the dynasty's founding. The state therefore reinstituted the "equal fields" system because it ensured a steady flow of tax revenues. The state parceled out land, all of which the emperor theoretically owned, in equal shares to the peasants. It allocated approximately thirteen and a third acres to all adult males between the ages of seventeen and fifty-nine, their working years. In return the farmers had to pay two kinds of taxes annually: an amount of grain equivalent to 2 or 3 percent of the annual harvest for each male adult in the family (women were tax-exempt), and twenty feet of silk or twenty-five feet of linen that their women wove. Males also owed the central government twenty days of compulsory labor (corvée) and the local government two months of special duty (corvée). Local officials took a census every three years and redistributed the land. They reclaimed 80 percent of it from men sixty years of age and, on the basis of it, redistributed it to men who had reached the age of seventeen.

The throne also took measures to establish a viable currency in the wake of large-scale counterfeiting that had broken out at the end of the Sui dynasty. In 621 the emperor ordered the minting of new coppers that had uniform shapes, weights, and metal content. He also imposed the death penalty on anyone caught privately casting coins. By 755 the government had eleven mints with ninety-nine furnaces producing coins in various places in China. Those coppers, also called cash, were small, round coins with a square hole in the center. The hole permitted the threading of coins on cords. A string of 1,000 coppers constituted the next higher unit of currency. Needless to say, large quantities of cash were very bulky and difficult to transport. Consequently, it was the prac-

**A Tang Copper**

tice in Tang China to make payments for large transactions in gold, silver, and silk.

In the seventh century Tang forces extended Chinese dominion over a territory greater in extent than previously known. By 661 the armies had established the dynasty's sway over Central Asia as far as a point north of Kashmir, on the border with Persia. In 668 a combined force of Chinese and southern Koreans (Silla) conquered northern Korea (Koguryŏ), a feat that had eluded both the last emperor of the Sui and Emperor Taizong. However, the Tang was not able to subjugate the country completely. Furthermore, a new and very powerful kingdom in Tibet began to encroach on China's western territories.

The era ended on a sad note. Due to floods, droughts, locust plagues, and epidemics, famine broke out in the two capitals in 682. The corpses of the dead lined the streets, and citizens resorted to cannibalism in order to survive. The scarcity of food drove the price of grain to unprecedented heights.

## USURPATION, OVERTHROW, AND CORRUPTION (684–712)

The period following the death of the third Tang emperor on December 27, 683, was unique in the annals of Chinese history. It was singular because a remarkable woman, Empress Wu, ruled the empire in her own right. Gaozong, her husband, suffered from a chronic illness, perhaps a stroke, that left him subject to dizziness, paralysis, and impaired vision. He was also weak-willed. Taking advantage of the situation, the empress assumed the power behind the throne by 660 and became monarch in reality if not in name. After Gaozong's death she deposed her eldest son, Zhongzong, and sent him into exile. Then she installed her second son, Ruizong, on the throne and governed for the next six years as a regent, the manner by which women in traditional China took control of the government. In 690 she deposed Ruizong, overthrew the Tang, assumed the throne, and established her own dynasty, the Zhou (690–705). She was the only woman in Chinese history to accomplish such a feat.

The daughter of a lumber merchant, Empress Wu was extremely gifted and intelligent and had a natural gift for politics, a superb ability to judge men, and an exceptional talent for manipulating them. However, she also was singularly ruthless and cruel. After a rebellion against her regime broke out in Yangzhou during 684, she initiated a reign of terror that grew in intensity over the next decade. She established a secret service to ferret out her enemies, or those supposed to be her foes, and in 690 established a special investigative office at a gate in Luoyang where her agents subjected suspected traitors to unspeakable tortures. The persecution culminated in the exile and executions of thousands. At first directed at members of the Tang clan (the Lis), it eventually came to encompass anyone she thought to be a threat to her power, from chief ministers to palace servants. Many, if not most, of the prosecutions during that period were unjust. Numerous innocent men and woman died as result of false accusations or the caprice of her agents. Others suffered from physical disabilities for the rest of their lives as a result of injuries inflicted by the empress's lackeys. A prince who spent ten years imprisoned in the palace received a beating several times a year. Afterward he could predict the weather. When it was about to rain, his welts would feel heavy and depressed. When it was about to clear, they felt light and vigorous.

The reign of terror ground to a halt in 693, and the empress enjoyed two years of relative calm. In 696, however, trouble erupted on China's borders. First, in the spring the Tibetans invaded from the west and inflicted a great defeat on a Chinese army less than 200 miles from Changan. Then in the summer the Khitan, a pastoral people living in the northeast, rebelled against their cruel and arrogant Chinese governor, and annihilated a Chinese force. The bodies of the slain soldiers filled a mountain valley near what is now Beijing. Then the rebels drove deep into Tang territory. The loss of Chinese troops in those battles was so heavy that the empress freed prisoners and emancipated private slaves who were willing to fight. She promised the new recruits rewards if they enlisted in her armies. To make matters worse, the Turkish khan seized several prefectures in the northwest during the fall. While holding off the Turks and Tibetans with skillful diplomacy and bribery, the empress sent a force of 200,000 troops to attack the Khitan in the summer of 697. The Khitan folded and fled to join the Turks. In the autumn of 698 the Turks invaded along a route similar to that taken by the Khitan. Empress Wu dispatched 450,000 soldiers to thwart them, but the huge force failed to expel the enemy. When she called for new recruits, less than 1,000 men responded. In desperation she recalled her eldest son from exile, installed him as heir apparent, and appointed him generalissimo of another army. Almost immediately 50,000 men volunteered to serve. Thereafter the empress was able to assemble a substantial force that compelled the khan to withdraw into the steppes.

After assuming the throne, Empress Wu instituted many changes that were intended to establish the uniqueness of her dynasty. Most of her innovations were superficial and short-lived. By and large there was no great break in the continuity of the government, society, or economy between the Tang and the Zhou dynasties. Life went on much as it had before her usurpation. Perhaps her greatest legacy was her elevation to office of men known for their intelligence and talent. A number of those men provided the government with able leadership for years after her death.

In 705 Tang loyalists deposed Empress Wu and restored Zhongzong to the throne. For the next eight years women enjoyed unprecedented power in court politics, and a dramatic upsurge in corruption occurred. Empress Wei, the wife of Zhongzong, who assumed the throne in that year, enjoyed his favor because she had given him steadfast support and talked him out of committing suicide while he was in exile between 684 and 698. Taking advantage of his goodwill and weak disposition, she promoted the rights of her daughters and sought to acquire for them the same privileges that royal princes enjoyed. At her insistence her husband established offices with staffs of officials—previously granted only to sons of the emperor—for his sister and his daughters in 706. In 709 Wei requested that Zhongzong grant women the right to bequeath hereditary privileges to their sons, previously a male prerogative only.

The princesses also pressed their causes. In 706 Princess Anle, the emperor's favorite daughter, asked him to name her heir apparent in place of his son, a request that he ignored despite his weak will. She, her sisters, and other women in the empress's clique arrogated to themselves the right to make appointments to their staffs without going through bureaucratic channels. Those commissions came at a price: the ladies charged 300,000 coppers per title. They made a princely sum from the enterprise, selling more than 1,400 appointments. They also peddled official ordination certificates to the Buddhist and Taoist clergy for 30,000 coppers apiece.[2] In 714 the authorities discovered that the women had fraudulently ordained 12,000 monks and priests. As time went on, their behavior became even more outrageous. They stole gold, jade, and priceless pieces of calligraphy from the palace treasury. The princesses also sent their servants out to abduct the children of commoners in order to enslave them for service in their households.

Empress Wei had pretensions of emulating Empress Wu, and planned to assume the throne in her own right. In 710 she had poison inserted into one of her husband's pastries. After he died, she placed a boy on the throne. Tang loyalists, however, were not about to endure another usurpation of the throne. Eighteen days after the enthronement, they stormed the palace and slew the empress and Princess Anle. For three more years another woman, Princess Taiping, the daughter of Empress

Wu, wielded great power at the imperial court. She, too, was brought down by Tang loyalists in the summer of 713, and forced to commit suicide.

## THE GOLDEN AGE (712–755)

The reign of Illustrious August (Xuanzong), as he was known popularly, was the longest (forty-four years) and most glorious epoch of the Tang. He had led the coups d'état that overthrew Empress Wei and Princess Taiping. When he came to power, he found the state's resources wanting due in part to the corruption in the preceding decades. In 714 the emperor established a policy of austerity with regard to palace expenditures, forbidding his empress, consorts, and the women of his harem to wear brocades, embroideries, pearls, and jade. He ordered his gold and silver vessels melted down to provide funds for his armies. To impress the people with his earnestness, he had the pearls, jade, and precious cloth in his treasury burned in front of a palace hall. Illustrious August also took measures against the Buddhist church. He forbade wealthy and powerful families to establish Buddhist monasteries, a means of evading taxation, and defrocked more than 30,000 spurious monks, returning them to lay life and the tax rolls.

To increase revenues, the emperor sent agents out to reregister runaway households, families who had fled the Khitan and Turkish invasions in Empress Wu's reign, military service, famines, and other hardships in the north. Most of the peasants fled south to occupy previously uncultivated lands. Being unregistered there, they evaded taxation. For those who voluntarily surrendered, the government offered six years of exemption from taxation and compulsory labor in return for a payment of 1,500 coppers. As a result the government reregistered more than 800,000 families and took in more than 1 billion cash by 724. Thereafter the government never suffered from a lack of revenue.

Illustrious August's reign was probably the most prosperous age in the Tang for the vast majority of the people. It was a period of low inflation that was in part due to the expansion of a system of granaries. Local officials bought grain when prices were low, stored it in their granaries, and sold it below market value when prices were high. That action stabilized the prices of food and prevented famines. Originally the granaries existed only in the capitals, but in 719 the emperor established them in other districts of the empire's northern, southern and western regions. Land reclamation during the period increased agricultural productivity, and a rationalization of the canal system reduced the cost of transporting grain and other commodities. Furthermore, the emperor's government efficiently maintained law and order so that there was little banditry. Travel was safe and trade flourished.

His reign was one of great humaneness and benevolence. The number of executions—the emperor had to approve all of them—carried out in the empire was only twenty-four in 730 and fifty-eight in 736. In 747 Illustrious August also abolished the death penalty. In 716, when he learned that venomous snakes were killing people in the southeast, he ordered local officials to cut down the vegetation for ten paces along both sides of public roads to ensure that serpents would not attack travelers. In 722 Illustrious August distributed lands attached to government offices to the poor, and in 744 he raised the age of liability for taxation and corvée from nineteen to twenty-two. Two years later the emperor granted tax exemptions to ten of the poorest families in every village throughout the empire. Later he raised the figure to thirty, about 5 percent of the population. During his reign he also expanded the school system and improved health care in the provinces.

A skilled musician, poet, and calligrapher, Illustrious August fostered the arts. He and his brothers patronized the most famous artists of their day, and his reign was the most glorious period of achievements in those fields. Illustrious August was especially fond of musicians, singers, and dancers. An accomplished performer on a Central Asian drum, he often personally instructed his entertainers, correcting errors that they made. The emperor was also responsible for integrating foreign and Chinese music. He was probably most renowned for establishing the Pear Garden Troupe that trained musicians and singers. Illustrious August personally selected 300 performers from a larger institution, the Entertainment Ward, and taught members of the troupe the proper way to execute choral and instrumental music. The emperor used the troupe to try out and create new music. It was his own personal company, and probably performed only at the palace in the emperor's presence.

Relative peace between China and its neighbors prevailed while Illustrious August was on the throne. The nomadic peoples of the north, as always, periodically conducted raids along the frontier to plunder. They stole grain, abducted people to serve as their slaves, and chased off livestock. Though vexing, the incursions did not endanger the security of the empire. Only the Tibetans posed a real threat, because they were intent on seizing Tang territory. The objective of their invasions at the time was not the land of China proper, but that of Tang's dependencies to the northwest. Chinese forces were usually victorious over the Tibetans during the epoch.

Peace on the frontiers was partially due to disarray among the steppe peoples, the Tang's pursuit of diplomacy rather than war, and China's lack of an expansionist policy. However, the peace was mainly the result of a defense policy that originated in the middle of the seventh century and was most vigorously pursued during the reign of Illustrious August. That policy established large, permanent armies manned by militia units and non-Chinese cavalry along the Chinese frontier. In the early eighth century the government began to appoint permanent military commanders to lead those forces so that they could mobilize quickly in the event of an attack. The commanders were given considerable discretion in governing their troops and the use of official funds to procure provisions and arms. In 737 the throne abandoned the policy of conscripting men into service. Conscripts served for only three years, during which they trained in warfare and fought battles. Once their terms expired, raw recruits replaced them and the process of training had to begin anew. The cost of moving men to the outlands was large, and the continuous instruction of green troops inefficient, so the state replaced the conscripts with long-service soldiers who were battled-hardened and had lived in the frontier garrisons for years. The defense forces became professional armies. By 742 the total number of troops in those armies had risen to nearly half a million.

While the throne was taking aggressive steps to bolster border defenses, it was ignoring the guards and armies in the capitals. By the middle of the eighth century they were ill-trained, undermanned, and led by inexperienced officers. In some instances wealthy merchants and townsmen enlisted in them to acquire tax exemptions, then hired substitutes to take their places.

Although he was a vigorous and conscientious ruler during his first decades on the throne, Emperor Illustrious August grew lax in his later years. After 736 he delegated great powers to two of his chief ministers, who assumed nearly dictatorial control over important state affairs. Furthermore, the emperor became obsessed with one of his son's wives. In 740 he ordered a eunuch to seize the woman from the prince's mansion. Then he ordained her as a Taoist priestess—no doubt as a subterfuge to forestall the scandal that the abduction would inevitably engender—and had her ensconced in one of his palaces. Five years later he defrocked her and raised her to the highest rank among his consorts. Yang Guifei, as she is known to history, was a distant descendant of the Sui's ruling house. A plump beauty, she was accomplished in music and dance, Illustrious August's passions. She and the emperor apparently spent most of their time indulging in pleasure. Yang Guifei used her immense influence over him to have her relatives appointed to some of the most important offices in the empire. Her life and its tragic end became perhaps the most famous love story in Chinese history. It was later recounted in poetry, drama, and fiction.

## TIME OF TROUBLES (756–804)

The halcyon age of Illustrious August came to an end with the rebellion of An Lushan. An's father was a Sogdian, an Indo-European people who lived in a kingdom far to the northwest of China, and his mother was a Turk. He was governor of three defense forces in the northeast with headquarters near what is now Beijing. As such, he was responsible for controlling the Khitan and other nomadic tribes in present-day Manchuria. He also enjoyed unprecedented favor from the emperor, who appointed him to high-ranking offices, dubbed him prince (a privilege usually reserved for members of the imperial clan), had a mansion built for him in Changan, and granted him the right to mint coins. By 755 An became aware that Chief Minister Yang, a cousin of Yang Guifei, in Changan was plotting to remove him from power and began to fear that he was losing the emperor's favor. Consequently, on December 16, 755, he rose in revolt with the expressed intention of destroying his enemy, the chief minister in the capital. With some 150,000 troops, An Lushan marched south, encountering very little resistance. There were no trained, battle-hardened forces to impede his way. The best of the imperial armies were stationed on distant frontiers, and recalling them would take a long time. Twenty-four days later An crossed the Yellow River, where he seized control of the Grand Canal and cut off funds and supplies to the imperial court from the south. Ten days after that, Luoyang, defended by hastily conscripted recruits, fell to his forces. Having captured a capital, the rebel was able to proclaim himself emperor and establish a new dynasty.

In the summer of 756 Illustrious August made a disastrous decision. He ordered the imperial forces that occupied a formidable defensive position at a pass on the Yellow River to advance and confront An Lushan's armies. The frontal assault turned into a debacle when the rebel troops ambushed the national armies on July 9. The way to Changan was open, and there was nothing left to defend the city. Consequently, Illustrious August with his heir apparent, Yang Guifei, Chief Minister Yang, and a small escort of troops skulked out of the capital in the predawn hours of July 14. When they reached a rapid relay station west of Changan, the troops rebelled, slew the chief minister, and demanded the life of Yang Guifei. The emperor had no choice but to order his most trusted eunuch to strangle the love of his life with a horse whip. His highness then proceeded over an arduous route to exile in Chengdu in the southwest, where he abdicated. The heir apparent made his way to a city in the northwest. Meanwhile, An Lushan had fallen ill. He suffered from deep-rooted boils on his face that caused acute pain, and he gradually lost his sight. As a result he became cruel and irascible, moods that disaffected his subordinates. In early 757 a eunuch entered his tent during the night and plunged a sword into his belly. An Lushan died from loss of blood. The rebellion, however, continued, first under the command of An's son and then of his former generals.

Although the Tang recovered its capitals in 757 and finally suppressed

An Lushan's successors in early 763, the effects of the rebellions were devastating. The first of them was the collapse of border defenses. In 756 the government withdrew troops from the south to fight An. The aborigines there took advantage of the opportunity. Their army of 200,000 men invaded the area east of Canton, burned Chinese settlements, and maintained control over the area for five years. Two years later a force of Arab and Persian pirates surrounded Canton, forcing the Chinese governor to flee. The brigands looted the government granaries and storehouses, burned dwellings, and sailed away. In 763 the Tibetans also took advantage of the Tang's military weaknesses, invaded from the west, and seized Changan, where they installed their own candidate, a Tang prince, on the throne. The occupation lasted less than a month, but it forced the court to flee again. The Tibetans continued to menace the capital, forcing the government to declare martial law in the city on four occasions between 764 and 768. They established a border between themselves and the Chinese that was only seventy-eight miles west of Changan, and repeatedly sent forces across it to raid and plunder for more than two decades. Furthermore, the Tibetans seized the northwest territories of China proper as well as Chinese settlements along the Silk Route in Central Asia. The loss of the northwest prefectures was a terrible blow to the Tang because they contained the best pastures for horses. Consequently the dynasty was short of mounts for its cavalry. It had to buy steeds from the Uighurs, who took advantage of the situation to sell the Chinese broken-down horses for outrageous prices. The Tang did not recover the northwest territories until the 840s, and warfare with the Tibetans continued sporadically until 851.

To recapture its capitals, the throne called upon the pastoral peoples of the northwest and west regions to render assistance. Of those peoples the Uighur Turks were the most able of the mounted warriors and the most important factor in the Tang's victories. In 757, as a reward for their aid in capturing Luoyang, the commander of the imperial expedition allowed them to loot the imperial treasuries and storehouses, pillage the markets, and slay defenseless citizens in the city for three days. Elements of the imperial army that thought of the city as rebel territory also participated in the plundering and carnage. The violence continued for three months. Luoyang fell to rebels once again in 759, and the emperor asked the Uighurs for further assistance. In 762 the Turks and imperial forces retook and plundered the city. The citizens of Luoyang, who were terrified of the Uighur, took refuge in pavilions at two Buddhist monasteries. The Turks set the structures ablaze, killing tens of thousands of people. The fires did not die out for many weeks. By virtue of their contribution to the restoration of the Tang, the Uighurs enjoyed something of a favored position in Changan for decades thereafter. That led to some outrageous and arrogant behavior on their part. In early 772 their legation, 300 horsemen, left the hostel for foreign emissaries without authorization and abducted boys and girls in the wards and markets of Changan. When officials tried to prevent the kidnappings, the Uighurs assaulted them. The throne sent a eunuch to mollify them, and they stopped their depredations. Seven months later the Uighurs again left the hostel without permission, chased a county commandant, and seized his horse. He dared not struggle with them, and departed on another mount. The throne tolerated their barbarous behavior because the Uighurs were essential to the success of the Tang's defense. It maintained friendly relations through marriage alliances of royal princesses to their khans.

War with the Tibetans and the vexatious relations with the Uighurs were not the most pressing problems that faced the dynasty in the late eighth century. Foremost of its predicaments was a policy of establishing military governorships in the interior of China precisely comparable to the frontier defense garrisons that Emperor Illustrious August created in the first half of the century. In order to bring a quick end to the rebellion of An Lushan, the throne appointed army commanders to raise troops in large areas of China proper. That entailed the creation of new administrative regions, called provinces, that encompassed from two to a dozen or more prefectures. By 763 there were thirty-four of them, and as many as fifty later in the century. That policy also caused the militarization of large areas of the empire. In 763 there were more than 750,000 men under arms in the new professional, standing armies. Their commanders could also call up local militia units under their control. The latter were low cost because they served on a temporary basis only and would tenaciously defend their homes. However, they were ill-trained for combat outside their native districts.

In 763, 75 percent of the governors in the provinces were military men, and 50 percent as late as 804. There were two types of commanders, the loyal and the disloyal (who were mostly former officers of An Lushan's armies). In order to avoid prolonging the campaign against the remnants of An's forces, the throne pardoned those of their leaders willing to cease hostilities and confirmed them as military governors of the territories under their control. Since the dynasty had no reliable armies of its own, except for the frontier garrisons in the northwest that could not be withdrawn in the face of Tibetan aggression until 780, it depended on the loyal governors for internal defense. Those forces, however, were not under the direct control of the court, and many of their governors submitted taxes irregularly because they needed funds to maintain their armies. As for the former rebel officers—occupying the northeast and portions of a region south of the Yellow River—they became semi-autonomous or autonomous. From 763 to 819 over thirty prefectures in the east and northeast appointed officials on their own authority and submitted no tribute or taxes. The government lost control of 25 to 30 percent of the population, as well as of the revenues that it would otherwise have received from those subjects. The court had effective control over four regions: the northwest frontier; the region around Changan; the south, including the Huai River and the Yangtze River basins; and a corridor along the Grand Canal. Except for two rebellions in 762 and 763, the south remained loyal to the dynasty and was its principal source of revenue during that period. For that reason the government made every effort to keep the Grand Canal open.

All governors acquired political control over the territories they occupied by virtue of their military power. In autonomous provinces, the military governors in many cases insisted on hereditary succession and passed their offices on to their sons. In other cases former subordinate officers fought it out to determine who would assume the governorship. The court was powerless to intervene in either event, and usually accorded de facto recognition of the new leadership. The governors of those regions openly defied orders from the central government, appointed their own followers to political offices in their spheres of influence, and levied illegal taxes. As a result, the quality of the local bureaucracy declined. Authority became decentralized, and the court in Changan was unable to prevent it because it lacked the military forces to impose its will on the governors. The throne adopted a laissez-faire attitude toward the provinces.

The next most pressing problem for the Tang was financial. When An Lushan seized the Grand Canal, he cut off the flow of grain, cloth, and money from the south to Changan. After his seizure of the capitals, the imperial government lost all of the cereals stored in its granaries and the wealth in its treasuries. As a result the court was in dire need of funds, especially to support its war effort. The throne resorted to the temporary expedient of selling ordination certificates for the Buddhist and Taoist priesthoods. In late 755 and early 756 one official collected 1 billion coppers from that activity in one northern city alone. After the recapture of the capitals the throne extended the practice to all areas of the empire and authorized the sale of titles for government posts, honorary bureaucratic titles, and noble titles as well. It also approved the sale of examination degrees that went for 100,000 cash each. Most of the purchasers of those instruments were merchants, the only group that could afford the large sums of money required to pay for them. The traders were eager to obtain them because the certificates exempted them from taxation. The court also appealed to merchants for a contribution of one-fifth of their wealth to support the war effort.

The old taxation and land systems completely collapsed after the rebellion of An Lushan. In the course of the wars many census records and tax rolls were destroyed or became obsolete because the peasants had become casualties or had migrated out of the battle zone. The government made little effort to revive the old systems after 766 and abolished them in 780. In the meantime it resorted to levying miscellaneous taxes to provide revenues for the public coffers. Those were so inadequate that the state had to reduce the salaries and other emoluments of officials as well as the incomes of the nobility. In 780 the throne abolished all of the taxes and instituted a simplified, rationalized biennial levy. Local governments collected it in the summer and autumn, when the peasants harvested their crops and were in the best position to fulfill the impositions. The law imposed the exactions on all productive classes, not just farmers. There were two categories to the biennial levy. The first was a household tax based on the size and property of the family. It was assessed on the basis of money, but often collected in kind—grain and cloth—because there was an acute shortage of coppers. The second was a land tax collected in kind that applied only to fields under cultivation. In 780 the central government sent commissioners out to establish quotas for provinces and prefectures, quotas that remained in force thereafter. Those fixed amounts applied even to regions not under direct control of Changan. The state took no interest in how local authorities collected the taxes or in how much they collected (it varied from place to place) as long as they forwarded its share to the capital. The law allocated the revenues from the biennial tax to the central government, the provinces, and the prefectures. In the first years (781–783) the funds from the new levies exceeded the total proceeds from all other sources. Although the amounts declined thereafter, the system was so successful that it survived for seven centuries.

By far the most lucrative source of funds for the central government in the late eighth century was the salt monopoly. By 780 it produced half the state's income. Commissioners ran the system. They controlled production at salt wells in the southwest, evaporation pans along the coast that processed seawater, and a small number of salt pools scattered throughout the empire. The officials recruited workers who had traditionally engaged in the occupation or chose migrants willing to take it up. In either case the salt workers were exempt from compulsory labor. The producers had to sell all of their salt to the government, which in turn sold it to merchants, adding a tax that was ten times the market value of the commodity. In addition, local officials charged the traders transit taxes as they conveyed their goods to market. Since salt was an essential item in the preservation of food, everyone needed it even if its price was exorbitant, and therefore the government profited enormously, at least when the monopoly was well run.

The half-century following the outbreak of An Lushan's rebellion was a dismal time of great suffering for the dynasty and its subjects. The rebellion wrought great destruction throughout northern China. Rebel armies destroyed libraries, stole art treasures, and abducted entertainers—singers, dancers, musicians, and acrobats. Changan and Luoyang suffered repeated lootings and became dangerous places to live from 756 to 786. Mutinies and assassinations occurred frequently in both loyal and separatist armies during those thirty years, and warfare laid waste to many areas of northern China. The latter caused many people, especially peasants, to migrate south, where peace and prosperity prevailed.

The efforts by the throne to suppress defiant, autonomous military governors, especially those of the northeast provinces, between 781 and 786 ended in disaster. At first the court was fairly successful on the battlefield, but it suffered a major defeat in 782. The following year border troops from the northwest, who were making their way to the front on orders from the emperor, rebelled when they reached Changan because the government had not issued them adequate provisions. They seized the capital, forcing the emperor to flee westward with a few of his counselors. Then their commander assumed the throne and established a new dynasty. In 784 a provincial governor seized control of the Grand Canal, completely cutting Changan off from its source of revenues and supplies in the south. The government resorted to imposing new property and sales taxes on the citizens of Changan, as well as forcing loans from merchants in the capital. Warfare came to an end the next year when the throne returned to the status quo ante by confirming the independence of the autonomous governors. That defeat humbled the emperor, and he did nothing to reassert central authority for his remaining twenty years on the throne.

## RECOVERY (805–860)

In 805 an aggressive and vigorous emperor, Xianzong, ascended the throne. He was bent on reestablishing central control over the recalcitrant autonomous provinces. In the pursuit of his ambition he had two advantages that his predecessors did not. First, the fiscal reforms of the early 780s had filled his coffers, at least during his first years on the throne, so he could afford to engage in military operations. Second, the emperor had an effective and well-trained army, the Army of Divine Strategy, under his direct control. Originally the Army of Divine Strategy, founded in 753, was a northwest border garrison. Between 760 and 761 the imperial court moved it to a base west of Luoyang, where it could defend the approaches to Changan. In 765 the throne had it transferred to the imperial park in the capital. The throne placed eunuchs in charge of it in 783, and they remained in control until the end of the dynasty. By 798 it had grown to 240,000 troops and officers. During Emperor Xianzong's reign the army participated in several expeditions sent out to quell autonomous provinces. It also defended the capital, preventing rebel forces from besieging the city.

Xianzong conducted seven major military campaigns against the autonomous, recalcitrant provinces between 806 and 819, and managed to reassert imperial authority over all but two of them. That meant the throne recovered its powers to appoint military governors (that is, hereditary succession came to an end) as well as local officials in those areas. The more than thirty prefectures in the east and northeast that the central government lost in 763 returned to the fold. Xianzong's achievements endured. After his death the empire enjoyed four decades of peace and stability during which only one revolt of any significance occurred.

Xianzong's successors proved less capable than he. The first two spent much of their time indulging in hunting, polo, and other forms of diversion. The third was frugal and more serious. He enjoyed reading and studying. However, neither he nor his predecessors were able to control the eunuchs nor instill awe in the most powerful mandarins at the capital. The eunuchs held enormous sway over the emperor in the palace while the mandarins led factions that caused strife in the bureaucracy.

Wuzong, who assumed the throne in 840, was more forceful than his predecessors, though he did not solve the problems of the eunuchs and bureaucratic factionalism. He was an ardent devotee of Taoism and intent on destroying nonindigenous religions. In 842 he launched a persecution of Buddhism as well as other foreign faiths such as Manichaeanism, Zoroastrianism, and Nestorian Christianity. His repression reached its height in 845 when the government closed 4,600 monasteries and 40,000 smaller chapels and shrines. It also defrocked all monks under the age of fifty and those over fifty who did not possess proper ordination certificates, laicizing over 250,000 clerics in all. Hysteria reigned, and rumor had it that the emperor had ordered the decapitation of all monks and nuns in the capital so that he could use their heads to fill a large pit from which earth had been excavated to build a terrace in his palace. The throne allowed only forty-nine monasteries with some 800 monks throughout the empire to remain open. During the proscription, when monasteries were destroyed, dismantled, or converted to other uses, the church lost its greatest murals, paintings, and statuary. Many of them were the works of the most renowned artists of the Tang.

The real motive for the proscription was economic, not ideological. The state was short of revenues, and the defenseless Buddhist church provided easy pickings. The government seized its slaves, cash, silk, and grain to pay the salaries of its officials. It expropriated all metal statues and bells, converting those of bronze into coins, those of gold and silver into ingots that found their way into the public purse, and those of iron into farming tools. The throne also demanded that lay owners of metal statues turn their images over to the government for destruction. The state defrocked monks and nuns in order to return them to the tax rolls, but the effect of the policy was not always what the emperor intended. Bereft of food and clothing, some of the laicized clergy formed gangs of bandits that plundered villages to steal food and clothing.

In the two decades after Emperor Wuzong's demise in early 846, his successors did much to reverse his suppression of Buddhism and restore the religion to vigor. Besides bestowing imperial patronage on the church, the throne permitted virtually everyone from the nabobs of the capital to the peasantry in the villages to restore old and establish new monasteries if they had the wherewithal to do so. Nevertheless, it is highly unlikely that Buddhism ever fully recovered from the proscription. In a scant twenty years the number of monasteries, the size of the clergy, and the extent of its landholdings and wealth could scarcely have reached the magnitudes that were the product of more than two centuries of development. The civil disorders that plagued the empire in its last forty years dealt further blows to the church, its property and its scriptures.

## THE DECLINE (860–884)

The first sign of serious problems for the dynasty appeared when a large-scale rebellion broke out in a region southeast of the Yangtze River between 859 and 860. The government quickly suppressed it, but the revolt was the outcome of disaffections that had been growing for years in the south. Half of the rebels, who numbered more than 30,000 at one time, were peasants who had abandoned their lands because of oppressive taxation and had turned to banditry for their survival. The dynasty was losing the support of the region that had been staunchly loyal since the An Lushan rebellion and had been the major source of its revenue. At the same time the Kingdom of Nanzhao, southwest of the Tang, invaded Annam (northern Vietnam, then part of China proper) after the military governor there forced them to sell their livestock at below market value and killed one of their leaders. Chinese forces finally secured the area in 866, but the Nanzhao continued to attack Tang borders farther north until 875. One of the side effects of the war in Annam was a disastrous mutiny. In 868 northern troops, whom the government had sent south to fight, revolted when the court reneged on a promise to let them return home at the end of their tours of duty. They marched into the northeast where they attracted large numbers of peasants, bandits, and alienated soldiers in the area. The rebels seized control of a large region on the east coast between the Yellow and Yangtze rivers, then took to liberating landowners and merchants of their wealth. With the help of the Turks and other steppes tribes, imperial forces quickly put down the

insurrection in 869, but again a once loyal and revenue-rich area was devastated and disaffected.

It was precisely in the region between the Yellow and Yangtze rivers that the rebellion which broke the back of the Tang originated. In 878 Huang Chao, who excelled in swordsmanship and mounted archery, took command of an army of insurgents and, in the face of stronger imperial forces, decided to head south—pillaging, burning, and slaughtering as he went. In 879 he took Canton, the great entrepôt of overseas trade, and slaughtered most of its 200,000 inhabitants. Huang, who lost 40 percent of his forces to malaria in Canton, then marched north, gathering new recruits for his army from mutinous imperial troops and bandits. He devastated the critical lower Yangtze region again. In late 880 Luoyang fell to him without a fight. Changan succumbed on January 5, 881. Emperor Xizong and his court fled to Chengdu in modern Sichuan province. Huang declared the establishment of a new dynasty.

## NOTES

1. The word "minister" always refers to a high-ranking official, never to a clergyman.

2. Taoism and Taoist always refer to the Taoist religion, not Taoist philosophy, unless otherwise specified.

# 2

# Society

## ARISTOCRACY

Although Tang China cannot be called feudal, at least in the sense that Europe of the same time was, it was a highly stratified, hierarchical society. The state regulated everything—the allocation of resources; access to education and political office; tax obligations and exemptions; legal accountability and punishment; and more—on the basis of an individual's status. Sumptuary laws dictated the quantity, quality, size, and adornment of clothes, transportation, homes, and other facets of life. The notion of equality, so cherished in modern times, did not exist in the Tang.

At the apex of society were, of course, the emperor and his family. The latter included both his nuclear and his extended families: grandfathers, grandmothers, mother, wives, sons, daughters, grandsons, granddaughters, brothers, sisters, uncles, aunts, nephews, nieces, and cousins. The throne bestowed nine ranks of noble titles, from prince to baron, on male relatives. It also conferred the title princess on aunts, sisters, daughters, the consort of the heir apparent, and the wives of princes. The court allocated portions of the annual tax revenues to them. Fiefs, estates that nobles controlled at the acquiescence of a king, had vanished long before the Tang. Grants of tax receipts replaced them. Those allowances were the grain and cloth levies that local officials collected from a given number of households in a given district. In the first half of the Tang, the government established offices with staffs of officials and clerks for princes. Those agencies coped with the grants and other matters. Before 682 the allowances, as a rule, were modest. Revenues ranged from 800 to 1,000 households for princes and 300 to 600 for princesses. During the reigns of Empress Wu and Emperor Zhongzong the amounts rose steeply. In 705 the emperor bestowed the taxes from 5,000 households on his brother and Princess Taiping, and the following year, generous grants of 4,000 and 3,500 households on his two favorite daughters. In 709 one of his ministers calculated that taxes from 600,000 households, about 8 percent of the taxpaying population, were going to pay for the incomes of the nobility. He reckoned that aristocrats received more silk from levies than the imperial treasury did. In the same year a report to the throne concluded that there were 140 nobles receiving incomes from fifty-four prefectures, roughly 15 percent of the empire. After Illustrious August ascended the throne and launched his program of austerities, he cut the incomes of the nobility. Another period of inflation occurred thereafter as the fiscal health of the government improved. According to statutes enacted before 739, the range of revenues granted the nobility ranged from 10,000 households for a prince to 300 for a baron. After the rebellion of An Lushan, the court could no longer afford such excessive expenditures, and the allowances dropped drastically.

The aristocracy also included extremely powerful clans who had monopolized high government positions in the dynasties before the Tang. Some of them, four from the northeast in particular, professed to have the finest Chinese pedigrees, married only among themselves, and considered the Lis (the royal house of the Tang) to be parvenus. As late as the early ninth century an emperor complained that a marriage to two of those families was considered superior to one with the imperial family. The members of those clans who held noble titles did not acquire them by virtue of their birth. The throne bestowed them for meritorious service or as expressions of favor. The power of the clans rested solely on social prestige and tradition. That strength was sufficient to secure them high-ranking positions in the bureaucracy until the end of the dynasty.

Except in the worst of times, the aristocracy lived comfortably. In the best of times they lived lavishly and extravagantly. Some princes were dissolute, indulging in hunting, drinking, and entertainment. In the early eighth century the son of one prince died suddenly because of overindulgence in wine and women. It was Zhongzong's daughters, however, who outdid all others in the prodigal expenditure of the enormous wealth that they had acquired by selling ordination certificates and office titles. Princess Anle expropriated the estates of commoners west of Changan to build a pleasure park. She spent enormous sums on adorning the grounds. Workers excavated a lake sixteen miles in circumference. Laborers piled stones to create a mountain resembling Mount

Hua—a sacred peak and scenic wonder east of the capital—dug a river channel in the form of the Milky Way, installed bridges, and paved roads with stone. Carpenters erected pavilions and covered walkways. Artisans decorated the structures with gold and silver, and inlaid them with pearls and jade. After the execution of the princess in 710, the government seized the property and turned it into a public park. Citizens of the capital visited it daily. Some princes were avaricious and accumulated large amounts of gold and other valuables in their treasuries. Occasionally, the throne punished a nobleman for violating sumptuary regulations. One emperor removed a prince from office because his clothes and ornaments were too extravagant. There were rare cases of frugality among the aristocrats. One preferred cheap hemp garments to the normal expensive silk robes worn by nobles, and ate nothing for three days on the anniversaries of his ancestors' deaths.

In the early years of the Tang, aristocrats were prominent officers in imperial armies. Three of Gaozu's sons played active and decisive roles in the military campaigns that founded the dynasty. One of his daughters also took part in the early stages of the Tang rebellion. She fled to her estate west of Changan on learning that her father was about to revolt. After arriving there, she distributed her property to recruit several hundred men hiding in the nearby mountains, so that they could assist Gaozu as he approached the capital. She sent a servant to a bandit, camped in a bamboo grove, who was killing travelers. The young boy convinced the highwayman to join forces with the princess. The servant also talked three more brigands, who controlled several thousand men, into placing their bands at her disposal. Her motley crew, known as the Lady's Army, managed to capture three prefectures. A number of princes and sons of princes served as military officers later in the seventh century. There was a warrior tradition in the imperial family at least in the early years of the dynasty.

Some later imperial appointments of aristocrats to military posts were disastrous. In 756 Illustrious August appointed one of his sons as military governor of the empire's southern regions. When the prince arrived at a city on the Yangtze River, he recruited an army of more than 200,000 men. Then he rebelled against the throne. Raised in the palace, he had no knowledge of or feeling for leading men. Government armies put down his insurrection and killed him.

It was the custom of the Tang court, especially in the first half of the dynasty, to appoint princes and other nobles to government posts. In many cases the offices were sinecures. The aristocrats held them in absentia and never performed the duties assigned to their offices or even left their mansions in the capital. In some cases, however, nobles actually went to the provinces and administered their districts as true officials. A few of them acquitted themselves admirably. One acquired a reputation for his fairness in adjudicating important legal cases. Another was so uncorrupt and severe in administering justice that criminals fled his jurisdiction. Yet another distinguished himself by quelling a rebellion of aborigines in southeast China without resorting to force. Others, however, were cruel governors. One prince who was serving as the governor of a prefecture assaulted a county commandant under his authority for no just cause. When one of his subordinates dared to reprove him for trampling the crops of peasants while hunting, he beat him.

Some aristocrats took to learning and the arts. Others fostered scholarship. An emperor appointed one of his sons to the post of director of the imperial library because he was so fond of learning. A prince in the early seventh century used his wealth to collect a large library that contained very fine editions as well as rare calligraphy and copies of stone inscriptions. In 641, another prince published a large historical geography of the empire compiled by a literary academy of scholars that he had established with imperial consent. In 677, a third prince submitted to the throne an annotation to an early dynastic history that his circle of learned men had compiled. Subsequently, one of Empress Wu's henchmen subjected him to severe duress, and he committed suicide. There were princes who excelled in music, painting, and calligraphy. Even distant members of the imperial clan were artists of some note. The most infamous chief minister of the early eighth century was a fine painter, as were his father and uncle.

Sometimes the character of aristocrats left something to be desired. Some were arrogant, overbearing, or self-indulgent. Others were ignoble; their behavior unseemly, criminal, indecent, or depraved. In 643 the heir to the throne created a scandal at court when he became infatuated with a boy dancer of an imperial troupe that performed at his mansion. The boy, who was about thirteen years old, was exceedingly good-looking and an outstanding singer. The heir made no effort to hide the love affair, and his father soon learned of it. The emperor had the boy put to death. The loss of his paramour devastated the heir, who took ill. He installed a statue of the dancer in one of his halls and made libations to it as acts of mourning. In the same year another prince had two officials on his staff assassinated when one was about to reveal his transgressions, and the other refused to have any part in the murder of the first. In 672 a son of an ailing prince took advantage of his father's weakened state to molest one of his concubines. Afterward the prince learned about the harassment and rebuked his son. Unrepentant, the son deprived his father of food and medicine so that he died of starvation. In 682 or 683 the throne ordered another son of a prince to commit suicide for bestiality, specifically for committing the crime of incest. One of Illustrious August's nephews and three of his friends murdered a man in the capital, partly to obtain his riches and partly to settle a grudge. In broad daylight they bludgeoned the man to death, boiled his flesh, and ate it. When the crime came to light in the summer of 739, the throne banished the nephew. It then ordered him to commit suicide when he reached a rapid relay station east of Changan.

The in-laws of an emperor could be as wicked as his clansmen. One of Empress Wu's nephews, a handsome fellow, had an abominable character and believed he could do as he pleased because he was a close relative of the empress. When the empress's daughter, then seven or eight years old, came to pay a call on her grandmother—who doted on the nephew and in whose mansion he lived—he seduced all of the young palace ladies in her retinue. That was outrageous enough and entirely illegal, but his transgression went unpunished because he enjoyed the protection of his grandmother. Unchastened, he committed an even greater offense. He broke into the home of a beautiful young girl whom the court had selected to be the heir apparent's concubine, and raped her. By that time his protectress had died. During the mourning period for her he brazenly cast aside his sackcloth and indulged in entertainment, seriously violating Tang law. Empress Wu had had enough of his deplorable and illicit behavior. She arranged to have him banished on the grounds that he had violated mourning regulations. She did not want her family's reputation besmirched by a conviction on the charge of rape. Her nephew committed suicide on the road to exile.

There were also some hard times for aristocrats. After the deposition of an empress in 655, her adopted son and former heir apparent was so afraid that Empress Wu or one of her cohorts would send an assassin to slay him that he took to wearing women's clothes as a disguise. It was not uncommon for an aristocrat to commit suicide when he believed that the throne would have him executed for being implicated in some plot. From 688 to 693 Empress Wu had hundreds, if not thousands, of the Tang's nobles put to death, frequently on baseless charges. In 752 the throne demoted the son of a prince merely because he sold a house to an official whom the throne had found guilty of plotting rebellion.

## BUREAUCRACY

In the Tang there were two types of officials: functionaries and mandarins. Functionaries, known as those "outside the current," were scribes, clerks, warehouse keepers, and other subalterns of the mandarins, those "within the current." They performed the routine tasks of administration—drafting correspondence and reports, compiling records and registers, maintaining inventories, and the like—that were beneath the dignity of the mandarins from whom they received their salaries.

The highest goal for an ambitious man of social standing and/or education was to acquire a position "within the current," to become a mandarin. There were basically three ways to acquire such an office. First, a man could assert hereditary privilege. The sons of officials were eligible for appointment to a post one grade lower than the highest office that their fathers held (or had held, if they were deceased). That form of advancement probably accounts for the fact that some high-ranking mandarins in the Tang were illiterate. In the early eighth century a minister of the Department of Households in Changan could neither recognize written words nor understand documents. He apparently had a low regard for those who could do so, for he called his subordinates "dogs" and "jackasses." Officials of that sort relied heavily on their subordinates to read and draft documents. It would be a mistake, however, to assume that all men who acquired posts by hereditary privilege were illiterate or incompetent. Second, he could receive a special appointment from the throne. In those cases, the emperor acted on the recommendation of an official or on information, oral or written, that he had received. In most instances he made his decisions on the grounds that the candidates had superior reputations, special skills, or exceptional qualifications. Last, an aspirant for a bureaucratic position could sit for civil service examinations and receive a post if he passed them.

One authority has called the Chinese bureaucracy a meritocracy because in principle it recruited and promoted officeholders on the basis of learning, skills, and other abilities—not on the basis of social status. That is certainly true for the Tang with some exceptions, notably mandarins who received appointments on the basis of hereditary privilege. After a man acquired a post, his superior annually rated his character according to four categories of attributes: his virtue and righteousness, integrity and prudence, impartiality, and diligence. He then assessed the subordinate's actual performance of his duties according to twenty-seven criteria, such as the selection of talented subordinates with good character for his staff, proper training and equipping of troops, just sentencing of convicted criminals, meticulous maintenance of records, prevention of fraud in the market, and rearing the animals under his charge so that they were fat and strong. An official's career depended on favorable evaluations, so he had to conduct himself prudently if he wished to advance.

There was a hierarchy of nine grades for offices and the mandarins holding them. The ladder of success for mandarins—who received elegant titles such as Grandee of Radiant Emolument and Bearer of the Gold Seal with Purple Ribbon on attaining new grades—conferred greater and greater prestige and privileges as they received promotions to offices with higher and higher rankings. The system was also the instrument by which the government fixed salaries, all of them tax-exempt, and allocated resources. In addition, the court ennobled high-ranking or meritorious bureaucrats, civil and military. It conferred titles—duke, marquis, count, viscount, and baron—on them and provided them with grants similar to those accorded the aristocracy but smaller in size (the revenues from 50 to 2,000 households).

Many of the Tang's officials were upright, diligent, and competent. A legal officer in one prefecture never imposed beating with the thick rod as punishment for crimes. When he rose to a post in the Department of Punition at the capital during the reign of Empress Wu, he was responsible for saving the lives of several thousand men whom the empress's cruel clerks had falsely accused. In the same period an official in the Service of the Supreme Justice—immortalized as Judge Dee in novels by a modern Western author—adjudicated 17,000 legal cases in one year, cases that had remained unresolved for years. Through his intervention he also saved the lives of 600 to 700 men sentenced to death for being implicated in the rebellion of a prince. A general of the Gold Bird Guard that patrolled the streets of the capital night and day personally passed judgment daily on more than 100 men caught violating the law. He was not lenient in applying punishments, so citizens, both nobles and commoners, feared him. Nevertheless, he was responsible for establishing order in the city. Exemplary local officials took a keen interest in the welfare of the people they governed. When one county commandant arrived in his district, he discovered that it had suffered from floods year after year, and that the river damaged a wooden bridge that had to be repaired annually. He had the dike along the river raised, and built a floating bridge to replace its wooden counterpart. Those actions prevented further calamities in the county. When an epidemic struck and killed livestock in his province, a governor-general devised a machine that peasants could push to plow their fields instead of using their cows.

Other local officials made efforts to repair schools and encourage students to pursue learning. When powerful and wealthy families in a prefecture illegally occupied land, depriving peasants of their fields, the governor gathered up a large tract of land and gave it to the poor and needy. One county commandant was extremely frugal, permitting his slaves only one meal a day. Whatever surplus his parsimony produced, he gave to the poor. A governor of a prefecture had a flour mill built at his own expense and donated the profits to the starving. In addition he had more than ten huts built along the sides of his dwelling for them to live in. It was common practice among people living in districts governed by worthy, exemplary, and humane officials to raise stone tablets in their markets or streets bearing inscriptions commemorating the good government of their mandarins.

Tang China also had its share of bad officials. The most common form of malfeasance during the dynasty was corruption. When the chief of some aborigines in what is now North Vietnam wanted to take a wife, the Chinese governor of the prefecture demanded 1,000 lengths of fine silk fabric before he would grant his permission. The chief was able to supply only 800 lengths, so the governor seized the bride-to-be and had his way with the maid for three days before returning her. Since he had deflowered the woman, the chief would not marry her. An imperial censor had a passion for eating beef. Consequently, while he was conducting an inspection tour in the region south of the Yangtze River, the number of cattle slaughtered in the area to feed his appetite was enormous. He was corrupt and would not conclude an investigation, whether it concerned a trivial or a grave matter, until he received gold for doing so. Consequently, the price of gold and silver rose sharply in the region. The people there called him the Gold Cow Governor. The throne took a particularly dim view of such offenses, and often had mandarins found guilty of the crime beaten to death before officials standing in the courtyard of the audience hall, to serve as a warning.

The Tang dynasty was a period of brutality and violence, but no more so than the twentieth century. A governor-general of the region northwest of Changan composed a declaration of war against a Turkish khan in which he rebuked the khan in very rude terms. Then he wrote the text on the stomach and back of a Turk, cut the words into the man's flesh, blackened the characters with ink, and cauterized the wounds with fire. The pain was unbearable, and the Turk screamed all day and night. Afterward the governor-general sent the man back to the khan. When the emissary returned with the khan's reply, the governor-general sliced off the man's flesh, piece by piece, until he died. When the same man was serving as a senior official for Luoyang between 705 and 707, the price of grain rose and thieves proliferated. He apprehended all of the robbers and had them beaten to death. Then he left the criminals' rotting corpses piled up before the gate of his office as a warning to the citizens of the capital. No one dared steal thereafter.

The army had the usual hierarchy of leaders, including generalissimos, grand generals, generals, and lower-ranking officers. During the Tang, military officers could earn honorary titles for meritorious service on the battlefield. The distinctions ranged from Marshal of War Cavalry, the lowest, to Superior Pillar of State, the highest. To qualify for the titles, the commander had to accumulate a certain number of commendations: the highest, Superior Pillar of State, required twelve. The Provost of Honors awarded commendations on the basis of a formula that combined the number of men killed or captured with the size of the enemy's army defeated in battle. There were three grades of merit for the former: 10, 20, and 40 percent of the adversary's troops slain or taken prisoner. There were also three degrees for the latter: victories won against superior, equal, and inferior forces. The highest number of commendations that an officer could earn in a single engagement was five, for a victory against a larger army in which his troops killed or captured 40 percent of the enemy. He could also earn three for stubbornly defending a stronghold or for surviving a particularly fierce battle. The Provost of Honors often relied on reports sent to him by the commanders who fought the wars. Some unscrupulous officers padded the figures for the numbers of enemy troops killed and the size of their adversary's forces when they forwarded their battle accounts to the capital. In the early seventh century one enterprising warrior chopped the noses off the men he slew and carried them back to his superior to avoid suspicion that he was exaggerating in his combat report. In some cases commanders claimed victories when they had actually suffered defeats. The court could grant the same honorary titles to civil officials for meritorious achievements that did not involve military action.

## EUNUCHS

Imperial eunuchs constituted another, small class of the privileged. They probably numbered no more than 5,000 at any given time during the dynasty, but had tremendous power and influence. Although by the mid-ninth century the throne required all regions to submit castrated boys, most came from regions along the southeast coast. The majority of them were sold by their parents and emasculated in their youth, before they were sent to the capital. After the boys arrived in Changan, a senior eunuch of the Service for Palace Attendants adopted them and gave them his surname. He also taught them whatever duties the throne assigned them. By and large eunuchs were illiterate, and most performed menial duties in the innermost, private quarters of the emperor. Some, however, had enough education to teach palace ladies the Confucian classics, Taoist philosophy, history, mathematics, law, poetry, calligraphy, and board games.

In the early years of the dynasty the throne restricted the number, power and privileges of the eunuchs. In the late seventh century Empress Wu eased the restraints. Eunuchs began to acquire mansions in the capitals as well as estates in the nearby countryside, take "wives," and adopt uncastrated children of both sexes so that they could bequeath their titles and property to their heirs.

Eunuchs were the guardians of the imperial harem, so employed because they could not spread their seed and spawn offspring that were not the emperor's. By the middle of the eighth century the number of women in the seraglio of Emperor Illustrious August soared to 40,000, with about one eunuch for every ten ladies. Because they governed the emperor's household, eunuchs had unique and frequent access to him. Illustrious August's most trusted eunuch slept in a curtained area along the side of the emperor's bedchamber. Eunuchs were solely responsible to and dependent on the emperor, but acquired enormous power over officials because of their unique access to him.

By the early eighth century the throne was employing eunuchs as generals. It sent one to northern Vietnam with orders to suppress revolts by aborigines. Between 722 and 728 he quelled three rebellions with the help of an army that he recruited from the natives. He took more than 80,000 heads and had the bodies of the slain stacked in pyramids, presumably to serve as a warning to men contemplating insurrection. He was a brutal man who terrified the aborigines because he took scalps and cut the skin from the faces of prisoners he had captured. He was not the only eunuch known for his cruelty. The citizens of Changan so despised one who had been a thief catcher in the capital that they stood by the road with bricks and stones to hurl at him when he departed for an assignment in the south. A chief minister at the time had to order market officials to disperse the crowd so the man could leave the city.

It was not until the rebellion of An Lushan that eunuchs began to exert great power over the court and the government. After 800 they came to control the flow of documents to and from the throne. Addresses to the emperor and decrees from him passed through their hands, and required their approval before implementation. They became involved in appointments of provincial governors and the operations of capital schools. By the ninth century the throne had placed eunuchs in charge of the palaces, the postal system, guest houses, the imperial treasury, and churches in the capitals. It also established a council of eunuchs responsible for conducting deliberations on public policy. As a result the power of eunuchs became so great that they engineered the enthronements of over half of the emperors in that century. Some of the hapless rulers in that epoch became puppets of the eunuchs.

## CLERGY

One of the largest privileged groups in Tang society was the clergy. In 845 there were 360,000 monks and nuns throughout the empire. The church attracted novices, not only because of their devotion to the faith but also because, once ordained, they were exempt from taxes and compulsory labor. It also attracted many landlords who wished to evade those obligations. Those "bogus monks" remained laymen, acquired ordination certificates, but did not practice celibacy, lived with their families, and reaped the profits from their fields or other enterprises.

The power of Buddhism rested on its control of land, industrial works, and money that were often tax-exempt. Its doctrines of compassion and salvation were the forces that led to the acquisition of wealth and property. Compassion required the clergy and laity to assist those less fortunate than themselves: the indigent, the frail, and others. That tenet of faith compelled the laity to donate portions of their wealth to the church as a kind of sectarian welfare. Salvation was individual and particular, in contrast to compassion, which was universal and altruistic (i.e., compassion applied to all people, regardless of their status or relationships). The motive of donors was to improve their lot and that of their ancestors in purgatory, and to elevate themselves or their ancestors to a superior station during their rebirth in the next state of existence. The notion was that a gift could redeem sins committed in this life, and thereby reduce or eliminate punishment in the afterlife. The size of such gifts was sometimes astronomical. In 767 a eunuch not only granted the church his estate, a prime piece of real estate east of Changan, but also contributed a billion coppers for the construction of a monastery on the manor.

The donors belonged to all classes of society from the emperor to the peasant, and gave all manner of property—land, mills, coppers, silk, slaves, and more. In addition, monasteries increased their holdings by purchasing fields and confiscating lands when debtors defaulted on loans. Except for Chan (Zen) Buddhists, the ordained clergy did not work the land. According to the Indian notion of nonviolence, the monastic rules of discipline forbade them from digging, irrigating, and harvesting because such actions might result in the killing of living things, in particular insects and microorganisms. Consequently, monasteries entrusted the working of the land to novices, tenant farmers who paid rent that was ten to twenty times the tax obligation that they would otherwise have paid to the government, bondservants who indentured themselves to pay off debts, and slaves. In 845, at the height of the persecution of Buddhism, the government confiscated 150,000 slaves from Buddhist establishments. The slaves did not fare well. The army took possession of those who had martial skills, civil offices took the old and enfeebled, and the government sold the young who had no skills. Officials divided their families, sending fathers in one direction and sons in another. In the provinces of central China slaves had no food or shelter. Corrupt officials or wealthy merchants often illegally seized them.

Monasteries augmented the revenue they received from their land with income from industrial enterprises. The most important were mills for hulling grains or grinding them into flour. These installations, operated on water power, were built along irrigation canals in uplands and were far too expensive for peasants to construct. Trip-hammer mechanisms, pestles attached to wooden arms and affixed to an axle, rose and fell as a waterwheel at the end of the axle rotated. When the pestles descended and struck the cereals, they pounded off the husks. Grist mills operated in a similar manner. A waterwheel attached to an axle turned an upper stone that revolved over a lower, stationary stone. That action pulverized grains placed between the stones into flour. Though monasteries owned the mills, they did not operate them. The clergy entrusted

A Water-Powered Trip-Hammer Mill

their construction and maintenance to millwrights and the production to millers. The millers, who may have been serfs, had to pay rent for the use of the mills. The revenues collected went into the coffers of the monastery.

Monasteries operated oil presses that extracted oil from sesame (hemp) seeds. As with the mills, they owned the equipment and were responsible for its maintenance, but entrusted the operation of the presses to laymen. They charged the operators rent for use of them. Contracts entitled them to seize the property of the lessees should they fail to pay the prescribed fees. Like millers, the oil producers were free to sell to the public any surplus in excess of the rents they owed, but the monastery imposed a tax on such sales. They were probably the greatest consumers of oil because they kept lamps perpetually burning in their Buddha halls.

The wealth accumulated by the church through donations, rents, and industries went first to the maintenance of monasteries and the support of the clergy. However, the normal expenditures of monasteries apparently required only one-fourth to one-third of their income. Some of the surplus went to the construction of new facilities and to the commissioning or purchase of paintings, murals, statues, and bells, as well as to furnish supplies for festivals. However, the monks employed a large portion of it to increase their revenues through commercial transactions. The first of them was pawnbroking, which appeared in Buddhist monasteries in the sixth century. A peasant in need of seed at the beginning of spring would deposit a valuable object, such as an iron cauldron, with the monastery as security for a loan of grain. If he failed to redeem the property by returning the seed after the autumn harvest, he agreed to forfeit all of his movable property. The monks charged him no interest for the transaction. If, however, the person was of a higher station and the transaction involved money, such as a woman who pawned her comb for 500 coppers, he or she had to return the principal with interest to redeem the pledge. Buddhist pawnshops did a thriving business. One monk in the early ninth century set up establishments that lent out more than 1 billion coppers a year against security. This astonished the emperor, who issued a decree in 817 that prohibited the nobility, officials, Taoist priests, and Buddhist monks from holding more than 5 million cash at a given time.

The second commercial activity was lending. There were basically two types of loans. The first type was short-term loans, usually for seven months, extended to peasants and consisting mostly of seed grain. Some farmers, either because they exhausted their stores during the winter or they had used their surplus to celebrate the New Year, did not have enough to begin sowing in the spring. If the borrower was a monastery's tenant, it advanced the grain to him without interest. He agreed, however, to forfeit his movable property if he failed to repay the loan after the autumn harvest. If the borrower was a free farmer, the monastery charged him interest, generally 50 percent, when he returned the principal. The second type consisted of loans extended to individuals of some station, officials or aristocrats. They were advances of silk, money, or processed commodities, such as oil and flour. The interest rates were substantially higher than those charged peasants. One contract established the rate for a loan of 1,000 coppers at 200 cash per month, for a total of 1,200 coppers interest when the loan fell due in six months. In other words, the borrower paid a rate of 120 percent when he returned the principal. The reason for such exorbitant rates of interest may be that the risk was higher, both because the value of the loans was greater and because there was a greater chance of default. Some officials failed to pay their debts, and monasteries were relatively powerless to compel them to make good. To reduce the risk, the monks usually drew up contracts with borrowers, including peasants, that were signed by guarantors who promised to make restitution should the borrowers default.

The income from commercial transactions must have been substantial. The ledgers of two monasteries in Central Asia record that 33 and 55 percent of their income came from interest. The returns to some prominent churches in the capitals and other large, prosperous cities in China proper were even greater. By and large Buddhists lived off the labor and product of the peasantry and other lower classes. However, they returned much of their income to the community as charity.

## PEASANTS

All Chinese dynasties regarded farming as the fundamental occupation, and rightly so since the economy was overwhelmingly agrarian. Farmers and their families constituted 80 to 90 percent of the population. The government relied on them to produce the revenues that enriched the royal treasury, supported the nobility, supplied salaries for officials, maintained armies, and funded public works, among other things. Consequently, during the early Tang the state took steps to ensure a minimum standard of living for the peasants and to bind them to their land. The latter required registration of the entire rural population. Local officials revised the registers every third year, taking a sort of census, to make sure that farmers still occupied their assigned plots. From the registers they then compiled tax rolls.

Adult males of rural households grew grain in their fields: wheat, barley, and millet in the relatively dry north and rice in the wet south. They also raised vegetables as well as domestic animals, especially pigs, cattle, and chickens. In addition the men hunted and fished to augment their diets. The Tang law code permitted private citizens to possess bows, arrows, swords, shields, and short spears. If the peasant had enough money to buy or the skill to manufacture them, he could supply himself with the tools for bagging game. There was a division of labor in farming families. The wives and daughters were responsible for weaving textiles. That task required them to process plant fibers and draw out silk from the cocoons of silkworms.

The peasant suffered from a large number of afflictions, both natural and man-made. Natural disasters were the worst. Floods as deep as forty feet inundated as many as sixty prefectures, or one-sixth of the empire. Some destroyed as many as 10,000 homes, forcing people to live on boats or nest in trees. They drowned thousands and laid waste to crops and farmland. Droughts struck as often as four years in a row. One devastated 14 percent of the empire, not only killing plants but also drying up wells, so that people died of thirst and disease. Hail, sometimes the size of a fist, flattened crops and killed men, horses, cows, and birds. Pests, too, were a threat to the livelihood of the peasant. Rats in packs of as many as 10,000 attacked the fields and burrowed into houses, where they ate clothing. Rabbits in similar numbers devoured the crops. The worst of the pests were probably the locusts that descended in enormous swarms and devoured all of the soft tissues of trees and plants. With nothing else to eat, the peasants sometimes resorted to stripping off the grasshoppers' legs and wings, in order to steam them for food.

According to traditional ideology, the emperor assumed personal responsibility for such disasters. He blamed himself for governing poorly and offending Heaven (nature). When a plague of locusts struck Changan in 628, the emperor seized a grasshopper in the Forbidden Park and, as he was about to eat it, declared, "Mankind depends on grains for life. If the people have committed sins, I am solely accountable for them. You should devour me only, and not harm the people." During a drought in 724 the emperor stood naked, exposing himself to the sun for three days, to elicit the sympathy of the gods while praying for rain at an altar in the palace. Some local officials also performed that rite. Those unusual acts were probably rare, but it was quite normal for the throne to dispatch officials to conduct religious rituals at temples in the capital and at holy sites, such as sacred mountains, throughout the empire.

The government undertook more pragmatic measures to relieve the distress of the peasants. It had a system of granaries situated at strategic sites throughout the empire. The granaries collected around three and a half bushels of grain from each landholder annually. When a natural disaster struck, causing famine, officials distributed the stored cereals to the starving population in the affected region. Furthermore, one of the Tang's statutes provided a graduated system of tax remissions to farmers who sustained losses. If 40 percent of a peasant's crops was destroyed, he did not have to pay the grain tax; if 60 percent, he did not need to render the grain or cloth levy to the state; and if more than 70 percent, he did not have to pay any taxes or perform compulsory labor.

Peasants also suffered greatly at the hands of their fellow men. There were large displacements of population in the north because the wars with the Khitan and Turks during Empress Wu's reign and the rebellion of An Lushan had devastated farmlands. Peasants also deserted their fields and fled to evade compulsory labor and conscription. Even when it involved public works, such as constructing dikes or repairing roads, that the farmer might benefit from, forced labor took him away from his land and family for extended periods. Far worse, except for rations that the government provided while he was traveling to and from the place where he performed the service, he had to bring his own provisions with him for the time, usually twenty days, that he spent working on the project. If he had the money—and most did not—he could hire a substitute. Peasants might protest when the undertaking did not involve their personal interests, the taskmasters were harsh, or the conditions of service were unbearable. During the construction of a prince's tomb, the peasants so hated the forced labor that they filled the road, raised a clamor, and threw bricks and tiles at the funeral cortege. Conscription was even more terrible because the term of service was three years, it might mean serving far from home on the frontiers, and it involved the risk of injury or death. The north suffered the most from absconding peasants in the first half of the Tang. According to one estimate, the north lost 28 percent of its population, and the south nearly tripled its population, between 609 and 742.

War and compulsory labor were not the only banes of the peasant's existence. Aristocrats, mandarins (both those in the capital and in the provinces), and eunuchs, as well as military governors, army officers, and merchants, were major sources of misery for free farmers. Beginning in the second half of the seventh century, powerful families, especially those in the region around Changan, built landed estates at the expense of independent peasants. Through the abuse of their authority as officials, falsification of land registers, sheer coercion, illegal purchases, and confiscation for nonpayment of debt, the upper classes and the wealthy seized peasants' plots. In the early ninth century a military governor in the southwest illegally confiscated 122 estates and 88 households. The government made efforts to halt estate-building and provide land for dispossessed farmers in the first half of the Tang with some success, but after 756 that sort of legislation proved futile. Furthermore, the state contributed to the problem. It owned estates that it rented to tenant farmers. By the late eighth century two reports from officials to the throne estimated that independent farmers constituted no more than 4 or 5 percent of the empire's population. This may have been an exaggeration, but the loss of free farmers was staggering nonetheless.

In the late eighth and early ninth centuries the biennial tax became a source of great distress for farmers. When the court instituted the tax in 780, it fixed tax rates according to the value of coppers in that year. At the time the economy was in the last throes of an inflationary cycle that had begun in 763. In 785, however, a long period of deflation began that lasted until 820. As a result the price of the peasants' grain and cloth dropped steadily as the value of money rose. Farmers therefore had to set aside increasingly larger amounts of their commodities to pay the levies imposed by the government. According to one estimate, their tax burden increased 500 percent in forty years. That, of course, caused more peasants to abandon their land. During that period a mandarin met a snake catcher in south China who submitted his vipers, which had black skins with white stripes, to the imperial physician in Changan twice a year in lieu of paying the biennial tax. When dried and preserved, the flesh of the serpents could cure leprosy, boils, and other maladies. Both the grandfather and father of the peasant had died while catching snakes. He himself had almost died a number of times during the twelve years that he had been gathering vipers. Out of sympathy for the man's plight, the official offered to intervene with the authorities and restore him to the tax rolls. The snake catcher pleaded with him not to do so. He preferred risking his life, because 50 to 60 percent of his neighbors who were liable for the biennial tax had abandoned their land and migrated.

Under such difficult circumstances the peasant had two options. First, he could stay where he was and become a tenant farmer or agricultural laborer. That was not an appealing alternative. Tenant farmers, as many as 200 families on a single estate, constituted the bulk of the landowner's labor force. The tenant paid half of the crops that he harvested as rent to the landowner, a sum much larger than the taxes he would have paid to the government had he been free. In addition, when the estate supplied him seed and food, it expected repayment and charged him a high rate of interest. It also imposed levies on other commodities, such as textiles, that he produced. Finally, the landowner required him to perform labor services, such as constructing or repairing walls, bridges, and buildings.

His second option was flight. Although that choice involved a certain amount of hardship initially—leaving one's ancestral home was excruciating and traveling was hazardous—the peasant was better off in the end. The south was the preferred destination because there were still extensive regions of rich land that had not been occupied. The problem of estate-building was also less severe in that part of the country. Finally, during the Tang the far south (present-day North Vietnam and the provinces of Guangsi and Guangdong) was rich in minerals, especially gold. Around 700 a peasant who had a flock of more than 100 ducks was cleaning their pen one day and saw the glint of something shining in their droppings. He sifted the dung in a basin of water and recovered fourteen ounces of gold. Afterward he followed the fowl to their feeding area at the foot of a mountain. He drilled into the spot and dug up more than 12,800 ounces of the precious metal. As a result he became a very wealthy man. Peasants were still extracting gold from the droppings of geese and ducks as late as the ninth century. Others used felt to sift gold from river water. Peasants ceased tilling their fields and ran away to the goldfields. Mining offered farmers their only hope of striking it rich and escaping from the miseries inflicted by estate owners and tax collectors.

## ARTISANS AND MERCHANTS

Aside from slaves and vagrants, the classes most subject to discrimination in the Tang were artisans and merchants, especially the latter. The basis for the prejudice against merchants on the part of the state, officials, and intellectuals was that traders were "leeches" who produced nothing. They lived off the surplus that the peasantry generated by dint of its hard labor. Furthermore, their pursuit of wealth was contrary to conventional ethics that frowned on materialism. Finally, their wandering lifestyle made it difficult for the government to control them. For those reasons merchants and artisans—the latter grouped with merchants because, although they were producers, they sold their wares for profit—occupied the lowest rung in the traditional hierarchy of classes. The government and the upper classes accepted them only because they were necessary for the operation of the economy.

Because of that bias the government enacted statutes that discriminated against merchants and artisans. The law prohibited them from having intercourse with officials and banned the upper echelons of the bureaucracy from entering urban markets. It forbade merchants and artisans to sit for civil service examinations, and therefore to hold public office. They had no access to political power. The state did not allocate land to them except in regions where there were vacant tracts, and even then it allowed them to occupy only half of the amount that it normally granted to peasants. It also forbade them to ride horses.

Landless merchants and artisans living in cities did enjoy some privileges when it came to taxation. There they had to pay only levies on their households and properties. However, after the rebellion of An Lushan the government occasionally subjected them to other exactions. During a crisis in 783–784, when the state was strapped for revenue, it compelled merchants in Changan to loan it money. Officials estimated that they could exact 250 million coppers from ten to twenty of the wealthiest traders without forcing them out of business. They also imposed a 20 percent excise tax on all goods sold in the markets. There were two further instances in the ninth century when the government resorted to exacting forced loans from merchants. Meanwhile, some provincial officials were also collecting excise taxes on goods sold by merchants.

Despite the discrimination and exploitation, some merchants made immense fortunes. In 734, when the state confiscated the property of a merchant living in Changan, his fortune amounted to 600 million coppers.

The government took a similar action against another merchant residing in a city on the Grand Canal in the early ninth century and seized 10 billion coppers from him. Those men were among the tycoons, a very small number of traders. There was a host of small vendors and peddlers who eked out a hard living with little return and never struck it rich.

The upper class's prejudice against merchants is difficult to understand, given the fact that aristocrats and mandarins were also parasites who, with some exceptions, sucked the blood from the peasants through rents and taxes. Like the traders they produced no concrete goods— grain, salt, cloth, metals, bricks, tiles, furniture, and so forth. Although the law barred mandarins from making a profit from their inferiors (i.e., commoners), they engaged in commerce anyway. Even the government of the early Tang relied on capitalism to pay the salaries of officials because the granaries and treasuries were empty. It allocated funds to all local governments. They then turned the money over to wealthy families, no doubt mostly merchants, who had experience in loaning money. Those families were responsible for making a profit on the capital at a rate of interest fixed by the government. The local governor then apportioned the revenues that he received to supply salaries for his staff. This form of bureaucratic capitalism continued into the ninth century.

At least one local official manifested some entrepreneurial talent. A county commandant met the elder of a hamlet and asked, "How many eggs can I buy for a copper?" The man replied, "Three." So the commandant purchased 30,000 for 10,000 coppers, but he did not take them with him. Instead he instructed the elder to have hens hatch them. After they hatched, the commandant had one of his underlings sell the chickens for him, and made 300,000 cash. He also asked the elder, "How many bamboo shoots can I buy for a copper?" The man replied, "Five." So the commandant purchased 50,000 of them. Then he told the elder to raise the shoots in the woods. When they grew into bamboo stalks in the fall, the commandant sold them for ten coppers apiece and made 500,000 cash.

Some officials of the court engaged in commerce. A director of palace workshops was an expert at making a profit. In 681 he reported to the throne that he had made 20 million coppers from selling horse manure. When the emperor asked for his opinion on the matter, a mandarin replied, "Even though the profit is great, I fear that later ages will call the house of Tang 'sellers of horse manure.' " So, despite the fact that profits went to his coffers, the emperor put a halt to the practice. In 687, when the superintendent of the Forbidden Park north of Changan was about to sell fruits and vegetables to make money for the throne, the governor of Changan protested that it was undignified for the emperor to sell such lowly goods. Consequently, Empress Wu forbade it. By the early eighth century the aristocracy was making money from flour mills that they had erected on their country estates outside of Changan.

In the late eighth century aristocrats and officials who had previously been reluctant to sully themselves with mercantile activities openly engaged in commerce. By 780 they had set up shops to trade commodities in Yangzhou, the great center of commerce and industry. At the time military governors and inspector generals in the south also got involved in establishing businesses. Under the guise of making money for their armies, they actually made a profit for themselves. By 831 even soldiers had established shops along the avenues of Changan.

In the same period that some officials were becoming merchants, some merchants were becoming officials. Although still despised by the upper classes, merchants were indispensable for producing revenue at a time when older sources, especially land taxes, were drying up. In their ceaseless search for funds, local governors, warlords, and others, sought out merchants and employed them because they had the talent to make money. Even the central government was not above using them. Furthermore, although a merchant might not take civil service examinations, it appears that by 803 large numbers of their sons were doing so, and also occupying most of the seats in the state colleges at the capitals.

## SLAVES

At the bottom of the pecking order were the slaves. There were two types: official and private. The imperial court and the government acquired slaves from several sources. During the early years of the Tang, large numbers of slaves were foreign soldiers and civilians captured in victorious campaigns that Tang armies conducted in Korea, Inner Mongolia, Central Asia, and northern India. In the first half of the seventh century the emperor sent an envoy to India who traversed the difficult road over the mountains in the southwest, gathered a force of Tibetans and Nepalese, plundered Magadha (the birthplace of Buddha), seized 2,000 men and women as well as thousands of cattle and horses, and returned to Changan with the king of India. Among his prisoners was a physician who claimed to be 200 years old and to possess a formula for prolonging life. When, however, he failed to produce the elixir, the emperor dismissed him. After Tang armies conquered northern Korea in 688, they brought back 200,000 prisoners. The descendant of one of the captives was Emperor Illustrious August's personal slave. In 713 the emperor freed him for his meritorious contributions to the deposition of Princess Taiping and appointed him to various posts in the imperial guards.

The second type of slave was family members of men sentenced to death for rebellion and sedition. The court confined the womenfolk of the condemned in the Flank Court, the western section of the central palace within the walls of Changan, and called them palace ladies. It was the custom for an emperor to free large numbers of the women when he ascended the throne. This no doubt accounts for the enormous size— 40,000 women—of Emperor Illustrious August's harem. He reigned for forty-four years, so there was no occasion for releasing the ladies, and their numbers mounted year after year. Many of the adult women were probably literate because they came mainly from the upper class. For those who had no education, the young perhaps, the throne provided instruction in the classics, writing, poetry, law, mathematics, chess, and other fields. They were also supposed to care for mulberry trees and raise silkworms, traditionally woman's work, to supply fabrics for the palace.

The third source of official slaves was foreign tribute, the obligation that monarchs and chieftains of subject states or tribes owed the Chinese emperor, who was their liege lord. Those gifts included skilled artists and entertainers. The king of Tokhāra, a nation north of modern-day Afghanistan and Pakistan, sent a painter of extraordinary skill to the Chinese court in the early seventh century. He was best known for his Buddhist icons, but also executed works depicting flowers and birds. The most celebrated of the slaves, however, were troupes of musicians, singers, and dancers who performed at court banquets and other functions. The kingdoms of Japan, Korea, what is now Burma, and several Central Asian states sent them periodically to Changan, where they were integrated into the court's music bureaus. Other gifts, however, were curiosities. A king of what is now Cambodia dispatched albinos to the emperor. In 669 an embassy from Japan presented some hairy Ainu archers who astonished the Chinese court.

Merchants supplied private slaves to wealthy customers for a price. Most of their goods were foreigners or aboriginal peoples living in the southern districts of China. The aliens included Turks from the northwest, who were prized for their abilities to ride horses and handle livestock; Persians captured by Chinese pirates in the southeast; and Korean women, whose beauty made them a hot commodity in the households of the well-to-do. It had been taboo since ancient times to sell Chinese, and the Tang law code imposed a stiff penalty for doing so. Kidnapping a person to sell as a slave was a capital offense requiring execution by strangulation. This applied, however, only to those who were enslaved against their will. Chinese debtors and tenant farmers who could not meet their obligations sold themselves or their sons for fixed periods, even for life, to relieve themselves of their burdens. Furthermore, the law did not apply to aborigines living in the southern prefectures of the empire. Those regions supplied the largest number of slaves in the Tang. Traders considered the native inhabitants of those regions to be barbarians, beyond the pale of Chinese civilization, and therefore not subject to the law prohibiting their abduction and sale. Neither the emperor nor local officials could stop the trade.

Slaves in the Tang, as elsewhere, were property. The Tang law code accorded them a status equal to that of domestic animals and inanimate possessions. Consequently, if a man abducted another man's slave, it prescribed a severe punishment of exile to the distant reaches of the empire. The same rule applied to someone who caught a runaway slave and failed to turn him in to the authorities within five days. A government slave who ran away was subject to sixty blows of the thick rod for the first day he was missing, and more the longer he remained at large. Male slaves could not marry the daughters of commoners (i.e., free men). If their masters permitted them to do so, they were subject to two and half years of penal servitude, and the marriages were annulled. On the one hand, the penalty for murdering a master was decapitation, or strangulation if the death resulted from an accident. On the other hand, if the master killed his slave for no legitimate reason, he received a sentence of one year penal servitude. However, if he did so because the slave committed a crime and he had not requested authorization to slay him, he was liable for a punishment of only 100 blows with the thick rod.

## FOREIGNERS

The Tang dynasty was one of the most cosmopolitan in Chinese history. Influences from abroad affected nearly every aspect of life, from music to medicine. Part of the reason for the tolerance of things foreign was Buddhism, which reached the height of its development and popularity in the Tang. The spread of the religion, which began about A.D. 65, continued into the seventh and eighth centuries. At least fifty-six Chinese monks made their way to India between 618 and 705, learned Sanskrit, and returned to China laden with hundreds of sutras that they set about translating. Conversely, monks from India and Central Asia made their way to China to spread their doctrines. During the eighth century three great masters of Tantric (occult) Buddhism arrived in Changan, where they received a favorable reception from the Tang court and transmitted the tenets of their school. Whether Chinese or foreign, the monks imported many facets of Indian culture to the Tang besides their scriptures and religion.

Another factor in the Tang's acceptance of things foreign was the nature of the ruling class. In the period of disunion from 316 to 581, after the nomadic peoples conquered north China, many Chinese aristocrats in the north and northeast, including the reigning Lis of the Tang, intermarried with the barbarians and assimilated their culture to a degree. After the founding of the Tang, the influence of the steppe cultures persisted. The best, or at least most infamous, case was that of Taizong's eldest son. He was so enamored of Turkish culture that he took up the language and dressed in Turkish clothes. He selected attendants whose appearance resembled that of the Turks, had them braid their hair in pigtails, don sheepskin garb, and tend sheep. He installed himself in a tent erected in his palace, outside of which he installed banners emblazoned with wolves' heads, the totem of the Turks, who thought of themselves as descendants of the beast. There he had lambs roasted whole, and carved the flesh off the sheep with his sword. He even re-created a Turkish funeral fit for a khan in which he lay on the ground while his attendants circled his body on horseback and shouted, in conformance with nomadic mourning rite. Few people of the Tang were so obsessively attached to Turkish ways as he, but the influence of that pastoral people was apparent in many facets of Tang culture.

During the Tang the government divided foreigners who decided to stay in China into three classes based on their wealth. Adults of the highest class had to pay a tax of ten silver coins; those of the second, of five; and those of the lowest, nothing. After they lived in the empire for two years, the law reduced the levy to two sheep for the highest class, one sheep for the second, and one sheep for every three households of the lowest. The state also required the aliens to supply horses in the event of military campaigns. Obviously the regulations applied only to the nomadic, pastoral peoples of the northern and western steppes, as well as to merchants from countries west of China who traveled overland. While the Arabs and Persians who rode the waves may have brought silver with them, it is unlikely that they brought sheep or procured them in the south, where the animals were scarce. The government was more tolerant of the "barbarous" indigenous peoples of the southeast, who practiced slash-and-burn agriculture that yielded meager harvests. It demanded only half the taxes it imposed on their Chinese neighbors.

The destination for the seafaring Arab and Persian merchants, as well as Malay and other outlanders of the south and west, was the great port of Canton. There were warehouses there for off-loading their cargoes that were exchanged for silk and porcelain, the Chinese commodities most desired by those aliens. The throne also set aside a special residential quarter south of the Pearl River for foreigners who chose to stay in China and trade or to wait for the northeastern monsoon to carry them out to their homes. The size of that community was quite substantial by the late ninth century. When Huang Chao sacked the city in 879, many of his 120,000 victims were foreigners—Persians, Arabs, Indians, Southeast Asians, and others. Like all foreign settlements in the Tang, that in Canton enjoyed a degree of autonomy and extraterritoriality. Designated elders governed the affairs of the community. Furthermore, under Tang law aliens who committed crimes against those of their own nationality were judged according to their own customs and laws. The state required Chinese magistrates to inquire what those mores and regulations were before passing sentences. If, however, they committed offenses against those of another nationality or native Chinese, the judge passed judgment on them according to Chinese law. Furthermore, if a foreigner married a Chinese woman while living in the empire, he could not take her back to his native country. This put him in a predicament, because if he died in China without a wife or an heir, the state confiscated all of his property.

Despite that deference to their native laws and customs, foreign merchants in Canton often suffered mistreatment at the hands of local officials. A governor in the late seventh century could not control his staff because he was weak and irresolute. When a foreign ship docked at the port in 684, his subordinates seized the cargo. The merchant lodged a complaint with the governor, who had the trader shackled and was about to imprison him. That enraged all of the foreigners in the city. One of their number, a Malay, strode into the courtroom, pulled a knife from his sleeve, and murdered the governor along with more than ten of his aides. He then fled, boarded a ship, and disappeared. In 761 a eunuch, whom the throne placed in charge of foreign shipping that entered the port, chased out the military governor and permitted his subordinates to plunder the city on a grand scale. More often, however, local officials milked foreign merchants for all they were worth. In the late ninth century a governor imposed a kind of private tax on them which was so lucrative that over an eight-year period his fortune grew to exceed the value of the empire's treasury. He was especially fond of rhinoceros horns, elephant tusks, and pearls. In 769 his graft was so great that the number of foreign ships entering the port dropped to four or five a year. When an honest official took charge, it increased to more than forty a year.

The Tang welcomed the wisdom and expertise of foreigners. Three clans of Indian astronomers/astrologers held posts in the imperial bureau of astronomy at the capitals during the late seventh and early eighth centuries. The most renowned and productive bore the name of the Buddha, Gautama Siddhārtha. The throne placed him in charge of compiling a massive compendium, which survives today in 120 chapters, of astronomy and divination, fields in which he was a master. Although it consists mainly of excerpts from ancient Chinese treatises, it introduced from India a symbol for zero, primitive trigonometry, and the division of the circle into 360 degrees. The influx of foreign medicinal substances from the west was so great that a Chinese pharmacologist compiled a treatise devoted solely to them. The government also prized the military abilities of outlanders. By 751 the commands of all armies on the north, northeast, and northwest frontiers of China proper were in the hands of foreign generals. Among those aliens was a Korean general who was remarkably successful in campaigns against Central Asians in the far northwest until the Arabs defeated him in 751.

# 3

# Cities and Urban Life

## CITIES

The word for "city" in Chinese literally means "walls and markets," an adequate if somewhat minimal definition of a traditional urban settlement. All cities in Tang China theoretically had ramparts and bazaars. Officially, according to the census of 754, there were 1,859 cities—321 prefectures and 1,538 counties—throughout the empire. The actual figure was somewhat smaller since prefectures were also the seats for some counties. A number of the prefectures and counties were located in poor backwaters that had neither the resources to afford nor the strategic value to justify the construction of outer walls. They also had populations too small to warrant labeling them "cities." Those settlements had bamboo fences or palisades instead of walls.

All cities—capitals, prefectures, and counties—were seats of government administration. Commerce, industry, transportation, and communication were important but secondary facets of their character. Cities never enjoyed any significant autonomy from the central government. Nor were they independent from the countryside that surrounded them. The figures for populations of county seats included both the citizens within their walls and the inhabitants of the villages within their jurisdictions. Unlike cities in classical and medieval Europe, they had only a hazy identity of their own. Most Chinese in ancient times thought of themselves as residents of villages or urban wards where their families originated, and where their ancestral graveyards were situated in the adjacent countryside. City walls were purely defensive; they did not serve as rigid boundaries between the rural and the urban. Cities did, however, drain wealth from rural sectors in the form of taxes and profits from trade. Rural riches provided the luxurious lifestyles that the urban upper classes enjoyed. The accumulated wealth also made cities the primary targets for pillaging rebels and marauding foreign invaders.

The greatest of the cities were the capitals, Changan in the west and Luoyang in the east. They housed imperial palaces as well as compounds—the August Enceintes—for the bureaus of the central government. Changan had been the main seat of the Tang since its founding in 618, and was probably the largest city in the world at the time, with a population of perhaps 2 million souls. Its prestige was so great that the Japanese adopted its layout for their imperial metropolis at Nara in the eighth century. At the beginning of the Tang, Luoyang, which had suffered greatly from destruction wrought by warfare, was the seat of a military governor and a prefecture. In 657 the emperor raised it to the status of capital because frequent famines in Changan, which suffered from a supply problem, forced the imperial court to move there. Luoyang, however, remained underpopulated until 691, when Empress Wu, who favored it over its western counterpart, had more than 100,000 families, half a million people, transplanted there from the region around Changan. Thereafter, it became the second largest city in China with a population of about 1 million souls. Luoyang sat astride the Luo River close to the end of the Grand Canal, so foodstuffs from the fertile south easily made their way into the city. Except during her reign it was the secondary capital of the Tang. Furthermore, the court never visited it after 743, when Changan's supply problem was solved. The dynasty also designated Taiyuan as its northern capital, but the city never became the seat of government.

Some cities were more than seats of government. They were also centers of economic activity. The greatest of them in the Tang was Yangzhou, located on the Grand Canal close to the Yangtze River, where commodities from the interior of China and overseas were transshipped and sent to northern metropolises. It was also the headquarters for the national salt monopoly as well as the greatest industrial town in the period. It produced admirable bronze mirrors; fine felt hats that citizens of Changan esteemed; sugar refined from cane; boats that sold for 5 million coppers; elegant, expensive furniture; and beautiful silk textiles. Canton was the greatest entrepôt of foreign trade. There ships from Persia, Arabia, and southeast Asia off-loaded rare perfumes, woods, jewels, plants, drugs, dyes, and other goods that Chinese merchants sent north to satisfy the tastes of the rich and powerful in the capitals. Chengdu in the southwest was the greatest center for the production of paper and printed books, both of which were Chinese inventions. It also served as a haven for emperors fleeing rebels who attacked and seized Changan.

Most Tang cities lay on flatlands next to rivers that served as the cheapest routes for transportation. That meant that spring floods periodically devastated towns as winter snows melted in the mountains to the west and raised the levels of rivers above the levees built to prevent inundations. Luoyang, which sat astride a river, was particularly vulnerable to such disasters. Floods on occasion destroyed as much as 18 percent of the city. The most readily available and cheapest building material in the lowlands where towns were erected was dirt. Consequently, engineers and laborers built walls by ramming thin layers of loose earth in wood frames to form the core of the ramparts. They then faced them with brick or stone to prevent erosion by rain and constructed battlements on top to provide for their defense.

The outer walls of Changan, the city about which we have the most information, were about eighteen feet high. They encompassed an area some five miles by six, about thirty square miles. The purpose of the ramparts was to provide security for the residents within. They were barriers for preventing intrusions by assassins and bandits, but not insurmountable obstacles, as Tang law recognized. Climbing over city walls was an offense punishable by ninety blows with a thick rod for walls of the counties and one year of penal servitude for walls of the prefectures and capitals. As defensive bulwarks for impeding attacks by foreign invaders and indigenous rebels, the ramparts were less than satisfactory. They rarely withstood prolonged sieges, and emperors usually abandoned their capitals at the first signs of imminent military attack. Furthermore, the efficacy of walls as impediments was somewhat dubious, for wild animals sauntered into cities from time to time. In 769 a tiger settled in the ancestral shrine of a chief minister in Changan, and a general dispatched by the throne slew it with a crossbow. Another tiger entered a ward of the city in 782 and wounded two men before it was captured. In 830 a bear lumbered into a Buddhist monastery in Changan. Deer were also frequent intruders at the capital.

Gates in the walls provided access to city interiors. Smaller metropolises probably had at least one gate for each direction, but in Changan there were three each in the east, south, and west walls, as well as a dozen or so in the north that opened onto imperial parks and palaces. Each gate had three portals, and since traffic traveled to the right in Tang times, men, horses, and carriages entered Changan through the right portal (as one faced the gate from outside) and departed through the left. The middle opening was no doubt reserved for imperial or ritual processions. Gates were weak points in city defenses and therefore were heavily reinforced. Their keepers shut them at dusk, when the curfew began, and secured them with cylinder locks. No one, except for couriers with imperial decrees of an urgent nature, could enter or leave the city during the night. Failure to fasten the bolts of the locks or destruction of them while opening the gates was an offense punishable by eighty blows with a thick rod. In the capitals, gates were also prominent urban monuments and often were topped with pillared halls. Emperors made progresses (journeys) to them to see officials off when they were traveling to new posts in the provinces or retiring from office, as well as to pay their respects to deceased ministers or other eminent persons when their funeral corteges were leaving the cities to make their way to tombs outside the city.

Inside city walls, thoroughfares divided the urban landscape into a grid. In Changan there were eleven avenues running from north to south and fourteen streets running from east to west. The roads were constructed of rammed earth and, being unpaved, turned to muddy bogs when it rained. The narrowest were 82 feet wide, those terminating in the gates of the outer ramparts were 328 feet wide, and the imperial way located in the exact center of the city, running from north to south, was 492 feet wide. The width of roads in the capitals, enormous even by modern standards, no doubt created excellent firebreaks in an age when water pumps for extinguishing conflagrations were unknown. Although terrible fires broke out in some sectors of the city—a fire consumed 4,000 homes, warehouses, and other buildings in the eastern market during 843—Changan suffered none of the citywide holocausts like the one that destroyed 17,000 homes in a southern city during 807. Roads in that town were unquestionably narrower.

The Tang law code established regulations for the control of traffic along urban thoroughfares. Fifty blows of the thin rod was the penalty for speeders, that is, riders or coachmen who raced their horses or carriages down a street or lane of a city into a crowd of three or more people. If they injured or killed a person, the punishments were sixty blows with the thick rod and execution by strangulation, respectively. If they injured or killed a domestic animal, they had to pay restitution to the owner of the animal. However, if the coachman or rider had just cause for speeding, such as summoning a physician to treat an illness or delivering an imperial decree, he was free from punishment unless he maimed or killed.

Precisely who maintained law and order in the streets of most cities during the Tang is unclear except for the capitals. There the responsibility fell to the Gold Bird Guards, who patrolled the thoroughfares day and night. Every intersection had a police post with thirty guards at major crossroads and five at minor ones. All gates had such posts with 100 men at the most important and 20 at the least important. The Gold Bird Guards were not always effective in carrying out their duties. In 838 some highwaymen shot at Chief Minister Li as he was making his way to an audience with the emperor in the predawn hours. Li suffered a slight wound, his retainers fled in all directions, and his startled horse raced back to his mansion. The thugs intercepted Li at the gate of his ward, assaulted him, and cut the tail off his horse. He barely escaped with his life. The emperor commanded army troops to take over guarding the streets of the capital. It was several days before calm returned to Changan.

Drainage ditches eleven feet wide and seven feet deep flanked both verges of the avenues and streets in Changan. The installation of the drains naturally entailed the construction of bridges, four at all intersections. The ditches were not sewers. Human waste was a commodity carted to the countryside and sold to farmers, who used it as fertilizer for their crops. There was a family in Changan that for generations had engaged in collecting night soil from dwellings in the city and had become wealthy from the trade. They had a beautiful mansion replete with fine furniture, a staff of slaves to do their bidding, elegant clothes for their women to wear, and herds of domestic animals to supply meat for their table.

From the founding of Changan in 582 emperors had trees planted—elms and junipers and pagodas—alongside the ditches to provide shade and elegance for the metropolis. Citizens were probably most pleased when the throne ordered the planting of fruit trees along the avenues in 740, an act that enriched their diets as well as their surroundings. Emperors periodically had to order the replanting of trees. Gales occasionally uprooted them. In 835 a great wind blew down 10,000. Heavy snow and rainfall in 820 toppled many. In addition, citizens chopped them down for fuel and building materials in times of unrest when the authorities governing towns were unable to enforce the laws.

Canals were essential fixtures of cities, more so in the south, which had more watercourses than the north. The great metropolis of Yangzhou, which was crisscrossed with canals, had more boats than carriages. Changan had five canals, all but one of which delivered water to parks in the outer city, lakes in the gardens of patricians, and the grounds of imperial palaces. The fifth, designed to transport lumber and completed in 742, flowed into the western market, where the wood was stored in a pool. In 766 the mayor of the capital extended one of the canals eastward across the city to furnish citizens with firewood and charcoal, which were in short supply. The channel was eight feet wide and ten feet deep. Canals were weak points in city walls, as Tang law acknowledged. Entering a city through a canal was an offense punishable by ninety blows with a thick rod and eighty blows if the trespasser was caught in the water but had not yet entered the town.

The area around Changan was overpopulated and suffered from a lack of grain from the early seventh century to the early eighth century. That was partly due to the difficult and expensive carting of the cereals that had to travel roads on the last leg of their journey. In 743 the Commissioner of Land and River Transport constructed a canal from the junction of the Yellow and Wei rivers to the capital, and dug a lake just outside the city to receive boats. The following year 1,750,000 bushels of grain arrived from the east and south. Changan rarely suffered a shortage thereafter. A canal also supplied Luoyang with its needs. It terminated at a lake inside the city where transport boats anchored.

## WARDS

Avenues and streets divided cities into square or rectangular wards—Changan had 110 of them and Luoyang 113—similar to blocks in modern American towns. Unlike their modern counterparts, however, they were far larger and walled. In Changan the size of the smallest was 68 acres and that of the largest, 233 acres. The wards encompassed houses, mansions, government offices, monasteries, temples, parks, workshops, and inns. In Changan, newly rebuilt in the late sixth century, the southernmost wards, four to the east and west of the main north–south avenue, had no great dwellings, at least in the early eighth century. Farmers raised crops there. In both capitals there were also gardens for cultivating medicinal herbs used in the palace; growing vegetables served at imperial feasts and sacrifices; and raising bamboo to supply the Department of Agriculture. The southern portion of one ward in Changan had no dwellings at all, only graves. Ironically, though the region surrounding Changan was overpopulated, the capital itself was underpopulated.

Walls of rammed earth, nine or ten feet high in Changan, enclosed the wards. Sometimes the walls were inadvertently erected in perilous locations. On July 30, 720, the walls of one ward in Changan collapsed during the night and a large pool formed. The disaster, probably caused by a sinkhole created when ground water eroded the limestone bedrock, destroyed more than 500 homes.

Each of the wards was crisscrossed by north–south and east–west roads that terminated in gates. Maintaining the integrity of the arteries was a difficult task for the government. Citizens encroached on the roads to plant crops, to excavate earth to build kilns for baking bricks or roof tiles, and to build walls and dwellings. The penalty for infringing on the streets was seventy blows of the thick rod, but only fifty blows with the thin rod if the infraction was committed to grow food. Enforcement of that regulation was not particularly effective in the late eighth century, however. In 776 the throne ordered all structures built in the roads of the wards and markets destroyed. The lanes of the wards were unpaved. In the late ninth century rain mired a road in one of them, and a jackass carrying firewood got stuck in the mud, blocking the way for a ruffian.

Infuriated, he picked up the beast by all four of its legs and threw it several paces into a drainage ditch.

Roads divided wards into quarters. The quarters had alleys that were crooked or serpentine, so the grid pattern favored by Chinese city planners since antiquity broke down at that point. A few names of the alleys—Felt Alley and the Alley of the Jingling Harness—survive in Tang sources.

The function of ward walls was to provide internal security by preventing the movement of people. The law clearly asserted the principle. Ninety blows with a thick rod was the punishment for climbing over ward walls. Each of a ward's roads terminated in gates that a headman, who was in charge of affairs within the ward, barred at dusk. As the sun went down in Changan, a tattoo of 400 beats on a drum signaled the closing of palace gates and a second, of 600 beats, the closing of ward and city gates. The length of the tattoos gave people ample time to return to their dwellings before the ward gates closed. In the predawn hours drummers beat another tattoo of 3,000 beats that was the signal for opening the gates. Each of the avenues also had drums that sounded at curfew. The law forbade citizens to travel on the main thoroughfares of the cities outside the wards during curfew, but it did not restrict their nocturnal movements within the wards. The statute, however, permitted public commissioners bearing official documents, as well as marriage processions, to use the avenues and streets after curfew. In both cases they had to obtain a permit from the county government first. It also allowed private citizens who needed to find a doctor or procure medicine for the treatment of the ill to travel, as well as those who needed to leave their ward to announce a death. However, they had to have a certificate issued by the ward headman. Anyone else found wandering outside the wards during the night by the Gold Bird Guard was subject to twenty blows of the thin rod. In 808, however, the throne had a eunuch who got drunk and violated the curfew beaten to death. The emperor also demoted the officer in charge of the Gold Bird Guard and banished him from the capital.

Woe betide the reveler or criminal who tried to ignore the hail of the night patrol. According to the law, if a guard encountered a traveler on the main streets outside his ward and the traveler failed to respond to his queries, the guard was to twang his bowstring. If the wretch refused to answer his second call, the sentry was to loose a warning arrow to one side of him. If the fool still did not reply, the watchman was to shoot him down.

Aristocrats and high-ranking officials preferred living in the wards of Changan's eastern half. One particular ward along the northeast wall of the city attracted their attention because during the Sui dynasty a clairvoyant declared that the place had the aura of nobility. No doubt the upper classes believed that a mansion there would perpetuate their good fortune and elite status. The western half of the city was far more populous than the eastern, and full of drifters and transients. It also appears to have been the district where foreigners lived. A Turkish prince and his wife had a mansion there, and most of the foreign churches were located in the northwest.

The lowest inhabitants of cities were the impoverished, who lived wherever they could find shelter and sought sustenance by begging from those better off than themselves. In the early eighth century a man led a cow that had a human hand more than a foot in length hanging between its forelegs through the wards of a city. He exhibited the mutant in the expectation that passersby would give him food. An impoverished woman and her father sang songs in the streets of wards to eke out a living. A general was so smitten with her voice that he took her as one of his private entertainers. Not all panhandlers were human. A clever artisan who was in charge of the imperial factories once carved a Buddhist monk from wood and placed it in the market of a provincial city. The automaton carried a bowl in its hand, was able to move on its own, and begged for money. When its bowl was full of coppers, a mechanized bolt abruptly shot out, locking the coins in the dish so that no one could filch them. The wooden monk could speak on its own and say "Alms." The market folk flocked to see the spectacle. Because they wanted the automaton to speak, the donations made to watch it perform filled the bowl several thousand times each day.

Emperors were not happy to have derelicts roaming the streets of the capitals. They considered the cities to be their own special domiciles. In 734 the throne banned beggars from the streets of the metropolises and consigned them to the Wards for the Sick, Buddhist foundations that cared for the ill, aged, orphaned, and poor. The government oversaw the wards and capital officials provided the money for their maintenance from their own funds. In 738 the emperor also assigned revenues from newly opened fields near Changan for the relief of the poor and of commoners who had returned to their lands after fleeing. Those welfare measures did not survive the rebellion of An Lushan in 756.

After the rebellion the structure of the wards broke down along with the political order. Previously only nobles and high-ranking ministers could legally construct gates for their mansions that opened directly onto the main avenues of Changan outside the wards. Afterward other citizens who had not enjoyed such privileges before followed suit. They began knocking down ward walls and encroaching on the roads to build their dwellings. In 831 the Commissioner for Patrolling the Streets reported that people having gates opening onto the avenues did not observe curfew carefully, opening them before dawn and closing them after nightfall. As a result it was easy for thieves to flee and hide on their property. So the official proposed that all private gates, except for those of the nobles and ministers, be barricaded.

## MARKETS

In theory every city had a market, but small and impoverished counties probably did not. Those that did, were official markets ruled by Market Commandants appointed by the central government. In 707 the throne issued a decree forbidding the establishment of markets outside cities. There were, however, exceptions. The state operated periodic markets along the northern frontier, mainly to purchase horses from nomadic, pastoral peoples. There were also unofficial rural markets, called "markets in the grass" (northern China) or "markets in the wilds" (south China). They arose spontaneously in the countryside to serve the needs of peasants living more than a day's ride from a city. The farmers traded their produce for goods—the most important of which was salt, which was not available in many places—supplied by traveling merchants. At first they had no stores, shops, or warehouses, but toward the end of the dynasty some of them acquired such facilities.

The government controlled all urban markets through the agency of Market Commandants and their small staffs. The duties of the commandants were to register merchants and their establishments; to inspect weights and measures to ensure that they met government standards; to weed out counterfeit coins; and to prevent the sale of inferior goods that did not meet official requirements for size, weight, and quality of materials or workmanship. The statutes required market officials to send all weights and measures to the imperial treasuries in the capitals or the offices of prefectures and counties in the eighth moon of every year so they could be tested to ensure their accuracy, and stamped with a seal. It was the responsibility of market officials to issue certificates of purchase for slaves, horses, cattle, camels, mules, and donkeys within three days after the transactions. In addition it was their duty to prevent price-fixing, monopolies, and other unfair market practices by merchants. According to regulations, they had to set the prevailing prices for all commodities every ten days. If they fraudulently acquired goods by setting the prices higher or lower than their real value at the time, the government ordered them to resign, stripped them of all their bureaucratic and aristocratic titles for a period of six years, and forced them to pay double the value of the property involved.

The greatest markets in the Tang were those in Changan. The capital had two of them, each of which was somewhat bigger than two of the largest wards (i.e., over 466 acres). There were two roads running east to west and two running north to south that were 100 paces wide each. The streets divided the markets into nine sectors. The office of the

Market Commandant was in the central block, as were those of two bureaus charged with stabilizing prices. The first of them was responsible for disbursing cereals during famines, when grain prices soared. It released reserves amassed from taxes and held in government granaries. Its duty was to flood the market with cereals at prices below market value so that the price of food dropped and people who were starving had enough to survive. Prefectures also had such offices as well as granaries. The second bureau, abolished in the 730s, was responsible for stabilizing prices of other commodities. It dumped surplus goods that government agencies had not used and property that the state had confiscated from nobles, officials, and others who had committed high crimes. The government was about the business of curbing inflation.

The nine sectors of Changan's markets, as well as other urban bazaars, were subdivided into lanes (*hang*), each of which was devoted to a single commodity and was required by law to erect at its entrance a sign with a title that designated its specialty. All retail shops or stalls that sold a given product were located in the lane with the appropriate sign. Warehouses and wholesale outlets lined the outer walls of the market. Only a dozen or so of the names for the *hang* in the capitals and other cities have survived in Tang literature: Meat (where a man once purchased the head of white cow to concoct a nostrum for curing some ailment); Iron (where one could find a clever fortune-teller); Apothecary (where an emperor once ordered ingredients for a Taoist elixir that would ensure his immortality); Ready-Made Clothes; Pongee (low-grade silk); Axes; Steamed Buns; Bridles and Saddles (that had a tavern); Weights and Measures; Gold- and Silversmiths; Fishmongers; and Greengrocers. Since the eastern market of Changan alone had 220 lanes, these titles represent a minute fraction of the goods and services offered in the lanes.

There were also businesses in the markets whose *hang* names are unknown. Some sold horses, mules, cows, pigs, and slaves that were kept in pens. The western market in Changan had a pig sty where a sow gave birth to a piglet with one head, three ears, two bodies, and eight legs in the summer of 813. A firm in the eastern market, the Jackass Express, rented donkeys to travelers who did not wish to walk to their destinations in the city. At another firm a patron could purchase foreign musical instruments. Brewers produced an ale called Melody of the Western Market, no doubt because that was the location of their establishment. A man in that bazaar sold porridge for a profit and made a fortune from his enterprise. In contrast, the wife of a wealthy merchant, who was a devout Buddhist and donated his mansion to the church for conversion into a monastery, sold excellent cooked cereals at a cheap price. There was an establishment that sold fried pastries and steamed dumplings in the western market, and also a restaurant or delicatessen.

By the beginning of the ninth century, a large increase in trade led to new developments in urban markets. Protobanks—there was one in the western market of Changan—emerged that offered a safe-deposit service. For a fee they took custody of gold, silver, and coins to protect them from theft. The firms issued checks to their customers, who could use them to draw funds from their stored valuables. The checks were the ancestors of the world's first paper currency, which a provincial government in China issued during 1024. Gold- and silversmiths also issued such promissory notes.

The hours for trading at markets throughout the empire were more restrictive than the curfew. According to a Tang statute they opened at noon with a tattoo of 300 beats on a drum and closed an hour and three quarters before dusk with 300 beats on a gong. However, night markets must have flourished in residential wards because the gates of the central markets closed before nightfall. There is little information about them, but no doubt they served the needs of customers who had neglected to purchase essential items during the day at central markets. The throne banned the night markets in Changan in 841, but, like many such edicts, that decree was probably ineffective because the bazaars were critical to the lives of urban dwellers.

Because the mansions of nobles, mandarins, and other eminent people were mostly located in the eastern half of Changan, the shops of the eastern market catered to the rich and famous by selling costly and exotic wares. Its warehouses held rare goods imported from all over the world. Although commodities sold in the western market were of a more utilitarian and pragmatic sort, it was not without its own exotic wares. It had a Persian bazaar. The Persians, whose empire fell to the Arabs in the early seventh century, specialized in stones, precious metals, gems, elephant tusks, sacred relics, and above all pearls. After the rebellion of An Lushan the western market also had a thousand or more "Uighur" moneylenders who adopted Chinese dress, apparently to conceal their ethnic identities. Several Central Asian peoples assumed Uighur names— no doubt to avail themselves of the extraordinary protection that the Turks enjoyed—to pursue the lucrative business. The moneylenders advanced cash to the sons and younger brothers of nobles, military officers, merchants, and commoners. The young men squandered the money on amusing themselves. The usurers made enormous profits from their transactions. In 831 a "Uighur" sued the son of a grand general who had failed to repay a debt of nearly 11 million coppers. Upset over the scandal, the emperor not only banished the general but banned all commercial dealings between Chinese and foreigners except for trade in livestock.

Merchants were not the only proprietors of shops in the markets. Buddhist monasteries also established retail outlets and businesses that made loans against security. The income from those enterprises was sometimes substantial, and found its way into the church's treasuries. The throne banned Buddhists from participating in such commercial activities in 845.

The western market of Changan also had a pond for releasing the living. A Buddhist monk had it dug and filled with water in the early eighth century. The notion was that by purchasing fish and freeing them in the pool, one could accrue merit for one's ancestors that would absolve them from sin, lead to liberation from purgatory, and assure their rebirth in a favorable existence, such as an official, in the next life. No doubt monks recaptured the creatures—as they have in modern times—to resell to the next supplicant seeking salvation. Buddhist monasteries had identical ponds in the Tang. Ironically, the government conducted most executions under the solitary willow tree near the pond in the western market.

Not all trading took place in the great urban markets. By the ninth century some retail establishments, such as shops that sold fine silk textiles, existed in residential quarters. Furthermore, throughout the Tang, peddlers roamed the wards of Changan. A hawker who acquired the nickname Camel because he was a hunchback, pushed a small cart from which he sold pastries in the streets. Once he crashed into an overturned wagon of bricks and spilled his snacks on the ground. When he removed the bricks with a mattock, he found a pot of gold. He became a very wealthy man and purchased a mansion in the capital. A fellow tradesman who was a westerner had a small shop by the gate of a ward. He lit his lamps and stove in the predawn hours to sell breakfast. A vendor peddled fish on the main north–south street of Changan. Villagers outside the capital brought firewood in from the country on the backs of donkeys to sell in Changan. Huineng, the founder of the southern school of Chan (Zen), sold firewood in a city near Canton because his father, a banished official, died when he was very young. While doing so, he was instantaneously enlightened after hearing the reading of a Buddhist sutra. There were also vendors of oil who carried their vats on their back and sometimes were as unwilling as the sellers of kindling to yield the road to an official.

Nor was manufacturing concentrated in the official markets. As previously noted, the makers of bricks and tiles were in the habit of digging up dirt from roads in the wards where their works were located. In the ninth century there was an iron forge in a ward just west of the eastern market whose blacksmith also dabbled in selling horses in the street. Some brewers also made fine ale at the Toad Tumulus, an ancient grave mound in a ward beside the eastern wall of Changan. A craftsman of fine musical instruments had a workshop in the northeastern section of Changan. Where water was plentiful, as in Luoyang, there were gristmills for grinding grain into flour inside the city. A Buddhist monastery in that city had one with four waterwheels.

Various shops in the roads of wards copied Buddhist sutras and cast statues that they sold to the faithful along with food and ale. The emperor forbade that commerce in 714, ordering the clergy in monasteries to transcribe scriptures for the laity who wanted them instead. Laws proscribing activities that had become popular were generally effective only in the short term, so the trade in such articles probably survived into later times. The throne had banned the manufacture of statues by craftsmen for public sale in the first half of the seventh century, without lasting success.

There was also a variety of services offered outside the main markets. The capitals had many inns, both private and public, to accommodate travelers. A ward along the west wall of Changan had a funeral parlor where one could hire square-faced (masked) exorcists who expelled demons at graves, as well as rent hearses and other equipment for funerals. Such establishments would, for a fee, provide professional wailers who keened during funeral processions. On occasion they held contests to determine which of their mourners was the greatest singer of dirges. According to a short story, such a match took place on a major thoroughfare of the capital and attracted tens of thousands of spectators. Two firms put up 50,000 coppers to pay for food and drink as a prize for the winner. The competition began at dawn with an exhibition of hearses and other funerary paraphernalia. At noon the singers entered the arena and sang their laments. The winner reduced the crowd to sobbing and weeping with his rendition of "Dew on the Shallots," a classic funeral elegy. An old madam in a bordello in the Gay Quarters was very wealthy and rented a large store of clothes and dishes to others of her profession who wished to entertain male guests. A physiognomist, who read people's faces to foretell their futures, had a place in one of Changan's southeastern wards. He was so good at his occult art that citizens flocked there in hordes.

Buddhist monasteries ran public bathhouses in cities. A monk erected such an establishment in Luoyang, and the citizens of the capital, clergy and laity, the wealthy and the destitute, thronged there. It was open only on the first five days of each moon, but it attracted a steady stream of patrons. Some 2,000 to 3,000 customers bathed in its waters yearly during the seventy or seventy-five days when it was in operation.

The markets had their complement of taverns, but there were also pubs scattered throughout cities. In Changan westerners operated taverns, favored by poets, in the wards along the southeast wall of the city. They employed white-skinned, green-eyed, blond women from Central Asia to sing and dance so that patrons would spend more money on ale. Aside from the taverns inside Changan's walls, there were pubs where villagers living along some nineteen miles of the eastern road outside the city sold ale to travelers. Sojourners called the drinks that those establishments purveyed "goblets for dismounting the horse." Since the Chinese rarely drank without eating, pubs were also restaurants or snack shops.

Taverns dispensed ale on credit, and their proprietors, sometimes women, entrusted the collection of debts to their waiters. In his youth the most renowned painter of horses in the Tang caught the attention of a great poet when he went to settle a bar tab at the versifier's home. While waiting for the money, he passed the time drawing men and horses on the ground. The poet was so impressed with his work that he bestowed an annual stipend of 20,000 coppers on the lad for more than ten years, to sustain him while he studied painting.

## OFFICES

Every city in Tang China had a government office. All of them were walled compounds. In the provinces they contained the local governor's reception hall, where he conducted all of his official business, including criminal trials. Both prefectures and counties had residences at the offices for the governors and commandants, as well as for their families, if they accompanied them to their posts. They might have gardens with an abundance of white flowers. The compounds included offices for subordinate officials and prisons where wardens kept close watch over witnesses and criminals. They also housed local schools, with shrines for Confucius and his disciples, where teachers instructed their charges in the classics.

In the courtyard before the prefectural governor's reception hall, officials, military officers, commoners, and clergy gathered and stood, in positions fixed by their ranks, on the east side to hear the reading of imperial amnesties. Couriers of the rapid relay system brought the decrees, written on yellow paper, from the capital. When everyone was settled, the governor emerged from his hall at the north end of the square with a military escort of twenty officers, and stood on a carpet facing west. Army officers brought a stand covered with purple cloth and placed it before him. A judicial official spread the imperial decrees on it. Two legal mandarins read parts of the edicts alternately in loud voices. The objective of this recital was to ensure that the emperor's subjects understood his will. When the reading concluded, the governor dismissed all in attendance.

The largest concentrations of public buildings were in the two capitals. Each had compounds for its mayor and two county commandants. They also had huge, walled compounds—the August Enceintes—that contained the bureaus of the central government. Official agencies were also located in wards outside that compound. The Directorate of the Sons of State, which governed the most prestigious schools in the empire, was just southeast of the August Enceinte in Changan. In the early eighth century the throne converted one entire ward of the capital, formerly a market, into a camp for training soldiers in the use of the crossbow. In the ninth century there were also military camps in the outer city of that capital. In the last years of the dynasty Changan's wards also contained institutes for training musicians and entertainers.

By far the largest number of offices in Changan's wards were the headquarters of prefectural officials who traveled to the capital and made reports to the throne on affairs in their districts once a year, in the autumn and winter. During 643 the emperor discovered that they had no quarters in the capital and were renting rooms where they lived together with merchants. He therefore ordered the agencies in charge of construction to build them mansions. In 691, 2,800 of the local officials arrived in Luoyang to attend court, so the number of their dwellings must have been substantial. After the rebellion of An Lushan, provincial mandarins no longer made annual trips to Changan. Military governors took over the mansions and turned them into transmission offices. They sent their dispatches there for forwarding to the throne. The bureaus also became credit institutions. Southern merchants who transported their goods north and sold them in the capital turned the money that they made from their transactions over to agents at the transmission offices of the districts from which they came. The officials then used the funds to pay the taxes that their provinces owed the central government and issued the merchants certificates, known as "flying money." When the traders returned to their homes in the south, they presented the certificates to local authorities, who paid them the amount of money specified on the certificates. The system saved the merchants the risk and burden of carrying their profits with them as they traveled, and spared the government the expense of transporting taxes to Changan.

## CHURCHES

All great cities in the Tang had religious establishments of one sort or another. In the early eighth century Changan had ninety-one Buddhist monasteries (sixty-four for monks and twenty-seven for nuns), sixteen Taoist temples (ten for priests and six for priestesses), two Nestorian Christian churches, and four Zoroastrian shrines. Those figures did not include small Buddhist chapels or the ancestral shrines of powerful families. Some of the monasteries and temples were immense, occupying entire wards in the capital. One of the Buddhist establishments there had more than ten courtyards with 1,897 bays (the space between pillars) where 300 officially ordained monks resided.

The size and magnificence of the churches in Changan were the result primarily of patronage from the throne, nobility, and eminent political figures, who usually endowed them in order to earn merit toward salvation for themselves and their ancestors. In 631 the emperor established a Taoist abbey in gratitude to priests who had cured the heir apparent's illness. The Tang dynasty had a special affinity for Taoism because the family claimed descent from Lao Tzu. When the throne dubbed a prince heir apparent in 656, it converted his mansion into an abbey whose verandas, halls, murals, statuary, and priests' quarters were beyond compare. In the early eighth century, when the daughter of a princess took vows as a Taoist priestess, the court converted her mansion into an abbey. In 747, when the husband of a princess died, she requested permission to become a Taoist priestess, and the emperor established an abbey for her. The third emperor of the Tang established the most famous Buddhist monastery in the city—it occupied a whole ward—in the memory of his mother. The mother of an emperor in the mid-ninth century endowed a Buddhist monastery with 200,000 cash and three carts laden with embroidered cloth to accrue merit for her son's deceased wife. Even enslaved palace ladies collected money among themselves to erect a pagoda. One official donated his mansion as an act of repentance for executing a monk who had been falsely accused of having intercourse with a maidservant. The most powerful eunuch of the early eighth century donated his mansion in Changan for conversion into a Buddhist monastery. After the casting of a bell for the church, he convened a vegetarian feast for members of the imperial court. He demanded that his guests contribute 100,000 coppers each time they struck the bell. Someone who wished to curry the eunuch's favor struck the bell twenty times and forked over 2 million cash.

It was also the habit of the throne to have buildings in palaces dismantled and given to churches, which reassembled them to construct religious halls. Empress Wu donated one of her dressing rooms to a Buddhist monastery, and in 713 the emperor gave his bedchamber to a cloister. In the early eighth century the throne presented a stage for dancing to a Buddhist cloister. In 730 the emperor bestowed perhaps the largest of such gifts when he wanted a Taoist abbey erected with utmost speed. He ordered four palace halls dismantled to construct two halls for venerating the gods, a meditation chamber, and gates. In the early ninth century another emperor had 300 men restore the same abbey at a cost of 1 million coppers. At the cost of 1,000 lengths of silk and 171 pounds of tea, he also had an enclosed passageway built from the palace to the temple. Then he paid 5 million coppers and 207 bushels of grain to sponsor a great rite at the church.

Some emperors had halls for their own portraits established at monasteries in Changan. In 713 the monarch allocated 20 million coppers and assigned 1,000 craftsmen to the construction of such an edifice. Not only did his likeness adorn the walls, but paintings of ghosts and gods that he had removed from the palace were installed there. A princess built a portrait hall that had landscape murals on its walls painted by a respected artist.

The wealth of Buddhist monasteries in Changan was enormous. In the early years of the dynasty, a monk set up an Inexhaustible Treasury—so named because its assets could earn interest indefinitely—in a monastery. Men and women of high standing brought cartloads of coppers and silk as acts of repentance. They left their riches on the premises and then departed without giving their names. By the middle of the seventh century the wealth derived from those donations was incalculable. Unfortunately, the prelates who governed the church placed a secular custodian, whom they judged to be of good character, in charge of guarding their treasury. The temptation was too much for him, and he made off with its gold. The monks were so trusting that they were unaware of the theft until he absconded, and never discovered how much he had stolen. Monks supervised the treasury thereafter. The monastery used the interest it earned from loaning the riches it accumulated to pay for the restoration of other monasteries throughout the empire, to feed the starving, and to sponsor religious rites. The monks did not require contracts from debtors, fully confident that they would repay them with interest. In 713 the emperor abolished the treasury on the grounds that its banking practices were fraudulent, and confiscated its treasury. He then disbursed the holdings to other Buddhist monasteries as well as Taoist abbeys in the capital for use in repairing statues, halls, and bridges.

All monasteries had at least one hall for worshipping Buddha: offering prayers, burning incense, and chanting scriptures. Some were enormous. A hall dedicated to the Buddha Who Is to Come was 150 feet high. Every hall had a statue of the Buddha, one of which was thirty feet tall. They were usually made of bronze, but also could be of precious metals and stones. One monastery in Changan had 600 small silver Buddhas, one figure of pure gold that was several feet high, and another of silver over six feet tall. A church in the capital had a statue carved from jade that came from Central Asia. Occasionally, emperors bestowed statuary from the palace collection on monasteries. In such cases they sent the images forth in corteges having 1,000 painted carriages escorted by troupes of palace musicians, singers, and dancers.

Emperors might also bestow paintings from the palace collection on churches. Most artworks in the cloisters served ideological and educational ends. Since the vast majority of Chinese were illiterate, Buddhist monasteries and Taoist abbeys commissioned artists to paint murals depicting aspects of their beliefs that the unlettered could grasp visually. The frescoes of purgatory that the greatest artist of the dynasty painted on the walls of a monastery in Changan were so horrific and monstrous that visitors felt their hair stand on end. He executed another mural of the underworld that was so terrifying, butchers and fishmongers who saw it changed their professions. They feared that they would suffer the hellish tortures depicted in it for the sin of slaying living things. One artist's depictions of the underworld were particularly marvelous because he had died, visited the infernal regions, and returned to life to paint what he had seen. Murals of paradise were no less vivid and realistic, though less sensational.

The most prominent structures of Buddhist monasteries were pagodas, a unique form of architecture developed by the Chinese. Purportedly based on Indian stupas, they more closely resembled ancient towers that had been the vogue in architecture centuries before the Tang. Pagodas were artificial imitations of the sacred mountain, and were the only highrise buildings in traditional times. Two, the Large Goose and the Small Goose, that rise to 210 feet and 149 feet, respectively, and are built of brick, are the only structures that survive from Tang Changan. The upper stories of pagodas provided excellent views of cities and became urban landmarks.

They also assumed an important role in the ancient Chinese art of *feng-shui*, or geomancy. The basis for geomancy was the belief that invisible forces (*qi*: breaths, vapors, energies) control nature and the destiny of people. They flow above and below. Human activities, such as digging and building, disrupt, obstruct, and injure the currents. As a result, natural disasters occur and, more important, one's luck takes a turn for the worse. In the early seventh century a Sui official observed that a large lake southwest of Changan was exerting an adverse effect on the capital, and suggested that the erection of a pagoda could counter its influence. In geomancy, water, the element of yin (the moon, dark, pliant, female) could exert either a benevolent or a malevolent force on the site of a city, dwelling, or grave, depending on its location and character. A river with a slow current that flowed south and turned to the east was a benign influence. In this case the lake was to the west and was not flowing at all. Therefore, it was stagnant and lifeless. To remedy such a situation, geomancers usually proposed interposing a tall object, often a tree for a home, that represented yang (the sun, light, rigid, fire, male) between the structure and the water. A pagoda was ideal for a city, given its height. So in 611 the emperor had a pagoda built of wood that was 330 feet tall and 120 paces in circumference at the southwest corner of Changan.

Monasteries had meditation halls where monks practiced their devotions, cells where they slept, baths where they bathed, as well as kitchens and dining halls. They had libraries where they stored their sutras (scriptures). One of them had a separate building that housed a revolving bookcase. The size of Buddhist libraries in Changan grew enormously when pilgrims returned from India with great loads of sutras. After they arrived home, they translated the scriptures at the churches in the capital. Monastic collections often included Taoist scriptures as well as secular works. One wise poet of the ninth century deposited editions of his collected works in monasteries on three different occasions, probably because he believed that the cloisters provided better security and would preserve them longer. The broad range of books in the churches may account for the fact that candidates for civil service examinations took lodgings in the monasteries of Changan while preparing for their tests.

Some of Changan's monasteries were repositories for Buddha's relics; four of his teeth were preserved in four different cloisters. One of them, which a Chinese pilgrim brought from India, was three inches in length. Those monasteries put the purported artifacts on exhibit with offerings of food, flowers, and incense. Citizens donated cereals, coppers, and other things as pledges of their reverence. The most revered of the relics was part of Buddha's finger bone, preserved in a cloister 100 miles or so west of the capital. On three occasions in the late eighth and the ninth centuries the throne had it brought to Changan, escorted by a grand cortege with monks and nuns trailing behind. Villagers from the surrounding countryside flocked to the city to watch the spectacle as the parade entered through the northwest gate, where the emperor greeted it from a pillared hall above. The leading families of the metropolis decorated their coaches in rich adornments to honor the relic. In 873 a zealous believer, a soldier, lopped off an arm and carried it along the road, his blood dripping on the street, as the cavalcade made its way through the boulevards. Many citizens bit off their fingers to manifest their devotion. A monk burned herbs on his bald pate. He shook his head and cried out in pain, but lads from the market gripped him tightly so that he could not budge. Finally, he fell to the ground when he could no longer stand the agony. After the relic arrived in the palace, the emperor ordered some 10,000 posts of incense, ten to twenty feet tall, erected throughout the city. Gold and jade adorned the first nine feet of the posts, which were made of earth. The fragrance from the incense wafted throughout the capital. Wealthy families built halls from silk cloth where they installed trees of gold and jade and pools of mercury. They also built floats of fancy textiles that carried singers and dancers. The floats paraded through the streets of the metropolis for the amusement of Changan's citizens.

Self-mutilation was a facet of Buddhist asceticism. Buddhists had little regard for the body, which they called "a bag of stinking skin." They thought of it as the ultimate source of the temptations that prevented the devout from attaining enlightenment and salvation. It is therefore not surprising that monks or the laity willingly sacrificed all or part of their bodies to express their deep devotion to their faith. They might burn off fingers, gouge out eyes, or cut off ears to make offerings to the

Buddha. Buddhist scripture promised the clergy who made such sacrifices that they would qualify for rebirth in the paradise of Pure Land. The most extreme form of such practices was autocremation. One Tang monk at the age of seventy-four set out with a disciple for a peak on a holy mountain. At his order the disciple wrapped him in waxed cloth and hemp, and poured oil over him. Then he set fire to his master. The flames consumed the monk's body from the top of his head to the soles of his feet.

Convents were not always the abodes of the chaste that they were supposed to be. In the mid-ninth century an emperor made a tour of Changan in disguise. When he arrived at a Taoist nunnery, he discovered that the women were attired in elegant gowns and heavily made up. Shocked and angered, the monarch ordered one of his officials to expel the priestesses from the place, and appointed two men to take charge of the abbey. The ladies apparently were courtesans.

## THE GAY QUARTERS

There was one special district, the North Hamlet, in Changan reserved for high-class courtesans who mainly served nobles, officials, graduates of the civil service examinations, and occasionally rich merchants. Prized more, or at least as much as, for their talents as entertainers at feasts than for their sexual services, they resembled Japanese geishas. They were superior to their counterparts in Luoyang and the barmaids who served drinks in the prefectures because they had excellent table manners and were extremely polite (or at least some were). They were official entertainers who had to register with the government and over whom the mayor of the capital exercised control. He regulated their sedan chairs and could stop them from leaving their quarters.

The North Hamlet was in the northeast quadrant of a ward that was adjacent to the eastern market, across from the August Enceinte and east of the national colleges. It had three winding alleys. The courtesans living in the North Alley were inferior in skills to the those residing in the Central and Southern alleys, who held them in contempt. The gates of the latter byways opened onto the north–south road of the ward. Newly appointed officials sauntered incognito there, looking for pleasure. The bordellos on those alleys were large and tranquil. They had three or more salons for receiving guests as well as smaller rooms hung with several layers of drapes. Flowers and shrubs grew in front of and behind the dwellings, where there were ponds with strangely shaped rocks. Not all of the courtesans there were well-to-do. The house of one who lived in the South Alley with her madam—who happened to be her biological mother—and two older, unskilled sisters was shabby. Since the women

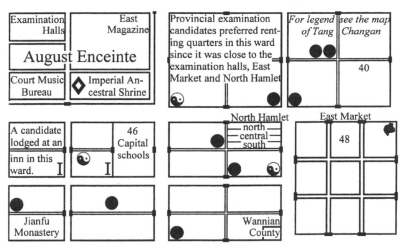

**North Hamlet, the Gay Quarters**

attracted few pleasure seekers, the women sold herbs and fruit at a small stall on their property.

The madams were, for the most part, foster mothers because the girls and young women over whom they exercised control were usually not their biological daughters. Some of the foster mothers were former courtesans who were too old to pursue their profession. They supported men who attended to their bedchambers, but the women did not treat them as their husbands. Madams were popularly called "exploding charcoal," perhaps because they often lost their tempers at their foster daughters. Foster mothers taught the courtesans the skills of their trade: singing and the rules of drinking games in particular. They flogged their trainees whenever they were negligent or lazy.

As for the courtesans, some had been raised as beggars in their youth, and others had been indentured to poor families in rural hamlets. Others came from good (i.e., wealthy or patrician) families that had betrothed them to obtain a bride price from unscrupulous men. Those scoundrels then sold the girls to madams in the North Hamlet, where they had no means of extricating themselves. When the girls entered the bordellos there, they took the surnames of their foster mothers. After training, at the age of eleven or twelve they received splendid gowns, a gift that signified they were fully fit to receive guests.

It was difficult for courtesans to leave their bordellos. The madams let them out only on the eighth, eighteenth, and twenty-eighth days of the moon to hear lectures on scriptures at a nearby Buddhist monastery, and then only after their daughter paid 1,000 coppers. On those three days young men of Changan gathered at the church to look over and meet the courtesans. If a woman went elsewhere, to attend a party at a park or to have a rendezvous with a man, a maid had to accompany her. The maid took her earnings and handed them over to her madam.

An important role for the courtesans was to supervise feasts. They were at ease with nobles, high-ranking officials, and candidates for the civil service examinations, but were especially punctilious in following the rules of propriety when receiving court officials who carried gold insignia. Whatever the case, the best of them were skilled conversationalists, poets, and singers who knew the rules of drinking games and kept a party convivial. They were also not above telling a guest that he talked too much when he was bragging about his accomplishments and spoiling the banquet for others. Some of them, however, had bad dispositions when offended. After a drunken guest made fun of one courtesan, she struck his cheek and inflicted a deep scratch. Some hostesses enjoyed great repute among their patrons even though they were homely. After hearing the fame of a courtesan, a graduate of the examinations named Liu became infatuated with her, sight unseen. He sent her gift after gift, but she refused to see him. Finally, he bribed an official with a gift of three and three-quarters pounds of gold flowers and silver goblets. The mandarin escorted the woman to the graduate's feast even though she was sick at the time. When Liu lifted the curtain of her sedan chair, he found an ugly woman who was disheveled, in tears, and older than he. He sent her back.

The normal fee for a feast at a bordello in North Hamlet was 1,600 coppers, and double that for a guest who was a newcomer and for a party that went on after the first candles sputtered out. Musicians who lived near North Hamlet were ready to perform for a feast at a moment's notice. The musicians charged 1,200 coppers for each round of drinks, but 2,400 if the revelry went on after the first candles died. When a guest came up short on the required fee to a madam, she might seize his carriage and clothes in lieu of payment.

In the early ninth century the North Hamlet could be a dangerous place to visit. A young member of the Gold Bird Guard named Wang encountered a drunk in one of the brothels and hid under the man's bed. Another man suddenly burst into the room with sword drawn and beheaded the drunk, believing him to be Wang. The murderer then threw his victim's head to the ground and lay down on the bed to sleep. Wang escaped with his life, presumably after spending an uncomfortable night on the floor, and never visited the quarter again. In the same period Linghu, a candidate for the civil service examinations sent to Changan from the provinces, spent much of his time in the Gay Quarters. One day the madam of a brothel asked him to leave because she was having a family gathering. Suspicious or curious, he went to the neighboring house to sneak a peek at the festivities. From its window he saw the madam and her courtesan slay a drunk and bury him in their backyard. The next day, he went to spend the night at the brothel, and in the middle of the night asked the courtesan about the murder. Alarmed, she seized his throat in an attempt to strangle him and called out to her foster mother. When he was on the verge of dying, the madam advised her daughter to stop. The next morning Linghu reported the matter to the authorities, but when they went to investigate, the pair had fled.

Some courtesans were not happy with their lives in North Hamlet and yearned to leave it. If they were lucky, a rich man might marry them, present them with gold and silk as a bride price, and take them away from North Hamlet. Nobles might, with the approval of their wives, take them as concubines. In one case, while a duke was occupied with affairs of state, his nephew had an illicit affair with his uncle's concubine and spent a month with her, neglecting his duties. When the matter came to light, the duke's wife sent her away with several hundred pieces of gold. The woman married a minor clerk, and before a year had passed, they had squandered the gold. Since her husband could not support her, she returned to North Hamlet to become a courtesan again.

The local governments of prefectures and larger administrations also maintained courtesans, who had to register and entertain officials. Camp courtesans provided amusement for military officers at posts around the empire. The proud father of a successful graduate of the civil service examinations opened the gates of his home in southwest China for a party at which all of the camp courtesans in his district appeared to enliven the festivities.

Not all courtesans lived in the Gay Quarters of Changan. One named Night Coming lived in a ward along the southeast wall of the capital. As a young woman her skills at amusing men, singing, and dancing exceeded all others. The sons of the nobility squandered fortunes to pay for a visit to her. One of the greatest poets of the Tang, a Taoist priestess and a courtesan, entertained her gentleman clients in the abbey where she lived. Both of those women probably were official courtesans, for they appear to have entertained only aristocrats and mandarins.

As for commoners, when the economy boomed in the second half of the Tang, public houses of prostitution began to appear in markets and other heavily trafficked places to serve the needs of merchants and others who could afford the pleasure.

A promiscuous man could catch a venereal disease in the Gay Quarters or in lower-class bordellos. Syphilis did not exist in China until Europeans introduced it in the sixteenth century. Tang physicians recognized some form of gonorrhea, however, and they knew that it was spread by indiscriminate intercourse with prostitutes.

## PARKS

The largest park in Changan was the Forbidden Park north of Chang-an. Though not the largest in the empire—that distinction belonged to its counterpart in Luoyang—it was forty miles in circumference and, as its name implies, off-limits to anyone but the emperor, his servitors, and his guests. Fed by rivers and canals that flowed from the mountains south of the city, it had lakes with fish and groves of peach, pear, and willow trees, as well as vineyards. The Department of Agriculture ran the vast complex that produced food for the emperor, his family, and his officials. The park was also an animal preserve where herds of animals roamed, and sometimes became prey during the throne's hunts. There were palatial halls and ball fields where the emperor amused himself and those whom he chose to honor.

Several parks existed in the districts outside the Forbidden Park and the palaces. The greatest of them was the Serpentine River in the southeast corner of the city. In the early eighth century the throne had the river flowing through the area dredged to form a lake so deep that one could not see the bottom. It was joined to a much older park called the Lotus Garden. After 756 it became the most popular spot for feasts that emperors bestowed on their officials. An Arab who visited the capital in the ninth century reported that it was off-limits to commoners (i.e., citizens who were not aristocrats, mandarins, or examination graduates).

The park had a two-story hall called Purple Clouds as well as a number of pavilions where a successful contender for a palace examination might convene a feast to celebrate his victory. The Serpentine River and Lotus Garden had willows, poplars, lotus, chrysanthemums, marsh grasses, and reeds. Wildfowl visited it in the fall when they made their way south for the winter. Esthetes liked to visit, watch the birds fly by, and listen to their cries. There were also a Buddhist convent and a monastery, as well as two ancestral shrines for high-ranking officials, within its precincts. In 835 the throne undertook a restoration of the park, ordering 1,500 soldiers to dredge its lake and rebuild its edifices. At that time the emperor bestowed grants of vacant land on officials so that they could build their own pavilions in the park.

Patricians could visit the Serpentine River at any time of the year, but they were particularly fond of going there during the spring. It was the custom for citizens of Changan to climb into carriages or mount horses and ride to parks in the city or scenic areas in the suburbs during the second half of the first moon. There they erected oiled tents and feasted to enjoy the arrival of spring. The waterproof tents protected revelers and their victuals from being soaked by rain. The third day of the third moon was an occasion that had special relevance to Serpentine River. Since the fourth century the educated had held drinking parties along winding rivers, and those festivities survived into the Tang (though then they took place on the banks of lakes). Patricians went to the Serpentine River, where they ate and drank under silk tents erected along the shores of the lake. High-ranking ministers could take their pleasure on painted boats that drifted on the surface of its water. The emperor, who sometimes attended such fetes, might provide entertainment in the form of music, song, dance, and acrobatics by lending his own performers to the revelers. The ninth day of the ninth moon was an occasion for visits to the park, where revelers spread out a picnic, roamed the banks of the lake half-drunk, and listened to the calls of ducks and geese.

# 4

# House and Garden

## DWELLINGS

The word for "home" in Chinese is a pictograph of a roof with a pig beneath. The roof was, of course, essential to any dwelling built above ground. A pig in an abode, however, was peculiar to China. Throughout most of China's history, even in the twentieth century, the pig has been the most prized source of meat, butchered and eaten on ceremonial or sacrificial occasions by even the most humble people. For that reason the lowly peasant made every effort to protect the creature from theft and allocated space for it within his house. Those with greater resources—rich peasants, merchants, officials, and aristocrats—had sties to house their hogs and did not keep them in their living quarters.

There were all sorts of dwellings in the Tang dynasty. Beyond the Great Wall pastoral tribes lived in yurts, round tents made of felt that they stretched over wood frames. They could easily dismantle the yurts and move them, loaded on their horses, to greener pastures for grazing their sheep. In northwest China, where trees were scarce and the climate was dry, people lived in artificial caves. The soil of that region was loess, dirt that the winds had blown in from the steppes of the north for centuries. The deposits were 150 or more feet thick, and fairly easy to work since they contained few rocks. The inhabitants dug chambers into the sides of hills or excavated deep, rectangular pits at the bottom of which they tunneled into the walls to fashion rooms. Cave dwellings reached a mature stage of development during the Tang. In southwest China aborigines lived in homes built on pilings to protect themselves and their property from moisture and flooding. Along the Yangtze River crews of transport vessels spent their entire lives on boats. Their craft even had gardens that produced vegetables for the tables of the boat people. Some merchants in central China had large ships on which they lived with troupes of female entertainers and complements of maidservants. In some southern districts nearly half of the population lived on boats.

Most of the information about houses in Tang sources concerns the great residences of the patricians in Changan and Luoyang. At the beginning of the dynasty, those mansions were spare and plain. Between 690 and 710, however, members of the aristocracy, especially princesses, began to erect lavish dwellings, striving to outdo each other in extravagance. That trend continued during the second half of Illustrious August's reign among imperial princes, high-ranking officials, and those who enjoyed imperial favor. In some instances the behavior of well-connected families during that period was as outrageous as that of Zhongzong's daughters in the early eighth century. One of Yang Guifei's elder sisters, who enjoyed imperial favor by virtue of her kinship to the emperor's beloved consort, arrived at the house of a former high-ranking minister named Wei. Dressed in a skirt and tunic of yellow silk gauze, she climbed out of her sedan chair and entered the mansion with more than twenty of her maidservants. She met Wei's sons and said, "I've heard that this dwelling is up for sale. How much do you want for it?" They replied, "This was the residence of our ancestor, so we could not bear to part with it." Before they finished speaking, several hundred workmen burst into the mansion, scaled the eastern and western wings, and began dismantling the structures from the roof tiles down to the timbers. Helpless to stop the pillaging, the Wei sons and their servants managed to rescue only their zithers and books. As compensation for seizing their halls, the woman gave them some two acres of wasteland. In contrast, when workmen finished building her main hall, using the materials from the Wei mansion, she paid them 2 million coppers for the job. In the end the lady met her just desert for abuse of the Weis. When An Lushan's armies descended on Changan, she fled into a bamboo grove, where her mother-in-law stabbed her to death before slitting her own throat.

During the rebellion of An Lushan many of the great houses in the capitals were razed or ruined. After 763 chief ministers, other powerful mandarins, and meritorious generals launched another period of extravagant building. One of them in the second half of the eighth century had two first-rate mansions—northern and southern—in Changan as well as more than a score of country estates south of the city. After his disgrace and execution the government had both of the mansions dismantled and seized the building materials to construct office buildings. The fashion of erecting grand mansions in the capitals continued during later times when peace and prosperity prevailed. There were, however, eminent officials who were frugal and lived on shabby lanes in homes that barely sheltered them from wind and rain.

Many of the mansions in Changan and Luoyang were actually the property of the emperor, who thought the capitals were his own personal domains. It was the habit of the throne to bestow mansions on nobles, mandarins, and eminent persons who enjoyed imperial favor. Some of the dwellings were enormous. The mansion of a prince might occupy an entire ward. When the emperor granted such gifts, he usually ordered a chief minister and/or general to escort the honored recipient to his new residence with the imperial fife and drum corps. The throne might also furnish a troupe of female entertainers, fancy fabrics, and silver vessels, as well as bestow a feast upon the honoree. Occasionally, an emperor would erect a dwelling for a favorite. Illustrious August had one raised in Luoyang for a singer whose voice he greatly prized. It was more lavish than the mansions of the aristocracy. Properties of that sort reverted to the state on the death of the occupant and were sometimes sold by the government. It was also the privilege of the throne to confiscate them if the person who received them committed a high crime or suffered some disgrace. Not all dwellings in the capitals, however, were in the hands of the dynasts. Such private real estate could be sold. One of the mansions in Changan was valued at 3.4 million coppers in 856, and another sold for 5 million coppers in the same period. In one instance an emperor of the early ninth century had to spend 2 million coppers to purchase a mansion so that he could return it to the impoverished descendant of a venerated chief minister who had lived in the early seventh century.

Ideally, a dwelling of the Tang dynasty faced south so that it received the warmth of the sun and the beneficent forces of fire—the element associated with that direction and a vitalizing force for the inhabitants of the house. This notion, derived from ancient cosmology and geomancy (*fengshui*), determined the location of a dwelling's main gate or door. The Chinese, however, also believed that malevolent forces, such as noxious vapors (*qi*) or ghosts, could enter through the portals. To obstruct such evil invasions, those who could afford to do so had a wall, called a shadow wall, built in front of their gates to prevent calamities from befalling their families.

Larger dwellings had outer walls to provide privacy and security. Builders used the same rammed earth technology employed in building the outer ramparts of cities. They did not, however, face home walls with brick or stone. That may explain why sixty days of continuous rain in the fall of 754 destroyed large numbers of houses in Changan. That type of construction had other defects as well. A thief needed only a pail of water

**Exterior Walls and Gates**

**Rammed Earth Wall Construction for a House**

for rubbing a hole in a wall to break in and make off with the owner's valuables. Furthermore, unless carefully tended to, earth walls developed cracks from settling or earthquakes. Nosy neighbors might then peek into the house next door.

Walls had to have gates. At the mansions of the upper classes they were tall enough to accommodate a mounted rider and wide enough to permit the passage of a carriage with its team of horses. They had two leaves like the doors to halls, and wooden bars on the inside to bolt them. Keepers manned them to prevent the intrusion of unwanted visitors. If they did not recognize the person knocking on the portal, they would demand a calling card from the stranger. Unscrupulous gatekeepers might also demand a bribe from the visitor. They would not inform their masters that someone had come to pay him a call otherwise. One of the honors accorded to the highest-ranking aristocrats and mandarins was the privilege of having lances with banners attached to them planted outside the gates of their homes and offices. Sumptuary regulations specified the number of lances, which varied, according to the rank of the man, from twenty-four for the emperor to ten for the governors of the smallest prefectures. Because the banners deteriorated over time, the Office of Military Arms replaced them every five years. The lances were markers of rank and made the dwellings of the elite who lived outside the palace readily identifiable to travelers on urban roads.

Depictions of gate gods, either painted directly on the leaves or on paper that was attached to them, were a means of defending the portals against the intrusions of evil forces. According to folklore, the deities were two generals who served Emperor Taizong of the Tang. One night the emperor took ill after hearing the sound of a demon heaving bricks and tiles at the door of his bedchamber. Two generals volunteered to stand guard in front of the emperor's door, and did so night after night until Taizong recovered. The emperor then had portraits of the officers painted and glued to the leaves of his gate, one for each panel, to prevent the demon from entering again.

The mansions of the rich and powerful in Tang China, like those before and after them, consisted of a series of courtyards. **Halls** Unlike the great houses, chateaus, and villas of the West, they were not single, massive buildings embracing parlors, dining rooms, kitchens, bedrooms, and so forth. Instead, they were compounds containing separate structures for different purposes. In general the main buildings, or halls, sat on a central axis that ran from north to south and were at the rear of the large courtyards. Smaller buildings sat on the east and west sides of the squares, and were joined to the halls by porticos, or covered walkways, that provided shelter from the elements for anyone moving between the structures. The courtyards were fairly self-contained, so that an owner could close one off and rent it to a lodger. The front or outer courtyard was the man's domain. It contained the largest and most formal hall, a parlor where the head of the household received visitors and conducted business. The rear or inner apartments were the woman's realm and were off-limits to men unless they were family members. In the seventh and early eighth centuries some of the patricians had eunuchs to guard those quarters, their harems. In 749 the throne abolished the custom with a decree that ordered all private households to send their eunuchs to the palace.

Most halls were rectangular with one longer side, the front, facing south. Occasionally, an official might have a crescent-shaped parlor built to receive his associates. Halls were usually one or two stories high, so mansions presented a horizontal aspect. Sumptuary statutes regulated their size. The halls of aristocrats and mandarins of the third grade and above could not exceed five bays (the space between two pillars) on the

long side and three on the short. The figures for nobles and bureaucrats of the fourth and fifth grades were five and three bays, and those for lower ranks and for commoners were three and one, respectively.

The halls rested on platforms of rammed earth that prevented floods from damaging the interior and its contents. Sometimes that precaution failed. In 817 a heavy rain in Changan collapsed a pillar in one of the palaces, flooded the markets with three feet of water, and destroyed more than 2,000 homes. That paled in comparison to a flood that struck a city in the northeast during 669. The waters rose to five feet and destroyed more than 14,000 homes. The wealthy had the foundations of their homes and the stairs leading up to them faced with polished stones that had beautiful grains. The burnish was so fine in some cases that visitors wearing leather boots risked slipping and falling. Stone, however, was not a preferred building material in ancient China. It was used mostly for steps, balustrades, bridges, and tombs.

A builder had to be careful where he obtained his materials, lest he disturb the *fengshui* of the site. When a ge- **Construction** omancer visited a chief minister in the early eighth century, he warned the mandarin not to have earth removed from the northeast corner of the property. A month later the man paid another call on the official, declared that the aura of the place was desolate, and suspected that a great deal of soil had been taken from the forbidden spot. When he and the minister went to the site, they discovered pits more than ten feet deep. The geomancer predicted that the mandarin would enjoy fame and fortune for twenty years, but thereafter his sons would suffer disaster. Greatly shocked, the official asked if the misfortune could be averted if the holes were filled. The master replied that soil from another place would not have the aura of the site and would not join with the arteries of energy running beneath the ground. As he had foretold, one of the chief minister's sons was later executed and the other was sent into exile for collaborating with An Lushan.

Craftsmen, using bamboo scaffoldings, raised wooden pillars that rested on stone plinths (footings) on the rammed earth platforms. Carpenters worked them into round shapes and then sanded them smooth. There were two materials for accomplishing the latter task. One was a plant appropriately called "wood thief," which grew in the marshes of the northwest and contained large amounts of silica. The other was the rough skin of sharks. The pillars, not the walls, bore all of the roof's weight. Only in peasant dwellings were walls load-bearing. Carpenters tied the pillars together by fastening square or rectangular beams on their tops. In very fancy halls, imperial palaces, or Buddhist monasteries, they might install elaborate systems of brackets on the beams to support the rafters. The eaves of the roof extended beyond the walls to cover porches that surrounded the building and provided shade. The entire frame—pillars, beams, rafters, and the rest—was made of wood, the preferred material for homes of patricians. Pillars, beams, and rafters were often painted bright colors. In some cases, however, roof beams made of cypress timbers were left untouched so that one could admire their fine grains. Of all the elements in traditional architecture, the roof was the crowning glory of the hall, its most expensive and striking feature.

Workmen laid semicircular glazed ceramic tiles on roof boards affixed to the rafters. Though much more expensive, tiles had a great advantage over other materials, such as thatch, commonly used in peasant dwellings. They were fireproof. Embers from a nearby blaze blown onto them by the wind would not ignite them. The holocausts that destroyed huge numbers of dwellings in some provincial cities during the Tang may have resulted from failure to install tiles on roofs. Canton, a primitive city by the standards of its northern counterparts, was repeatedly ravaged by fires until 806, when a governor ordered its citizens to use tiles. There were some disadvantages to tiles, however. They were so heavy that when a gale blew them off roofs, they crushed people to death. They also attracted unwanted guests. Snakes had a nasty habit of taking up residence under them.

The spaces between the pillars of halls were filled with a variety of materials, such as wood and bricks. The mansions of patricians sometimes had double walls or concealed rooms in which valuables or fugitives were hidden. In the aftermath of a chief minister's assassination in 815, the emperor ordered authorities in Changan to search for such secret places in the homes of nobles and mandarins, in an attempt to find the murderers. The probe failed to locate the culprits. Another chief minister living in the same period was a connoisseur of fine things and paid high prices for them. He acquired rare books and paintings that he had mounted on gold and jade rollers. He stored them in holes gouged from a wall hidden behind another. After his death a thief broke into his vault, stole the treasures, removed their gold and jade rollers, and abandoned the books and paintings, which were probably far more valuable, on a road. Generally speaking, a hall's interior did not have walls that divided it into smaller rooms.

Windows provided ventilation and light. Glass panes did not exist in Tang China. For those of modest means, paper sufficed for windows, preferably oiled paper because it was translucent and therefore admitted more light. For the more affluent, silk—dyed scarlet, green, or some other hue—might serve the purpose and tint the sunlight falling on the floor inside of the room. In either case the materials could not withstand the force of strong winds. Consequently, carpenters built wooden lattices to which they glued the paper or cloth. They used pine, wood that was too soft for structural members of the building, for the frames. There was a wide variety of patterns for lattices, a feature for which Chinese architecture has been justly renowned. In exceptional cases small pieces of glass or mica that sparkled in the sunlight might be inlaid in the frames.

It was customary to fit windows and doors with blinds that provided privacy while allowing air to circulate when the windows or doors were open. Made of long bamboo slats and cord, they rolled upward. Carpenters also installed latticework on the upper portions of doors. Princess Tongchang had the lattices of her doors adorned with jewels, and

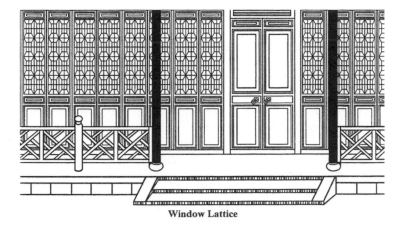

**Window Lattice**

a powerful minister of the late eighth century had his embellished with gold and silver.

Workers covered the masonry walls inside and out with plaster. The owner of a mansion might have a famous artist paint cranes, horses, a landscape, or a rendering of a famous dance on his walls. A renowned calligrapher might brush a line or two of poetry or prose on the walls of his host's abode during a feast. Ancient Chinese thought of graffiti as a means of beautifying, not defacing, a room—or, for that matter, nature. Many rocks on scenic mountains have inscriptions chiseled into their surfaces. In 681 a director of the court's workshops adorned the walls of a hall that he had built for the emperor in a controversial manner. He installed mirrors on all sides. After the emperor went to look at the place, he asked one of his ministers what he thought of it. The official replied that heaven did not have two suns, nor earth two rulers. The mandarin thought that the multiple images he saw in the chamber were terribly inauspicious. They were signs that new rulers would rise to challenge the Tang and split the empire into several kingdoms. The emperor ordered the mirrors removed immediately. In 825 another emperor had a new hall built that required 100,000 pieces of gold and silver leaf to decorate its walls and ceilings.

The truly extravagant had their halls plastered with aromatics. In the early eighth century a sybaritic minister who was a member of Empress Wei's clique had a new mansion built, and ordered the workmen to apply a paste of aloeswood and red powder to the walls. When one opened the doors, a heavy fragrance burst forth from the interior. Aloeswood was the rotten portion of trees that grew in Southeast Asia. It was impregnated with a richly scented resin and very expensive in northern China. Emperor Illustrious August had a pavilion of aloeswood in front of which there were peony trees with red, pink, purple, and white blossoms. One of his chief ministers outdid him. There was a pavilion of aloeswood at his mansion at Changan that had sandalwood (another aromatic tree that grew in Southeast Asia) railings and walls plastered with a paste of musk and frankincense. In the spring, when the peonies were blooming, he assembled guests in the pavilion to admire the flowers growing outside.

**Rooms**  The private quarters of a mansion, including its bedchambers, were usually located in courtyards behind the parlor. A high-ranking official bought a property in Luoyang during the eighth century and had it modified over the years. At the center stood a hall for his first wife, who had died. It was spare and unadorned. To the east of that was one for his elder brother's wife (the brother presumably had passed away). To the northeast was another for his elder sisters when they came to visit. It was not uncommon in the Tang for brothers to live together. In that case the head of the household would allocate a whole courtyard to each so that they could live with their families yet have a degree of privacy.

Some halls served special purposes. Aside from the parlor there were libraries where educated men spent their leisure hours reading and writing. In the early Tang the literate had to transcribe books themselves or purchase them from a store that employed scribes. The texts were copied by hand on sheets of paper, the text written from the top of the page to the bottom and from right to left. Afterward the sheets were pasted together to form a scroll and rollers were glued to an end of the scroll so the book could be rolled up for storage. Longer books had many scrolls that constituted chapters. It was the custom to measure the size of a library not by the number of titles in it, but by the number of scrolls it had. Some of the collections were quite large. In the late eighth century a chief minister had 30,000 scrolls in his library and at least three other men had 20,000. A collector in the early eighth century acquired so many books that they overflowed his shelves. He had to pile the excess on his windowsills. The heaps there grew so tall that they totally blocked out the sunlight. An aficionado of music could also have a special two-story hall devoted solely to playing the drum.

The mansion of a wealthy patrician might have its own treasury. The grandson of Empress Wu's uncle had one that was 500 paces long and had more than 100 coffers where he stored the riches that he had collected. He used that wealth to curry favor with other courtiers and officials. One night the building burned to the ground, destroying everything inside.

A mandarin had a shrine built in the southwest corner of his mansion for worshiping his ancestors. The truly powerful living in Changan, however, had separate ancestral shrines erected in other parts of the city.

Patricians had separate bathhouses. The washrooms had pitchers, basins—made of metals such as bronze or gold—and towels for washing the face and hands. They also had tubs, the humblest made of wood and the grandest of porcelain or metal. A bathhouse might also have a couch, mats, and a screen to shield women from men's gazes. Peeping Toms were not unknown. In the fifth century a Buddhist nun stayed in the home of a powerful general. He stole a glance at her while she was bathing and completely naked. As he watched, the woman took out a knife, cut open her belly and removed her organs, lopped off her feet, and beheaded herself. In a short time she restored herself to her original state.

The grandest of all baths during the Tang were those at hot springs on Mount Blackhorse, a day's ride east of Changan. The second Tang emperor favored the springs, which he visited eight times for seven to ten days in the winter and spring. He had a palace built there so he could avail himself of the healing powers of the waters, which contained arsenic and sulfur. It was, however, Emperor Illustrious August who made the place his home away from home. He sojourned there thirty-eight years out of forty-four that he was on the throne. After 740 his visits during the cold seasons grew longer and longer. He lingered at the hot springs for three weeks, four weeks, five weeks, sixty days, and finally for three months.

Since Illustrious August spent large amounts of time at the springs, he had a city built on the site. Whenever he made an excursion to Mount Blackhorse, his court went with him. That entourage included not only his harem, members of his family, and guards, but also the whole bureaucracy of the empire that usually worked in the capital. The complex at the springs was therefore huge, for it included mansions for nobles and mandarins, offices for all of the central government agencies, and quarters for underlings and servants as well as warehouses, kitchens, and other support facilities. Construction of the complex entailed erecting a wall around it. In the end its cost must have been enormous.

Two springs formed the core of the palace. The Hall of Nine Dragons, appropriately named because the dragon was traditionally the emblematic beast of the emperor, was for the personal use of Illustrious August. The second, called the Lotus Blossom Spa, was Yang Guifei's bath hall. She also had her own multistoried hall for grooming and applying cosmetics. The pools had linings of exquisite stones with elegant grains. When he still enjoyed imperial favor, An Lushan presented the emperor with fish, dragons, ducks, and geese carved from white stone, as well as stone bridges and lotus flowers. When the emperor disrobed to enter the water, the creatures that An furnished seemed about to take flight. That frightened Illustrious August, who ordered them removed. The baths must have been fairly large, because the emperor had boats of lacquered wood chased with silver and oars inlaid with pearls and jade made so that he and Yang Guifei could cruise upon the waters. He also had an island made of precious stones and aloeswood erected in the middle of a pool. There were also sixteen baths for the imperial concubines, who seem to have been careless about their baubles. Their pearled tassels and jeweled cords floated down the "Gold Drain," out of the palace and into the drainage ditches along the streets, where poor folks snatched them up daily.

There were structures in mansions that did not qualify as halls. Kitchens were essential fixtures in homes where the lord frequently entertained his guests with feasts, but little information about them has survived in Tang literature. The well-to-do traveled on horseback or in horse-drawn carriages, so their dwellings had stables and garages. There were also quarters for the servants that even families of modest means required.

All great houses had privies. In most homes they were crude structures that were not the objects of much embellishment. They consisted of a pit and a wooden outhouse installed above it. The outhouse had an opening in the floor over which the user squatted. They usually reeked until the local collector of muck came by to empty them, and therefore probably were installed far enough from the living quarters that their stench did not offend anyone. There was a means of thwarting malodorous assaults on the olfactory senses when one had to use the outhouse. It was the custom to stuff dried jujubes (Chinese blackthorns) up the nostrils before entering it. A thoughtful host might provide his privy with a wooden lid to hide the filth from his guest's sight. The task of removing the waste from a latrine was sometimes assigned to a student by his mentor, as an act of discipline. For example, a young man, who later wrote the classic book on tea, offended a Buddhist monk with whom he was studying, so the monk ordered him to clean out the monastery's privy as punishment. Assassins availed themselves of the pits to dispose of their victims' heads because lawmen were reluctant to search through their contents. The cousin of a poet thought so little of his verses that he tossed them into his latrine. In the homes of the wealthy the privy might be fancier, having an antechamber furnished with a couch. In 819, when a subordinate of a military governor made up his mind to dispose of his superior, he sent troops to bring him in. They found the governor and his two sons hiding beneath a couch in a latrine at their home.

A man had to be careful about where he installed his privy. There was a haunted house in Changan during the Sui dynasty. All of the previous occupants had died there. A man named Wan, who did not believe in ghosts, took over the place without a second thought. One night a spirit dressed in very fine robes appeared to him. Wan asked the spirit why he had come. The specter replied that he had been a general centuries before, and that his grave lay near the home's privy. He had always

**A Chinese Privy**

suffered from the foul odor there, so he asked Wan to do him the favor of having his remains removed to another place. The ghost promised to reward him liberally for his efforts. Wan agreed, and asked the spirit why it had slain the previous occupants of the dwelling. The specter replied that they had all died of fright; he had killed no one. Wan dug up the coffin and interred it elsewhere. The following night the specter appeared again, predicted that Wan would become a general, and vowed to provide assistance on all of his campaigns. As predicted, Wan became a commander of Sui forces, and every time he went into battle, he sensed the presence of spirit warriors aiding him. He always won his battles.

The privy had its own deity. According to a tradition recorded in the fifth century, she was the second wife of a provincial official. In a fit of jealousy the man's first wife slew her by throwing her into the pit of a latrine during the Lantern Festival, the fifteenth day of the first moon. Later the ruler of heaven took pity on her and dubbed her the goddess of the privy. Mortals knew her as the Purple Maiden. It became the custom on the fifteenth day of the first moon to welcome the Purple Maiden at one's latrine by uttering the words, "Your husband is not at home and his first wife has gone out. So, little damsel, you may come out [of the privy]." It was also the custom for householders to shine torches into wells and latrines on the last day of the first moon to expel all ghosts.

The homes of the wealthy had to have wells to provide water. Although there appears to be no notice of them in Tang sources, **Wells** every ward in all cities must have had public wells. Digging them was expensive—well beyond the means of the lower classes to pay for—and carrying water long distances was extremely difficult, if not impossible, unless one had the means to purchase a horse and cart. Devout Buddhists established wells in the markets of the capitals and privies at their four gates for the convenience of people. Use of those wells, however, was beneath the dignity of the upper classes. They installed their own wells on their property. Some patricians went to extreme lengths to embellish them. In the ninth century Princess Tongchang had a railing of gold and silver built around her well. Wells usually had covers to prevent dirt, vegetation, and animals (lizards, rats, insects, and children) from falling into them. Even so, an annual cleaning of them had been the practice for centuries. Some wiser minds tossed sand into their wells to filter out impurities seeping from the ground. Others dumped cinnabar and arsenic in them, hoping to acquire immortality. A chief minister in the ninth century had a well with a gold and jade railing that he kept securely locked because he threw jade and pearls into it. After he was beheaded, it was discovered that his bones had turned a golden yellow because he had drunk the well water for years.

Wells were not always reliable. During a great drought in 785, the rivers flowing toward Changan from the mountains to the south of the city dried up, and so did all of the wells in the capital. Sometimes wells collapsed. They also served purposes other than those for which they were intended. Women often committed suicide by leaping into them. Sometimes they provided handy hiding places for valuables. In 613 the family of a rebel threw their gold into a well, no doubt because they feared the government would confiscate it in reprisal for his uprising.

## FURNISHINGS

In the early Tang, couches were the primary pieces of furniture in parlors. They were low, large, raised platforms, usually made of wood, that had no backs or armrests. People sat on them cross-legged and used low tables for writing and eating. The emperor's throne, called the "dragon couch," was certainly the heaviest and no doubt the most magnificent. It was made of gold and bronze. The throne was "mobile" in the sense that imperial servitors, probably a good number of them, transported it to various locations for important occasions. On the last day of the moon and during solar eclipses, the attendants carried it to the Altar of Soil, where the emperor attended to state rituals. They also carried it to the examinations for mounted archery. Another fancy imperial couch came from Persia as tribute. It was made of carnelian, a stone that is usually some shade of red.

Outside of the palace the most extravagant couch in history, or so one observer claimed, was one that a favorite of Empress Wu had made for his mother. Fashioned of ivory, it sat in a tent adorned with gold, silver, pearls, jade, and every sort of precious stuff. It had coverings of woven rhinoceros horn, sable cushions, cricket-mosquito felt and dragon whisker and phoenix pinion mats (rush or reed mats made in China).

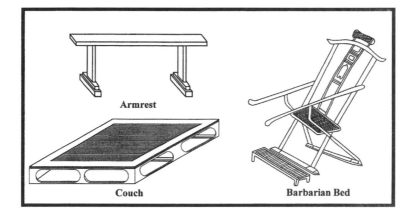

Armrest

Couch

Barbarian Bed

When the son was beheaded in 705, the throne enslaved the mother in the palace.

Tents, or perhaps more appropriately curtains with canopies, surrounded couches of the wealthy in formal settings such as parlors. The materials used to make them could be as humble as bamboo or as extravagant as pearls and jade. In 873, when the emperor had the finger bone of Buddha brought to the palace, he had it ensconced behind drapes of pearls and jade. A chief minister in the late eighth century settled his favorite concubine in a tent with curtains of gold thread. He had another tent made of shark silk. According to folklore the shark people living beneath the Southern Sea, who wept tears of pearl, wove it. The fabric may have been *pinikon*, a cinnamon-colored cloth made in South Asia from the tough filaments that mussels use to attach themselves to underwater surfaces. Whatever the case, the material purportedly provided warmth in the winter and coolness in the summer.

The Chinese had known of the chair since at least the first century. It was a folding seat and clearly of foreign origin, for it was called the "barbarian bed." The fashion of sitting on chairs did not catch on for centuries, perhaps because people preferred sitting cross-legged. Whatever the case, the first true chairs appeared in the Tang. In the middle of the eighth century a courtier made a frame to lean his back against out of tree limbs. When he made one that resembled a dragon, he presented it to the throne, and thereafter such pieces became the rage among patricians. It is not clear whether the man attached his invention to a couch or not, but chairs had definitely become common pieces of furniture for mansions by the ninth century. Small, round stools and long benches for sitting at dinner tables also appeared in the home about that time.

Screens were common fixtures in the homes of patricians. They were movable and installed behind seats to block drafts. Their surfaces pro-

**Screen**

vided convenient spaces for inscribing texts. Taizong had ten criticisms of him submitted by a righteous minister affixed to a screen so that he could read them in the morning and evening. He recorded the names of all prefectural governors on another, which he consulted on rising and retiring—apparently so he could memorize the officials' names. During his reign one of his ministers, who was an outstanding calligrapher, copied the text of a book devoted to biographies of virtuous women on a series of screens. Nor was that the only such work. A monastery in Changan possessed a set of fifteen screens with the text of a Buddhist scripture engraved on it, the characters inlaid with precious stones. Palace ladies had entrusted the treasure to the cloister for safekeeping during the rebellion of An Lushan, along with pearl-lidded jeweled caskets for storing them.

Screens were also the objects of aesthetic adornment. A man of means could commission an artist to paint landscapes or scenes of the four seasons on them. Yang Guifei had one on which pictures of beautiful women from former times had been engraved and their clothes inlaid with precious stones. A chief minister who lived just after her had a screen with images of famous and beautiful female entertainers of the past chased on it and decorated with tortoiseshell and crystals.

Beds were couches with poles affixed to their four corners, and curtains hung from the poles. The drapes for imperial use were exquisite. Empress Wu bestowed a set made of embroidered silk gauze on one of her ministers after visiting his home and learning that he slept behind curtains of inferior silk. He spent an uncomfortable night in his new surroundings. The next day the mandarin reported to the empress that a face reader had told him when he was young that he ought not be extravagant. He therefore requested her permission to return to his old, humble drapes. The servants of a sybaritic chief minister in the eighth century hung his and his wife's nightclothes over twelve gold and silver braziers during the day to infuse them with aromatics for a pleasant sleep at night. Taoists recommended that beds be at least three and half feet high, so that damp air and demons emanating from the ground could not attack sleeping people. They also counseled against placing a bed against the northern wall and advocated removing the left shoe first when retiring for the night.

Pillows were made of porcelain, wood, stone, and other hard materials. An official in charge of the government's monopoly on iron and salt had one encrusted with lapis lazuli that he placed on his gold bed. Those made of rosewood were said to cure headaches. Pillows were rectangular, with a dip in the middle for resting the neck. A noble lady in the early eighth century had a "night shining pillow" that glowed in the dark so she did not have to rely on lamps or candles. Pillows, according to the Taoists, should not be too tall because they could diminish the number of years allotted to one. They were also magical in Chinese folklore. The younger sister of Empress Wei had one in the form of a leopard's head that warded off evil, and another in the shape of a prostrate bear that would ensure the birth of a male child.

There were no closets in Tang homes. They had pegs on which one could hang one's apparel temporarily. Bamboo hampers were used for long-term storage of clothing. An auspicious omen appeared in one of them during the spring of 708. The palace reported that a multicolored cloud rose from one of Empress Wei's skirts that was lying in a bamboo hamper. The emperor had his artists paint a picture of the portent to show his bureaucratic corps. One of his ministers suggested that he have the illustration promulgated throughout the empire. He agreed, had copies made, sent them to localities, and bestowed an amnesty on his subjects for good measure.

The mansion of a powerful man might have a treasure chest. Academician Wang, a really ugly man who enjoyed the emperor's favor,

**Bed, Bedding, Pillow, Candle, and Ghost**

sought only to enrich himself by collecting bribes from patricians seeking his influence at court. The gentlemen flocked to his gate, and some who could not gain admittance during the day had to sleep overnight in pastry shops and taverns. Wang accepted nothing less than 1,000 coppers just to let them into his dwelling. He had a large chest in his house that had no lid, only a hole through which he passed the gold and silk that he received. His wife sometimes slept on it.

Foreign rugs graced the floors of patrician dwellings in the Tang. At least two ancient centers, Bukhara and Persia, that were renowned for their carpets then as now, sent them as tribute to the court. Such goods were also commercial wares, transported on the backs of camels across the deserts of Central Asia to Changan. They made their way to shops in city markets. China had its own works for weaving rugs, as the following anecdote attests. When Chief Minister Yang installed a pavilion made of sandalwood at his mansion in Changan during the ninth century, the son of a provincial official secretly sent a man to measure its floor. Afterward he had a carpet woven and presented it to the chief minister at a party the mandarin threw for relatives and friends to mark the completion of the pavilion. Unfortunately, when Yang fell from power, the gift of the rug implicated the son with the chief minister, and he, too, suffered punishment.

Chamber pots were standard fixtures in the homes of the well-to-do. In order to curry favor with a notorious favorite of Empress Wu, a poet of some renown carried his urine bucket for him. In 683 a governor, who wished to gain the empress's favor, falsely informed Prince Li Ming, who had been banished to his district, that she had bestowed suicide on him. Terrified, the prince hanged himself. Later, while the governor was sleeping during the night, an assassin sneaked into his quarters, decapitated him, and fled with his head. Subsequently, Empress Wu had Li Ming's sons executed. While officials were taking inventory of their property that the government had confiscated, they found the governor's skull. It had been lacquered to make a chamber pot and inscribed with his name. It was only then that the authorities learned the prince's sons had commissioned an assassin to murder the governor in order to avenge the injustice that he had done to their father.

Tang dwellings in northern climates were cold. They were drafty and had no insulation. Stoves or braziers were the only source of heat from late autumn to early spring. The fuel for the heaters was either firewood or charcoal. If a man was an aristocrat, bureaucrat, or military officer, the government provided a monthly supply of fuel for him. Clever members of one chief minister's household in the mid-eighth century mixed coal dust with honey and kneaded the dough into the shapes of paired phoenixes. They placed sandalwood in their stoves, put the phoenixes on top, and set them ablaze. Braziers apparently were not very effective at warming the chill, or at least some patricians thought so. A chief minister of the mid-eighth century had the largest and fattest of his concubines and maids form a line in front of him to block the wind during winter months. He called the array a "formation of flesh." When the winds and snows became bitterly cold, one prince had female singers crowd closely around the sides of his seat to protect him from frigid drafts. He called them the "chanteuse band." Another prince, when his hands were cold during the height of the winter, and he was far from a fire, would thrust his hands into the bosoms of his lovely female singers and caress the flesh of their breasts. He called the ladies "hand warmers."

In the Tang there were three ways of starting a fire. First, one could strike a flint knife against a flint stone to produce sparks that ignited tinder. Second, one could use a metal fire drill, twirling it rapidly to generate flames on wood by the heat of friction. Last, one could use a concave bronze mirror to focus the rays of the sun on dry kindling.

The latter method had the disadvantage of not working on cloudy days or at night.

The humble had to make do with fans for relief from the heat of summer. There were other ways for those with means. A princess once ordered her servants to hang silks dipped in clean water along the southern veranda of her mansion, to cool her guests during a party at the height of summer. On the hottest days the sons of an official in the early eighth century had artisans carve blocks of ice into the shapes of phoenixes or other animals, and sometimes decorated them with gold rings and colored ribbons. When the carvers completed the work, the sons placed the ice sculptures on platters and sent them to princes, dukes, and great ministers. They hoped to curry the favor of those powerful men by providing them the means of cooling themselves. For the truly rich and powerful there was a form of air conditioning built into halls. Emperor Illustrious August had a cool hall built. When one of his mandarins strongly denounced him for doing so, he ordered a eunuch to summon the man. It was summer, and the heat was intense. When the minister arrived at the cool hall, the emperor was sitting on his throne, behind which water struck fan-wheels creating a chilly breeze that wafted around the sovereign's clothes. Water pumped to the four corners of the hall fell in a curtain that splashed on the floor. The emperor invited his critic to sit on a stone couch that contained ice and supplied him with a cold drink. Soon the official was trembling from the cold. His belly rumbled thunderously. He had to repeatedly implore Illustrious August to let him retire before the monarch would grant his permission. The coldness to which his body had been subjected so disturbed his system that the bureaucrat wet his pants when he reached the hall's gate. As in other matters, high-ranking ministers sometimes adopted the fashions of the throne. After the execution of a censor in the mid-eighth century, clerks sent to inventory his property found a "pavilion of automatic rain" from the eaves of which water cascaded down on all four sides. During the summer Yang Guifei's throat became parched from the heat. To remedy the problem, she sucked on a jade fish.

There were four types of implements for lighting in Tang China: torches, oil lamps, candles, and lanterns. Torches provided illumination for courtyards and for travelers. Made of faggots and installed at the foot of stairs leading into halls, they provided enough light to turn night into day. Without them nocturnal feasts, polo matches, and hunting were impossible. Lanterns, made of light bamboo frames to which paper or silk was pasted and in which lighted candles were placed, supplied light for short trips in the dark.

Candles and lamps provided interior illumination for halls. The fuel used in lamps—burned in flat metal or ceramic pans—was usually hemp oil. Some exotic fats, such as whale and seal oil, also were used. A fish caught in the oceans off China's southern coast was more fat than meat. Its flesh was rendered to provide oil for the lamps lit at banquets or that illuminated looms. (Apparently women wove at night.) Lamps so fueled were called gluttonous fish lamps. Medical canons discouraged the use of pork and bear fats for lighting because smoke from their flames caused nearsightedness. Patricians might have fancy stands made for their lamps. A royal prince of the early eighth century had dwarf slaves carved from wood and painted polychrome hues to set before his bed. Each of the statues held lamps in its hands that burned from dusk to dawn.

Unlike Europe, where animal fats were the chief constituents of candles, the substance for candles in medieval China was usually an oil derived from the berry of a plant that was mixed with beeswax. Patricians might have aromatic candles that had various fragrances mixed into the wax, and filled their bedrooms with marvelous scents all night. They might also have elegant holders for them. A prince of the early eighth century had lads carved from wood and clothed in green robes that held candles in their hands. He placed the figures around his banquet mats whenever he dined with other princes and nobles. Some candles were graduated so that people—probably Buddhist monks performing nocturnal devotions—could determine the passing of time. Buddhists also introduced incense clocks to Tang China. The wood or metal devices had channels in the shapes of Sanskrit characters that were filled with incense. Monks could tell the time because as the incense burned, it passed marks along the channels. Each mark represented one of the night watches: 7 to 9 P.M., 9 to 11 P.M., 11 P.M. to 1 A.M., 1 to 3 A.M., and 3 to 5 A.M.

The ambience of an upper-class home was extremely important in Tang China, especially with regard to its scent. To broadcast fragrances, homes of the wealthy had braziers in which they burned aromatics. A sybaritic prince of the early eighth century had two sculpted, dwarf lads bearing bejeweled braziers in their hands placed before his bed curtains so that they would dispense their fragrance throughout the night as he slept. The Tang materia medica recommended mixing dried bat dung with frankincense and cassia, and burning the mixture to repel mosquitoes.

## GARDENS

Patricians went to extreme lengths to provide themselves with grand gardens. Bai Juyi, one of the greatest poets of the ninth century, contended that gardens should occupy at least half of the land for a stately home, and should include a lake as well as 1,000 stalks of bamboo. In 823 he purchased a mansion in the northwest corner of a southeastern ward in Luoyang, a section of the city he considered to be the most scenic. The residential quarters sat on only 18 percent of the property's nearly two and a half acres. The remainder of the tract was a garden with a lake (29 percent of the land) and an enormous bamboo grove (53 percent of the land).

After retiring from office in 829, Bai set about the business of renovating his garden. To the east of the lake he built a granary to store 1,700 bushels of cereals that he had amassed while serving in his last government post. To the north of it he erected a library to house the cartload of books that he had collected, and to the west of it a zither pavilion, with a large stone jug for ale, that served as a site for the many parties that he threw. Bai had three mountains—perhaps in imitation of the three holy mounts in the Eastern Sea on which the immortals dwelt— raised in the middle of the lake. He built bridges between the islands and the shore, and laid out a road that encircled the lake. While serving as governor of Hangzhou and subsequently of Suzhou, districts just south of the mouth of the Yangtze River, the poet collected items for his northern garden. In Hangzhou he procured a strange rock from India and a pair of cranes. In Suzhou, a district long famed for the beauty of its scenery, he acquired white lotus and pleasure boats for sailing on his lake. He also shipped back from there five fantastically shaped stones formed by erosion on Grand Lake. Bai's friends contributed to his endeavors. One built a bridge for him. Another supplied him with a recipe for brewing a very delectable ale. A third gave him a zither with an extremely clear timbre. A fourth taught him a serene tune to strum on the instrument. A last donated three square, smooth bluestones large enough for sitting or reclining.

Bai passed the last eighteen years of his life at the mansion, frequently entertaining his friends in its garden. Whenever he threw a party, he and his guests went for a sail on his pleasure boats. Trailing along behind the craft underneath the water were 110 waterproof sacks containing ale and roasted meat. Whenever the party exhausted the contents of one bag, the poet's attendants would retrieve another for the pleasure of his companions. Bai also had a troupe of ten singers, dancers, and musicians. When the strumming of the zither was over and his guest were merrily drunk, he sent the entertainers to pavilions on the islands in the lake, where they performed the introductory section of "Rainbow Skirt," a famous piece of music that, according to legend, Illustrious August learned while on a trip to the moon.

As the account of Bai Juyi's garden indicates, the cultured elite of the Tang greatly prized bamboo and rocks. Some were not above embellishing the stalks of the woody grass. A sybaritic prince of the early eighth century had pieces of jade tied to his bamboo so that he could listen to their tinkling as the wind knocked them together during the night. When

**Peony and Garden Rock**

the groves were large, they provided convenient places for assassins or other outlaws to hide from the authorities. Patricians in the Tang had a passion for rocks, especially those from Grand Lake near Suzhou. They appreciated stones that gave the appearance of being miniature mountains with grottoes, cascades, and streams. These gentlemen did not shy away from defacing them. One eminent official of the ninth century had the phrase "Possessing the Way" carved on a rock in his famous garden. Some rockeries were quite valuable. One with a grove of trees at a princess's mansion in the early eighth century was worth 20 million coppers.

The crown jewel of Tang gardens was the peony—the most esteemed flower of the time, known as the King of Flowers—and Luoyang had the most magnificent varieties. According to one source the reason was that Empress Wu banished them to the city after a visit to a rear garden in the palaces of Changan, where she noticed that they bloomed later than other flowers. There were two forms of peonies, a plant and a shrub (the so-called tree peony). They had large, showy blossoms, sometimes as much as seven or eight inches in diameter, and came in yellow, red, white, and purple, as well as pastel versions of the same colors. A clever Taoist in the ninth century created hues for them artificially. He applied chemicals such as lac, a secretion of an insect that infested trees in Vietnam and Cambodia, to the roots of the plant. Within a few weeks blue, purple, yellow, or red flowers bloomed, according to various formulas that he used. In the same period the peony had become so admired that the price of a single graft from a magnificent shrub could fetch tens of thousands of cash. There was a tree peony in the palace that had 1,000 petals. It attracted more than 10,000 white and yellow butterflies at night, and the ladies of the palace tried to catch them with nets.

A gentleman's garden might have lotus growing in one of its ponds or lakes. The plant was an import from the west, probably India, and its blossoms were usually pink or white. There was an unusual yellow variety that clever gardeners in the region south of the Yangtze delta may have bred. Blue lotus flowers were even more rare. Apparently a family of dyers from the same region produced the peculiar blossoms by applying their stains to the plant. Other flowers that found their way into Tang gardens included white and purple magnolias, three varieties of cassia (Chinese cinnamon) trees that produced white flowers with red centers as well as pale yellow and purple blossoms, a fragrant bramble with yellow blossoms (the color of ale, to which it was often added for flavor), azaleas, chrysanthemums (favored because they bloomed in the autumn), redbuds (misnamed because they had small purple flowers), and many more. Patricians also esteemed two nonflowering evergreens, the pine and the cypress. Evergreens were symbolic of long life because they never turn color in the fall or winter, and thus they were essential elements of a good garden.

Many Tang gardens served both aesthetic and practical ends. Patricians planted Chinese apricots that bloomed in the spring with fragrant, light pink or white sprays, peaches that had deep pink blossoms, and crabapples with rose-red flowers. The owners of some mansions raised geese and ducks on their ponds. One had a pool that produced fine fish. Gardens provided fruit and meat for the table.

Architecture was an essential element of gardens, an artificial intrusion in a natural landscape. There were thirty-six pavilions in a garden at a mansion in Luoyang during the Tang. Such structures were often the sites for banquets and other amusements. However, some might serve as refuges from the maddening crowd. One mandarin built himself a studio in a secluded area of his garden so that he could get away from company to hum and whistle. Another fancy addition to a man's private park might be a stone for floating ale goblets. The custom of floating goblets originated with a party that China's most celebrated calligrapher threw for forty-one friends and relatives on April 22 (the third day of the third moon) in 353. The festivities took place on the banks of a winding river where guests sat on mats. In the course of the feast the host had goblets of ale set adrift on the waters. When a beaker touched the spot on the bank where a guest sat, he had to retrieve it, drink its contents, and write a poem. In the Tang, patricians continued to hold such drinking parties. By that time it had become the custom of some to have channels carved into large slabs of stone in imitation of the winding river. Presumably, goblets floated on water flowing through the channels to seats where guests sat ready to seize them, drink, and write poetry. Or perhaps they were only ornaments.

The grandest of all gardens during the Tang were those of the emperor in Changan. All palaces had areas devoted to woodlands, lakes, streams, and bridges. Some came equipped with winding rivers for celebrating the third day of the third moon. The walls of the Forbidden Park encompassed the ruins of the ancient capital of the Han dynasty and pavilions where the emperor entertained his guests. It was also a reserve where wild animals such as white deer roamed free, so that his majesty and his guests, foreign envoys in particular, could enjoy themselves hunting. The game they shot usually provided meat for sacrifices, especially those at the imperial ancestral shrine. The park had mews for hawks, eagles, and other raptors, as well as kennels for hounds that were employed in the hunt to chase down or catch quarry. It also had pens for exotic creatures—lions, leopards, elephants, and rhinoceroses—sent as tribute by foreign nations. A Tang manual on government states that there was not a bird, animal, vegetable, or fruit that was not raised there.

Many of the flora and fauna in the Forbidden Park and other imperial gardens were native to China. Sometimes the method by which the throne acquired plants and animals did not endear the emperor to his subjects. Eunuchs were sent to the provinces, especially those in the south, to procure rare and beautiful things. In 682 a party of the gelded servitors went to find extraordinary specimens of bamboo. As they sailed up and down the Yangtze River in a boat that carried the grasses for transplantation in the Forbidden Park, they treated the locals cruelly. When they arrived at one prefecture, a senior administrator would have none of their tyrannous behavior and imprisoned them. He then sent an address to the throne severely criticizing the dispatching of such expeditions. After receiving the remonstrance, the emperor put an end to the expedition. In 716 Emperor Illustrious August sent a company of eunuchs to collect exotic birds, pond herons and tufted ducks, in the south. The agents caused great annoyance among the inhabitants of the region. When his servitors reached the northern end of the Grand Canal, a governor of a prefecture sent an address to the court, reproaching the emperor for his wish to fill the Forbidden Park with rare fowl. Illustrious August acknowledged the fairness of his remarks, set the birds free, and bestowed forty lengths of silk on the man.

In the mid-eighth century some hedonistic scions of the upper class devised a sort of mobile garden. The sons of a chief minister hunted down celebrated flowers and extraordinary trees during the spring and planted them on the floor of a wooden cart. Beneath the carriage was a set of gears attached to the axle. As the vehicle moved forward, pulled by slaves or servants, the base on which the foliage rested rotated so everyone could see all of its wonders without changing their positions.

# 5

# Clothes and Hygiene

## FABRICS

In 815 an assassin waylaid Pei Du, a chief minister, near his home and struck him on the head. Pei fell off his horse and landed in a drainage ditch. A member of his entourage grabbed the killer from behind and raised the alarm with a loud bellow. The desperado cut off the man's arm and fled before the authorities could apprehend him. Although the blow to his head inflicted a wound, Pei survived the assault because the felt of his hat was so thick.

Felt, made from wool, was a tough material, as this anecdote demonstrates. It was used for tents, saddle covers, and boots. In the Tang it seems to have been particularly suited for making hats. Early in the seventh century a high-ranking minister who was the brother-in-law of the emperor devised a new kind of felt hat made from the wool of black sheep. It became the rage among patricians in the capital. The original homeland of the fabric was Persia, and it was sent to China from Central Asia during the Tang. By that time some northwest prefectures of the empire also produced it.

There was a host of fabrics available for making clothes in the Tang. Prefectures in the northwest sent camel hair, a very soft cloth, to the Tang court. The Tibetans presented the throne with a woolen fabric made from otter fur as tribute during the ninth century. Southeast Asia, Tibet, Japan, and Korea sent bombycine, a textile woven from the remnants of the cocoon that the wild tussah moth cut its way out of, to the Tang court. In the southeast, people made fabrics from banana fibers by treating them with lime. They were soft and yellowish-white, inferior to bast fabrics (such as those made from hemp) produced in the rest of China. The Chinese of the Tang knew of cotton, but only as an article of commerce. It was indigenous to Pakistan and India, but made its way gradually along the Silk Route into Central Asia. Cotton was expensive to produce and inferior to silk so it was not until the thirteenth century, when technology improved its manufacture and lowered its price, that it became an important fabric for clothing. Under extreme circumstances the people sometimes wore garb made of materials not normally used for garments. When a military governor was on his way to Changan to attend an imperial audience in 767, he allowed his troops to plunder a district just east of the capital. They laid waste to an area of thirty-three miles, stripping it of all its wealth, even clothes. As a result mandarins and functionaries had to wear apparel made of paper.

Princess Anle had the imperial workshops make two skirts from the feathers of 100 birds. When one looked at them from the front, they had one color; from the side, another; in the sun, yet another; and in the shade, a fourth. The dressmakers wove the images of a hundred birds into the "fabric." Afterward the fashion caught on with officials and commoners. As as result, hunters went into mountain valleys to capture extraordinary birds for sale in the market. The numbers killed in their nets were countless. Nearly all of the extraordinary fowl of the Yangtze River valley and the southeast were exterminated. In 713 Emperor Illustrious August had the princess's skirt burned in front of a palace hall.

All of these fabrics were exotics, and some of them made it no farther than palace warehouses. Except for felt, few played a major role in Chinese clothing of the Tang. In that period there were really only three types of cloth: wool made from animal fur, linen made from woody (bast) fibers, and silk made from insect filaments. Woolens were probably the easiest to manufacture because there were few steps between shearing the sheep and spinning the thread. Commoners wore clothing made from the fabric during the Tang.

The making of bast fabrics from the fibers of hemp, ramie (a plant of the nettle family) and kudzu (a creeping vine) was more complicated. For example, preparing hemp required soaking the plant in water, peeling the skin off, scraping it, soaking again, washing, drying, beating, combing, splitting, beating again, spinning, steaming, and drying again. Hemp was a northern plant that grew in colder climates and produced seeds that, when pressed, yielded the most prevalent oil for cooking and lighting in the Tang. Hemp cloth was a coarse fabric favored for mourning clothes (sackcloth), bandages, sheets, and shrouds. It was also the cloth for the garments of the lowest classes and recluses. Both ramie and kudzu were southern plants. Ramie was superior to hemp because a farmer could get two to three times the yield from it on the same amount of land. Cloth made from it had a brilliant luster like silk and dried easily in climates of high humidity. Southerners wore it in the summer because it was light and cool, and absorbed sweat.

The most difficult and expensive fabric to manufacture was silk. It required, first of all, a grove of mulberry trees. Pickers stood on ladders or platforms to pluck the leaves from the trees. They collected the leaves in baskets and carried them to sheds for feeding the insects. Women took charge of raising the silkworms. When the eggs hatched in the spring, they spread the worms on hemp mats in trays or on shelves so the grubs could feed on the mulberry leaves. The heat from a fire burning in a pit dug in the floor of the shed could reduce the time of the worms' maturation by as much as five days. The preferred fuel was dried cow manure because it did not smoke while burning. The ladies frequently fed the grubs large amounts of leaves and constantly moved them from one container to another, to clean out their droppings. After thirty-three days or so, the caterpillars begin to weave cocoons with filaments excreted from the glands located along their sides. They completed their task in about four days. To obtain the best quality of silk thread, reeling began immediately while the moths were alive. The women had to unravel the filaments from the cocoon before the moths started chewing their way out. If there were not enough hands to accomplish the work task quickly, they killed the moths. There were three methods for doing that: drying the cocoons in sunlight, drawing out their moisture by salting them, and steaming them. The latter was superior to the others. The ladies allowed only a select few of the moths to gnaw their way out of the cocoons. They bred and laid the eggs for the next generation of silkworms.

The Bureau of Weaving and Dyeing in Changan recognized ten types of textiles. Two of them were linens and woolens. The remainder were various types of silk—chiffons, damasks, satins, and the like—differentiated by the character of their weaving. Gauze was one of the finer varieties. It was an open weave in which spaces were left between the warp and woof threads. Gauze was probably the fabric preferred for summer apparel because it was light and permitted air to circulate around the body. In the simplest weaves the warp threads passed over and under the woof threads. By varying the interlace—for example, passing the warp threads under two woof threads, over three, under two—weavers could create different patterns. Known as figured silks, the designs might include flowers, birds, talons, clouds, or tortoise shells. Brocade was produced when the weaver used threads of different colors to produce the design. Embroidery was yet another method of adorning cloth with images created by threads of various hues.

Color was a very important factor in Tang clothing because it was a mark of status and distinction. The Bureau of Weaving and Dyeing recognized six hues: purple, blue, red, yellow, black, and white. Dyers usually tinted fabrics with vegetable dyes to create the first five colors, and used bleaches to produce white. The secretions of the lac insect were used to dye deer skins red. In 630 the emperor issued a decree that fixed the order of hues: the robes of mandarins third grade above were purple; fourth and fifth grades, red; sixth and seventh, green; and eighth and ninth, blue. Wives wore frocks of the same color as their husband's robes. The throne conferred purple robes on men of exceptional distinction, including Taoist priests, Buddhist monks, recluses, and others. White was the prescribed color of garments for commoners. That class included scholars who were candidates for civil service examinations. It was also the color of mourning garments. Commoners in the seventh century apparently were not happy with the color imposed on them by the statute. They took to wearing short, inner tunics of purple, red, green, and blue under their outer garb. Some went so far as to remove their white robes and parade around in their colored underwear when they were in their villages. When the emperor learned this in 674, it upset him because the proper distinctions between the noble (patricians) and the base (commoners) were not being maintained. He ordered everyone to wear inner garments of the same color as their outer garments. During the Sui dynasty the law required butchers and merchants to wear black, but it is not clear if the rule still applied in the Tang.

Dyers could apply their tints to threads or to whole cloth. They could also stamp it onto the fabric. The process involved carving the desired design on a block of wood. The dyers strung two cords horizontally between two poles and hung the fabric on the lower one. They swabbed their tints on two blocks, suspended them from the upper cord and pressed them on the stationary cloth. Then they moved the block farther along the upper string and repeated the process. Stamping reached its maturity in the Tang, when dyers began imprinting cloth with multicolored designs. The innovation required multiple stampings, one for each tint applied. The process was an important precursor to the invention of printing in the Tang, an operation that involved inking engraved wooden blocks and pressing paper on them.

## FASHIONS

Commoners—farmers, artisans, merchants, and scholars not in government service—wore loose, baggy trousers (similar to modern pajama pants), tunics that opened in the front, and sashes tied at the waist. By law the hems of their tunics, which often had round collars, could not fall below the thigh, and the fabrics used for all of their apparel had to be white hemp cloth. Slippers made of rushes, straw, or hemp thread, and sandals secured to their feet by straps, served as shoes. Some shoes were made of wood. Medical authorities recommended using camphor because it dispelled foul foot odor. In the fields peasants wore large-brimmed, bamboo hats that protected them from the sun and rain.

How seriously the state prosecuted violations of sumptuary regulations is open to question. Enforcement was probably more rigorous before the rebellion of An Lushan than after. In 693 a chief minister had an official beaten to death in the imperial audience hall for amassing brocades that the throne had forbidden private persons to own. After 756 the government probably overlooked infractions, especially with regard to the merchant class. By the ninth century there were complaints that the wives of traders had ample supplies of silk and wore gold bracelets. Their daughters sported pearl necklaces.

Most of the information about clothing that has survived in Tang sources concerns the attire of aristocrats and mandarins, and their women. Ceremonial vestments were numerous and elaborate. There were fourteen different regalia for the emperor alone: raiments for worshiping Heaven, enthronements, sacrifices to former rulers, offerings to the gods of the seas and mountains, worshiping the deities of soil and grain, audiences on the first day of the moon (new moon), feasting officials, hunting, audiences on the fifteenth day of the moon (full moon), memorial services at tombs, passing legal judgments, horse riding, and funerals. Nobles and officials also had formal dress for religious rituals, audiences with the emperor, and banquets. Ceremonial attire for emperors included mortarboards with chin straps and strings of pearls dangling from the front and rear; robes with embroidered badges depicting dragons, holy mountains, and other symbols; leather belts fastened with jade hooks; ceremonial swords, some of which were embellished with gold and jade; silk pouches for carrying seals; jade girdle pendants; and silk slippers with upturned toes. The stitching of imperial robes was so fine that one could not see the seams. The size, number, color, quality, and decoration of those articles differed according to the rank of the wearer. A renowned court painter provided the designs for the formal attire of the emperor and officials as well as those for palanquins, parasols and fans.

Formal dress, whether worn at court or otherwise, resembled modern bathrobes. Gentlemen wore a set of two made of silk. They folded the right lapel of both over the left. The outer was the smaller, so it exposed the lapels and sleeves of the inner. Men wore unlined robes in the summer and lined robes in the winter. A sash or belt secured them at the waist. The sleeves of the clothing were quite voluminous, and sometimes hung down from the wrists and forearms to well below the knee. When meeting people, men and women covered their hands with their sleeves. If they needed to use their hands, they folded the sleeves back across their forearms. Those sleeves were ideal places to hide daggers if one

**Ritual Regalia**

Robe          Tunic, Seal Pouch, Jade Belt

**Tang Patterns for Men's Clothing**

Turbans

Late Tang    Court Headdress    Early Tang

**Mens' Hats**

had a murderous intent. Men's skirts were tied at their waists. The hems brushed the floor and covered the feet, exposing only the toes of shoes.

The everyday apparel for patricians was much plainer. In fact, it was very similar to that for commoners: baggy trousers and tunics with round collars. However, there were no restrictions on the lengths of the tunics nor on the kind of fabric for them. Silk was, of course, the preferred cloth. The standard headgear for men was a cloth cap or turban that wrapped around the forehead and rose up at the back to form projections in various shapes above the head. It was tied in a knot at the back, and the ends of the excess material hung down like tails. Sometimes the ends were starched or lacquered so that they jutted out vertically like wings. Boots were common footwear because horseback riding was an essential mode of transportation for the upper classes. The skin of a deer that roamed the forests of the south supplied the best leather for them. The hides were dyed red before the bootmakers set to work.

Peasants wore raincoats made out of reeds or straw that hung down from their necks and covered their bodies. The well-to-do used oiled cloth to protect themselves against downpours. A collection of medical prescriptions had a bizarre formula for waterproofing cloth: Place spiders in a pot and feed them pork lard for 100 days. Then kill the arachnids and rub the grease exuded from their remains on a towel. Presumably, the towel was placed on the head during storms. Physicians warned that wearing clothes drenched with water or sweat caused sores, rashes, and itchiness. They recommended changing garments immediately and powdering the body.

Women's clothing was similar to the formal wear of men. It resembled the kimono that is still worn in Japan today. In some fashions the outer skirt was tied across or above the breasts and flared out from the sides of the body. This fashion survives in traditional ceremonial wear for Korean women. At certain times it was fashionable to bare the shoulders and don a shawl of sheer fabric that fell to floor. Some styles revealed cleavage, an immodesty uncharacteristic for Chinese women. Perhaps they were outfits worn by courtesans or entertainers. Judging from mortuary figures, some female dancers performed topless. When they did not, fluttering the long sleeves of their gowns was an important feature of their choreography.

Women wore types of jewelry common to most cultures: earrings, finger rings, necklaces, and bracelets. It was their preference for baubles that set them apart. One finds virtually no references to the gems—diamonds, rubies, emeralds, and sapphires—as precious stones for jewelry. Diamonds were known to the Tang, but only as an industrial material for grinding stones and perforating pearls. The three most popular objects for personal adornment were jade, pearls and kingfisher feathers. Some types of jewelry were peculiar to China, notably the hairpin. It was a long piece of gold, silver, or ivory that resembled a dagger or letter opener. The shaft was for inserting into the hair. The hilt was the object of adornment, often flaring out in floral designs. Pearls or pieces of jade on string sometimes dangled from their ends. Bright blue kingfisher feathers were used to create gorgeous hair pieces. Some women believed that the wings of an emerald-green beetle were love charms, and pinned them to their frocks to attract men.

Taoist alchemists had two methods for making artificial pearls. One of them called for boiling the nacre (mother-of-pearl) removed from oyster shells in vinegar and pulling it into threads after the liquid had cooled. Roll the nacre into spheres the desired size and perforate with a pig's

Big Sleeves       Low-Cut

Dancer's Costume      Western

**Tang Patterns for Women's Gowns**

bristle for stringing. Insert the spheres into the belly of a carp and steam the fish until overdone. Bring the milk of a white goat containing mica to a boil several times. Then remove the mica, bring the milk to a boil again, and place the pearls in it. Leave them in the milk overnight. Rinse them the next morning.

For men, jewelry was an element of formal court wear. Aside from the girdle pendants and jade belt hooks that had a long history in China, they also wore leather belts studded with jade plaques. According to sumptuary regulations the emperor's belt had twenty-four plaques of white "mutton-fat" jade; those of nobles and mandarins, fifteen of pale green jade.

The influence of foreign cultures had a profound effect on fashions throughout the Tang. At the beginning of the dynasty the riding habits

for palace ladies was a sort of burnoose that the Chinese had adopted
from the Tu-yü-hun, a pastoral people who lived on the northwest frontier of China proper. It was a large sheet of cloth that the women draped
over their heads. The mantle fell across the shoulders to the feet, covering
most of the body and leaving only a small break between the edges for
the women to see through. The purpose of the apparel was to prevent
men on the streets from leering at the women. It had one drawback from
the government's point of view. It provided a convenient disguise that
rebels donned when they wanted to escape from the authorities who
were hunting them down.

Women began to abandon the burnoose in the middle of the seventh
century. Emperor Gaozong took a dim view of the trend, believing it to
be a serious decline in public decency. In 663 and 671 he issued decrees
that attempted to revive it, but to little avail. The mantle continued to
lose favor with palace ladies and disappeared completely by 705.

When Gaozong issued his edicts, women had taken up a new fashion
as a substitute for the burnoose. It was the curtain bonnet, a broad-
rimmed hat with a veil that ran around the sides and back and fell to
the shoulders. The fabric of the veil was a gauzelike material, and the
fancier veils were adorned with jade and kingfisher feathers. Alternately,
women might wear a hood that exposed only the face. In either case the
headwear did not cover the face, a fact that disturbed the emperor. The
curtain bonnet was another foreign import, an article of clothing native
to Tokâra, a nation in the far northwest, outside the empire's borders.
After 705 the hat became extremely popular not only among palace
women, but also among the wives and daughters of commoners who
followed their lead. However, it lost favor, and by 742 women were
wearing hats that concealed nothing of their face or lower hair. Some
did not even bother to don headgear when riding horseback in public.

Western dress became fashionable in the 740s and 750s. It is not clear
from which westerners the Chinese adopted the style. They were probably Central Asians, but they may also have been Persians. Men sported
leopard skin hats, and the women wore hairpins with trinkets that jin-
gled when they walked. The apparel for women had tight sleeves and
collars. After 705 women had adopted masculine attire, boots in particular, according to the customs of the pastoral peoples living northeast of
China. After the rebellion of An Lushan the influence of Uighur culture
grew along with Uighur military power. Women began to fix their hair
in the Uighur style, to wear Uighur dress, and to ride Uighur horses.
For the most part it was the high society of Changan that succumbed to
foreign fads. It is impossible to determine how much effect they had in
the provinces.

## APPEARANCE

A pleasing appearance was extremely important to the women of the Tang. It could be obtained naturally or artificially. The natural method involved applying or ingesting animal or vegetable matter that improved the look of the skin. According to a pharmacologist, bat brains applied to a woman's face removed blackheads. A Sui dynasty manual on aromatics for women in the imperial harem gave the following formula for attaining a fair skin tone: Pulverize dried tangerine peel, white melon seeds, and peach blossoms, strain the powder through a sieve, and ingest a spoonful thrice daily for thirty days. Another, from a collection of prescriptions to relieve discomfort, supplied directions for a mixture that would improve the complexion and slim the waistline: Dry blossoms from three peach trees, crush them, and sift the powder. Mix the powder with ale and take a spoonful before eating thrice daily. The collection also recommended a face cream that would make the face glow and protect it against harsh cold in winter: Boil apricot pits and pulverize them with skinless sesame seeds that have been fried in their own oil. Blend those ingredients with Chinese powdered hemp seeds until the mixture turns creamy white. Another facial cream called for steeping three chicken eggs in fine ale, sealing the mixture in a pot, covering the jar tightly, and letting it stand unopened for twenty-eight days. There was an even simpler potion: Smear the face and body with the blood of a black-boned, silky bird on the seventh day of the seventh moon. Apply the gore three times.

Cosmetics were, of course, the artificial means of beautifying the countenance. There were several powders that Tang women applied to their faces to give them color. One of the oldest was ceruse, made of a lead oxide, which tinted the skin white. Women also applied it to their breasts. Poets called such makeup "lead face" and "lead flower." Women may also have applied minium, another lead oxide, as a rouge to redden their cheeks. It is more likely, however, that they used vermilion (mercuric sulfide), a bright red pigment, or safflower which has large orange or red blossoms. Rice flour served as the base into which the minerals or flowers were mixed. The lac insect from southern Vietnam and Cambodia yielded a dye for rouges as well. Since the sixth century Chinese women dabbed their foreheads with a powder containing massicot, a third lead oxide, that imparted a yellow color to the brows. They may have used golden arsenic for the same purpose. A yellow forehead was extremely popular in the Tang, perhaps because face readers asserted that a yellow aura around the forehead was extremely auspicious. Conversely, sometimes the character of makeup could be a portent of a calamity. In the early eighth century, Illustrious August's concubines applied ceruse to their cheeks in a pattern suggesting tears. Those in the know considered that to be a bad omen. The rebellion of An Lushan broke out thereafter. There was a simple and quick method of perfuming face powders: placing whole cloves in their containers. In the early ninth century, when Tibetan fashions became popular, patrician ladies abandoned face powders and rouges entirely, a change not welcomed by some men.

There were also lotions for making the skin glossy. A formula from the sixth century calls for wrapping four aromatics, including cloves and nutmeg, in a piece of silk and immersing the packet in fine ale. Let the liquid rest for one night in the summer, two in the spring or autumn and three in the winter. Pour the ale into a copper pot and add sesame oil and lard. Bring the liquid to boil for a few minutes and then reduce to a simmer. Add the scent packet and continue simmering until the fluid is completely evaporated. The salve is done when you stick a piece of burning wood in the mixture, and it does not sizzle when the potion extinguishes the flames.

In the Tang women applied beauty marks to their chins, cheeks, and foreheads. Painted on with red, yellow, black, and other pigments, they took the form of crescent moons, coins, birds, insects, flowers, leaves, and the like. The fashion was an old custom that dated back to the second century, but it did not come into vogue during the Tang until around 700. A woman who had been enslaved in the palace, and by virtue of her extraordinary literary talents rose to become a secretary to Empress Wu, reintroduced it to high society. It was a means of covering facial blemishes and scars. Beauty marks did not always mask natural flaws or accidental wounds. Before 766 the wives of patricians were extremely jealous. Whenever female slaves or concubines committed the slightest offenses, they branded their faces.

It was the habit of women in medieval China to pluck all their eyebrows and paint in new ones with tinctures. The best-known style, called moth eyebrows because their shape resembled the wings of the insect, apparently originated in the Sui dynasty. It became so fashionable at the court in the early seventh century that officials had to supply a daily ration of twenty-seven quarts of a pigment to the ladies of the emperor's harem. The pigment was derived from conch shells. In the Tang, women seem to have preferred a greenish blue. In the late eighth century, palace women were using indigo, a blue dye of Persian origin. In the early ninth century, under the influence of Tibetan culture, they began to paint thin eyebrows in the form of inverted Vs that gave their faces a sad expression. The style was called "convict," "tear," or "mourning makeup." A decade later they were drawing three or four red or purple lines above and below their eyes. They called the fashion "blood halos."

One jealous wife in the Tang devised her own style of eyebrows.

  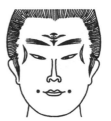

**Beauty Marks and Eyebrows**

Madam Fang would not permit her husband's slave girls to wear thick makeup or do their hair up in tall chignons. A recently purchased maid-servant did not yet know the rules or her mistress's temper. She made herself up a bit too attractively for the wife's taste. The mistress said to her, "So you like makeup? I will make you up!" At which point the woman had someone slice open the slave's eyebrows and fill the incisions with blue pigment. Afterward she heated a metal door bolt until it was red hot and burned the corners of the servant's eyes. The scorching caused the skin to roll up. The wife then applied red powder to them. When the scabs fell away, the scars looked just like made-up eyebrows.

Red was an important color for facial cosmetics. Women brushed rouge on their cheeks directly under their eyes. Cinnabar (mercuric sulfide) imparted the red color to ladies' lip glosses. A powder ground from the horny plate that closes the shells of mollusks lent an agreeable scent to lip glosses in the Tang. The influence of Tibetan culture briefly led to the abandonment of red glosses. In the early ninth century black lip glosses became fashionable in high society. Pigment from impatiens, a flowering plant, blended with aluminum sulfate and garlic supplied a dye for women's fingernails. Both men and women wore their nails long. Some medical authorities warned that cutting fingernails and toenails too frequently weakened muscles.

Six gods governed women's cosmetics, ornaments, and attire: the first, ointments and pomades; the second, eyebrow tinctures; the third, face powders; the fourth, glosses; the fifth, jewelry; and the last, gowns. Whenever Yang Guifei did her face and hair, she would call out to each one of them by name while she was engaged in the procedure appropriate to that particular god. It would seem that she was appealing for divine assistance to beautify herself so that she would not lose the emperor's favor. His favor extended not only to her, but to her older sisters as well. He provided the women with an annual stipend of 1 million coppers to be used solely for purchasing powders and glosses.

There were a substantial number of hair styles for women in the Tang. Some were enduring. Others were passing fancies that surfaced for a

Tall Bindings                    The Conch                    Deserting the Family
**Tang Hairstyles for Women**

short time and developed from specific historical or sociological causes. One recent authority has uncovered twenty-four of the most popular fashions from his study of poems, histories, and other sources.

*Tall bindings* consisted of hair drawn to the top of the head and formed into "piles" in a large variety of shapes. The height of the hairdo was as much as a foot. The style was the most common in the Tang. Some women, notably Yang Guifei, achieved the effect without going to the trouble of doing her hair. She had wigs.

In the *conch*, the hair was drawn up to the top of the head, bound at the base with a ribbon, and the ends curled backward into a spiral resembling the shells of certain mollusks. Sometimes women combed their hair into double spirals.

In *jeweled bindings*, women wove gold, silver, and jade ornaments, often in the shapes of flowers, into their hairdos.

In *flower bindings*, women inserted or wove flowers into their tall bindings. The blossoms in question were probably peonies because they were the favorite flowers of the Tang period.

In the *convict cinch*, the hair was tightly pulled to the top of the head, bound at the base, and the ends done up in a bun. Although the style had been around for some time, it became fashionable among palace women in the reign of Xizong (873–888), especially during his exile in Chengdu. The name apparently derived from the fact that the ladies felt like prisoners in that city.

In *deserting the family*, the hair at the temples was pulled down along both sides to embrace the face. The fashion came into vogue at the very end of the Tang, when everyone clearly recognized that the dynasty was about to collapse and widespread dislocations of the population would occur in its wake. At the time it became chic to wear hairpins made of

**Tang Mirror**

lapis lazuli. That, too, was an ill omen, for the pronunciation of the word was the same as that of the phrase "wandering away," another expression connoting one's loss of home.

*Uprooting the grove* was a style similar to the preceding, except that the hair forming the frame for the face was disordered, and that from the top of the head was allowed to fall and cover the eyes. It emerged from the same sense that the Tang was doomed.

Girls did not do their hair in tall bindings, perhaps because their elders would not allow it. They did their hair up in a style called "anticipating immortals," which required them to draw two braids up from the back of the neck, pull them over the head and tie their ends above the hairline to form loops. Girls also wore bangs.

Combs were essential for keeping the hair in place when tall bindings were worn. The style required as many as ten of them. Made of gold, silver, jade, rhinoceros horn, and ivory, combs were small and had curved backs. A woman might also insert as many as twelve hairpins to fix her hairdo.

Every woman needed a mirror to apply her cosmetics and do her hair. In ancient and medieval China, mirrors, usually round, were made of bronze, not glass. The front was a smooth, flat surface that reflected images because it was highly polished. With time the surface dimmed and it had to be refurbished. There were craftsmen who did the job by burnishing it on a grindstone. The backs of mirrors were almost always ornamented. The designs could be purely decorative or they might be occult. Mirrors were magical. In the Tang the citizens of Changan would point them at the moon during lunar eclipses, hoping to save the orb from being eaten up. To enhance mirrors' mysterious, reflective powers, artisans often cast symbols, such as constellations and mythical beasts that had supernatural powers, on their reverse sides. Mirrors required stands. They were fairly tall when people sat on mats or couches, but later they were affixed to cosmetic chests that were fairly short.

Emperor Zhongzong had the grandest mirror of all. He commissioned the ateliers in Yangzhou to make a ten-foot-square mirror and cast a bronze cassia tree for its frame. The tree was adorned with gold blossoms and silver leaves. Each time the emperor mounted a horse, he looked at his reflection in it. The mirror was large enough to encompass both horse and rider.

Women stored their cosmetics, combs, hairpins, and all the rest in partitioned chests usually made of wood. In the early eighth century a skilled craftsman built an automated cosmetic case for the empress. It had a stand for a mirror and two compartments beneath. When she raised the lid to make herself up, a door to one of the compartments opened, and a wooden lady with a towel and a comb came out. After she finished, the empress replaced the items, the statuette returned to her niche, and its door closed. Then the other door opened, and a wooden woman emerged bearing rouge, eyebrow tincture, and hairpins. It, too, returned to its compartment, and the door closed, when the empress completed her makeup. Gold and silver decorated the painted box, and the wooden automatons wore robes of exquisite fabrics.

In the Tang some men also adorned their bodies. Their embellishments were skin deep. In general the Chinese did not approve of tattooing because it was a mutilation of the body, which ought to be returned to the grave in pristine condition, and because it was a custom practiced by the barbarians. There were, however, some men who defied social conventions. They were mainly the residents of markets, strongmen, and thugs. One of the ruffians in Changan spent 5,000 cash to have an artist prick his chest and stomach so that he could sport a landscape replete with gazebos nestled in the mountains, pavilions soaring over rivers, trees, birds, and animals. In the ninth century a band of juvenile bullies, more than thirty in number, terrorized and robbed people by force in the streets of a market at Changan. They entered a tavern carrying snakes and assaulted patrons with the shoulder blades of sheep. All of the hooligans had their heads shaved and tattooed with all sorts of images. The mayor of the capital ordered some ward headmen and their lackeys to apprehend the culprits. After their arrest, he had all of them beaten to death in the market. Thereafter market people with tattoos had them effaced by burning. At the time there was a strongman in one of the city's wards who had tattoos on his shoulders. That on the left read, "In life I do not fear the mayor," and that on the right, "In death I will not fear the king of hell." He paid for his insolence. The mayor had him beaten to death as well.

Some men paid to have their entire bodies tattooed. Others, despite their violent character, had a literary bent. A tough guy in the market of Jingzhou, a man who never flinched from a blow, had some verses by Bai Juyi tattooed on his torso from the neck downward. Others preferred religious motifs. The governor of a prefecture in southwest China imprisoned a troublemaker from the market who was prone to fighting. His underlings went to beat the man in his cell, but they could not bring themselves to do so because he had the image of the Buddhist god of wealth tattooed on his back. When he learned this, the governor was furious and had the thug brought to the courtyard in front of his office. Then he ordered his bailiff to thrash the man with a new bamboo rod that had a head three inches in circumference. Ten days later the ruffian was wandering the streets with his upper torso bared and begging for money. A soldier and strongman also had an image of a Buddhist deity tattooed on his back. On the first and fifteenth days of every moon he took his shirt off, sat with his back to his family, and had his wife and children worship the icon on his skin as they would have venerated a statue in a monastery.

A provincial inspector, who had excelled at playing polo on jackasses in his younger days, had a snake tattooed all over his body in his youth. The image of the serpent began in his right hand, where the jaws of the beast drawn on his thumb and index finger gaped. The body of the snake wound around his wrist, arm and neck. Then it slithered down his chest, stomach, thigh, and shin, where it terminated with a tail. Later in life the mandarin kept his hand hidden until he was merrily drunk. Then he would expose it and grab entertainers between his thumb and index finger, saying, "The serpent is biting you!" The performers would howl and pretended to suffer painfully. The inspector thought it was amusing.

## HYGIENE

There was not much tolerance for body odor in the Tang. In that period the word for the stench was "barbarian B.O." The barbarians in question were westerners, mainly Persians, but also Indians and other peoples living outside the empire, to the west. Those peoples earned such a notorious reputation for their offensive smell that their foulness became synonymous with body odor. One of Illustrious August's female acrobats, a westerner, suffered from the ignominy of it. It was perhaps not so much that the outlanders were naturally malodorous, as that they did not take measures to remedy the problem. The Chinese, at least the upper classes, were more sensitive to the problem. Women and men perfumed themselves. Palace ladies applied scents so lavishly that when they went out on an excursion, the redolence of their cortege permeated the air for miles. During the eighth century a courtesan in Changan was so skilled in applying scents to her body that her fragrance lured bees and butterflies, which followed her wherever she went. Yang Guifei wore cicadas and silkworms molded from camphor in her robes. It was also the custom for people of high station to attach small cloth bags filled with aromatics to their waist sashes. They favored slipping sweet basil into the pouches. They might also attach storax to their girdles. There was a rare, but more lasting way of perfuming the body. A madam, who raised a young girl to become a courtesan, fed her aromatics when she was a child. After she grew into adulthood, her body naturally exuded a delightful odor all of the time.

Medical authorities had their own solutions to the problem of body order. One of them was a deodorant made of lime, frankincense, cloves, sweet gum (the fragrant resin of a tree that grew in south China), and birthwort (an aromatic root). The compound was packed into small bags that were slung under the armpits. The authorities also recommended washing the armpits with urine on New Year's Day. One might also concoct a deodorant for internal consumption: Pound together cloves, patchouli (a Malayan mint), sweet basil, costus root (an import from Kashmir or Sri Lanka), Chinese spikenard (an aromatic from a Southeast Asian plant of the valerian family), two kinds of Chinese angelica (a fragrant member of the carrot family), the inner bark of the cassia tree, seeds from the areca (betel) palm, and musk from the glands of the male musk deer. Sift the fine powder, add honey, pound again with a pestle 1,000 times, and shape into pills. Take twelve pills during the day, dissolving one pill at a time in the mouth and three during the night. The body will exude the perfume of the mixture in five days, and it will scent clothes and bed linens.

Bad breath was also a social taboo among the upper classes. Cloves were an ancient remedy. In the Han dynasty the throne required its ministers to suck on a few cloves when they appeared at audiences to make their reports, so they did not offend the emperor. The clove was also a soothing balm for toothaches. Its active ingredient, eugenol, was a painkiller. In pre-Tang and Tang times southerners preferred chewing Chinese olives because they considered them superior to cloves as a breath freshener. The fruit was sour, but people steeped them in honey to make them more palatable. If one had the wherewithal, he might avail himself of more exotic scents. A sybaritic prince of the early eighth century chewed on a mixture of aloeswood and musk whenever he spoke with his guests. After he opened his mouth and began conversing with them, a lovely fragrance wafted over the mats on which they sat. As for dental care, a medical treatise of the early eighth century recommended rubbing teeth after getting out of bed in the morning, flushing the mouth with water several times after eating, and rubbing the teeth again before retiring. Failure to follow those directions would lead to rot. The introduction of Buddhism brought the Indian custom of using a stick to clean teeth.

The Chinese of the period 206 B.C.–A.D. 1000, especially those who lived in the north, the drainage basin of the Yellow River, had an ambivalent attitude toward bathing. In the sixth century a fastidious man at the very least washed his hands and face when he got out of bed in the morning, and his body every fifth day. Bathing every fifth day had been the custom since the Han dynasty (206 B.C.–A.D. 220), when the government provided a day off for officials to wash their hair. Chinese wore their hair long, so it was the focus of attention because it was prone to collect dirt and oils from the scalp. The Tang, following the precedent of a southern kingdom in the sixth century, was less generous than the Han, providing its officials with one day off out of every ten (on the tenth, twentieth, and last day of every moon). The casual term for a bureaucrat's salary at the time was "subsidy for clothing and hair washing." After the rebellion of An Lushan the government abandoned that liberal policy because of the frequent emergencies that required the services of its officials for long periods of time. Taoists did not believe in frequent bathing because they thought of it as a source of illness.

There were, on the one hand, fanatics about bathing. A scholar of the sixth century washed ten or more times a day and thought even that was insufficient. On the other there were men notorious for their uncleanness. An author who lived at the beginning of the Tang and enjoyed the favor of the emperor immersed himself in meditation and did not use a wash basin for ten days at a time. Bai Juyi, the renowned poet of the early ninth century, wrote that he did not wash or bathe for an entire year. When he finally did, he discovered how wasted his body had become.

The prevalence of body lice is perhaps the best evidence for the lack of cleanliness among many Chinese during the Tang. They were so common that one author of the period declared that you could predict the fate of an ailing man by the movements of the pests. If the vermin crawled toward their host, he would live. If they scrambled away from him, he would die (rats deserting a sinking ship, as it were). An authority on medicine recommended that the hair of children be regularly combed and washed, lest lice multiply on their scalps. Some adults infested with large numbers of the vermin were in the habit of disposing of them by biting and eating them. The lice then formed a mass in the stomach that only the ingestion of the ashes and boiled water from old combs could expel.

The bathing customs of foreigners were the object of some disdain on the part of Chinese. They found the habits of Cambodians strange because they bathed twice a day and applied musk to their bodies. The Koreans, too, washed themselves twice a day, and considered Chinese filthy because they were so remiss in their attention to personal cleanliness. Worse still, from the Chinese point of view, were the outlanders' customs of communal bathing. Men and women bathed together in the nude in both Korea and Cambodia. The authors of those opinions were mostly northerners (from the drainage basin of the Yellow River). A cold climate and fewer water resources were probably important factors in shaping their bathing habits and prejudices. An ancient philosopher from that region declared that people did not wash in the winter because doing so was unsuitable for the body. In other words, it was dangerous to the health. Taoists in the Tang opposed frequent bathing as well as bathing in rooms with drafts, too much heat or too much cold, because such conditions gave rise to disease.

It was the practice among some people in the Tang to scent their bathwater. There were officials in the emperor's household responsible for his tub. They inspected the water to determine if it was clean and properly perfumed. They also tested its temperature to ensure that it had the proper warmth for their lord. A Taoist scripture on liturgy instructed priests to bathe in the Waters of the Black Clouds before performing their rituals. Mix four ounces of green wood, seven ounces of sandalwood and two ounces of ginseng with three pecks of water and boil it until the liquid clears. The water was suitable for bathing in the summer, but had to be heated during the winter. Other Taoist scriptures called for bathing in waters scented with a compound of aloeswood, frankincense, sandalwood, birthwort, cloves, and Borneo camphor. Besides perfuming the body the scents had the power to bring down the spirits from the five directions (east, south, west, north, and center). Taoists also added boiled orchid and chrysanthemum flowers to tubs of hot water in which they bathed. They believed that the aromatics would prolong their lives.

The Chinese did not have true soaps (that is, soaps made from animal fats) until modern times. Instead, they relied on detergents made from the beans of the soapbean tree. Detergents act by forming films between cloth or the body and the dirt or oil on it. The films lift the filth off. Pharmacists mixed the pulverized beans with flour, powdered minerals, and perfumes. Then they rolled the compound into balls for use in washing and bathing. At the beginning of the Tang, apothecaries kept their formulas secret. They forbade their children to reveal them or, in some cases, would not pass them down to their offspring at all. In the early eighth century an author compiled a collection of prescriptions in which he supplied recipes for making some 200 products of various kinds for cleaning. Among them are two for washing the face, five for the hair, and eight for the body. The upper classes washed their hands in water containing bath beans after using the privy. The unsophisticated were ignorant of the custom and sometimes disgraced themselves. After one man's marriage, his wife's slave girls brought a basin of water with a

**Bath Beans**

silver casket full of the beans to him every morning. He poured the contents of the casket into the water and ate it for breakfast.

A Zen koan (paradox) from the Tang period irreverently declared, "The Buddha is nothing more than a dung-wiping stick." As the paradox indicates, the Chinese of the time were still using sticks to clean themselves after using the privy. However, at the time there was a superior material for accomplishing that: toilet paper. The Chinese invented paper in the first century or earlier, and soon put it to good use in the latrine. The oldest reference to toilet paper appears in a ghost story recorded in the fifth century. When a Mr. Yu was using the privy, someone extended his or her arm into the outhouse with a handful of "grass paper" so he could wipe himself. He never saw the body of the person who rendered the service. Later, when he was in the outhouse and waited in vain for someone to send in the toilet paper, he heard a struggle outside. He peeked out and saw the ghosts of a male slave and a female slave arguing over who would be the first to offer the paper. When the male inched ahead, a fight broke out between the two. When Yu was ready to leave, they were still at it. So he shouted at them in a harsh voice, and they vanished, never to return. An Arab merchant in the late Tang did not think much of Chinese cleanliness, observing that they did not wash their hands after using the privy, but merely wiped themselves with paper. Clearly, the people that he encountered were not among the most sophisticated.

# 6

# Foo∂ an∂ Feasts

## FOODSTUFFS

In the late eighth century a general declared, "There is nothing that cannot be eaten. Making things edible is only a question of skillfully blending sweet, sour, bitter, salty, and peppery flavors while cooking." Once he cooked the worn-out mudguard of his saddle, and declared that his dish was very tasty.

In short, an adept chef could turn even tough, old leather (the mudguard) into delectable fare. More to the point is the general's comment that everything is edible. It is probably fair to say that the Chinese have been the most omnivorous people in the history of the world. There were several reasons for that, the most important of which was geographical. The Tang empire stretched from the arid grasslands of Inner Mongolia to the lush, humid tropics of northern Vietnam; from the fish-rich seacoasts on the Pacific Ocean to the fertile plains on the border with Tibet as well as the deserts and steppes of Central Asia. The range of animals, plants, and minerals was greater than that of Japan, Korea, India, Persia, Arabia, Byzantium, and Europe in medieval times. Consequently, the number of edible things was larger than elsewhere.

Differences in climate, soil, availability of water, and other factors led to the development of regional variations in food and cuisine. The major geographic division in the Tang was that between the north and the south. The relatively arid north, essentially the drainage basin of the Yellow River and the steppes beyond, favored the cultivation of millet, which had been the major cereal in the Chinese diet from ancient times; barley, which was a preferred ingredient for soups; and increasingly wheat, which supplied flour for pastas and pastries. Turnips, a northern root vegetable, were delectable when cooked with mutton. Gourmets of the capital prized a summer garlic that flourished in the vicinity of Changan. The best pears, called Phoenix Roost, grew north of Luoyang. Grapes, apricots, peaches, Chinese pears, Chinese apples, persimmons, pomegranates (an import from the west), and jujubes (Chinese black-thorns) were also native to the region. Rhubarb grew in the northwest. The finest hazelnuts came from the region west of Changan; pine nuts, from the east of the capital; and chestnuts (dried, roasted, or ground into a flour) from the northeast. Walnuts, an import from the west, had taken root in northern orchards. Aside from pork, the most ubiquitous and most often eaten meat throughout the whole of the empire, the meat of choice in the north was lamb. Northerners also enjoyed the flesh of the Bactrian camel, especially the hump which was broiled or boiled. Bears inhabited the mountain valleys in the region south of Changan but were difficult to catch. A recipe for steamed bear called for boiling the meat and head of the creature until rare, and then marinating it in fermented soybean paste overnight; steaming sticky grains that had soaked in fermented soybean paste until they turned a reddish yellow; mixing the meat and cereal with scallions, ginger, dried tangerine peel, and salt; and steaming the mixture. Northeastern prefectures sent bamboo rats, so named because they fed on bamboo roots and were the size of rabbits, for the emperor's table. The peoples of the northwest captured marmots, whose flesh was fat and savory, to eat. The natives of the northeast ate sea otters, the size of dogs, which had waterproof skins. Eating roasted snow pheasant from an area northeast of Luoyang was said to make one courageous and robust. The natives of Shu (modern Sichuan) in the west ate flying cockroaches.

The south, stretching from the drainage basin of the Yangtze River to the southern border of what is now northern Vietnam, had the greatest variety of fauna and flora because it was warm and moist. Animals and plants also suffered less from human depredations because the region was still underpopulated. The major staple there was rice, most varieties of which grew in flooded paddies that required the great water resources. The construction of the Grand Canal in the early seventh century facilitated the transportation of rice north and made it readily available, at least to patricians and the rich, in the capitals. A palm tree produced another starch, sago flour, that southerners prized for making cakes, though they used rice more often. Bamboo shoots grew everywhere in Tang China, but those of the southern spotted bamboo were the tastiest of all. Yams and taro were southern root vegetables. A recipe for taro soup of the early sixth century recommends boiling lamb and pork with the root; flavoring it with scallions, salt, ginger, vinegar, and fermented soy paste; and thickening it with glutinous rice. Several varieties of seaweed were a foodstuff along the seacoast. Overindulgence in eating the purple leaf variety caused stomachaches and gas, but a blue-green variety facilitated urination. Islanders off the east coast of China from Korea to the southeast ate a purple-reddish kelp because they did not have other vegetables. Northern Chinese who consumed it, however, took ill.

The south was the great homeland of fruits, a paradise of sweets. Bananas grew there, but the crown jewel of the region was the litchi. It had a coarse, reddish skin and a dark pit. Its flesh was sweet and aromatic. Southerners prized it so much that they established a festival to celebrate the ripening of the fruit. Occasionally a northerner developed a passion for it. Because Yang Guifei loved them, she had the government's rapid relay system transport them to the imperial palace thousands of miles from their native district. Court musicians composed a song in honor of the fruit. Less flavorful, but closely related to the litchi, were dragon eyes, which were smaller, had a smoother skin, were greenish-yellow, and were less sweet. Although litchi enjoyed the greatest esteem, it was not the most common fruit. That honor belonged to citrus fruit. Oranges, mandarin oranges, tangerines, kumquats, and loquats all graced the tables of southern diners. As early as the fourth century, markets in the southeast sold rush bags, as thin as silk, filled with reddish-yellow ants that attacked insect pests when hung from mandarin orange trees and saved the fruit from destruction. This is probably the first instance of using insects to control insects in human history. In pre-Tang times southern Chinese women carved the citron, imported from southwest Asia, into the shapes of flowers and birds, then stewed them in honey for edible table decorations. That practice probably continued into the Tang. A variety of oak yielded a sweet acorn that slaked thirst and arrested diarrhea. A climbing woody plant bore a nut three to four inches in length, with white pulp and a black kernel, that was sweet and edible.

If the south was the richest region for fruit, it was also the most bountiful area for seafood. Southerners enjoyed jellyfish cooked with cinnamon, Sichuan pepper, cardamom, and ginger; oysters boiled and eaten with ale; fried squid flavored with ginger and vinegar; horseshoe crabs prepared as a sauce or pickle; red crab seasoned with the five flavors (sweet, sour, bitter, salty, and peppery); live shrimp served with vegetables and heavy sauces; and soup prepared from a gelatinous substance obtained from the shells of the green turtle. The natives also ate puffers, fish that Tang men called "river piglet" (though some species also lived in the sea). When frightened, the fish inflate a bladder and float to the surface of the water, where they are easily gathered. The puffer is extremely poisonous, having a sac of toxin near its spine. The Japanese today eat it raw, sometimes with disastrous results; a small number of people die every year when chefs improperly prepare it. However, Tang cooks cleaned, then boiled it in a pot of hot water that presumably leached out whatever poison remained in the flesh.

Mammals, reptiles, and insects also made their way to southern tables. Some, such as the sambar deer, were common and fairly recognizable to northerners. Others were bizarre. The elephant, slain with poison arrows, produced twelve cuts of meat, the best of which was the trunk, whose crispness after cooking made it a favorite for barbecuing. Southerners in pre-Tang times made a broth from the head of the macaque monkey and probably continued to do so in the Tang. In the Tang they also boiled the flesh of the proboscis monkey with the five flavors to make a soup that they claimed cured malaria. According to a northern exile, the meat of the white-throated partridge was sweet and plump, superior in flavor to that of chickens and pheasants. Eastern barbarians, the aborigines of China's southeast coast who lived in mountain valleys, ate the native green peacock—it tasted just like duck—not to be confused with the flamboyant Indian peacock. They also made jerky of its flesh. Nor did the southerner exclude reptiles from his diet. The locals of many areas relished frogs. They also considered python hash flavored with vinegar a delicacy. Snakes were such common fare in some districts that a northerner who lived there for ten years had never encountered a single serpent because the locals had eaten them all. The natives of certain areas were fond of eating hornet larvae roasted with salt, cooled, and dried. Wearing protective overcoats made of grass, they smoked out the insects, climbed the trees, and brought down the nests, which had several hundred tiers of combs. That delicacy was sent to Changan as tribute for the emperor. Chieftains of southern tribes were in the habit of presenting a sauce of ant eggs and salt to honored guests as a treat.

By far the greatest factor in the diversity of the Chinese diet, then as now, was the search for substances that could cure illnesses, prolong life, and confer immortality. The search for things to promote health and longevity led medicine men to investigate and classify the benefits of all sorts of animals (dogs, asses, tigers, porcupines, badgers, wolves, hedgehogs, bats, whales, humans), birds (storks, goatsuckers, cuckoos, crested mynahs, goshawks, owls), fish (carp, eels, sharks, cuttlefish, stingrays, sea horses), reptiles (alligators, geckos, pit vipers, sea snakes), amphibians (toads), insects (praying mantises, bombardier beetles, spiders, dung beetles, fireflies, mosquitoes, centipedes, lice), plants (chrysanthemums, camphor, eggplant, hemp, ferns, jasmine), and minerals (gold, silver, mercury, arsenic, mica, copper, iron, lead, jade, coral, pearls). No doubt those who searched for these products were also largely responsible for introducing all sorts of parts from animals and plants into the cuisine of China. For example, the ubiquitous pig yielded its head, lard, brain, heart, liver, spleen, kidneys, pancreas, stomach, bladder, intestines, tes-

ticles, feet, snout, lips, tongue, teeth, tail, and nails, as well as various
fluids and excreta, such as blood, milk, sweat, bile, and feces, for healing
prescriptions. Not all of the substances or parts listed ended up on the
table, but many did. A clear distinction between drugs and food did not,
and does not, exist in Chinese fare.

Another factor in the omnivorous appetite of Tang Chinese was a passion for exotics. Some of the foodstuffs, such as bear's paw, reached the
table because they were hard to obtain and venerated since antiquity.
Others were foreign imports and sometimes difficult to acquire. Golden
peaches that came from far off Samarkand took root in the imperial gardens north of Changan, and probably graced the tables only of the emperor and his favorites. Pistachios arrived from as far away as Persia.
Tang dietitians contended that eating them made a person fat and robust.
By the ninth century farmers in southeast China were growing them, so
they had become a native nut. Korea contributed the best pine seeds and
ginseng roots. Dates from palm trees—sweeter than jujubes—and figs
made their way from Persia. Both trees took root in the southeast by the
ninth century. Mangoes were exotic because they were imported from
Southeast Asia and probably were enjoyed only at the tables of exiles
banished to the prefectures of the south. Finally, there were dishes that
were noted for their bizarre preparation. Southerners, always known for
their odd customs, stuffed infant mice with honey and let them loose on
the table, where they scurried about, peeping. Guests invited to such
banquets snatched the "honeyed peepers" with their chopsticks and ate
them alive. Southerners also boiled taro and, when the water bubbled,
dropped live frogs into the pot. The frogs, attempting to escape the scald-
ing heat, embraced the taro and were eaten when fully cooked. Sometimes bamboo shoots replaced the taro, and the dish became something
like an amphibian Popsicle.

Authorities on Chinese history and culture have probably overrated
famines—at least forty-two of which (approximately one every seven
years) occurred during the Tang—as a source of diversity in Chinese
cuisine, but famines did compel people to eat things that they would
normally scorn. In 621 Tang forces besieged Luoyang and erected earth-
works around the city to prevent anyone from leaving or foodstuffs from
entering the metropolis. After consuming all of the grass roots and tree
leaves in the city, the citizens turned to making cakes of mud and the
powdered residue of grains, with unfortunate results. Everyone who ate
the pastries took ill. Their bodies swelled, their legs weakened, and they
died.

Cannibalism was another last resort for surviving famines. In the winter of 618–619 the army of a warlord, some 200,000 troops in all, surrounded a district south of Luoyang and exhausted all the stores of millet
there. The price of grain rose to 10,000 coppers per peck, and one could

not find any to buy even at that price. Famine broke out, so the natives began to devour each other. The rebel soldiers were also starving, so they took to abducting children, whom they steamed and ate. That led the warlord to conclude, "Of all the delicious things to eat, none surpasses human flesh. As long as there are people in neighboring districts we have nothing to fear from famine." He had a large bronze bell with a capacity of 200 bushels inverted, stewed the flesh of children and women in it, divided the meat, and gave it to his officers. The worst famines occurred in cities under long sieges. In 757, when An Lushan's forces surrounded a town and its provisions ran out, the inhabitants ate all of the horses, birds, and rats they could find. Then they turned to paper, tree bark, and tea leaves. Afterward they ate their children, breaking and roasting their bones to get at the marrow. The general in command of the armies in the city slew his concubines in front of his troops, in order to feed his men. He forced them to eat the flesh of his women. When that food ran out, he rounded up all the women, and finally the young and old men in the city, to supply his soldiers. In all, 20,000 to 30,000 people died to feed the troops.

Sometimes cannibalism was not an act of survival but a form of punishment. That was especially true in cases of disloyalty to the throne. In 643 a general had a governor chopped in two at the waist for treachery. Then he ripped out his heart and liver, and ate them. The emperor was upset because the general had not asked his permission in advance, but he did not punish the officer. Devouring the flesh of rebels, traitors, and barbarians was quite acceptable. Chastisement need not involve high crimes. A chieftain in southeastern China during the late seventh or early eighth century threw a feast to entertain some guests, and ordered a dandy to serve the ale. The fop committed some offense that enraged his master, who ordered him dragged out and murdered. Then the chieftain had the poor fellow's remains boiled until they were tender, and served the soup to his guests. Some time later, as the level of the broth dropped, the dandy's hands appeared in the bowl. The sight shocked the guests, who clutched their throats and vomited.

Vengeance was also a motive for cannibalism. Sometimes a son felt compelled not only to assassinate his father's murderer, but to devour his heart and liver.

And some men just developed a taste for human flesh. In the late seventh or early eighth century, a marshal got a moneylender and his slave, who had arrived at a hostel in his city, drunk; murdered them; and carved up their flesh. He mixed the meat with mercury and fried it in oil together with their bones, which he had pulverized. Afterward he wanted to eat the moneylender's wife as well, but, aware of his intentions, she fled. The county commandant investigated the matter thoroughly and uncovered the facts of the case. In due course the supreme court in the capital handed down a verdict ordering local officials to beat the marshal to death.

Despite the general's assertion that all things were edible, there were bans on certain foodstuffs. Several principles underlay those proscriptions. Some were political and religious in nature. Generally speaking, the throne encouraged the avoidance of eating beef and butchering of cows, on the grounds that the bull was the principal draft animal that farmers employed to plow their fields. In one extreme case the emperor, who favored Buddhism, banned the slaughter of cattle from 831 to 833. Despite those occasional decrees, people ate beef during the Tang. In the south women slaughtered water buffalo. They tied the beasts to trees, scolded them for refusing to plow, and then beheaded them. Perhaps the cattle were aged and no longer able to perform the task assigned them. Cattle were not the only creatures subject to the humane regard of the throne. At various times emperors banned the butchering of chickens, dogs, asses, birds, and insects. They also prohibited fishing. The underlying justification for such edicts was usually secular, but no doubt the Indian notion of nonviolence and reincarnation that Buddhism brought to China had some effect as well. Whatever the case, the throne banned the slaughter of animals on various Buddhist fast days and Taoist holy days as well as during certain months.

Other bans on eating foods derived from medical canons and dietary manuals. Some that called for abstaining from meat that was contaminated or diseased—meats thought to be poisonous—were related to sanitation: do not eat horses or cows with boils, any animal slain with a poison arrow, the flesh of domestic animals that dogs refuse to eat, any meat allowed to sit overnight without being boiled, underdone boiled meat, meat that floats in water, perforated hearts or livers of pigs and sheep, domestic animals suffering from diseases or scabies, sacrificial meat that moves on its own accord, the flesh of a rabid dog, moist jerky under a leaky roof, and jerky that fails to dry when set out in the sun. Another set of prohibitions concerned toxic combinations of foodstuffs, at least in the opinion of the dietitians: do not eat plums with the meat of small songbirds or honey; pheasants with walnuts; the eastern speckled quail with pork; turtle with pork, rabbit, duck, or mustard; leeks with beef or honey; and mussels with melons or radishes. A third class was religious, and included strong-smelling vegetables. Both Buddhists and Taoists eschewed consuming onions, garlic, scallions, leeks, coriander, and the like. In principle their monastic rules also forbade them from eating meat and drinking alcohol. In reality some of the clergy indulged anyway.

A fifth class was cosmological in character: never eat heart in the summer, liver in the spring, lungs in the fall, kidneys in the winter, or spleen in any season. Apparently the notion was that one ought not to consume organs in season: the heart was the governing organ of summer, the liver of spring, the kidney of winter, the lungs of fall, and the spleen of the entire year. One also should not devour the flesh of the animal that was one's astrological sign (ram, bull, rabbit, rat, etc.). Finally, there was a large number of taboos that defy logical explanation. They were probably superstitions based on ancient folklore: do not eat black cows or sheep with white heads, white sheep with black heads, white horses with black heads or hooves, deer with white armpits, any animal with red feet, black flesh taken from beneath the saddle of a horse, horse liver, sheep with a single horn, horses that grow horns, domestic animals that died of natural causes with their heads facing north (presumably it was permissible to eat the meat of those whose heads faced south), domestic animals that died of natural causes with their mouths open, and animals with forked tails.

As with many other aspects of life in Tang times, the imperial court bestowed foodstuffs on nobles and officials according to rank. For the purpose of distribution the government grouped the nine grades of that elite into four categories. As might be expected, the highest class— mainly royal princes—enjoyed the richest, most varied, and largest quantities of such gifts. The number and types of food diminished with each downward step of the pecking order. The princes received a monthly ration of twenty head of sheep, thirty-seven pounds of pork, and thirty fish (each of which was one foot in length). The lowest order got no meat at all, and those in between, very meager daily portions of mutton only. The princes were also the only recipients of honey, pears, chestnuts, and rice flour. The throne also provided varying amounts of charcoal and firewood for cooking food as well as for heating the home.

## PRESERVATION

In ancient times there were basically two means of transforming raw food into edible fare, preserving and cooking. The preservation of foods was important in all parts of Tang China, but especially in the temperate zones of the north, which were subject to harsh winters. In those climes refrigeration was available. The best of the coolers, of course, were those of the emperor, ice pits located in the massive parks of the capitals. Each year his minions carved 1,000 blocks three feet by three feet and a foot and a half thick from the frozen creeks of mountain valleys, and had them transported to the imperial "iceboxes" where they kept perishable delicacies fresh and succulent—chilled melons were particularly popular during the summer—throughout the year. No doubt nobles and high-ranking officials also had pits for storing ice since they were wont to follow the ways of the court. According to an agricultural manual, even a peasant could avail himself of a simple method of cooling his produce.

Dig a ditch four or five feet deep next to the south side of a wall between late October and early December. Pack vegetables into the trench, one variety to a layer, and intersperse with layers of soil. When the pit is three-fourths or four-fifths full, press earth and straw on top of it. The vegetables so stored would survive the winter in the cool, insulated depths and, when retrieved, were as crisp and fresh as they had been in the summer. Similarly, a farmer could dig a pit in the ground under the roof of a shed and carve holes in its side for depositing clusters of grapes that would last through the winter when covered with earth.

The latter method was effective only during cold seasons and useless for preserving meats, but there were many processes for preventing spoilage of flesh, fruits, and vegetables by rot, bacteria, and maggots. In some cases, apparently, simply drying was sufficient to accomplish the task. The flesh of the river deer, cut into slices the size of a person's palm, or boiled fish could be laid out to dry in the shade. Raisins were made by mixing grapes with honey and oil, boiling four or five times, straining, and spreading out to dry in the shade. Honey enhanced the flavor. The raisins would last throughout the summer without spoiling. Usually, however, preservation required heat, salt and ferments.

Salting fish required removal of gills and guts: Fillet, wash, and rub the fish with salt (more salt during the summer than other seasons). Press two fish together, skin sides out, and cover with a mat (or seal in a jar if preparing in the summer). The fish are ready to eat when the meat turns pink. To eat, wash the salt off and boil, steam or bake the fish. Brining was another means of preserving: Shove sticks into the mouth of unscaled and undressed snakehead fish, and push them down to the tail to prevent the fish from curling. Pour an extremely salty brine with a powder of ginger and Sichuan pepper into the body cavities, thrust a rod through the eye sockets of ten fish, and hang the rod under the northern eaves of the house for two or three months during the winter and spring. Remove the viscera and steep the fish in vinegar to eat. Salted apricots, called white apricots, were a snack eaten while drinking ale: Pick the fruit in the summer, after it has changed to a yellow color, and rub them with salt. After the salt has extracted the juice, salt the fruit again and dry them in the sun. When ready to use them, rinse the salt off and soak them in honey.

Jerky had a long history in China, and during the medieval period the process was applied to beef, mutton, venison, and wild and domestic pigs. The procedure was as follows: Slice the meat into strips. Prepare a clear stock by boiling cracked lamb or beef bones, and skim the scum off the top. Cook fermented soybeans in the broth and add finely minced shallots with a powder of Sichuan pepper, ginger, and tangerine peel. After the meat sits in that marinade for three nights, string the slices on a cord and hang them under the eaves on the north side of the house to dry. Afterward, wrap the jerky in paper bags to prevent flies and dirt from spoiling it, and suspend it in an empty storeroom. Various species of fowl—chicken, duck, geese, pigeon, and more—were preserved in the same manner.

Pickling with vinegar was a common method of preserving vegetables in medieval times. The liquid for it was usually made from spoiled ale, moldy cooking grains, salt, and honey; rotten Chinese peaches also served the purpose: Seal the fruit tightly in a jar; they will decompose in seven days. Strain out the skins and pits, and seal the jug tightly again. Twenty-one days later the peaches become a delicious vinegar. Vegetables preserved in vinegar included leafy greens (mallow and mustard), tubers (rape turnip, garlic, and ginger), melons, mushrooms, and even ferns. Ale was also used as a preservative: Fill a jar with jujubes (Chinese blackthorns) and pour ale over them. Seal the jug tightly with mud. The fruit will last for several years without spoiling.

There was an unusual method for preserving duck eggs that entailed the use of a plant peel also employed as a poison that was thrown into ponds or streams to kill and harvest fish effortlessly: Boil the skin to extract its sap, and mix the liquid with salt. Let it cool, then pour it into a pot holding the duck eggs. The eggs are edible after they have been steeped for one month. Boil until well done and serve with ale or food. The sap dyed the eggs a reddish-brown.

## COOKING

The most prevalent form of cooking was boiling because it was the means of making plain cereals, gruels, stews, soups, vegetables, and beverages. Turtle soup had a long history as a gourmet dish in China: Boil a softshell turtle whole, take it out of the pot, and remove its shell and innards. Return the meat to the water, and add mutton, ale, spring onions, the bark of the lily magnolia tree, and ginger. Boil the mixture until done, and adjust the seasoning with salt and vinegar. A recipe for rabbit stew called for boiling it in ale and lily magnolia bark. Sheep's lungs required a double boiling. After the first remove the lungs, finely mince them and finish cooking in a thick mutton soup with a little sticky rice and fresh ginger. Pig's feet required boiling the meat to a pulp, removing the bones, and flavoring with vinegar, spring onions and fermented soybeans. The ingredients for "sour stew" included pig's intestine and malt sugar. Another for pig's intestines called for clotted sheep's blood as an ingredient. Vegetable soups included taro with pork and mutton, the leaves from a gourd vine with chicken, and pickled bamboo shoots with fish. In areas blessed with hot springs, people cooked pork, mutton, and eggs in their boiling waters, thus avoiding expenses for fuel and the labor for drawing water.

Steaming was another widely used method for preparing all sorts of things, including bear: Clean a bear's head, boil it with some of its flesh until half done, and steep overnight in fermented soybeans. Soak glutinous rice in fermented soybeans, and cook. Mix the meat with the rice, ginger, salt, and dried tangerine peel. Steam until done. The head of a fresh pig also lent itself to such treatment: Debone it, boil, and mince the flesh. Add clear ale, salt, and fermented soybeans. After steaming, sprinkle it with dried ginger and Sichuan pepper. A recipe for sweet lotus root called for cutting off the top of the tuber, filling its cavities with honey, and sealing it with flour. After steaming, the flour was removed and the honey was poured out. Then the root was peeled and sliced.

Roasting, broiling, and barbecuing were common forms of cooking in medieval China, and suckling pig was a traditional favorite: Scald the pig, remove its bristles with a knife, cut a small hole in the belly, pull out the viscera, and clean thoroughly inside and out. Fill the stomach and chest cavity with grass, impale the pig on a stout wooden spit, and roast it over a fire, turning the spit quickly and ceaselessly. While roasting, baste it with clear, filtered ale, fresh rendered pork fat, or sesame oil until golden brown. Cooked this way the pork melted in the mouth like snow. Basting ensured that the skin of the pig was crispy, the most prized quality. The procedure for roasting beef was different: Impale a piece of meat from the back of an adult cow or the thigh of a calf on a spit and place it close to the fire, cooking one side at a time. When the meat turns white, immediately slice it off and roast another side. This method ensured that the beef was juicy, tender, and delicious.

Beef, lamb, or pork liver marinated in scallions, salt, and fermented soybeans, as well as beef tripe (appreciated for its crispness when done), lent themselves to roasting when strung on sticks and cooked over open fires. There was a barbecued sausage made from the large intestines of sheep and filled with minced lamb flavored with finely chopped scallions, salt, fermented soybeans, ginger, and Sichuan pepper. A kind of haggis found its way into medieval cookbooks from the west, no doubt through the pastoral peoples of the steppes: Clean the stomach of a one-year-old lamb and turn it inside out. Fill it with thin slices of mutton and mutton fat, along with ginger, black pepper, fermented soy paste, salt, and other condiments, and sew it closed. Dig a pit and build a fire in it. Remove the embers, place the stomach in the bottom, arrange the coals on top, and roast until done. Meatballs also had a place among the roasts: Slice pork and mutton into a fine julienne; mix it with fresh ginger, dried tangerine peel, scallions, and melons; pound to a pulp; roll into balls; and roast. Balls of minced meat from a young goose were also good fare: Mix goose meat with scallions, ginger, Sichuan pepper, and other condiments; form into balls; and string on bamboo. Baste with the whites of ten chicken eggs and then with the yolks. Roast rapidly over a very hot fire. When the juice oozes out of the meat, it is done. One could also wrap minced and stir-fried goose, duck, deer, pork, or lamb flavored with various condiments around a bamboo tube, six inches in circumference and three feet long, from which the green skin and nodes had been scraped off. A chicken or duck feather was used to apply egg whites and yolks. The cook held one end of the tube and turned it rapidly over a fire. When the meat was done, the meat was cut into six-inch pieces. Oysters and giant clams roasted in iron pans were served on the half shell with a little vinegar for flavor. Roasting was essential to finish burnt cakes, a pastry filled with a mixture of fried mutton and scallions.

Two brothers earned a reputation for a bizarre and cruel form of roasting. They were the favorites of Empress Wu in the early eighth century and competed to see which of them could invent the most outrageous form of cooking. The first had a giant cage made. He placed geese and ducks, and a bronze basin containing a sauce of five condiments inside and lit a charcoal fire at the center. As the fowl circled the fire, they got thirsty and drank the sauce. The birds whirled and turned in pain as the fire roasted them. When they were cooked inside and out, all their feathers had dropped off, and their flesh was pink and warm. Not to be outdone, the second installed a live jackass in a small chamber furnished with the sauce of five condiments and lit a charcoal fire. In both instances the animals presumably marinated from the inside out. The brothers received their just deserts when, after their executions in 705, the citizens of Luoyang happened upon their corpses, which had been thrown in the street, and as an act of vengeance carved up their flesh. When the people discovered that it was as white as the fat of pork belly, they roasted and ate it. At the time people said that the terrible manner in which they met their fate was retribution for their cruel treatment of animals.

Frying, too, had its place in the culinary arts of the medieval period. There was, for example, a recipe for a kind of crispy, sweet-and-sour fish that may sound familiar to those acquainted with modern Cantonese cooking: Gut a golden carp but do not remove its scales. Marinate it in a mixture of honey and vinegar, and add salt. Fry it in oil until the color changes to pink, and serve it whole at the feast. Another probably has no parallel in modern Chinese cuisine. Emperor Illustrious August ordered an archer to slay a deer, and had the meat fried in its blood. He bestowed the dish, called hot Luo and Yellow Rivers, on An Lushan and other generals. Frying was a method for cooking pastry. A recipe for rich (fat) rings called for a dough of glutinous rice flour, water, and honey that was rolled out like a large noodle. The ends were pinched together to form a doughnut, and it was fried in oil. Another recipe for fine ring cakes had the same ingredients and cooking method, but required the addition of cow and sheep milk, which made the pastry crispy.

Baking was not as prevalent in medieval China as it is in modern times, perhaps because ancient Chinese stoves did not have baking chambers. A recipe for marrow cakes, however, calls for it: Mix marrow fat with honey and flour. Form cakes four or five inches thick, plaster them to the sides of a western cake oven and cook until done. Do not turn. They are fatty and delicious. Baked fish required an even more primitive method: Wrap a fish in grass and cover with clay. Place on hot embers and cook. When done, remove the grass and clay, wrap in leather or cloth, and beat to tenderize. The flesh was white as snow and tasty, a true delicacy for a meal or as a snack while drinking ale. Sometimes baking was done in an underground pit: Clean a sheep's stomach and turn it inside out. Mince mutton, fill the stomach with it, and sew the stomach closed. Heat the earth in a pit with torches. When the torches are consumed, remove the burning charcoal. Place the sheep's stomach in the bottom of the pit and cover it with the embers. The virtue of this method was that the resulting sausage cooked in its own juices.

The most important skill in Chinese cooking throughout the ages has been cutting, slicing, and chopping; and the most important tool, the cleaver. In an ancient classic a master chef described his art. He worked with his mind, not his eyes. By so doing, he glided through the natural interstices of the meat, gently applying his blade without overworking it. The average cook had to change his cleaver once a month and a proficient chef once a year, but he had not needed a new one for nineteen years. Cutting meats and vegetables was a critical aspect of cooking because the Chinese had only two eating utensils, chopsticks and spoons. The cook did all of the slicing and chopping in the kitchen, and he made sure that the pieces were small enough for the diners to pick up with chopsticks.

Aside from rice, which was usually served plain, a large number of Chinese dishes were stews, mixtures of meat, vegetables, and/or fruits. That allowed the cook to develop fare that derived its savor from the natural flavors of the foods he combined. It may also explain why there was such a narrow range of seasonings employed in medieval Chinese cooking: garlic, raw ginger, tangerine peel, preserved Chinese apricot, cooked chestnut meat, salt, honey, sugar, ale, pepper, onions, fermented soybean paste, and vinegar. There were two kinds of pepper used in the cuisine of the Tang, the native Sichuan pepper and an import from India. Patricians prized the latter over the indigenous variety. When a chief minister fell from power in the eighth century, officials took an inventory of his possessions that the government was going to confiscate and discovered 1,400 bushels of the Indian pepper in his mansion. The size of the cache indicates that the foreign pepper was not just a commodity, but a store of wealth like silk, and that it derived its value from a high level of demand among the upper classes in the capital.

## FEASTS

The greatest of all feasts were those that the emperor bestowed. He had bureaus with ample personnel to provide victuals and drink for such occasions. The palace food service had a staff of seven cooks and helpers under the direction of sixteen supervisors and eight dietitians who oversaw and prepared the food served daily to the emperor and members of his household. The supervisors and dietitians were responsible for ensuring that the content of the meals conformed to the seasons and to dietary regulations, as well as for managing the delicacies sent to the court as tribute. It was a rather small agency compared to the Service of Radiant Emolument, which was in charge of banquets for imperial relatives, officials, and foreign legates as well as the food for state sacrifices. That bureau had a kitchen staff of 2,000 under the direction of 10 supervisors and 15 recorders. It included 30 ale brewers, 120 ale servers, 23 makers of sauces, twelve makers of vinegars, twelve makers of fermented soybean paste, eight makers of pickled vegetables, and five makers of malt sugar. When the number of guests at feasts was particularly large, the throne called on both agencies to prepare the meals. In 644 the throne feasted 1,100 elders from the region around Changan, for 3,500 officers of the Divine Strategy Army in 768, and for 1,200 women of the palace and members of the imperial family in 826.

There were two types of occasions for which the throne bestowed feasts in the Tang: the regular, whose dates were fixed by the calendar, and the irregular, which took place as circumstances dictated or at the whim of the emperor. The former included festivals and imperial birthdays. The latter encompassed a host of events that were worthy of celebration. Feasts commemorating military victories and the voluntary submission of foreign nations were common in the seventh century. Throughout the dynasty the state provided banquets for emissaries sent from abroad to present tribute and pay homage to the emperor after he received them in audience. The sovereign usually attended such festivities only when the envoys represented a powerful neighbor such as the Turks or Tibetans. Normally officials in charge of foreign affairs handled such matters.

Certain ceremonies—enthronements, the installation of an heir apparent, a military review, or the performance of time-honored rituals—were also worthy of a banquet. More frequently an emperor bestowed a feast to celebrate a happy event in the life of his family, such as the birth of a son or grandson, the marriage of a prince or princess, a princess's or empress dowager's move into new quarters, or a court visit to the mansion or estate of a brother, son, or daughter. Imperial excursions and journeys, including hunts and visits to the estates of high-ranking officials, entailed regaling members of the imperial entourage with food, ale, and entertainment. Sometimes the throne conferred feasts as send-offs for generals sent to the frontiers to bolster defenses, officials leaving for Luoyang to make sacrifices at an ancestral shrine or returning to their posts in the provinces (including one for An Lushan), or monks who enjoyed imperial favor. Other diverse occasions for such festivities included the recovery of the emperor from an illness, honoring former aides, the completion of construction of a palace for the heir apparent, abundant harvests, and celebrations for the appearance of auspicious omens, such as red birds nesting in a palace gate.

The sites for feasts were as diverse as the occasions for them: palace halls, a palace or city gate, palace gardens, the former estate or residence of the emperor, a famous lake west of Changan, the Wei River north of the capital, the homes of princes and princesses, government offices, Buddhist monasteries and pagodas, the private mansions and country estates of officials, and even palace polo fields. In 729 Illustrious August established a new practice. He instructed officials to find a scenic spot for convening feasts on their days off (one out of every ten, the length of the week in the Tang). He promised to provide them with the money to pay for the festivities. He also ordered the appropriate agencies to supply tents and prepare food. That innovation became a custom in later reigns. The location most favored by bureaucrats was the Serpentine River park in the southeast corner of Changan. Emperors rarely attended parties there, but they were willing to supply funds for them. In 788 the throne established the following budget for each of three major festivals during the year:

500,000 cash for chief ministers and officials in perpetual attendance

100,000 cash for the court academicians

1,000,000 cash for (officers of?) two imperial armies

200,000 cash for generals of the imperial guards

100,000 cash for other reporting officials.

The court was to disburse the funds—a total of 1.9 million coppers five days before each festival, and the regulation was to be effective for future festivities. The throne also forbade the mayor of Changan to interfere with officials traveling about and feasting. On occasions when the emperor was not in attendance and the party took place outside the palace, the throne dispatched eunuchs to convey food and ale to the site of the feast.

Sometimes the guest list for imperial feasts included the entire bureaucratic corps present in the capital at the time. At other times the throne invited only a very small number, officials of the fifth grade and above, or those of the third grade and above. In some instances the emperor summoned local officials, such as governors of prefectures and county commandants, to his table. In others, invitations went out to mandarins holding specific positions—the Minister of the Department of Personnel, the Commissioner for Transport or the mayor of Changan—and officers of particular armies—commanders who fought in northern Korea or led palace forces.

The rank of guests determined their place in the seating arrangement at imperial feasts, and they became upset if they found themselves assigned to places they believed were beneath their dignity. In 730, when the legate of the Turkish khan in the north arrived for a banquet, he discovered that the emissary of a Turkish tribe that lived in the west had a higher seat than his. He declared, "Your nation is small and was originally our vassal, so you cannot occupy a place superior to mine." The other envoy retorted, "This feast was arranged for me, so I cannot take an inferior seat." To resolve the matter, Emperor Illustrious August had two curtains hung, the one on the east side for the legate of the Turkish khan and one on the west for the envoy of the smaller tribe. The Chinese, too, could be sensitive about their status. In 632 the governor of a prefecture arrived at a feast and learned that his assigned place was lower than another's. He angrily bellowed, "What rank have you, that you should sit above me?" A prince who occupied the next place beneath the governor's admonished him, but he would have none of it and beat the prince with his fists until the noble's eyes nearly swelled shut. The incident displeased the emperor, who terminated the festivities. However, he did not punish the offender, but only reproved him. Afterward the governor became more prudent and got control over his anger.

The entertainment at imperial feasts in the Tang could include tightrope-walking, pole acts, juggling balls with the feet, sword dances, dancing horses, trained elephants, tugs-of-war, football, polo, wrestling, and even board games. However, the most common form of diversion that the court provided was the performance of the Nine Ensembles. The troupes consisted of seven to thirty-one musicians and two to twenty dancers. Two of the ensembles represented native Chinese music (one a mixture of Chinese and foreign that developed in the northwest during the fourth century), one Indian, one Korean, and five Central Asian. A tenth was added in 642 after its king submitted to Tang suzerainty, but it never caught on and vanished shortly afterward. The foreign troupes were gifts sent to China by foreign kings as tribute to the emperor. Each ensemble, native and foreign alike, had its own unique tunes, instruments (strings, winds, and percussion), costumes for both musicians and dancers, and choreography. Some of them had a difficult time preserving their scores. The Koreans, who had twenty-five airs in Empress Wu's reign, later lost all but one. One of the ensembles came from fabled Samarkand, beyond the pale of the Tang empire. In one of its numbers, the

Western Spinning Dance, young women dressed in scarlet tunics with brocaded sleeves, green damask trousers, and red leather boots advanced, retreated, and twirled atop wooden balls on a stage. Their feet never touched the ground. The sound of the rolling balls resembled that of thunder. In the early eighth century the court had a troupe of several hundred that all performed at once. It became so popular that Yang Guifei and An Lushan learned to perform it.

At feasts, guests dined in the open courtyard of a hall where the entertainers also performed. Consequently, when the weather turned bad, the court canceled the festivities and rescheduled them. Deaths, burials, droughts, and sieges of cities were also causes for calling off banquets.

Normally, feasts were all-day affairs. Some lasted well into the night, so guests dined by the light of torches. On one occasion a banquet for a high-ranking official went on for three days. Another that the throne bestowed in 906 lasted five days.

It was customary for the throne to bestow gifts on its guest at the conclusion of a feast. The most frequent article given was cloth: brocade, silk, polychrome silk, or linen. In 620 the emperor, who was ecstatic over a military victory that recovered his former base north of Changan, sent his guests to an imperial magazine, where the official in charge presented them with his entire stock of polychrome silk. On another occasion a sovereign bestowed silk on all infants in the empire at a banquet commemorating the birth of his son. The throne also gave millet and cash to guests. The emperor allocated the presents in amounts according to the ranks of the recipients, those of higher grades receiving more than their inferiors. Other gifts of a diverse nature, not disbursed according to the status of the guest, included ginseng, gold seals with purple ribbons (for two officials as a mark of favor), robes for officials, gold and silver vases and platters, twenty-five cartloads of fodder and grain (on a military governor; presumably for the use of his troops), and horses.

Tang sources rarely mention the fare at feasts. However, two menus have survived from the early eighth century. One is a list of fifty-eight courses served at a "tail burner." Emperor Zhongzong bestowed it on an official after appointing him to head the secretariat in charge of the six departments of personnel, households, rites, the army, justice, and agriculture. Folklore had it that when a tiger transformed itself into a man, its tail did not change, and had to be burned off to complete its metamorphosis. The notion was that the feast marked the end of an official's former career so that he could assume the dignity of his new one. Zhongzong's feast took place on the banks of a lake in eastern Changan. The entertainment for the occasion was a boat race. Each craft represented one of the six departments, and the Department of the Army's took first place. The dishes served at the banquet included: shortbreads cooked in separate compartments of a steamer; Noble Consort's

**Strumming the Zither**

Rouge (pink, flavored clotted cream); the Queen Mother's Imperial Yellow (cooked grain with a covering of sculpted and imprinted lard); sausages of beef intestines filled with mutton fat and marrow; Glistening Shrimp Roast; twenty-four varieties of wonton; thinly sliced crab rolls; cold frog (actually clam) soup; octagonal cold food cakes formed in wooden molds; perch; fish fry; strands of sheep hide a foot in length; fish fermented in milk; onion and vinegar chicken; roasted sheep and deer tongues; shredded goose; Snow Baby (water frogs with beans); the Immortals' Slices (chicken marinated in milk); rabbit; pigeon roasted alive; and a platter of lamb, pork, mutton, bear, and deer. A significant proportion of the dishes served at the feast were pastries, dumplings, cakes, and breads. The fare resembled what the Chinese now call *dianxin* or *dimsum*, an often large variety of tasty snacks that come in small sizes so diners can enjoy a wide range of foods, textures, and flavors.

There were also private feasts on a much smaller scale and far less lavish than those given by the throne. The occasions for such festivities were festivals, marriages, births, birthdays, send-offs, and more. The sophisticated elite, hosts and guests, entertained themselves with performances on the zither, mouth organ, or other musical instruments. Most nobles and officials had troupes of female singers and dancers that provided diversion at banquets. The second menu from the Tang is for a private banquet. It appears in a novelette that relates the tale of a love affair between an official traveling to a new post and a young noblewoman. The bill of fare included rice, chicken broth, pheasant soup, softshell turtle hash, quail soup, a plump piglet, delicate carp, goose eggs, duck eggs, pure white bear meat, pure yellow crab preserve, fish

**Mouth Organ**

hash, cold liver, grapes, sugarcane, jujubes, pomegranates, red oranges, crabapples, melons, pears, plums, peppers, and purple salt.

It was customary at both imperial and private feasts for guests to write poetry to commemorate the occasion. Those exercises were often competitions in which versifiers strove to outdo one another. In 709 the emperor made an excursion to a lake west of Changan and commanded his courtiers to compose verses during the banquet. After they finished writing, he gave the pieces, over 100, to his secretary to judge. She climbed up a tower made of bamboo and polychrome silk and read the poems. A moment later the papers started drifting down, and the authors scurried to retrieve their works. When only two were left, she hesitated for a moment before dropping one of them. The skill of both poets was equal, but the winner's poem, which she retained, took first place because it ended more vigorously.

Finally, there were Buddhist feasts, which were always vegetarian. Judging from popular literature, two of the greatest sins for that religion were the taking of animal life and eating meat. This notion went against the grain of traditional Chinese culture because meat played a huge role in festivities of all kinds. The occasions for vegetarian feasts included Buddha's birthday (the eighth day of the second moon), birthdays of emperors, anniversaries marking the deaths of previous sovereigns, the completion of construction or renovation of a monastery, the installation of a new statue, thanksgivings for rain or abundant harvests, compensation to a monastery for providing room and board, and funerals. The sponsors included the throne, wealthy donors, monasteries, and societies of laymen organized by monks for that purpose. The feasts were sometimes called "Limitless Fasts" because there was no restriction on who could attend. The number of guests who attended was usually 500, 1,000 or 5,000. In exceptional cases, those subsidized by the emperor, the figure rose to 10,000.

Most feasts were times for joyous celebration. Occasionally, they were the scenes of violence. On November 2, 619, the founder of the Tang invited the khan of the Western Turks to an inner palace hall for a banquet. When the eating and drinking concluded, the emperor sent his guest to a secretariat, where the legate of the Eastern Turks, the enemies of their western brethren, murdered him. Gaozu permitted and abetted the assassination because the Eastern Turks were very powerful and had provided him with assistance during his march on Changan. The episode was a black stain on the history of the dynasty.

Sometimes guests became the fare at a feast. In 619 the throne sent a commissioner to mollify an infamous rebel who had just submitted to the suzerainty of the Tang. To reward him for accepting vassalage, the court bestowed the office of governor-general on him and raised him to the dignity of prince. During a banquet held for him, the Tang envoy drank too much and tried to make a fool of the former rebel. "I have heard, sir, that you are fond of eating human flesh. How does it taste?" Not one to take a taunt lightly, the new prince delivered a riposte. "Eating the flesh of a drunkard is just like eating the meat of a swine marinated in the dregs of brew." Beside himself with fury at the explicit insult and the implicit threat, the commissioner upbraided his host. "You demented brigand! You have become a member of the court, which makes you a servant of the throne, and yet you would revert to eating human flesh!" Tired of this sport and no doubt inflamed by his guest's fit of pique, the prince gathered up the envoy and more than a score of men in his service from their seats, and had them boiled to feed his intimate aids. Then he fled to Luoyang, where he placed himself at the service of a Tang enemy. Fate eventually caught up with him. When Tang armies captured the city in 621, they beheaded him.

## BEVERAGES

The most common drink of the Tang was water. One medical authority of the early eighth century described the virtues of twenty-six varieties, from rain to water found in pig troughs. He claimed the latter would heal wounds left by snake bites when applied externally. Dew collected from plants in the autumn improved one's complexion. Frost gathered and melted in the winter could dispel the heat and redness of the face resulting from drinking too much alcohol. Winter snow was an antidote to all kinds of toxins, but spring snow contained "bugs" and was therefore harmful to the health. Tang people also highly prized mineral waters. Streams that flowed through "jade"—actually any sort of prized rock—possessed life-sustaining powers. Drinking from such a brook that cascaded down from Mount Hua just east of Changan prolonged the lives of local people. Quaffing jade water also prevented the graying of hair, a sure sign of advancing old age. Streams flowing from limestone caves with stalactites also promoted health. People who imbibed such waters were fat and robust, and did not grow old. On the southern island of Hainan, where springs and wells were scarce, the natives drank water extracted from creeping vines.

The Chinese also had instant fruit juices in medieval times: Dry jujubes in the sun, and boil them in a wok. Strain out the liquid and mash the fruit in the bottom of a basin. Place the pulp in gauze and squeeze out the juice. Plaster the mash on a plate or the bottom of a bowl, and dry it in the sun. Then rub it into a powder with the fingers. When ready for a drink, mix a spoonful of the powder into a cup of water. This sweet-and-sour ade was just the thing for slaking the thirst while traveling. There were similar, but simpler, processes for making powders from apricots and crabapples that one could reconstitute as a juice. Vinegar water was another thirst quencher drunk on hot summer days. Some "fruit juices" came directly from the husk. Southerners drank coconut milk, which did not cause intoxication.

Although 80 percent of modern Chinese do not have the enzyme in their stomachs to properly digest milk, it was a beverage in the north during the Tang, perhaps because so many Chinese there had intermarried with the pastoral peoples of the steppes in Tang and pre-Tang times. Tang medical authorities contended that many northerners were plump and robust because they drank cow and goat milk. Milk strengthened and fattened their bodies.

Tea was originally a medicinal substance, but by the sixth century southerners had taken to drinking it as a beverage. The homeland of the plant was in the southwest near the Tibetan border, but it took root in many areas to the east on the lower reaches of the Yangtze River. Imbibing it as a beverage did not reach the north until the early eighth century, when a Buddhist monk on Mount Tai in modern Shandong province sipped it to keep himself awake while he practiced meditation. His example led many others to take up the habit, first in neighboring districts and then in Changan. Soon many teahouses selling boiled tea opened in the markets of northern cities. It even captivated the Uighur, who, when they came to Changan, rushed off on horseback to buy it in the markets before doing anything else. Barges and wagons carrying the stuff from the Huai and Yangtze rivers supplied the demand of northern aficionados. Lu Yu, a southerner raised in a Buddhist monastery, wrote the oldest, surviving manual on tea shortly before 761. His work further popularized the beverage. Tea merchants were so grateful for his assistance in promoting their trade that they had images of him molded in clay and installed on their kilns. They worshipped him as the patron deity of tea.

The processing of tea in the Tang involved plucking the leaves from trees in the spring. Then workers steamed, pounded, patted, and roasted them in ovens or kilns. Afterward they packed them in paper bags to preserve the flavor, and repackaged them in bamboo leaves or tree bark for shipment. Roasting the leaves may have reduced or eliminated the natural bitterness of the foliage and made it palatable to drinkers. Even so, some aficionados took to mixing additives—onions, tangerine peel, ginger, jujubes, pepper, mint, even clotted cream—to flavor it. In whatever form, everyone appreciated it for its caffeine—a stimulant that relieved depression, drowsiness, and fatigue.

The most prevalent form of tea at the time was brick tea, now popular only in Tibet. Brewing involved crushing the brick into small fragments or grinding it into a fine powder, and infusing it in boiling water. Not all varieties were the same. Some districts produced superior leaves because of better soil, climate, or other factors. Furthermore, the quality of the brew depended on the quality of the water used. In the ninth century a scholar compiled a short list of the best rivers, springs, wells, and pools to draw water from. The vast majority of them were in the south. Heat was also a factor. One author wrote a short treatise on the best ways of boiling water, sixteen in number, for making tea. Clearly, brewing had become a ritual that only the leisure class or proprietors of teahouses had the time to pursue. As the art developed, specialized implements evolved for preparing and serving tea. Lu Yu described and provided illustrations of twenty-four utensils essential for those purposes.

Wine was not unknown to the Tang people. Centuries earlier the grape made its way from the west to China, where three varieties—yellow, white, and black—grew. Cuttings for a fourth—the purple "mare teat," so called because of its elongated shape—were brought back from Central Asia for transplanting in the emperor's park north of Changan. Several districts in north China grew grapes, and a monastery in Changan had a vineyard. There was a small, native variety. Northerners also prepared wine from pears and jujubes. Although the art of making wine had taken root in the lands of the Tang, it was a rare beverage, and drinking it never became a widespread custom.

Northerners, at least in Changan, enjoyed koumiss, fermented mare's milk, a gift from the pastoral peoples of the steppes. Southerners made a wine from the fruit of the "chinese strawberry," though Tang herbalists warned that it injured the teeth and muscles. Natives of the south also produced toddies from various palms, such as the flowers of the banana and the sap of the areca (betel nut) trees. Among the preferred alcoholic beverages in a list compiled in the ninth century were also three ferments from different species of the myrobalan, a fruit native to India that took root in the vicinity of Canton during the Tang or earlier.

One might occasionally imbibe those exotics, but the real drink of choice for the men of Tang was ale, known best in the west as rice wine. It was an alcoholic beverage made from cereals—millet in the north and rice in the south—in a manner similar to brewing beer. Making wine is a simple process because fruits contain sugar that naturally ferments once the juice has been extracted and bottled. The vintner can sit back and wait for the molds in the juice to convert its sugar to alcohol. The conversion of grains into alcohol is more complicated because its starches must first be transformed into a sugar. This involves the manufacturing of starters, ferment cakes, from air-borne molds.

The procedure for making one type of ferment cake called for separately grinding equal measures of raw, steamed, and lightly roasted wheat to a powder, and then mixing them: Have a lad draw water before sunrise and stir it into the flour. Boys then form the dough into rounds two and a half inches in diameter and almost an inch thick. They must complete the task the same day. In a thatched hut with a floor of firmly tamped earth and no loose dirt or moisture, divide the ground into four squares separated and encircled by paths. Lay the cakes out to dry. Make effigies of the gods of the five directions with upturned hands. Place jerky, wine, pastry, and broth on their palms as a sacrifice, and pray. Then seal the wooden door of the hut with mud to prevent drafts from entering. After seven days open the hut, turn the cakes, and reseal the door. Fourteen days later open the hut, stack the cakes, and reseal the door. After twenty-one days remove the cakes, place them in an earthen jug, cap it, and seal it with mud. Twenty-eight days later, drill holes in the cakes, string them on cords and dry them in the sun. When they dry totally, store them for use.

The process for brewing ale was nearly as complex as the manufacturing of the starter. One method called for grinding the ferment into a fine powder in a mortar and steeping it in a vat of water for three days, until bubbles formed on the top. Then the brewer added half-steamed millet, twenty-one parts to one part of ferment, in four stages over four days and covered the pot. When the mixture smelled right and ceased bubbling, it was ready to drink. Some varieties took little time to mature. Cock Crow acquired its name because a brewer could mix it one day, and produce ale by the time the cock crowed the next morning.

As with tea, water was a critical factor in brewing ale. River water was the best, especially that collected at the time of the first frost in November or so. If it was drawn in other months, the brewers had to boil it five times before using it. Sometimes rainwater was an ingredient. Thunder Ale was a variety of brew that relied on water collected during summer thunderstorms. In localities where it was available, mineral water was a prized element in brewing. Many people used water from limestone caves that had stalactites because its alkaloids cut the acidity of the ale.

Drinkers were not always satisfied with taking their brew straight, so a variety of additives were used to flavor ale during the Tang. One of the drinks favored on New Year's Day was Black Pepper ale. A recipe for that blend dating from the third century called for powdering seventy kernels of pepper with dried ginger, mixing it with the juice from five pomegranates, pouring it into fine spring ale, and heating it until warm. It was palatable when drunk hot or cold, and prolonged life. A man of great capacity could drink a liter or more of it. It had the added virtue of curing a hangover. Another version of that recipe substituted honey for pomegranate juice. One might also flavor ale with ginger, lotus or bamboo leaves. One aficionado of exotic ingredients served Fish Ale at the height of winter. He had camphor carved in the form of small fish. When his wine came to a boil, he would toss one of the fish into it, thus imbuing his brew with a fragrance that his contemporaries greatly esteemed.

There were regional differences in the quality of ales. In the early ninth century an author compiled a list of the sixteen best alcoholic beverages, twelve of which were varieties of ale. Topping the list was Fu River, produced in a prefecture of south central China. When an official discovered how good it was in the early eighth century, he informed the emperor. Thereafter the court recruited master brewers only from that district to make ale for presentation at its feasts. Actually, Fu River had an ancient reputation for the quality of its product. Changan produced three varieties—Melody of the Western Market, Courtier's Clear Ale of Toad Tumulus, and Old Woman's Clear Ale. They apparently were not superior brews, for their titles appear at the bottom of the list. Brewing was not a monopoly of professionals. An authority in the Tang declared that men who got drunk on home brew were superior to those who did so on the ale served at taverns in the lanes. In the early seventh century a renowned hermit, who was erudite and given to drinking, employed several slaves for the purpose of making ale for him in the spring and summer. In the mid-eighth century the household of an imperial prince had a method for producing an ale called Sweet Dew. Both of those men wrote manuals on brewing as well.

## DRINKING

Ale was an essential offering at all rites, both the grand public rituals of the court and the private observances of ancestor worship, in the Tang. That fact explains why there was little stigma attached to drinking and drunkenness among the upper classes. Custom dictated that the host of a drinking party supply his guests with more than enough brew. In one case a prominent official of the early eighth century had a serpentine structure built for drinking that he called the Ale Grotto. On each of the bricks, some 50,000, in the structure's floor he placed a bowl of ale to completely satisfy the thirst of his friends when they came to visit.

The occasions for drinking were virtually the same as those for feasting. There were, however, several rites and celebrations in which drinking played a predominant role. One was the village drinking ritual, which dated back to ancient times. Each year the governors of prefectures and commandants of counties invited the elders of their districts to a banquet in the winter. The government supplied the food and liquor as well as the musical entertainment. The custom disappeared after the An Lushan rebellion. Festivals celebrating imperial birthdays, at least from 730 to 755, were also occasions when the throne called for drinking by all of its subjects.

It was permissible to drink almost anywhere: palaces, mansions, Buddhist monasteries (despite the fact that their rules forbade imbibing alcohol), rapid relay stations, parks, even government offices. On the first day of 822 the throne demoted an imperial counselor and sent him out to a provincial post after revelry at the office for compiling histories. It was not the official's inebriation that disturbed the emperor, but the fact that he had insulted a chief minister while drunk. There was, however, a certain risk to letting oneself go while inebriated. An emperor might excuse a man of talent for appearing before him drunk, but the offender might also lose imperial favor for it. The throne would not tolerate a sot who was drunk all day in his office. Such an offense was cause for dismissal. It was also acceptable to drink at almost any time. In the winter a host might convene a party at dawn, to dispel the chill of the previous night with ale before eating breakfast. The warming effect derived not only from the alcohol but also from the fact that it was the custom to drink ale warm. Generally speaking, however, day was the proper time for drinking and night for sobering up, though there was plenty of nocturnal imbibing.

Although servants, courtesans, waiters, and barmaids generally served ale to guests at a banquet or to customers in a tavern, there were also machines for delivering it. In 647, at a feast for legates from several Central Asian tribes, the emperor had a tall stand with a silver pitcher on top installed before a palace hall. From a reservoir in an eastern pavilion ale flowed through a hidden conduit to the leg of the stand and bubbled, like a spring, upward into the pitcher. When the brew reached a certain level, the pitcher tipped to fill a huge silver basin below. Waiters ladled ale from the bowl to fill goblets for the guests. The emperor employed the device to impress the barbarians with the cultural (i.e., technological) superiority of China.

However, that machine paled in comparison to the inventions of a county commandant who was both clever and fond of ale. He carved a wooden monk from wood and dressed it in a suit of coarse, colored silk. At the commandant's parties the automaton poured brew and handed goblets to guests in a fixed order. He also made wooden chanteuses that could sing songs and play the mouth organ. They were able to play and sing in perfect accord with the rhythm of the music. If a guest did not drain his goblet, the wooden monk would refuse to take the cup back for a refill. If the guests had not finished drinking, the wooden chanteuses would sing and play the fife to urge them on.

Another ingenious craftsman fashioned an ale mountain in the early eighth century. The mountain, which had extraordinary and marvelous peaks, was three feet tall and had a hidden, interior reservoir that held more than sixteen quarts of brew. It sat on a lacquered wooden basin four feet, five inches in circumference that rested on a large tortoise. In the belly of the turtle were a pump and a machine that drove the device. An ale pool encircled the base of the mountain, and a ring of hills surrounded the pool. Lotuses with blossoms and leaves of wrought iron rose from the pool. The opened flowers and unrolled leaves took the place of platters for serving jerky, meat jellies, and rare fruits to be eaten with the ale. Midway up the southern side of the mountain was a dragon with the front half of its body protruding from the slope. The beast opened its mouth and spit brew into a goblet seated on a large lotus leaf beneath. When the cup was 80 percent full, the dragon ceased spewing ale, and a guest immediately seized the goblet. If he was slow in draining the cup and returning it to the leaf, the door of a pavilion at the top of the mountain opened and a mechanical wine server, dressed in cap and gown, emerged with a wooden bat in his hand. As soon as the guest returned the goblet, the dragon refilled it, the wine server withdrew, and the doors of the pavilion closed. Dragons of the same sort on the other three sides of the mountain also disgorged brew. At two places on the mountain there were tilting bowls. When empty, they tipped, and the dragons filled them with ale. When half full, they rose to an upright position, but when brimming, they tilted again. A pump siphoned the ale that flowed into the ale pool through a hidden hole and returned the brew to the reservoir inside the mountain. It was so efficient that not a trace of ale remained in the pool by the end of a feast.

There were also nonmechanical, but bizarre, contrivances for serving wine. An aristocratic lady of the eighth century had deer guts suspended from the beams in one of her halls. Whenever she threw a party, the lady ordered her servants to climb up to the beams and pour ale into the intestines. Guests who wanted to drink needed only to untie the lower end of the guts to fill their goblets.

Most cups in the Tang were made of porcelain, an ancient Chinese invention. In the early eighth century the palace treasury had a goblet, azure in color with a pattern like raveled threads, that was as thin as paper. On its foot there were incised words filled with gold: "self warming goblet." Whenever the emperor ordered ale poured into it, the chalice heated the brew automatically. One record indicates that a type of porcelain, now called eggshell, was produced in Tang times. Another type of vessel was made of lacquered wood, a kind of ware that the Chinese had used for cups for a millennium before the Tang. More extravagant were cups of silver and gold. Southerners turned the shell of the nautilus with a red and blue-green surface into ale goblets. They adopted carapace of the tiger crab with a red-and-yellow striped exterior and a pearly interior for the same end. Nor did southerners leave birds in peace. They turned the skulls of hornbills into cups for imbibing ale. They also filled coconut husks with brew.

Then, as now, the Chinese rarely drank without eating. Snacks eaten to "put the ale down" could be quite substantial. A list of them, from the novelette whose dinner menu appears above, included gray mullet from the Eastern Sea, deer tail, deer tongue, dried fish, roasted fish, minced wild goose relish, preserved vegetables, quail soup, cinnamon-flavored gruel, meat pies, bear's paw, rabbit's haunch, the meat from a pheasant's tail, and jackal lips. Those fourteen dishes were hors d'oeuvres presented before a meal of some twenty-three courses. Either the portions were small or the capacity of the diners was large. Another food eaten while drinking was the crabapple. Southerners soaked the fruit in honey and cinnabar (mercuric sulfide), and served it as a dessert with ale. One snack that drinkers avoided while imbibing was the persimmon. Medical authorities advised drinkers to abstain from nibbling on it because it made one drunk quickly and caused heart pains so severe that one wished to die.

In the Tang, drinking among the patricians was a contest. There were a considerable number of games, including dice and riddles, designed to keep the ale flowing and the guests inebriated. In one a host, guest or courtesan spun a top carved in the image of a western barbarian. When it stopped twirling, it fell over, and the guest at whom it pointed had to drain his goblet. The largest variety of drinking games were the Ale Rules. One involved a silver canister filled with lots in the shape of oars with round handles and flat, rectangular ends. Guests drew the lots from the canister in turn and had to obey the instructions, commands, inscribed on the rectangular ends. The commands designated the person who had to drink at that moment: the puller of the lot, the most honored guest, the highest-ranking official, the taciturn, the talkative, the host of the party, the drinker with the greatest capacity for ale, the youngest, the last to arrive, and so forth. Some, however, were blanks that apparently gave the drinkers a short respite from imbibing. The instructions also specified the amount of ale—one, five, seven, ten, and forty measures—that the designated tippler had to quaff.

To ensure that parties did not get out of hand, three officiants presided over the game and assumed the responsibility for maintaining order: a governor, who reviewed penalties; a registrar of the rules, who knew the regulations and had a great capacity for ale; and a registrar of the horn (flagon). When a guest disturbed the gathering by laughing or talking too boisterously, was rude or impolite, or rose from his seat, the registrar of rules threw down a lot. The offender then confessed his transgression and drank a penalty cup. If he continued to violate the regulations, the registrar of the horn threw down a small, silver flag. The guilty man acknowledged his error again and downed another goblet. After the assessment of the third fine the governor stepped in to review the case. The intent of this judicial system was to ensure a convivial atmosphere in a situation that could easily become rowdy, given the inebriated state of the guests.

Sometimes the fines and penalties levied at such games were so heavy that violators could not endure them. A famous poet of the early ninth century said that in his youth he had been out drinking for several months in a row and had regularly served as the registrar of the horn. On one occasion a guest arrived last and continued to commit infractions of the Ale Rules. After downing twelve penalty cups, he could stand it no longer and fled the party. The fraternity of the goblet had little sympathy for such cowardice. One regulation called for abandoning such deserters, that is, not inviting them to further drinking bouts.

As might be surmised from this discussion, drinking was not only an acceptable custom among patricians in Tang times, but also a necessity for those who wished to be accepted and advance socially. One author advised his contemporaries to increase their capacity for ale so that they could win more contests and enhance their reputations. That counsel presumed a certain amount of self-control on the part of the person indulging. Outright drunkenness was not rare among the upper classes. In the spring of 732 the emperor threw a feast for his corps of officials on an island in a lake at the imperial park of Luoyang. At the conclusion of the festivities the guests were so drunk that his majesty provided litters with quilts to carry them home. Some artists apparently believed that inebriation contributed to the excellence of their work. Wu Daoxuan, the greatest artist of the Tang, always got drunk before painting. He is said to have painted the outer facade of a gateway to a Buddhist monastery in a single night while intoxicated. When the abbot of a Buddhist monastery wished to entice him to execute murals for the walls of buildings that he had just erected, he arrayed vats containing 100 gallons of ale on the porticos of the monastery and offered them to Wu if he would set his brush to work. The quantity of the brew so impressed the artist that he was only too happy to oblige. A painter of the ninth century would get drunk and splash ink on a scroll, laughing and singing as he worked. Sometimes he applied it with his hands. At other times he would dip his long hair in the ink and brush his tresses on the silk to execute his masterpieces. Some poets were also renowned sots. It was the custom for the literate to write verses at imperial feasts and private repasts while in a state of semi- or total inebriation. The second most famous poet of the Tang, Li Bai, was a confirmed alcoholic as well as a knight-errant who on several occasions cut down men to avenge injustices. When Emperor Illustrious August recruited him to serve as a drafter of imperial documents about 744, he was invariably drunk while on duty. Attendants had to throw water on his face to awaken him. Nevertheless, he accomplished the task assigned him immediately, despite his intoxication. According to legend, he died while drinking on a boat in a river. Seeing the reflection of the moon in the water, he reached over to embrace it, fell in the stream, and drowned. It is more likely, however, that he expired at the age of sixty-one from overindulgence in ale.

Medical authorities recommended soaking in hot water as a means of curing a great drunk as well as for overindulgence in melons and other fruit. There was also a plant with purple leaves that grew on the southern banks of a lake in a palace at Changan that reputedly could sober a sot immediately if he passed by it. One of the great medical compendiums of the seventh century contains formulas for dispelling a hangover (i.e., a headache)—a soup of bamboo roots boiled with five chicken eggs—and for allowing a person to imbibe without getting drunk—a powder of cypress nuts and hemp seeds mixed with ale. The text also supplied several prescriptions that would make sots give up alcohol: Mix the milk from a white dog with ale and drink it. Combine the sweat scraped off a horse with brew and imbibe it. Drop a powder of willow blossoms and the skin from a rat's head into your libation and quaff it. A writer in the ninth century warned that intemperance led to poverty and the destruction of one's family. He also cautioned the official who drank to take care in drafting his documents, so that he would not bring disgrace upon himself.

The peoples of southern China as well as Southeast Asia had a different means of ensuring a convivial atmosphere at their festivities. They chewed betel nuts—the acrid, slightly intoxicating fruit of a palm tree. The natives peeled the nut and rolled it in the leaves of the betel pepper along with lime derived from oyster shells. They believed that it was an aid to digestion, and always presented it to guests at feasts.

# 7

# Leisure and Entertainment

## FESTIVALS

There was plenty of leisure during the Tang, more so than in later dynasties. By the middle of the eighth century Tang statutes recognized twenty-eight holidays on which the government granted a total of fifty-eight days of leave to all mandarins throughout the empire. The rest of society—peasants, merchants, and artisans—also celebrated festivals, though probably with less time off. As already noted, the regulations provided officials with one day off every ten days (a Tang week). In addition the state gave its high-ranking employees fifteen days off in the fifth moon as a "farming holiday" and another fifteen days in the ninth moon as a "holiday for the bestowal of robes." In all of those instances government offices closed, permitting their personnel to spend their free time at home or in places of amusement. Finally, there were irregular vacations granted to officials individually. Those included the following:

1. Thirty days off every three years for a visit to their parents, if they lived more than 1,000 miles away, or fifteen days, if they lived more than 167 miles away (travel time not included)
2. Nine days for the wedding of a son or daughter, and five, three, or one day for the nuptials of other close relatives (travel time not included)
3. Three days for a son's capping (manhood) rite or one for another close kinsman's ceremony.

Besides the time off allocated by statutes, officials sometimes found themselves in posts that required very little work and permitted them to pursue their favorite diversions. Mandarins in Tang China were the leisured class in every sense of the word.

There were two sorts of festivals in Tang China. The first were solar, such as the summer and winter solstices. The second and more numerous were lunar, and often fell on double digits such as the third day of the third moon. (Since it is the convention to refer to the twelve divisions of the year in the solar calendar as months, we use the term "moons" to designate the twelve divisions of the lunar year.) The lunar calendar began sometime between mid-January and mid-February, the exact date differing from year to year. There was scarcely a moon without festivals to cheer the lives of the people.

**New Year's**  The first day of the first moon, also called the day of the chicken, was the grandest of all festivals, a holiday of seven days for government officials. The court held a levee, a grand audience, in the early hours of the day that civil and military officials, as well as nobles and foreign emissaries, attended. It was an occasion for reviewing the omens and disasters or blessings of the preceding year, for displaying the tribute submitted by prefectures and foreign nations, and for the presentation of candidates whom provincial governors had recommended for national examinations in the capitals.

Throughout the land, however, New Year's was mostly a private affair celebrated in the home. It was a festival for dispelling evil, to ensure a fortuitous future in the coming year. Householders rose at cockcrow and threw segments of bamboo into fires that they had lit in a courtyard or in front of their houses. When the heat expanded the air captured inside the segments, the bamboo exploded with a loud bang. Folk beliefs maintained that the noise drove away a malicious, one-legged specter that was somewhat over a foot tall, was unafraid of humans, and caused chills and fevers. After the eleventh century, firecrackers replaced the bamboo segments. To further protect their abodes, people hung willow branches on their gates to prevent ghosts from entering the premises. Some county officials took extraordinary measures by slaughtering a sheep, hanging its head on a gate, and covering it with a butchered chicken. The sacrifice of the sheep, which ate the sprouts, and the chicken, which ate the seed, would enable crops to grow. On New Year's Day it was the custom for people to drink an ale called Killing Ghosts and Reviving Souls, into which special herbs had been mixed. Imbibing the brew would ensure that they would not contract any illnesses in the coming year. They also ate a platter of five bitters—onions, garlic, leeks, and the like—because it fortified their internal organs.

This three-day event, held on the fourteenth, fif-
teenth and sixteenth days of the first moon, was the **Lantern Festival**
only occasion when the government lifted the curfew
so that citizens could freely stroll the streets outside their wards during
the night. It was a festival of light when the moon was full, and patricians sought to outdo each other in providing the grandest lamps. An
aristocratic lady of the mid-eighth century had a lamp tree with several
hundred branches that was eighty feet tall. When she lit it on Lantern
Festival, its light was visible for miles. It could not compare, however,
with that of Emperor Ruizong. He had a lantern wheel 200 feet tall
erected outside a gate of Changan in 713. The apparatus was clothed in
brocades and silk gauze, and adorned with gold and jade. When he had
its 50,000 oil cups lit, the radiance burst forth like the blooms on a flowering tree. There were over 1,000 palace women present. They wore
gauze trails, embroidered brocades with lustrous pearls, kingfisher hairpins, and fragrant makeup. Any one of their coronets or gowns was
worth 10,000 coppers. The cost for outfitting a single chanteuse was as
high as 300,000 cash. The court also skillfully selected more than 1,000
young female entertainers from Changan's two counties whose dress,
figured hairpins, and makeup were not inferior to those of the palace
ladies. The singers danced and sang under the lantern wheel for three
days and nights. Three years earlier Zhongzong had let several thousand
palace women—those enslaved there for the crimes that their menfolk
had committed—leave their confines to view the lanterns. Most of the
ladies took advantage of the opportunity, and fled.

This one-day festival took place on the third day of the
third moon (double-three). In ancient times that had been an **Lustration**
occasion for repairing to a river and bathing in waters
scented with the aromatic orchis plant. It was a rite for dispelling evil
and washing away defilement. By the Tang dynasty it had become a
time for merrymaking, specifically for drinking ale. As already noted, a
famous party in 353 established the conventions—feasting, drinking, and
writing poetry—for such festivities. During the Tang the throne presented deep-fried pastries to officials on double-three, perhaps at the
Serpentine River park.

This festival, so named because custom forbade the lighting of fires for three days, and therefore people ate cold **Cold Food**
food, was a solar celebration that fell on April 5. On that **Festival**
occasion people went to the tombs of their ancestors to
sweep them, sacrifice to their forebears, and have a picnic. It was also a
time for indulging in diversions. Ladies amused themselves on swings.
Palace women as well as new graduates of the civil service examinations
played football. An imperial workshop manufactured the balls—proba-

bly leather spheres filled with feathers, as in previous times—and presented them to the throne during the festival. Tugs-of-war and polo were also part of the entertainment during the festivities. In 710 Emperor Zhongzong had his chief ministers, sons-in-law, and generals participate in a tug-of-war. When two of the oldest ministers fell to the ground, the monarch laughed. Cold Food Festival also had something of the character of Easter in the West because it was the custom in the Tang to dye chicken and duck eggs then. The throne presented porridge to officials for their holiday.

**Fifth Day of the Fifth Moon**  This official one-day holiday commemorated the suicide of a famous, upright statesman in the third century B.C.E. who seized a rock and leaped into a river because his king had banished him for his criticisms. According to folklore, witnesses to his drowning boarded skiffs and rushed out in a futile attempt to save him. That tradition was apparently the reason for the boat races, now called dragon boat races, during that festival in Tang times. The special food for the fifth day of the fifth moon was a dumpling made of glutinous millet or rice wrapped in leaves and boiled. Officials in the capital received their portions from the palace. If it was raining on the fifth day, some people cut a piece of bamboo to make a tube for collecting the "divine water." Then they mixed rain water with the liver of an otter to form a ring that they ate to cure certain illnesses.

**Seventh Night of the Seventh Moon**  This one-day holiday for officials was a festival celebrating the love affair between the cow herder—the deity of the star Altair in the constellation Aquila—and the weaver maid—the spirit of the star Vega in the constellation Lyra. Separated by the Milky Way, they could cross it only once a year on a bridge of magpies. When they finally met, they consummated their relationship during the evening. The festival was basically for women, who prayed for enhancement of their skills at sewing and weaving. In the palace at Changan during the early eighth century, servitors erected a 100-foot-tall hall by knotting brocades (to a bamboo frame) and laid out melons, other fruits, ale, and roasts as offerings to the two stellar lovers. The emperor's concubines faced the moon and threaded polychrome thread into needles with nine eyes. The ritual was called "praying for skill [in sewing and weaving]." The ladies also captured spiders and placed them in lidded cases. The following morning they opened the boxes to see whether the webs were loosely or tightly woven. Those whose cases contained tightly woven webs would be skilled at their craft, and the others, inept. Commoners also performed the ritual.

The All Souls' Feast developed from the legend of the bodhisattva (savior) Mulian, who found his sinful mother suffering in the purgatory of hungry ghosts. There she starved, because when she put food in her mouth, it changed into burning charcoal. When Mulian **Fifteenth Day of the Seventh Moon**
informed Buddha, the latter instructed him to make a sumptuous offering, especially of fruit, on the fifteenth day of the seventh moon for monks everywhere. The collective virtue of the clergy was powerful enough to effect the salvation of seven generations of ancestors from hell, from existence as hungry ghosts, and from rebirth as animals. By dint of his effort Mulian saved his mother. Thereafter he asked Buddha to make the day a permanent festival, and he agreed. The story became the subject of a sutra translated into Chinese during the third century, and the basis for the custom of the devout laity making offerings to monks. Monasteries took the opportunity of All Souls' Feast to make ostentatious displays of their treasures, probably to attract large numbers of donors. They also gave dramatic performances for the diversion of the crowds.

This midautumn festival was a three-day vacation for officials. Today Chinese call it the Moon Festival. In Tang times it was an occasion when esthete gentlemen admired the moon during the night, at least when the weather was clear enough to see it. They **Fifteenth Day of the Eighth Moon**
saw in the moon not an old man, but a hare who was hard at work grinding ingredients for an elixir, using a mortar and pestle. (That was a Taoist image, for alchemy was Taoism's special field of endeavor.) Not everyone agreed on what the craters and plains of the lunar surface depicted. Some saw a toad there. The moon was also the site of the ice palace for the moon goddess and her court. In the folklore of the Tang, a magician escorted Emperor Illustrious August to that palace across a silver bridge that he had conjured up by tossing his staff into the air. During his sojourn there, on the fifteenth day of the eighth moon the emperor witnessed a performance of the "Air of the Rainbow Robe and Feathered Skirt" by immortal maids. He memorized the music, and on his return to earth taught it to his performers. The tale is incredible, but the piece was composed during the emperor's reign—an adaptation of an Indian dance, and the most famous in Tang history. Whatever the case, patricians and plebes alike enjoyed the festival. Those who lived in the country, where the curfew did not apply, might repair to a mountain to drink and feast throughout the night.

Another three-day holiday, this was an occasion, like the Cold Food Festival, for picnicking in the countryside, specifically on a high elevation such as a mountain. Urban dwellers, however, might convene **Ninth Day of the Ninth Moon** their feasts at the top of a pagoda or at the Serpentine River park in Changan. There was an intimate association between the festival and the chrysanthemum. The plant was thought to promote longevity because it blooms in the autumn and mimics the life-giving sun with its yellow center and white petals. During the Tang it was the custom to imbibe chrysanthemum blossom ale during the festivities. The stems and leaves of the plant were gathered on the ninth day of the ninth moon, added to fermenting grains, and allowed to brew for an entire year. Drinking the ale on the festival the following year prolonged one's life.

**The Last Day of the Twelfth Moon** On this night the well-to-do invited Buddhist monks or Taoist priests to recite scriptures at their homes. Then they prepared ale and fruit to send the god of the stove on his way. It was that deity's duty to record the sins of the family throughout the year and report them to heaven on the last day of the year. Families hung an image of the god painted on paper above their stoves on New Year's Day, and it remained there all year long, noting all the transgressions committed by the house-holders. On the eve of the last day of the twelfth moon, the god of the stove left the home and journeyed to the celestial realm. That was not a pleasant thought to families, so they rubbed the dregs of ale on the mouths of their images to get the deity so drunk that he could not make his report to heaven.

## GRAND CARNIVALS

The roots of Tang carnivals lay in grand bacchanals that the throne bestowed beginning in the late third century B.C.E. In 222 and 221 the first emperor of China decreed that everyone in the empire should en-gage in great drinking revelries to celebrate his conquest and unification of China. At the time there was a statute with the inscription "Three people or more congregating to drink without cause are to be fined four ounces of gold." The emperor's edict suspended the regulation tempo-rarily. His act belonged to a special class of indulgences known as "Blessed (or Felicitous) Bestowals," which emperors throughout Chinese history conferred periodically to celebrate momentous occasions and manifest their benevolence toward their subjects. In the following cen-tury, when an emperor assumed the throne, he issued an amnesty that granted a grand revelry of five days and bestowed beef and ale on his subjects. The grand revelry thus became a sort of grand feast linked to the promulgation of amnesties.

By the Tang dynasty the great feast had evolved into a more complex form of diversion, though it still retained some of its older features. The throne bestowed food and ale at least three times during the period. However, the great feast had assumed the character of modern, Western carnivals in three respects. First, it was an occasion for eating, drinking, and merrymaking, though not in anticipation of fasting afterward. Second, like Mardi Gras in New Orleans, it took place in the streets and included parades. Last, the entertainment resembled that offered at carnival sideshows, where professional performers did their acts in tents.

However, Tang carnivals differed from those in the West as well as from other forms of celebrations in China. They had no fixed dates (as festivals did), no special foods, and no specific religious connotations. Their existence depended solely on the emperor's generosity and special circumstances.

The throne bestowed sixty-nine carnivals between 628 and 758, approximately one every twenty-two months. One emperor granted one every seven months of his reign, but Empress Wu took the prize for the most, seventeen. Seventy-two percent of them were granted in conjunction with grand amnesties. The first celebrated an abundant harvest following a disastrous drought and famine that forced families to sell their sons and daughters to survive. The last commemorated the Tang's recovery of Changan, which had fallen to An Lushan the previous year. The most frequent occasions for bestowing them were performances by the emperor of great state sacrifices to the gods. Other circumstances worthy of such imperial gifts were events involving the heir-apparent (installation, birth, and marriage), and the assumption of new honorific titles by the emperor. In every case the throne bestowed the boons to the entire empire, so every district throughout the country celebrated.

The court usually limited the celebrations to three days, but under certain circumstances indulged its subjects with carnivals of five, seven, or nine days. They were all odd numbers since they corresponded to the great powers of the cosmos: the gods of heaven, earth, and man; the five planets that govern the elements; the seven stars in the Big Dipper; and the nine heavens. On at least one occasion the emperor suspended the curfew, and the carnival went on day and night.

Unlike the ancient Greeks and Romans, the Chinese did not erect arenas, hippodromes, or amphitheaters to provide sites for their citizens to enjoy the entertainments. There were entertainment "plazas" at Buddhist monasteries, but they could not accommodate the huge crowds that attended carnivals. In general the only large areas of empty space to which the populace had access were city avenues. The best description of how street parties were organized dates from the Sui dynasty, a decade or so before the founding of the Tang, and concerns not carnivals but New Year's celebrations. Each year the emissaries from the myriad nations that recognized the Sui as their suzerain came to court for the Great Levee on New Year's Day, and stayed on in the capital until the fifteenth day of the first moon. During that period the main avenue in Luoyang from the southern gate of the government compound to the southern gate in the city's outer rampart was transformed into a vast, continuous amusement area. That avenue, sometimes called Heaven's Ford Street, was some 2.5 miles in length and 492 feet in width. Chinese cherry, pomegranate, Chinese elm, and locust trees lined its verges, and an imperial way fenced off by a wall three feet high ran down its middle. On those occasions the officials from a government bureau erected tents where as many as 30,000 singers, dancers, and other entertainers performed to amuse the foreign legates and the citizenry of the capital.

In Changan an avenue that ran east to west between the central palace compound and the government compound was the site of a carnival in 713. Although at 1.75 miles it was shorter than other streets in the capital and its counterpart in Luoyang, it was more than twice as wide at 1,447 feet. The area was also more secure than the avenues of the outer city since the headquarters for fourteen imperial guard units were located south of the avenue. The authorities could easily call on those soldiers to handle crowd control in the event of trouble. Two other areas in Changan served as entertainment centers. One was a huge plaza in front of the main hall at the Daming Palace. That was more or less a public area of the palace where the emperor received officials, foreigners and commoners. The other was a square that Emperor Illustrious August had constructed to the west of the Xingqing Palace in early 737. The work basically involved broadening the street by demolishing parts of neighboring wards. That plaza was not as secure as the others. At one grand carnival held during the emperor's reign, the people in the square became unruly. They pressed in on the zone where entertainers were performing and clamored. Gold Bird Guards rained blows on the spectators with their staves, but failed to quell the disturbance. So the emperor, on the advice of a eunuch, summoned an official named Yan who had a reputation for being a cruel clerk. When he administered judicial beatings with the thin rod to the condemned, they could not rise afterward and feared that they would not die. When he applied the thick rod to the convicted, their blood flowed on the ground, and they wished to expire. After the brute appeared in the plaza outside the Xingqing Palace, he strode around the circumference of the arena, and with a wooden plank drew its boundaries on the ground. Then Yan declared, "Anyone who crosses this line will die." On each of the carnival's five days he stood in the square and imposed order by virtue of his reputation for savagery.

Gates in the capitals played an important role in the grand carnivals, because it was from their upper stories that the emperor viewed the performances that went on below or outside of them. They were essential not only because the ruler in ancient China always sat above his subjects, but also because they provided security. Imperial bodyguards always stood before them to prevent rebels, assassins, and madmen from approaching the throne.

As with modern carnivals in New Orleans and Rio de Janeiro, a parade of floats drawn by horses or cows was one of the highlights of the festivities. At least as early as the third century, China had entertainment wagons on which acrobats performed flying stunts at the top of poles fastened to the wagons. However, they paled in comparison to Tang floats, whose size and grandeur may have derived from great four-wheeled carts—some five stories high—that peoples of India and Central Asia rolled into the streets on Buddha's birthday, the eighth day of the second moon. By the early sixth century Buddhist monasteries in China had similar vehicles for parading statues of Buddha and other holy persons through the streets on holy days. The floats at Tang carnivals were called mountain carts or drought boats. The former were wagons that had superstructures hung with colored silks formed to resemble mountains. The latter, also draped with colored cloth, were ships made of bamboo and wood. Men inside the boat floats carried them along the avenues. Since they did not float on water, they were called drought boats. Musicians rode on the tops of both vehicles and performed as they moved along. Other carts carrying musicians, dressed in rich fabrics and summoned from counties as far as 100 miles from the capital, were drawn by bullocks covered with tiger skins or outfitted to look like rhinoceroses and elephants. Early in the seventh century an official in charge of the music bureau composed music for grand carnivals. It was perhaps his compositions that musicians on floats performed. On occasion the emperor offered a prize for those entertainers that he deemed the best. By the mid-eighth century powerful families in Changan took to building their own entertainment wagons, lofty structures covered with colorful fabrics. They carried a score or more of female singers and musicians and made their way around gardens. Both the carnival floats and private floats disappeared in China centuries ago, but vestiges of them survive in Japan, where young men pull them down the avenues of Kyoto during the July Gion Festival, which is supposed to dispel pestilence.

Grand carnivals died out with the An Lushan rebellion. For some time after 758 neither the court nor local governments had the funds to sponsor such lavish entertainments. Furthermore, the insurrection dispersed the performers to the provinces, so it was difficult for the throne to provide entertainment for them. It was not until after 960 that grand carnivals reemerged.

## ENTERTAINERS AND THEIR ACTS

The most numerous of all performers were professionals known as "independent entertainers." In ancient China the term denoted a class of performers who were not under the control of the imperial court or government bureaus. Since they did not receive support from the state, they made their livelihood from whatever fees or donations their patrons or audiences were willing to pay. However, by the beginning of the Tang dynasty the court had incorporated some independent entertainers, no doubt the best to be had, into a palace agency known as the Instruction Ward. That bureau provided diversions for banquets and special occasions. Thus the performers were wards of the state and received support in the form of stipends, food, and living quarters from the treasury. In some cases a powerful prince might have his own troupe. Emperor Illustrious August had such a company before he ascended the throne. It assisted him in deposing Empress Wei in 610. Strongmen were among the performers.

Nevertheless, the vast majority of independent entertainers in the Tang were not bound to the court. The state always viewed them with a jaundiced eye because they were itinerant. They arrived in a locality, exhausted whatever surplus it had to spend on amusements, and then moved on to greener pastures. The government saw them as vagabonds who made their living from the surplus income of hardworking peasants. In an effort to control them, it promulgated a statute that required all of them to register with local authorities and obligated them to perform a certain number of days each year for the state, as their share of compulsory labor service. The latter regulation gave local authorities a ready supply of performers on which they could draw for diversions at grand carnivals and other occasions, free of charge. Furthermore, in 714 the throne forbade independent entertainers from traveling from village to village where the government's control of the population was weakest. It had no offices in the hamlets. Violators of the proscription were subject to a beating of thirty strokes with the thin rod, a rather light punishment. From the state's point of view the independent performers were suspect elements of the population, like Gypsies in Europe, who might turn to crime when times turned bad.

Finally, the independent entertainers suffered from a stigma imposed on them by the classicists and moralists. In their view, the performers did not provide the sedate, restrained, and cultured music, song, and dance of the age-old rites maintained by the state. They were unorthodox, and therefore illegitimate. Independent entertainers did not conform to natural law, and as a result upset the balance and harmony of the cosmos. In other words, they were boisterous, raucous, uninhibited, and free. The distinction between the two classes of performers in the Tang was rather like the distinction in modern times between opera singers and circus clowns. Tang highbrows also objected to imperial patronage of independent entertainers on the grounds that the throne was wasting precious resources on frivolous amusements.

The term for the performances of the independent entertainers was, literally, the "hundred acts." As the phrase indicates, it encompassed a host of diversions—snake charmers, sword swallowers, fire eaters, and weight lifters, as well as more dignified music, singing, dance, and acting. Dwarfs played a role in the variety shows and were permanent fixtures at the Tang court, as well as in the mansions of the patricians. No more than three feet tall, they came from a southern prefecture. The district sent them to the emperor as tribute until the late eighth century, when the throne abandoned the practice at the instigation of an upright governor.

There were a number of acrobatic acts, two of which fell into the death-defying class. The first was tightrope-walking. **Acrobats** Some performers, most of them women, sauntered along the line with wooden platform shoes on their feet; others paced it on painted stilts, five or six feet in length, bound to their shins. In one act the acrobats formed a human tower of three or four performers, and the anchor man nimbly danced along the rope in time to the music. In another the acrobats in the pyramid somersaulted off the shoulders of those below, one after the other, and landed on the rope without falling to the ground. Still others juggled balls, turned somersaults, or fenced with double-edged swords.

The second, and more spectacular, were the pole acts. Those feats required an anchorwoman—most of the names for the performers that have survived are feminine—who placed a tall, painted pole 70 to 100 feet long on her head. The shaft normally had a crossbar affixed to its top on which slim young girls performed acrobatic moves such as hanging by their chins or doing handstands and somersaults. In one act the pole was crowned with a wooden mountain carved to resemble the fairyland of the immortals. A child climbed to the top and cavorted among the peaks while singing and dancing. In another, five young girls balanced themselves on five taut bowstrings stretched across a frame at the top of a shaft. They performed a martial dance that involved manipulating lances and spears. While all of that was going on aloft, the burly anchorwoman walked about, weaving back and forth to enhance the suspense in the audience.

Taoists had their own special acrobatic act, climbing the sword ladder. They planted two very tall poles in the ground and bound rapiers between them to form rungs. Then a priest climbed the ladder on his bare feet and brandished a saber while balancing on the top rung. In the middle of the eighth century a Buddhist prelate complained to the throne about the act, and requested permission to have monks perform it in order to outdo their rivals. He later claimed that the monks surpassed the priests in their skill at climbing the ladder, not exactly an unbiased opinion. Whatever the case, Taoists were still performing the stunt in southeast China during the nineteenth century, claiming it was effective in dispelling epidemics.

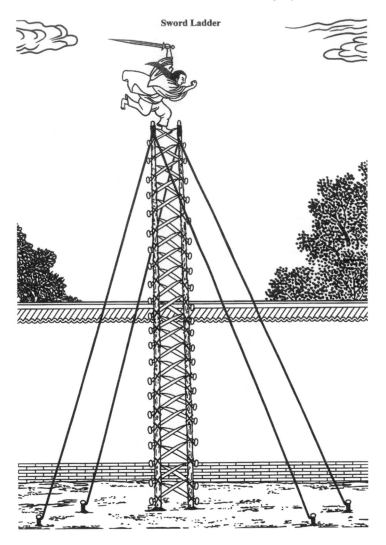

Sword Ladder

Other acrobatic acts—juggling props such as swords, plates, pillows, or pearls—involved feats of dexterity. Some performers kept small bells in the air by kicking them with their feet. The best of the entertainers must have been an armless panhandler in Luoyang who lived in the second half of the eighth century. He begged money from passersby at a bridge in the city by inscribing texts with a writing brush that he grasped between the toes of his right foot. Before he set his pen to paper, the mendicant tossed the brush a foot or more into the air two or three times and never failed to retrieve it with his foot before it fell to the ground. His calligraphy was not inferior to that of official scribes.

Boxing was a sport in the Tang, but it seems to have been an exercise for military training rather than a form of enter- **Wrestlers** tainment. Wrestling was a different matter entirely. It was one of the diversions that spectators could expect to enjoy at carnivals. Known as "horn butting," it originated in the fourth or third century B.C.E. During that period of disunity in China, wars increased in scale, frequency, and brutality. The existence of a kingdom came to depend on the quality of its warriors and that required improved methods of training. One of the methods was wrestling. By the third century a new term for it emerged, "paired shoving." In Japanese the term is pronounced *sumo*. Although usually thought of as a uniquely Japanese art, it existed in China at least a millennium earlier than in Japan. Depictions of the sport in Chinese art from 220 B.C.E. through the Tang show wrestlers stripped to the waist and their bodies pressed shoulder to shoulder. Their arms are wrapped around one another, and their hands grasp their opponent's sashes from behind. It would be erroneous to assume that the rules of the contest then were the same as those in Japan today, but it seems clear that the objective of throwing your opponent or tossing him out of the ring was the same.

In the Tang "horn butting" remained an exercise for training troops, but it was also a diversion. During the early seventh century two wrestlers, Peng and Gao, were members of opposing teams that were competing to determine which was superior to the other at a carnival in an outlying prefecture. Peng grabbed a live suckling pig and gnawed it from its head to its neck. Then he placed it on the ground, and it fled squealing. Not to be outdone Gao picked up a cat and devoured it from its tail up, completely consuming its intestines and stomach. All the while the creature whined and screeched. At that point Peng docilely conceded defeat to Gao. Bravado was apparently an added attraction of wrestling matches, in China then as in America now.

Some wrestlers were violent men. In 822 a cavalryman went to collect a debt from a sumo wrestler. The wrestler, who was drunk, refused to pay, and nearly beat the soldier to death. At that point the cavalier's fourteen-year-old son picked up a chunk of wood and struck his father's assailant on the head, cracking his skull. The wrestler died three days later. In 828, 300 commoners sued for the return of their land in a ward of Changan that had been confiscated. The throne had bestowed it on them more than forty years before, and they had paid no taxes on it. A eunuch ordered fifty wrestlers to arrest the citizens. When they went to carry out his command, they provoked a prolonged riot in the roads of the ward. After the emperor heard of the matter, he returned the land to the townsmen.

**Illusionists**
Magic was most popular with Tang spectators. According to ancient historians, masters of illusion made their way to China from India when the Silk Route was opened in the second century B.C.E. In the early fourth century an Indian who could sever his tongue as well as spit fire arrived in south China. The residents of the area gathered to observe his act. When he was about to cut off his tongue, he would stick it out to show the audience. Then he severed it, and his blood flowed out, covering the ground. He placed the amputated piece in a bowl and passed it around to show the people. The spectators could see both it and the stump still in his mouth. Afterward he replaced the tip of his tongue and rejoined it to the stump. Then he sat down to permit the gathering to see that his tongue was just as it had been before.

Buddhist monks from India who came to China with the intention of converting the natives to their faith also practiced illusions to attract followers. In the early fourth century a monk from Central Asia had a hole four or five inches in diameter beside his left nipple that he plugged with some cast-off cloth. On fasting days he hastened to a river, removed the rag, pulled out his intestines, washed them, and then restored them to his belly. At night, when he wished to read, he plucked out the cloth, and his inner light flooded his room.

Other foreign religions also practiced magic as part of their rituals. The Manichaeans from Persia had two churches in Luoyang where each year western merchants prayed for wealth, cooked pigs, and slaughtered sheep. They danced in a drunken revelry to the accompaniment of the balloon guitar, drums, and fifes. After paying their respects to God, they enlisted one of their number to be master and gave him cash. He seized an extremely sharp sword, thrust it into his belly until it exited from his back, and shook over and over. Blood flowed from his guts. In the twinkling of an eye he withdrew the blade, spat water on it, and blessed it with an incantation. His body was as it had been before.

Tang emperors did not always appreciate acts that involved simulated mutilations of the human body. In 656, at a grand carnival marking the installation of a new heir-apparent, Gaozong saw a westerner lift a blade and pierce his stomach. Revolted, he put an end to the performance and subsequently issued an order to his border guards forbidding them to allow magicians whose acts involved such illusions to cross the frontiers of the empire. The proscription was short-lived.

China had its own well-developed tradition in the arts of illusion, a tradition as old as the second century B.C.E. A Chinese magician who flourished between 670 and 674 had a trick in which he suspended a water jug from a beam and chopped the rope with a knife. Although he severed the rope, the jar did not fall. He also installed a jug of water in an empty room, placed a sword horizontally across the top of it, and closed the door tightly. Sometime later spectators entered the room to

**Balloon Guitar**

have a look. There they saw the dismembered body of the magician that had been cut into five pieces (torso, arms, and legs). The jug no longer contained water. Instead it was full of his blood. After they left and closed the door, the magician reassembled his body and appeared to them in his original state. He sold fortunes in a market and made 100 coppers a day. Later someone filed charges against him at court. The magistrate sentenced him to death. While he was being led to the market for execution, the expression on his face was composed, and there was not the slightest sign of fear on it. The magician ordered paper and pen to compose a brilliant final statement.

There was also a Taoist priest named Ye who was adept at performing illusions. He placed peach and willow branches on the stomach of a volunteer. Then he cast a magic spell on his sword, and with all of his might brought the blade to bear, chopping at the man's stomach. Although the sword severed the branches, it did not injure the flesh. That was just for openers. Afterward, wielding a pair of swords, he cleaved a woman in two. Her blood flowed everywhere, and her family wept copiously. Then the priest rejoined the halves of her body, spat water on them, and cast a magic spell. In the twinkling of an eye the woman was healed and returned to her original state.

Vanishing acts were also in the magician's repertoire. One morning, while riding down a small lane in a ward of Changan, Li Jiabo saw ahead of him a short girl wearing mourning clothes who was about three feet tall, but spoke like a woman. She was babbling as though she had some grievance. "Patience! Patience! We will have a decisive battle in the end! In the end I will not release him!" She snapped her fingers several times and muttered, "Really strange. Really strange." Confounded by her behavior and not daring to make inquiries, Li rode away. For two days the woman bewildered people on the streets. When Li next encountered her, a large crowd surrounded her, and at the center countless children pressed around her seat. When the dwarf woman came forward, she had a veil over her head and spoke irrationally. The children laughed at her. If anyone got close to her, she clutched them, so the children withdrew. At noon, when she saw that she had attracted a throng, she sat down. A child thrust himself forward and tore off her veil. The woman had disappeared. Only a three-foot-long stick of green bamboo with a skull hanging on it remained. The irrational behavior of the performer was apparently a come-on to attract spectators.

Another disappearing act purportedly permitted its performer to escape jail. While arranging for the performance of variety acts at a grand carnival in the early eighth century, a county commandant and his prison warden competed to see who could find the finest entertainer. The prison officials were very keen on the idea and had their minds set on winning. So they interrogated the inmates to find out if any of them could perform an act. One convict smiled and said, "I can do a clumsy rope trick." When the warden heard that, he asked what the inmate's crime was. His clerk told him that the man had been implicated in the theft of tax cloth. The warden asked the inmate what was special about his act, and he replied, "The herd of rope artists all tie both ends of their ropes to the ground and then walk, stand, turn, or whirl on the rope. I, on the other hand, need only a rope fifty feet in length and the thickness of a finger. I do not have to tie it down. I climb into the sky on it and frolic. There is nothing I cannot do on it." The warden was pleased. The next day a guard led the prisoner to the carnival grounds. After all of the other performers finished their acts, he ordered the inmate to demonstrate his trick. The convict walked into the arena with a coil of rope measuring more than 100 feet in length. He placed the coil on the ground, took one end of the rope, and hurled it into the sky. It straightened out like a writing brush. The inmate climbed twenty or thirty feet up, then forty or fifty feet. The rope rose straight, as if someone was pulling it from above. The crowd of spectators was truly astonished. Finally, when the prisoner climbed to a height of more than 200 feet and he reached the top of the rope, he acquired the power of a bird. He flew alongside the rope for a while. Then he soared away into the distance and vanished. Indians still perform this illusion, though they never climb to such spectacular altitudes or fly.

Vanishing and reappearing was yet another trick in the repertoire of Tang magicians. "Penetrating the Pot" was a Korean act adopted by the Chinese. One performer descended into a jar on a table, and another later emerged from a second jar on another stand. That illusion is not difficult to understand, but "Penetrating the Horse's Belly" is. The act, as depicted on a Japanese scroll of Tang entertainments that dates from the twelfth century, apparently required three performers. One held the reins of the steed, another entered the charger's anus, and a third emerged from its mouth. The illusion must have used some sort of apparatus and employed two children or dwarfs.

Animal acts played an important role in diversions, carnivals and otherwise. The largest and most awesome were those involving elephants. Although some of the creatures **Animal Acts** still survived in southern China, those that performed at entertainments in the capital were probably tribute sent from the countries south of the empire to the court in Changan. When they arrived in the metropolis, the throne assigned two grooms to care for them and supplied them with rice, soybeans and salt for feed. Since the animals could not tolerate the cold of the north, their keepers clothed them in sheepskins and felt during the winter. When the emperor called on them to entertain—in particular at the New Year's levee—they danced and bowed in homage to the strains of music. Incredibly, there were also tamed rhinoceroses that performed the same act as their fellow pachyderms. When Changan fell to An Lushan in 756, he had the beasts brought to Luoyang, his capital. To impress envoys from foreign lands, he declared that the animals had rushed north in response to his having received the mandate of Heaven. They would dance and pay homage to him as their sovereign by bowing. Then he ordered his servitors to lead in the elephants. However, when they arrived, the pachyderms stared at him in anger and refused to perform. Chagrined and enraged, An ordered his attendants to herd them into a pit and roast them alive. The fate of the rhinoceroses is unknown.

Dancing horses performed for the amusement of the court. In the early eighth century the emperor had trained steeds prance at a banquet for Tibetan emissaries. The coursers were tinted with five shades of pigment, adorned with silk trappings and gold fittings, and fitted with saddles decorated with images of unicorns and phoenixes. The chargers danced in perfect response to the music until they came to the central piece. At that point musicians presented them with ale, and they took the goblets in their mouths to drink. Then they lay down and rose again. The most famous troupe of horses was that of Emperor Illustrious August. Numbering 100, they were dressed in figured embroidery, adorned with pearl and jade ornaments attached to their manes and forelocks, and outfitted with gold and silver halters. The coursers performed to the "Music of the Upended Goblet," which had ten parts. In the course of their act they

**Penetrating the Horse's Belly**

knelt, reared on their hind legs, clutched goblets in their mouths, and got drunk. The denouement of the steeds' performance was when they ascended a three-tiered platform and whirled around on top of it. Sometimes robust men lifted the platform while the chargers pranced. Some of those admirable animals, like the elephants, met an unhappy fate. They fell into the hands of An Lushan after he seized Changan, and he sent a number of them to his base in the northeast. There they came into the possession of a subordinate officer who did not understand their value. One day at a feast the chargers took up dancing in response to the music being performed. Believing that the beasts had gone berserk, their ignorant grooms beat them with brooms. The chargers, thinking that they were out of order, strove all the more to conform to the rhythm. When the matter was reported to the officer, he ordered them thrashed. The more the grooms beat them, the more the horses strove to conform to the standard movements to which they had been trained. Finally they succumbed to the beating.

Perhaps the most amusing of all animal acts were those involving monkeys because their cavorting most closely resembled the behavior of humans. They performed pole acts, at which they were most adept, as well as somersaults. A man from western China excelled at training them and had at any given time more than ten of the creatures, large and small, in his care. Purportedly they were able to utter human speech because he fed them mercury sulfide. In one act, wearing hats and boots, they rode dogs. Spurring their mounts on with whips in their hands, they shouted as they passed from the front to the rear of a hall. They also performed a skit in which they emulated drunks and fell to the ground. Despite efforts to revive them from their stupor, they would not rise even when their master told them that the street patrolman was coming. Only when he whispered to them that Attendant Hou—a fierce official whom all men feared—was on his way would they jump to their feet, eyes bulging in fright, and feign terror at hearing those words. Everyone laughed at that.

Mountain man Wang had an insect act. While visiting an official's home, he pulled a segment of bamboo and a small drum from his bosom. Then he removed a plug from the bamboo tube and beat a tattoo on the drum with a broken twig. More than twenty spiders marching in a line emerged from the tube and split into two companies facing each other, as if they were forming a battle line. Sometimes Wang struck the drum three times, sometimes five. Whenever they heard the sound, the spiders maneuvered into a new formation. After performing more than twenty of the configurations, they reformed their original companies and marched back into the bamboo tube. Some animal handlers even managed to train hedgehogs. Citizens of Changan gathered in the streets to watch a pair of them face each other and dance to the rhythm of music.

If one did not prefer the real thing, he might enjoy the mechanical. There was a clever Japanese craftsman who appeared at court in the early ninth century. He pulled a wooden box from his bosom and took out several hundred red spiders that he arrayed in five troupes. The artisan told the emperor that they could dance to a tune. His highness summoned his musicians to play the piece. The toys then wheeled and turned to the music without skipping a beat. Whenever the air called for lyrics, they chirped. At the end of the music, they assumed positions according to their ranks in a file and withdrew into the box.

Dancing was an important form of entertainment, especially among the nobility. Imperial princes received instruction in it at **Dance** a very early age. For example, in 690, when he was five years old, Emperor Illustrious August performed "The Long-Lived Lady" during a banquet given by Empress Wu. At the same feast another prince, who was four years old, danced "The Prince of Lanling." The Prince of Lanling was a northern general of the sixth century who won a great victory. Afterward his troops composed a song called "The Prince of Lanling Breaks Through the Battle Formation" to celebrate his triumph. During the Sui and Tang dynasties the air evolved into a dance pantomime. By the early eighth century it depicted the general as having the face of a beautiful woman, so he wore a mask to strike terror in the minds of his foes when he went into battle. In the course of its performance the dancer brandished a weapon as though thrusting and stabbing at his adversaries. By the ninth century a whip replaced the weapon, and the performer wore a purple costume with a gold girdle. It was a "vigorous" dance in the Tang's system for classifying music.

Another vigorous dance was "The Prince of Qin Smashes Battle Formations." After Taizong, then Prince of Qin, defeated a rebel army in 622, his troops composed an air with that title to commemorate his triumph. Entertainers first performed it at a banquet in 627. In 633 Taizong drew a diagram for a dance that had a round formation to the left and a square one to the right. He ordered one of his courtiers to train dancers to perform it according to his drawing. The piece had three movements, each consisting of four formations. Clad in silver armor and carrying crescent-shaped spears, 128 boys pummeled and pierced to simulate the ebb and flow of battle. After the first performance in that year, the emperor had his ministers compose lyrics for it and renamed it "The Dance of Seven Virtues."

Military men also learned the art of dancing. In fact, dancing may have been part of their training to handle weapons. In early 622 a rebel commander captured Governor-General Li. The rebel admired the governor's talents and wanted to make him a grand general in his army, but he refused. Some of Li's former subordinates regaled him with food and ale, perhaps as a farewell before his execution. At the feast he said to them, "Gentlemen, you wish to console me with food and ale because you lament my difficulty and disgrace, so I shall carouse with you one last time." When they were all quite inebriated, Li spoke to the guards who had him in custody. "I can perform the sword dance. Would one of you be willing to loan me a blade?" One of them handed him a rapier. When he finished dancing, Li heaved a great sigh. "How can a great man, who has proved himself incapable of protecting that which he was entrusted with to defend, live and breathe with honor in this world?" Then he seized the sword and stabbed himself. His blood gushed out of his stomach, and he died.

In the early eighth century General Pei Min asked Wu Daoxuan to paint some murals on the walls of a Buddhist monastery in Luoyang. The artist agreed to do it on the condition that the general inspire him by performing the sword dance. Pei leapt on his horse. At a gallop he wheeled to his right and then to his left, brandishing his rapier. Then he abruptly tossed the sword hundreds of feet in the air. As it descended, he extended his scabbard to catch it, but it fell through a roof instead. Wu seized his brush and executed a mural that was the wonder of the world. Earlier the general had put his skills to a more practical purpose when he found himself surrounded by the Turks during a campaign in the north. He did his dance standing on the back of a horse, and cut down arrows shot at him by the enemy. They were so awestruck by the feat that they left the field of battle.

There was a form of the sword dance performed by women. The greatest of its artists—indeed, the only one who truly mastered it—was a lady in Emperor Illustrious August's troupe during the early eighth century. She taught the secrets of her craft to at least one other woman.

Entertainers of that sort may have brandished two swords, but some writers said they wielded silk ribbons with luminous objects at each end instead.

The grandest of the "supple dances" was "The Air of the Rainbow Robe and Feathered Skirt." Despite the legends of Emperor Illustrious August acquiring it from the moon palaces, it was in reality a form of entertainment that he adapted from Indian music. He often had it performed on his birthday. The female dancers wore costumes made of kingfisher feathers—hence its title—and necklaces made of gems. They were supposed to look like immortal maidens. In the ninth century they also wore hats with strings of pearls hanging down. A single lady like Yang Guifei or a troupe of them might dance it. In 836 300 women under the age of nineteen from the emperor's Ward of Instruction performed the act at court. The ballet was largely a palace entertainment, but occasionally the emperor bestowed treatises that contained instructions on how to perform it on meritorious ministers.

Tang dramas, if they can be called that, combined dialogue, music, and dance. The only difference between them **Theatricals** and other forms of musical entertainment was that they had something of a story line. *The Walking, Singing Wife* was based on a sixth-century tale of a man who had an ugly, pockmarked face and claimed to be an official when he was not. He was a lush who beat his beautiful wife every time he came home drunk. She resented his abuse and sued him in her village. A male actor wearing women's clothing played the wife and strode gravely onto the stage, singing as he went (hence the title). A choir sang responses. The husband, whose face was painted red to represent inebriation, entered next and battered his wife. Despite the serious nature of the subject, the drama was a comedy.

Puppetry in the Tang was very similar to drama, in that it involved song and dance as well as dialogue. There were **Puppetry** marionettes carved from wood, one of which was an old man with chicken skin and white hair. Apparently the most popular of the characters was Master Guo, who was completely bald and always opened the show. He excelled at jokes and jests. Master Guo was so popular that a man had a tattoo pricked onto his right arm that depicted the head of the puppet protruding from a bottle gourd. Unfortunately, there is no information on the plots of puppet plays.

Storytelling seems to have emerged as a form of professional entertainment in the Tang. The performers, men or **Storytelling** women, told their tales in the palace and on the streets. Sometimes they had paintings that they unrolled to illustrate their talks, visual aids of a sort. The scrolls sometimes had the texts of the poetry that the entertainers read written on the back. Parts of some stories were songs. If the audience was pleased with the performance, they would toss coins to the narrator and shout "Bravo!" In the early eighth century the military governor of a province in the southwest used storytellers to draft troops from the unwilling lower classes. When the plebes flocked to see the spectacles, his agents seized those of the audience who were poor or had no relatives, placed them in fetters, and sent them off to the wars.

The tales could be secular or religious, but the story of Mulian's journey through purgatory in search of his mother was probably the most popular. It evoked popular sentiments of filial devotion to parents that were very strong among ancient Chinese. Furthermore, some versions contained vivid descriptions of hell that no doubt titillated audiences. Metal barbs stabbed men in the chest, awls punctured women in the back, iron rakes gouged out eyes, copper pitchforks plunged into their loins. The pulverized flesh of sinners flew everywhere, and their blood soaked the roads. Such gory details were no doubt included to attract as large an audience as possible.

## SPORTS

In medieval China the mastery of archery was not merely a question of acquiring a skill that enabled one to bring down game or slay enemies. Among the ruling class, proficiency in it was a mark of manhood as well as social status. There were three orders of difficulty: standing, sitting, and mounted. Mounted archery required the bowman to let loose of the horse's reins and guide his mount by the pressure of his knees only while he shot. Even women mastered the skill. The art no longer exists in China, but survives in Japan among a small number of aficionados.

The imperial arsenal manufactured four types of bows from the wood of the mulberry tree: a long bow and a short bow for use by the infantry, the "horn" bow strengthened with horn and sinew for use by the cavalry, and a colored bow for use by imperial guards on ceremonial occasions. It also produced seven types of crossbows. The arsenal made the shafts of arrows from bamboo and wood. The wooden ones were reserved for target practice and hunting. The bamboo had an iron head for piercing armor.

Archery contests, known as Great Shoots, enjoyed classical sanction. Tang emperors revived the ancient rite. From 619 to 664 and 711 to 733 they issued decrees authorizing the performance of the ritual at halls or gates of the imperial palaces. They invariably took place on the third day of the third moon or ninth day of the ninth moon. On one occasion in 712 the contest lasted eight days. The throne specified the rank of officials who had to participate in the event: sometimes the entire corps, but at other times only those ranking fifth grade and above or third grade and above. Whatever the case, mastery of the skill was clearly a requirement for being a mandarin.

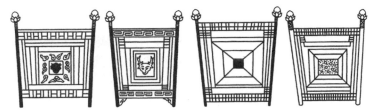

**Targets for Ceremonial Archery (Great Shoots)**

Proficiency with the bow varied greatly. On the one hand, an archer in the early eighth century could without fail hit goose feathers tossed into the wind while mounted on a horse. On the other hand, some officials who participated in the Great Shoots had virtually no skill at it. The worst was a kinsman of Empress Wu. When an official who had served the Turkish khan returned to the capital, the empress was furious at his treachery and ordered the bureaucratic corps to fill him with arrows while he was tied to a post. A grandson of her uncle, whom she had dubbed prince, loosed three arrows from a distance of seven paces and failed to hit him once.

Hunting, as entertainment, was a sport for aristocrats and mandarins. In the early Tang they pursued it with passion. **Hunting** One prince declared, "I can go without eating for three days, but I can't go without hunting for a single day." The grandest hunts were the emperor's. They took place in the Forbidden Park north of Changan, in regions close to the capital, or in wilderness areas near a city that he visited. In all cases the court went with him and set itself up at a clearing. Beaters drove the game toward the open field where the emperor and the courtiers shot it down. Some of the rulers excelled at the sport. Taizong once shot four arrows at a herd of wild pigs charging from the woods and brought down four of the animals. Illustrious August once bagged two wild boars with one arrow. Afterward he ordered an artist to paint a scene of his remarkable feat on a wall of the palace's northern gate.

Like medieval Europeans, the upper classes of the Tang used raptors to bring down prey for them. Because of their size, they used eagles to hunt large mammals such as foxes, wolves, and small deer. Their falcons, which knocked victims from the sky with clenched talons, attacked fowl; the saker took herons and larger birds, while the smaller peregrine struck down ducks and smaller game. Goshawks were the most favored of all the raptors during this period because they were fierce and the most competent in attacking prey, usually rabbits and pheasants. Sparrow hawks, smallest of the raptors, killed their prey, usually lesser fowl such as quail, by gripping them with needle-sharp claws and pinning them to the ground.

Naturally the throne had the finest collection of raptors, along with the best hounds and hunting leopards. Their keepers, eunuchs, were not always scrupulous. In 806 they released goshawks in the mansions of wealthy families in Changan and then demanded handsome compensation for retrieving them. About the same time they were in the habit of spreading nets over the gates or wells of the well-to-do so that the residents could not enter their homes or draw water unless they forked over coppers or cloth.

**Football**  Football was an ancient game in China that was still popular in the Tang. There were football fields in the palaces of the emperor and the heir-apparent at Changan. The mansion of a princess had one that was sold to the residents of its ward after her fall. In the early eighth century the emperor abolished the ancestral temple for the daughter of his predecessor and bestowed the property on a favorite, whose mansion was just to the north, for a football field.

The ball was probably a leather sphere filled with feathers, as it had been in previous times. As in modern soccer, the objective of the game was to keep the ball in the air by kicking it with the feet. The players, who performed for the pleasure of the throne, were often soldiers in imperial armies or members of the Gold Bird Guard. One military official could loft the ball halfway up the height of a pagoda. However, intellectuals might also indulge in it. While an imperial academician was playing football with his brothers at their mansion in Changan, the ball struck him on the forehead and inflicted a slight injury. Just then he received an urgent summons from the throne. When he arrived at the palace, the emperor noticed the wound and asked him about it. The scholar told him how he got it. His highness then bestowed two trays with ten gold bowls on each. Altogether the bowls held twenty-five pints of ale. The academician drank every last drop of ale, but showed no signs of being drunk. When a courtier had no skill at the game, he might ask the emperor to appoint him scorekeeper.

**Polo**  Polo, a sport imported from the west (Persia or Tibet) in the seventh century, was immensely popular among the upper classes in the Tang. There was a polo field in an imperial park and another at a palace in Changan. Some mansions of the upper classes in the capital also had such facilities. In the early eighth century the sons-in-law of the emperor sprinkled oil on the ground to make the surface as smooth as possible, so horses would not suffer injuries. Many provincial cities also had polo fields. In 819 a general in the imperial army ordered his troops to round up all the people in the market and wards of Yunzhou who had given aid to a rebel and herd them into a polo field. Then he had his soldiers behead them, more than 2,000 men in all. A similar incident occurred at a field in Luzhou during 844. It appears that polo fields had become convenient execution grounds for the military.

At the imperial court, two teams of sixteen men dressed in elegant outfits competed in a match to accompaniment of music provided by a military band. Astride well-trained horses, competitors struck the ball with mallets that had crescent-shaped heads. The objective was to put the ball through a circular goal one foot in diameter that was set ten to thirty feet above the ground. The sport was also played on asses. Imperial armies selected talented troops to engage in the sport for the emperor's amusement. However, virtually anyone—eunuchs, officials, graduates of the civil service examinations—could play if he had a horse and riding habit. One remarkable player could set up a string of ten or more coppers on a playing field and, at a gallop, strike each with his mallet, knocking them sixty or seventy feet in the air.

Polo was a dangerous sport for man and animal. In the early eighth century a prince who fell off his horse was knocked unconscious. In 826 the emperor held polo and sumo matches at a palace. The entertainment went on into the night and resulted in cracked heads and broken arms. Emperor Illustrious August was something of a fanatic about the sport. In 710, before he assumed the throne, Zhongzong ordered him and three others to compete against a Tibetan team of ten that had defeated the court's team. Illustrious August charged east and west like a whirlwind so no one could get in front of him to block his shots. As a result he and his teammates vanquished the Tibetans. During his reign he pursued his passion to such a degree that horses suffered injuries and died.

Sports that involved pitting animal against animal— ducks, geese, dogs, and elephants—were quite common **Cockfighting** in the Tang. In the late ninth century a prized male goose was worth 500,000 coppers. The most popular form of such entertainment was cockfighting. In the early seventh century all royal princes were aficionados of it. It enjoyed its golden age in the reign of Emperor Illustrious August because he was born under the astrological sign of the cock. He established special coops for more than 1,000 of the birds in Changan and assigned 500 young soldiers from his armies to train and care for them. As usual, aristocrats and even citizens of Changan emulated the throne and took to the sport, sometimes going broke in pursuit of their amusement. At the beginning of a match, their keepers led the cocks out, and the birds arrayed themselves in a row, raising their feathers and flapping their wings. Then they went into battle with metal spurs attached to their legs. A single bird might fight more than once in a day. A keeper might revive an injured gamecock by spraying water from his mouth on it. When the contests were finished and the keepers led them out, the winners took the lead with the vanquished trailing in the rear. A superior bird could fetch 2 million coppers in the late ninth century, when most emperors were fond of the sport and at least one was fond of gambling on the matches. The Cold Food Festival was a favorite time for cockfighting, but the sport also had a role to play at grand carnivals.

## GAMES

The history of games in China is very old. Although the names of many survive in ancient literature, with some exceptions the rules for playing them have not. Some people did not play them solely for relaxation, but for money as well. Although gambling was illegal in the Tang, the law was probably unenforceable and unenforced. One emperor and his princes in the late ninth century loved to wager on dice. In the early seventh century one ace at a board game won several hundred thousand coppers from a friend in his village and, when the friend could not pay the debt, he took his wife. However, the champion had already committed adultery with the woman, who was pregnant with his child. In the early years of Illustrious August's reign the women of his harem gambled by throwing gold coins to determine who would serve his highness that night.

**Weiqi**    One board game that was popular in the Tang, and has remained so today, was *weiqi* (encirclement chess), better known in the West by its Japanese name, *go*. The game requires a board and stones, or round pieces. The board has a grid of nineteen vertical and nineteen horizontal lines that yields 361 intersections. There are 361 stones: 181 black and 180 white. The game begins when the player having the black stones places one at an intersection, and proceeds with black and white taking alternate turns. Stones never change their positions or leave the board unless captured. The winner is the player who surrounds the most territory and captures the largest number of his opponent's pieces. It is a purely intellectual game of strategy. The game was extremely popular in the Tang. One ace obtained a post in the most prestigious imperial academy in Changan by virtue of his reputation at playing the game. In 805 he led a clique that took over the government for several months.

**Pitch Pot**    Pitch pot was one of the oldest games in China. A Confucian classic supplied an early set of rules for playing it. It required a bronze pot one foot tall with a mouth three inches in diameter. Attached to the neck of the vessel were two ears, tubes, that were one inch in diameter. The base of the pot was heavy and filled with beans to prevent it from tipping over when struck and to keep arrows from bouncing out. Each player received twelve arrows at the beginning of the game. Made from mulberry branches, they were two feet, four inches in length. Two men sat on mats and alternately tossed missiles at their pots, to the accompaniment of zither music. The total number of arrows landing in the pot and the difficulty of their placement—missiles

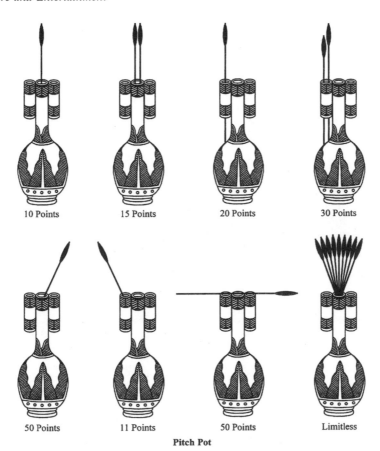

| 10 Points | 15 Points | 20 Points | 30 Points |

| 50 Points | 11 Points | 50 Points | Limitless |

**Pitch Pot**

falling into the ears counted more than those penetrating the mouth—determined a player's tally. A guest kept track of the points with counters, and 120 was a winning score. Although it appears to have originated as some part of military training, pitch pot was a gentlemen's game, an amusement for parties. Unlike *weiqi* it required dexterity and hand-eye coordination. Some players were amazingly adept at it. One who excelled at it in the early Tang boasted that his arrows never missed. He could toss the missiles over his shoulder into a pot behind him. For every 100 throws, 100 arrows struck home. His tosses were like "dragons rising and hawks soaring."

His physical prowess, however, could not match that of a general in the late eighth century. At one of his banquets a guest picked beans, counters for a game, out of a bowl and hurled them at flies, never missing his target. Not impressed, the general said, "Quit wasting my beans." Then he snatched flies out of the air by their hind legs.

# 8

# Travel and Transportation

## ON LAND AND WATER

In the late seventh or early eighth century a county magistrate stopped at a prefecture in southeastern China during a journey. The governor of the district, who entertained the magistrate daily with sumptuous feasts, offered to purchase two of his maidservants, but the magistrate refused to sell them. After the magistrate's party departed, the governor sent a band of brigands to pursue them. The bandits stole everything and slew everyone, returning only with the magistrate's wife and daughter. The wife begged to be taken in as a slave, but the governor rejected her plea and had her strangled. He spared only the daughter, whom he took for himself. Subsequently, he treated every official's family that passed through his district liberally throughout their stay. Then, after they went on their way, he sent his marauders out to track them down, steal their property, and murder them. No one escaped. Travel in Tang China was not only arduous and time-consuming, but also perilous even in peaceful times.

The most common means of getting from one place to another was shank's mare. Walking was cheap and therefore readily available to all classes. By modern standards it was incredibly slow. According to official regulations the distance that a walker or rider on a jackass should cover in a day was only seventeen miles. The government established standards of that sort to provide minimal requirements for the transportation of official goods, especially the revenues from grain and cloth taxes, in

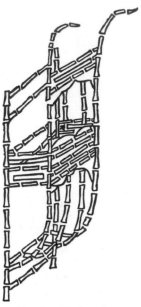

**Bamboo Backpack**

the provinces. Ennin, a Japanese Buddhist monk who visited the Tang between 838 and 847, traveled long distances on foot through northern China. He walked twenty to thirty miles a day, considerably more than the statutory limit. The distance a traveler on foot could make in a day varied greatly according to the strength of the individual, the nature of the terrain, the weather, and other factors. The fastest were the relay runners, some 9,200 of them, who carried highly perishable items, such as seafood from the southeast coast, to the imperial court at Changan. Goods transported in that manner might have sped along at 60 to 100 miles in twenty-four hours.

Transportation was equally simple. Peasants, urban laborers, and slaves carried loads in baskets suspended by ropes from the ends of long poles that rested on their shoulders behind their necks. Their spine and legs bore all of the weight. When the weight was too heavy, two men shouldered the pole, one at each end, with the burden suspended from the middle. Poles were used to transport virtually everything that was not too heavy or bulky—from grain, produce, and pigs to luggage, household furnishings, and coffins (empty or full). Backpacks, bamboo frames, were convenient for toting light loads long distances. Buddhist pilgrims favored them for conveying sutras from India to China across the deserts. Women carried their infants on their backs. They tied the bottom edge of a cloth around their waists, pulled it up over the child, and knotted the upper edge of the cloth to the lower edge in the front.

The next step up, literally, from shank's mare was the litter. In its simplest form it was a wooden platform with poles attached to the sides. Two or more servants—sometimes palace ladies—lifted it by the poles and carried the rider, who sat on top. It also served as a stretcher for moving the sick or injured. Fancier types were chairs with poles affixed to their flanks. Deluxe models had canopies to protect the passenger from the elements or curtained cabs that offered privacy as well. The latter, known as palanquins or sedan chairs, became popular in seven-teenth- and eighteenth-century Europe. In Tang China the bearers held the poles at waist level or placed them on their shoulders. The litter, in whatever form, was a vehicle for the upper classes who owned slaves or could afford to hire porters. The emperor had seven types of palan-quins with fifty-seven bearers and other attendants. He rode them for short distances, specifically from his apartments to the main palace hall for the grand levees on New Year's Day and the winter solstice, and to shrines or altars outside the palace for major sacrifices. He also employed them for short trips around his palaces. Emperors provided them for ministers who had trouble walking, so that they could attend audiences in the palace. In one case a prince was so obese that the emperor ordered him to ride in a palanquin when he came to court. Patricians probably also rode in palanquins when they had to ascend mountains where trails were too narrow, steep, or rough to accommodate carriages.

Men and women of means could avail themselves of several types of mounts. Gentlemen in north China kept double- **Mounts** humped Bactrian camels for travel and transportation. They were absolutely essential to merchants who traded along the Silk Route that passed through the deserts north of Tibet. The beasts could sniff out underground water and could detect the approach of deadly sand storms (they snarled and buried their heads). The government was also in the business of raising camels. It maintained herds of them in its pasture-lands to the northeast and northwest of Changan, and assigned one herder to care for seventy dromedaries. The state's most pressing need for camels was military. They provided the means for transporting pro-visions and equipment to garrisons stationed along the northern frontiers and beyond. Camels, along with horses and elephants, strode in parades along the boulevards of the capital on special occasions.

Camels were not the principal mounts for patricians, couriers, or sol-diers. Jackasses and horses were far more common. As might be ex-pected, the government raised the largest number of horses. At the beginning of the Tang, the dynasty had only 3,000 stallions and mares, which it had recovered from a marsh. Placed under able management, the number grew to 76,000 by 666, and much more afterward. In 681 one of the commissioners for herds reported the loss through death and theft of 180,000 horses, along with 11,600 cattle, in his district north of

Changan over a two-year period. The horse thieves, probably Turks, also killed or captured more than 800 herders and overseers. By 713 the northwest pastures had 240,000 head. In 725 they had 430,000 horses along with 50,000 cattle and 286,000 sheep. The numbers declined thereafter. In 754 the commissioner for the herds in the same region reported that he had in his charge a total of 605,603 animals, of which 325,792 were horses (including 200,080 colts), 75,115 were cattle (of which 143 were yaks), 563 camels, 204,134 sheep, and one donkey. Those figures were for one area only. The totals for animals raised in the south, east, and north are not available. There was a huge demand for horses by the army and the rapid relay postal system. After the Tibetan invasions in the mid-eighth century, the state lost all of the herds and pastures in the northwest. Horses were hard to come by, and the government had to buy poor-quality mounts from the Uighur at staggering prices.

Herdsmen were in charge of caring for the animals, which they branded with the name of the inspectorate that cared for them. If more than seven camels, six asses, ten horses, or fifteen sheep out of 100 died in a year, herders were subject to a punishment of thirty blows with the thin rod for the first animal, and more if the number exceeded one. They received the same punishment if the animals did not produce sixty foals or calves for every hundred female horses, cows, and asses. Annually, herders of the northwest pastures selected 50 fine horses and 100 of lesser quality to send to the imperial stables in the capital. The emperor had six stables and twelve corrals staffed with 5,000 grooms, 500 trainers, and 70 veterinarians. Tang statutes demanded that their caretakers be respectful of the animals and not beat them.

In terms of comfort and speed, the horse was a major advantage over shank's mare. The traveler did not have to exert himself or strain his leg muscles. According to statutes, official goods transported on horseback had to travel twenty-three miles a day, six more than by foot. That pace was very leisurely compared with the speed required of official couriers. When they were carrying copies of the Great Acts of Grace from the capital to prefectures, the throne expected them to make 167 miles a day. If they traveled both night and day, they were making seven miles an hour. If not, they galloped along at a much greater rate of speed. When horses sickened or were injured, couriers or officials who were riding them were required to leave them at the nearest prefecture for medical attention and feeding.

**Wheels** Even the peasant had wheels to relieve him of transporting heavy burdens on his back. The Chinese invented the wheelbarrow by the third century, a thousand years before it appeared in Europe. Unlike its Western counterpart it had no barrow. Instead, the load rested on a framework built on shafts above the axle and on either side of the wheel. Consequently, most of the weight fell

**Wheelbarrow**

on the axle, and the man pushing it was mainly responsible for keeping it from tipping. It could carry a heavier burden—a year's supply of food for a soldier—and move faster than a porter carrying the same load: twenty feet in the time that it took him to move six. To move a heavier load faster, the peasant could hitch a horse or ox to the front of it. People even rode on the wheelbarrow if something of equal weight was placed on the side of the frame opposite them.

There were many types of wagons, carts, and carriages in the Tang. The government depended on wagons—drawn by horses or oxen—to transport grain and cloth levies where there were no waterways or boats. In the early eighth century the state fixed the maximum load of each cart at 1,500 pounds and the fee at 900 cash for a distance of thirty-three miles. Taxpayers paid for it through a supplemental levy. The cost was incredibly expensive: in contrast, the charge for transporting a load on the Yellow River was fifteen coppers when the barges sailed upstream and six when they floated downstream. Overland haulage was also very slow. The statutory minimum was ten miles a day, seven miles less than loads carried on foot. Carters were permitted to transport forty-five pounds of their private possessions on their vehicles.

Patricians owned carriages for getting around the city and countryside. In the early Tang, women rode in them to avoid exposing themselves to the ogles of men on the street. The emperor had five different types: one for performing sacrifices and wedding an empress, which was azure and adorned with jade fittings; a second for making offerings to the gods and archery contests, which was red with gold fittings; a third for traveling, which was yellow with ivory fittings; a fourth for making inspection tours, which was white with leather fittings; and a last for hunting, which was black with lacquer fittings. These did not include ceremonial coaches that rolled along the streets of the capital during grand processions. On such occasions imperial garages also dispatched special, fancy carriages for mandarins to ride in.

Two vehicles with practical functions accompanied imperial parades and progresses (journeys). The first was an odometer. There was a drum in the center of it, and wooden figures of men with drumsticks in their hand before and behind the drum. When the cart had traveled one Chinese mile, the figures beat the drum. Emperors apparently were concerned with measuring the mileage that they traveled. The instrument may also have been used to gauge distances along the empire's roads. Highways had milestones, and government records contained figures for the exact distances of prefectures from the capital and of counties from prefectures. Odometers would have been excellent means for calculating such distances. The second was the south-pointing carriage. It had a wooden figure of a man with an outstretched arm at its center. As the vehicle moved along, the arm always pointed south, regardless of which direction the cart went. In short, it was a compass. The primary direction in ancient China was south. Maps were drawn to be read from north to south, that is, north was closest to the body and south farthest from it. Both the odometer and the south-pointing carriages had mechanisms beneath their beds that rotated the wooden figures by gears attached to their axles.

**Roads**    The Tang had an official road system of perhaps 13,500 miles. The highways ran in all directions, but did not reach a large number of cities, especially those directly south of Changan. There must have been roads to those places, but they may have been constructed and maintained at private expense. The method of construction was the same as that for building walls: rammed earth. Roadways were bowed in the center to force rainwater to the verges, and were lined with trees. In mountainous areas with cliffs, engineers built plank roads by applying fire to the rocks. The heat cracked the stones and created holes. Workers inserted horizontal wood beams into the sockets and laid boards on top to make a pathway on which men and horses could walk. When highways crossed rivers, local governments built and maintained bridges and ferries. Some spans were made of stone, but there were places with pontoon bridges, favored because they did not wash away during floods. Some pontoon bridges consisted of large boats linked together with iron chains. At crossings on broad rivers like the Yellow and Yangtze, only ferries would do for transporting men, horses, and wagons. Where the traffic was heavy, the crossings had large numbers of boats.

The longest of the roads, the Silk Route, stretched from Changan to the far end of the empire north of Kashmir. It had two branches. The southern, though shorter, was more dangerous because it passed through parts of the Takla Makan Desert, where the traveler might stumble on the bleached bones of men and animals that had perished in the heat for lack of water. The longer, northern route, one that skirted the desert was somewhat less inhospitable, and therefore preferable. The government maintained forts manned with soldiers along the way to defend it against marauding tribes that were wont to attack caravans laden with rich goods. The highway was mainly an avenue of trade.

Although internal roads also served as commercial arteries, the state did not establish them to facilitate trade. Two-thirds of the highways in the Tang ran north from Changan and Luoyang to the frontiers, a fact that reflects the state's primary concern for providing the means of transporting troops, weapons, and supplies to those areas most in need of defense. Its second concern was to provide channels of communication between the capitals and the provinces. To satisfy that need, it established the rapid relay system, a kind of a pony express. The system had 1,297 stations, one every ten miles along public roads, that kept mounts readily available for couriers carrying orders from the capital and reports from the provinces. They also provided room and board for the messengers as well as officials. One hundred officials in the capital administered the system, which had 21,500 station masters and riders throughout the empire.

The state was very sensitive about the speed and integrity of its postal system. Couriers who were a day late delivering the mail were subject to a punishment of eighty blows with the thick rod. As the length of delay increased, so did the penalty. The harshest was two years' penal servitude, meted out to riders who were six days or more behind schedule. If, however, the message concerned military matters requiring greater speed, the punishments were more severe: from one year penal servitude to exile at a place more than 666 miles from the man's home district. If the courier's tardiness resulted in the loss of a battle, a city, a fort, or the life of a single citizen or soldier, judges imposed a sentence of execution by strangulation. Riders carried transmission tallies in the shape of dragons and made of bronze or paper, on which the number of stations that a messenger was to pass appeared: the higher the number, the faster he had to ride. The law also prescribed punishments for couriers who turned documents over to others for delivery, conveyed them to an incorrect address, took the wrong route, or used a horse when a donkey was required. If, as a result of his passing a station without changing horses, the animal died, the rider had to pay restitution to the government. The state permitted couriers to carry only the clothes and weapons that they needed for their journey, as long as the weight of them did not exceed fifteen pounds. The reference to arms is another indication that travel was less than safe in the Tang.

At strategic places along highways and waterways the state set up barriers where it collected customs. They were also checkpoints where officials examined the credentials of travelers. Tang subjects were not free to move as they pleased. The punishment for passing through a barrier without the proper travel permits was one year of penal servitude, and for going around a checkpoint, one and a half years. Local officials issued such documents. The government was specifically concerned with preventing the movement of soldiers and criminals. Officials at the barriers also inspected baggage, wagons, and other objects to intercept contraband. Prohibited articles included armor, crossbows, long spears, lances, astronomical instruments, star maps, and books on military matters and omens.

Smugglers in the Tang sometimes employed coffins to move illicit goods because it was customary to ship the remains of the dead back to their ancestral villages. No doubt officials were reluctant to open caskets because they did not wish to disturb the dead or be exposed to decaying corpses. In one instance guards at a ferry stopped a group of people attempting to transport twelve coffins across a river to a district suffering from famine. When the military governor of the district learned that their cortege contained an abnormally large number of coffins, he grew suspicious, had his men break them open, and discovered that they contained rice. It is not clear why transporting grain was illegal at the time. In another instance a band of five thieves tried to ship weapons in a casket across a river so they could rob the residents of a neighboring district. A garrison commander discovered their plot and had all of them executed. Some thieves smuggled their loot out of the capital in a coffin and buried their plunder in a grave to hide it.

**Boats**   The Tang had plenty of boats, at least inland. In 764 a great windstorm struck a city on the Yangtze River in central China during the night. The gale spread fire, probably from an oil lamp, to boats moored there and destroyed 3,000 of them. Then the flames leaped ashore, consumed more than 2,000 houses, and killed between 4,000 and 5,000 people. Earlier, in 751, a fire broke out in government transport barges on the Yellow River and burned up 215 vessels along with 1,750,000 bushels of rice; 600 boatmen lost their lives. Several hundred merchant ships also went up in flames. Those figures represented just a fraction of the total number of boats in the empire; only those moored at two cities. All of the navigable rivers and lakes had watercraft, but the southeastern region had the largest number.

Virtually nothing is known about shipbuilding in the Tang until after 756. The rebellions of the mid-eighth century destroyed much of the government's shipping along the Grand Canal. The court sent one of its economic wizards south to deal with the problem in 764. He established ten shipyards at a county on the Yangtze. Their managers competed with one another to construct barges with a capacity of 1,750 bushels of rice at a cost of 1 million cash each. Over a period of fifty years the competition drove the price down to 500,000 coppers. For transporting grain to the capital, ten barges were roped together. By 874 the quality of production at the shipyards had greatly declined. They were building barges with a capacity of only 875 bushels and using cheap, thin wood to make them. The official shipyards manufactured only one type of vessel. There were many other kinds, from small, painted pleasure craft on which courtesans entertained their patrons to the Great Mother Ships that could carry more than 15,750 bushels of grain. The latter had crews of several hundred that spent their entire lives, from birth to death, on board. Those giants made one round trip a year on the Yangtze and Huai rivers, but reaped enormous profits. Private shipyards along the great rivers must have built them along with a variety of other types, though there appears to be no mention of them in Tang sources.

Tang statutory limitations for the transportation of goods on water provide some notion of the minimum speeds that boats made on the currents of Chinese rivers.

By a loaded boat traveling against the current

| | |
|---|---|
| On the Yellow River | 10 miles |
| On the Yangtze River | 13 miles |
| On other rivers | 15 miles |

By an empty boat traveling against the current

| | |
|---|---|
| On the Yellow River | 13 miles |
| On the Yangtze River | 17 miles |
| On other rivers | 20 miles |

By a loaded or empty boat traveling with the current

| | |
|---|---|
| On the Yellow River | 50 miles |
| On the Yangtze River | 33 miles |
| On other rivers | 23 miles |

Again, speed on the waters, like traveling by shank's mare, depended on several variables. Wind was a critical factor when the vessels had sails. A strong breeze on the Yangtze could move a ship along at a much faster clip than the official numbers given here. Conversely, weather could be an impediment. Gales and flooding brought travel to a halt. Physical strength, human and animal, was another important element. Men and oxen towed the barges that floated up and down the Grand

Canal. Two water buffalo could pull forty barges lashed together by hawsers.

Rapids were serious impediments to travel and transportation on some rivers. The most infamous in the Tang were the Three Gate Rapids on the Yellow River west of Luoyang. They interfered with the movement of barges carrying grain to Changan. In the early eighth century Yang, an imperial engineer, proposed constructing a plank road on the precipices at the gorge so towers could haul the heavily laden boats upstream over the cataracts. The throne approved the project. Yang was a "cruel clerk" who did not pay the towers' wages, and beat them to death when tow ropes or planks on the road broke.

All of the navigable rivers in ancient China flowed from west to east. That was an enormous problem for the imperial government, which needed to transport heavy loads of tax revenues from the rich regions of the Yangtze River to the north. Yangdi, the second emperor of the Sui dynasty, solved it by constructing the Grand Canal, China's second greatest engineering achievement next to the Great Wall. He joined older canals and had new branches excavated to form a more extensive system some 1,560 miles in length. It began at Hangzhou on the east coast, south of the Yangtze, and ran north and west to a point east of Luoyang. From there, branches stretched eastward to Mount Tai and northeast to a point southeast of present-day Beijing. On the southern route the emperor had his crews build paths for towers, plant trees, and erect palace halls. He loved Yangzhou in the south and several times transported his court there in flotillas of more than 5,000 vessels. In Tang times no emperor ever traveled south. For the most part the dynasty used the Grand Canal to transport grain and silk from the south.

There was a certain risk to traveling on inland waterways. Skippers might steal the goods of passengers who rented their vessels. In one case a boatman saw a merchant hide ten ingots of silver in his baggage. He filched the trader's sterling and sank it in the water at the mooring. The next day the boat sailed thirty-three miles and stopped at a military post. Officers inspected the merchant's luggage, and the loss came to light. The trader informed the authorities, who arrested the skipper. The commander of the garrison then sent some troops back to the embankment where the craft had moored the previous night. The soldiers dragged the river with hooks and brought up a basket containing the silver. It still had the merchant's seal on it.

Although the Tang had a navy large enough to transport 100,000 troops across the sea for an invasion of southern Korea in 660, it was not a dynasty noted for maritime enterprises, public or private. Foreign vessels carried trade and travelers to and from China by two routes. Manchurians, Koreans, and Japanese sailed southward from their home ports and landed along the eastern coast. The best of the seamen at the time were the Koreans, who established large settlements on China's seaboard as well as along the Grand Canal and the Yellow River. Japanese "traders," often members of the crew or the embassies that their ships transported, mainly purchased manufactured goods with gold or other valuables. They appear to have had little in the way of wares that the Chinese found attractive. It was the merchants who arrived from the south that brought the exotic commodities desired by the upper classes in the Tang. Those sailors and traders were mainly Persians and Arabs who sailed from as far away as the Persian Gulf in the winter to catch the winds of the northeast monsoon that would carry them across the Indian Ocean to Southeast Asia. From there they turned north on the winds of early summer. The ships picked up goods from the countries that they passed through—frankincense and myrrh from Arabia, cloves from Indonesia, pepper from Burma, coral and pearls from Sri Lanka among other things. Those were the wares that they sold after they arrived in the empire of the Tang.

The largest of the oceangoing vessels—some 200 feet long and capable of carrying 600 to 700 men—came from Sri Lanka. They had multiple decks and towed lifeboats. The sailors believed that their rats were divine because the rodents would desert a ship ten days before it capsized. They also carried homing pigeons that could fly a thousand miles and inform the people in their home ports that their vessels had sunk. Foreign shipbuilders in Southeast Asia did not use nails to build their craft. Instead, they lashed planks together with fibers from palm trees and caulked them with oil derived from a fruit.

Sea voyaging was very hazardous. Ships had no power of their own to propel them out of danger. When the vessel of Ennin, a Japanese monk, arrived off the coast of China, a wind blew it onto a shoal and waves crashed into the hull, threatening to break it in two. Instead, the rocking back and forth on the sandbar smashed the bottom of the boat and it settled into the water, drowning the cargo. The Japanese monk was fortunate. He did not encounter the great typhoons that doomed many a vessel.

## WAYFARING AND WAYFARERS

Imperial journeys were progresses, large processions marked by all the pageantry proper to the throne. In China any trip outside the palace, even to a temple or mansion in the capital, was a progress. The court often made short excursions outside the city to nearby palaces, spas, and hunting grounds. In such cases the entourage was small. Less frequently, the destination was a considerable distance from the metropolis. Emperor Taizong made the longest when he personally led his military forces into northern Korea to conquer that kingdom. On his return he

visited Taiyuan, his father's base of power before the founding of the
Tang. Taizong was away from Changan for seventeen months between
644 and 646, but part of his court remained in Luoyang during that
period. Twice, in 665–666 and 725–726, the imperial cortege traveled to
Mount Tai, where Gaozong and Illustrious August performed the sacrifices to Heaven, the state's most powerful deity. The mountain was
around 357 miles from Luoyang, and the court took forty and twenty-
six days, respectively, to make the trip. In 665 the cortege included military and civil mandarins, foreign legates—Turks, Persians, Indians,
Japanese, Koreans, and others—with their entourages, army troops,
guards, and wagons carrying ritual paraphernalia. It stretched out for
more than sixty miles. Horses and camels carried men, women, and baggage; cattle and sheep supplied food; and felt yurts and tents provided
shelter.

The most frequent long-distance journeys for the court in the early
Tang were those between Changan and Luoyang, undertaken to prevent
famines when food ran short in Changan. Between 637 and 735 the trip
of 285 miles, back and forth, was made no less than twenty-nine times.
It took twenty to twenty-five days to cover the distance. At eleven to
fourteen miles a day, the pace was slower than the minimum statutory
limit for walking or riding a jackass. On each occasion the government
and the court accompanied the cortege. So frequent were the visits to
the eastern capital that the aristocrats and ministers had mansions there.
The journeys were not only extremely expensive for the government, but
also very burdensome to the people along the route. They had to provide
provisions and labor for the imperial entourage. The throne frequently
bestowed tax remissions to subjects who lived in the districts along the
road, to furnish some relief for the hardships that they endured.

Traveling the road between the capitals could be dangerous even for
the emperor, who never went anywhere without a large body of guards.
In 682, when the court had to move to Luoyang because there was a
great famine in Changan, it feared that many bandits were lurking in
the underbrush to attack his cortege. So the emperor appointed a patrolling censor to take matters in hand. The man released a criminal who
was exceptionally eloquent from a prison in Changan. He took the convict's fetters off, dressed him in cap and gown, provided him with board
and room, and had him lead the imperial entourage. The ploy was so
successful that when the procession arrived in Luoyang, not a single
copper had been lost by the more than 10,000 members of the cortege.
However, many members of the entourage starved to death for lack of
food along the route.

Even the guards could pose a threat. In 641, while emperor Taizong
was making his way to Luoyang, two guards who detested serving on
compulsory travel duty shot arrows into the palace at the warm springs

on Black Horse Mountain during the night. Five of the missiles landed in the courtyard of the emperor's sleeping quarters. That was an act of great sedition for which the guards paid with their heads.

The most prestigious visitors to the Tang were the emissaries of foreign nations. Local officials met those who arrived by sea, and sent word to the capital. The envoys then waited for authorization from the throne before proceeding to Changan or Luoyang. Those who traveled overland along the Silk Route from the west had to have credentials, which they applied for in advance. The credentials, twelve in number, took the form of bronze fish in two parts. The government sent one half of each to the foreign nation and retained the other. Both halves had the name of the nation involved and a number specifying the moon (month) in which the envoys were permitted to enter the capital. Thus, if an emissary arrived in the fourth moon with a tally bearing the date third moon, he would not be received. If he arrived at the appropriate time, foreign affairs officials matched his token with that kept in the capital to verify that he was authorized to attend court. After 695 the government provided provisions for the envoy and his party. The amounts differed according to the distance of the state from the Tang capitals: six months' worth for India, Persia, and Arabia; four months' for the states of Cambodia, Sumatra, and Java; and three months' for a nation in what is now southern Vietnam.

Emissaries did not always fare well with local officials when they arrived in China. In the mid-eighth century, after a Japanese ambassador with a retinue of 500 men in ten boats disembarked, the local governor met him, lodged the emissary and his party in a government hostel, and abundantly supplied them with all their needs. He would not, however, permit them to leave their quarters. During the night the governor seized all their gifts and sank their ships. The next day he informed the ambassador that all of his craft had floated away on the tide and their whereabouts were unknown. After he reported the matter to the throne, the emperor ordered him to build ten new boats and assign 500 sailors to send the Japanese home. As they were about to set sail, the governor addressed the Chinese crews saying that since Japan was far away and the waves on the ocean large, they should seize the opportunity. With that hint the sailors set off. After traveling for several days, the crews slew the Japanese and returned home. Foreigners could also, however, be troublemakers. In the early seventh century some westerners robbed Chinese citizens in one of Changan's wards.

After an emissary arrived in the capital, the government saw to all of his needs: lodging, sleeping mats, food, and medicine—as well as a funeral, should he pass away. An official from the bureau of cartography in the Department of the Army visited him to inquire about the geography and customs of his nation, so that he could draw a map for submission to the throne. The interrogation was a form of intelligence-gathering; the information obtained would be of use against the envoy's nation should war break out. In the seventh century court artists painted scrolls depicting the emissaries bearing their tribute, standing outside the main gate of the palace while waiting to be admitted for an audience with the emperor. No doubt the work was helpful in identifying the nationalities of envoys who came afterward.

On an appointed day the emperor received the envoy at an audience. The emissary then kowtowed as an act of homage to the Son of Heaven and presented his tribute. On such occasions renowned artists of the court might paint the peculiar—from the Chinese point of view—appearances of the outlanders to commemorate the ceremony. All states or tribes, whether within the borders of the empire or not, were vassals of the Tang throne as far as the state was concerned. As such they had to tender gifts of their goods to their liege lord, as a symbol of their submission to his authority. In return the emperor bestowed a title, seal, state robes, and reciprocal gifts from his stores, generally more valuable than those received from the aliens. Some of those presents conferred on Japanese embassies still survive in a treasury at a Buddhist monastery near Kyoto. After the formalities the government hosted a banquet for the foreign dignitary, and with that he made ready to depart China and return home.

Tributary missions were important to the Tang court because they affirmed the suzerainty and power of the dynasty. In practical terms, however, they were far more significant to the vassal states. In the first place, members of the envoy's party carried on trade even though doing so was illegal under Chinese law. In the second, artisans, scholars, and monks accompanied the missions. While in China, they acquired valuable knowledge of advanced technology and ideas that they carried home to develop their cultures. Such, at least, was the case for the Japanese.

Officials were frequent travelers, moving to new posts in the provinces, making inspection tours, and so forth. One of them, Li Ao, wrote a diary, the oldest surviving example of the genre in China, of his journey from Luoyang to Canton. It took him and his family 169 days to cover the 2,500 miles, much of it by boat. However, they were in transit only 117 days, so they traveled an average of twenty-one miles a day. That was well in excess of the eighty days mandated for officials moving to new posts that far from the capital. The family's pace was leisurely. Like many mandarins, Li took time out for sight-seeing—visiting scenic mountains, lakes, and places of interest. Many of his compatriots made such stops, not just to take in the countryside, but also to visit friends and feast with them. The court sent legates to foreign nations who wrote accounts of the places and peoples that they had seen. The adventurer who brought the king of Magadha back to Changan in the early seventh century left a work in ten scrolls on the Indian kingdom. In the same period Emperor Taizong sent an emissary to invest a western Turk with the title of khan. After he carried out his charge, he discovered that some tribes had cut off his only road home. He spent three years in Central Asia, and put the time to good use by writing an account of the customs and products in the various lands he visited. Since he had no access to paper, he tore up his clothes and penned the record on the fabric.

The state provided transportation for the families of officials moving to new posts in the early eighth century, before the rebellion of An Lushan.

| Rank | Porters | Carts | Horses | Donkeys |
|---|---|---|---|---|
| 1 | 30 | 7 | 10 | 15 |
| 2 | 24 | 5 | 6 | 10 |
| 3 | 20 | 4 | 4 | 6 |
| 4 and 5 | 12 | 2 | 3 | 4 |
| 6 and 7 | 8 | 1 | 2 | 3 |
| 9 | 5 | 1 | 1 | 2 |

As usual, rank had its privileges, and the government dispensed its resources on the basis of status, not need.

In the Tang there were many books about foreign lands—Korea, Manchuria, Southeast Asia, Tibet, and Central Asia—but almost all of them have perished. The most notable exception is the record of the western nations written by a renowned Buddhist monk who spent sixteen years on the road and in India. His account provides a rare glimpse of the government, education, towns, clothes, science, customs, manners, fauna, and flora of India and the nations of Central Asia during the seventh century. Monks were also frequent travelers in China, where they moved to find masters who had acquired reputations for their wisdom, or made pilgrimages to sacred sites. Ennin, a Japanese monk who journeyed and lived in eastern and northern China between 838 and 847, has left the most valuable account of daily life in the empire. Unfortunately, not a word has survived from the greatest of all travelers in the Tang, the merchants who spent their lives on the roads or waterways, inside China and outside.

## ACCOMMODATIONS

There was a wide variety of accommodations, from palaces to tents, for travelers. There were a number of detached palaces in the countryside around Changan that provided the court with lodgings when it ventured out for a hunt or other recreation. In 738 Emperor Illustrious August ordered the construction of palace halls along the route from Changan to Luoyang. Ironically, neither he nor any of his successors made another progress east to the second capital until 904, when a warlord had his troops cart the emperor from Changan to Luoyang.

Stations of the rapid relay postal system also provided lodgings for travelers. Some of their overseers made great efforts to ensure that they had sufficient provisions for guests. The manager of a station located south of the Yangtze River gave the local governor a tour of his facilities and showed him three rooms for storing ale, tea, and pickled vegetables. Outside of each was a painting of the patron deity of the goods stored within. The god of ale, for example, was the mythological discoverer of brewing. The governor thought the elaborate scheme was unnecessary. A traveler needed a permit issued by a local official to stay at a station. During the early ninth century, an inspector impeached a bureaucrat in southwest China for illegally furnishing such a certificate that allowed the family of a military supervisor to stay in a station with the coffin containing his remains. Sometimes the quarters were insufficient for the demand, a condition that could cause violent conflicts between guests. The same inspector involved in the preceding case was lodging at a station between Luoyang and Changan. He had already taken off his shoes when a eunuch arrived and demanded his room. When he did not get it, the enraged eunuch kicked in the gate of the hostel, led the inspector's horse out of the stable, and threatened to shoot him with his bow and arrows. The inspector, in his stockings, fled to the rear of the station, where the eunuch caught up with him and struck him with a whip, inflicting a wound on his face. There were also official inns in large cities.

For those who could not acquire permits to stay in government quarters, there were private, commercial lodgings. Stores provided rooms and meals to travelers. Some were located near bridges or post stations. An innkeeper in southwest China poisoned a wealthy merchant who was lodging in his hostel for the night. After the trader died, he stole his money. Later, when a second merchant at the inn took sick and died, the military governor of the district became suspicious. He had the merchant's ledgers examined, but the audit yielded no evidence because the innkeeper had altered its entries. So the governor secretly interrogated the residents of the ward and the people in the hostelry. His inquiries uncovered the truth. He learned that the innkeeper had covered up his crime by bribing over twenty functionaries in the district with more than 1 million coppers. The governor had the innkeeper and the venal officials beheaded.

Buddhist monasteries and Taoist abbeys offered accommodations to travelers. When the clergymen were on the road, they could receive room and board in the cloisters free of charge. However, on occasion monks paid for vegetarian feasts as a form of compensation to the church, especially when they lived there for extended periods. Smaller and poorer monasteries were less than pleased to receive visitors. Ennin sometimes got a cold reception from abbots when he stayed overnight. Once two monks were downright hostile and drove him away several times. He had to force his way into the cloister and prepare his own meal. To their credit, the Chinese monks later warmed up to their guest and made noodles for him. Lay travelers also could find accommodations in monasteries. Students were particularly prone to reside in them for long intervals. In that case they rented rooms. Sometimes the members of foreign embassies stayed in them. In some cases the clergy had abandoned monasteries, they had fallen into disrepair, and laymen had taken them over as living quarters. In one case an innkeeper had taken over a monastery with two pagodas in front and converted it into a commercial hostelry.

A network of national monasteries and abbeys was launched during Empress Wu's reign and revitalized by Emperor Illustrious August in 738. They also offered room and board to lay travelers. A mandarin traveling from Luoyang to take up a post at Canton stopped at one of the monasteries in 809. His pregnant wife could not go on, so the family stayed there while she gave birth to a daughter and recovered from the ordeal. They lived in the cloister for fifty-two days. Since the government funded monasteries and abbeys, one Taoist and one Buddhist in all 321 prefectures, it is probable that officials did not have to pay rent for their stay in them. Sometimes government personnel occupied all of the cells in a monastery, and monks could not find a room to stay in.

Finally, a pilgrim could find lodging in Common Cloisters run by Buddhists on the major routes to Mount Wutai northeast of Changan. They were located three to ten miles apart and provided room and board for monks, nuns, and laypersons at no charge. Some accommodated as many as 100 visitors. During famines, however, they had no food for guests, so travelers had to carry their own provisions with them.

A traveler who found himself off the beaten path where there were no inns might find accommodations in a private home. The degree of hospitality varied greatly. Ennin was able to find lodgings with generous and friendly Chinese, but he also stayed with hosts who were surly and stingy. On one occasion, after passing thirty houses without finding a room, he forced his way into one and spent the night there. The Japanese monk's perceptions of Chinese hospitality were colored by his presumption that he was entitled to free board and room even in private homes.

# 9

# Crime and Punishment

## CRIME

Upon returning from a nocturnal fox hunt on January 9, 827, Emperor Jingzong caroused in the palace with twenty-eight eunuchs and captains of his polo teams. After he got merrily drunk, the emperor retired to change his clothes in another chamber. Suddenly all of the lights in the hall went out, and his drinking companions slew him in the dressing room. This regicide was the fruition of a conspiracy whose objective was to depose the king and install his uncle on the throne. A rival clique of eunuchs, however, had other ideas. They induced Jingzong's brother to issue an order authorizing the execution of the assassins. Imperial troops duly entered the palace and massacred the murderers the same day.

Jingzong's assassins were guilty of plotting rebellion, the first of the Ten Abominations. The Ten Abominations were the most heinous offenses in the Tang law code and covered four categories of crimes, the largest number of which pertained to the emperor. Threats to the sovereign's person included not only plotting or carrying out a rebellion, but also endangering his life or health through incompetence or malpractice. Servitors guilty of the latter offenses included physicians who failed to follow the proper formulas when composing the emperor's medicine and palace chefs who violated proscriptions in the *Food Canons* when preparing the emperor's meals. The *Food Canons* were dietary manuals that enumerated cooking taboos, such as mixing softshell turtles with greens or jerky with glutinous millet. Other crimes against the throne were acts that undermined the emperor's authority, such as unfounded criticism of the sovereign or forging his seals, and those that involved the destruction or theft of his property—palaces, carriages, quilts, cushions, clothes, and the like.

The second encompassed crimes against the state: switching allegiance to a foreign ruler, betraying a city to a rebel, attempting to flee China, and killing a superior civil or military official. Since the emperor was the embodiment of the state, most of these were also offenses against him. One of the most prominent prosecutions for treason occurred in the wake of the An Lushan rebellion. Some eminent officials, who found themselves trapped behind enemy lines, accepted appointments to posts in An's government. After Tang forces recaptured Luoyang, more than 200 of the traitors fell into their hands. The throne sentenced thirty-nine to death. The emperor ordered the entire bureaucratic corps to assemble at the execution grounds to observe the beheading of nineteen traitors beneath the solitary willow.

The third involved offenses against the family: beating or murdering grandparents, parents, uncles, aunts, elder brothers or sisters, and husbands; selling close relatives into slavery; lodging accusations against paternal grandparents, parents, or husbands; failure to provide elders with adequate support; and incest. The power of elders was the same as that of the emperor and his governors, who thought of themselves as the parents of the people. In the interest of maintaining social stability, the state made every effort to maintain the authority of household heads. Legally, it was perfectly acceptable for a father to flog his son, but a son found guilty of whipping his father was subject to death. While hunting in 662, the son of a chief minister trespassed on a farmer's fields and shot the enraged man with a whistling arrow. As punishment the minister beat him 100 blows with a rod. When word of the incident reached the throne, the emperor cashiered the chief minister, not for whipping his son but for failing to report the son's crime to the proper authorities. Fathers also held the power of life and death over their sons, though they might be subject to penal servitude for the murder. In 680 the emperor instructed General Gao to admonish and reprimand his son for his association with an heir to the throne who had been convicted and deposed for plotting rebellion. When the son returned home and entered the gate, his father thrust a dagger into his throat, his uncle stabbed him in the stomach, and a cousin lopped off his head. The men then dumped the son's remains in the streets of Luoyang. When the emperor learned this, it displeased him, so he demoted the general to a post as prefect in a district 940 miles from the capital.

The final category comprised depraved crimes. Those offenses included slaying three or more members of a household if they were not guilty of a capital crime; dismembering or burning a body before, after, or in the process of murdering the victim; and sorcery with special reference to *gu* poison. *Gu* poison was made by placing venomous creatures such as snakes, toads, scorpions, spiders, and centipedes in a pot. According to tradition, the animal that survived combat with the others and devoured them was the most noxious, by virtue of having absorbed the others' toxins. When the sorcerer or sorcerers decided to kill someone, he or she secretly injected the feces of the creature in the intended victim's food or drink. The poison then destroyed the victim's organs and caused him to vomit blood. No one who consumed it survived. Sorcery included other forms of black magic as well. Carvers of dolls who stabbed the hearts, nailed the eyes, or bound the feet and hands of their effigies to inflict harm on their intended victims were subject to the death penalty. So too were conjurers who uttered curses to cause misfortune and death.

The term "Ten Abominations" was a designation invented by legalists to single out crimes that the state and society considered to be the most reprehensible. Not all of the crimes were punishable by death, nor were other grave offenses subject to capital punishment considered to be abominations.

## ARREST

The duty of apprehending culprits fell to the Gold Bird Guards in the capitals and to thief catchers in the prefectures and counties. The latter included soldiers and constables who were underlings on the governors' staffs. Those men usually had some experience in apprehending outlaws, but the government did not rely solely on them. The law demanded that bystanders apprehend and convey to the appropriate authorities suspects who committed assaults resulting in broken teeth and fingers or more severe wounds, as well as thieves and rapists. Passersby on highways and byways, who were strong enough to subdue culprits, were subject to punishment if they did not come to the assistance of thief catchers who needed help. The neighbors of victims whom lawbreakers had robbed or murdered had to assist the government in apprehending and prosecuting the outlaws. However, the law allowed relatives of the culprit, people who dwelt with him, and his slaves to conceal his offense from authorities. It also prohibited prosecution of the same people when they informed the suspect that the authorities were searching for him. Those exemptions did not apply when the crime involved rebellion, sedition, treason, murder, or robbery by force.

Thief catchers, public or private, were not legally accountable if they slew an armed criminal who resisted arrest, if they killed him in the course of pursuit, or if the fugitive committed suicide. They were, however, subject to punishment if they injured or slew an unarmed suspect who did not resist arrest.

In extreme circumstances the throne resorted to extraordinary measures to capture criminals. In 815 assassins slew Chief Minister Wu in Changan as he was making his way to an audience with the emperor. Afterward the murderers sent written messages to the headquarters of the Gold Bird Guards as well as the capital's municipal and county offices: "If you do not arrest us quickly, we will kill you first." The threat dampened the ardor of thief catchers, who did not rush out to chase down the culprits. A great panic then broke out in the city, forcing the emperor to station additional guards at all gates. To protect other chief ministers he ordered dragoons of the Gold Bird Guards to escort them with strung bows and unsheathed swords whenever they proceeded to or retired from the palace. Left to their own devices, other officials armed their servants to serve as bodyguards. Several days later, when all efforts to apprehend the perpetrators had failed, the throne offered a bounty of 10 million coppers to anyone who captured the killers. The throne also issued a decree imposing the death penalty on officials fifth grade or higher and their clansmen who dared to hide the culprits. So empowered, the authorities ransacked the capital, searching every nook and cranny in the mansions of nobles and ministers. Seven days after the assassination, constables hauled in eight men who were staying in Changan without proper passes. The suspects, soldiers or officials loyal to Governor Wang, confessed and implicated eleven others. Despite great doubts as to their guilt, the emperor ordered all nineteen executed. Less than two months later an investigation into another rebellious plot uncovered the innocence of the condemned, or so it seemed.

## IMPRISONMENT

After arresting suspects, thief catchers hauled them off to jail. In 754 there were somewhat less than 1,900 prisons with well over 10,000 administrators throughout the empire. Incarceration in Tang China was not a form of punishment in itself. Jails were simply places for holding the accused while the authorities investigated the crime and imposed the sentence, a period rarely more than a few months. Abuses, however, occurred now and then. In the early ninth century governors of one district had incarcerated more than ten men for failure to render the total amount of taxes they owed the government. The prisoners had languished in jail for many years, so long that their wives had taken to begging in order to provide them with food or had remarried. When inmates died, the authorities seized their sons to take their places in the prison. They remained incarcerated for such a prolonged period not be-

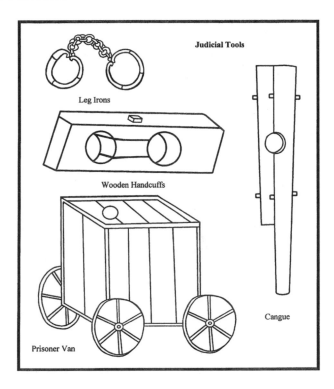

cause they were serving time, but because magistrates had not resolved their cases or imposed sentences upon them.

Ancient prisons probably differed little from those of nineteenth-century China. They were a series of cells having three masonry walls with a fourth opening barred by undressed timber. In the Tang, patricians occupied cells apart from plebes, and men and women were separated, at least in the jails of the Service for Supreme Justice at the capitals. Furnishings were spare: thick layers of rush mats for sleeping and probably a bucket for collecting human waste. The law prohibited family or jailers from providing prisoners with pens, paper, alcohol, gold, knives, or staves. The intent of the statute was to prevent the incarcerated from escaping by bribery, force, or other means.

Since Tang jails were not the formidable stone, concrete, and iron dungeons of the West, escape could not have been difficult. To prevent that, the law required wardens to keep dangerous inmates in fetters. The restraints for male prisoners charged with capital crimes were cangues and wooden handcuffs. Women subject to the death penalty and all suspects charged with crimes punishable by exile or penal servitude wore cangues only. There were exceptions to the rules. Mandarins ranked seventh grade or higher enjoyed the right of wearing chains only. Dwarfs, pregnant women, the disabled, and inmates over seventy-nine years of age awaited judgment unfettered. Prisoners suspected of minor crimes subject to punishment by thrashing or scourging were kept in loose confinement, that is, without restraints.

Tang statutes set standards for the sizes of fetters that differed according to the gravity of the offense. Those regulations set the lengths of chains at eight to twelve feet long, and wooden handcuffs at one and a half to two feet. The cangue consisted of two rectangular jaws made from wood planks with a semicircular hole cut in one side of each. Wardens joined the jaws around the prisoner's neck to form a kind of collar and locked them in place. It was a sort of a pillory without a post. According to law, cangues were two and a half feet long and sixteen to eighteen inches wide. Inmates so outfitted found it difficult to eat, sleep, or perform any other bodily function.

It was the responsibility of the prisoners' families to supply them with food and clothing. Only in cases where the accused landed in a jail far from home did the authorities provide for such needs. Even so, when his kinsmen arrived at the place of his detention, the law required them to reimburse the government for the expenses incurred in caring for the inmate. During the heat of summer, wardens allowed prisoners to bathe once a month and supplied them with vinegar water to slake their thirst. The code established standards for the humane treatment of the sick in all prisons. When an inmate took ill, the administrators had to supply him with medicine. If his condition was grave, they removed his fetters and admitted a relative to care for him in his cell. In the case of the highest-ranking mandarins, third grade or above, wardens permitted two relatives—wives, daughters, sons, or grandsons—to enter and attend to him. In the first moon of each year the central government sent agents to the provinces to examine the fetters, rush mats, and provisions for the sick in local prisons. Wardens who violated regulations governing the treatment of the ill were subject to punishment.

Jailbreaks occasionally occurred during the Tang. In the autumn of 775 a Uighur gutted a man with a knife in broad daylight at the East Market of Changan. Bystanders seized the assailant and dragged him off to the county prison. When the culprit's chieftain heard about the arrest, he rushed to the jail, rode in, and chopped the wardens with his sword. Then he freed his compatriot and fled with him. The punishment for inflicting wounds during a jailbreak was death by strangulation. However, the Uighurs were powerful allies of the dynasty, so the emperor made no further inquiries into the affair, permitting the offender to go unpunished.

Sometimes unscrupulous officials engineered the release of a prisoner. In 656 Li, a powerful minister, took a fancy to a beautiful woman incarcerated in the jail of the Service for Supreme Justice at Luoyang. The minister, who wanted to take her as a concubine, ordered Bi, a judicial review officer in the agency, to free her, in violation of the law. After the matter became public, and the throne ordered an investigation, Li intimidated Bi so severely that the official hanged himself in the prison. Even though a censor lodged an indictment against the minister, the emperor did not pursue the matter because Li enjoyed his favor.

## TRIAL

A trial began with the incarceration of a suspect whom thief catchers had caught in the act or with the lodging of an accusation by a victim, witness, or informant. In the latter event the magistrate who received the complaint incarcerated the accuser if the crime was serious. Then he dispatched thief catchers to arrest the accused. The pursuers had thirty days to apprehend the suspect, after which they were subject to punishment.

Magistrates had to take great care in cases initiated by allegations because many accusers filed false charges for personal gain, vengeance, or other reasons. A court official in the late seventh century had a maidservant named Bewitching Damsel who was not only beautiful, but adept at singing and dancing. The Prince of Wei, Empress Wu's nephew, borrowed her on the pretext that he wanted her to teach his women how to apply makeup. Then he took her for a concubine and refused to return her to her former master. The mandarin sent her a poem lamenting his loss. Three days after receiving the verses, Bewitching Damsel threw herself into a well and died. When the prince had her body pulled from the well, he found the poem in her sash and flew into a rage. To get even, he induced an informant to lodge false charges against the mandarin. The man was convicted and beheaded. Some plaintiffs went to extraordinary lengths to establish grounds for their falsehoods. In 639 the emperor discovered that accusers were maiming their eyes and ears to provide evidence for their lies in court. To prevent this, he added a thrashing of forty blows to whatever punishments the courts had imposed on the culprits.

The most infamous period for lodging false accusations was the reign of terror under Empress Wu's regime. That was due to three factors. The empress encouraged informers by offering them rewards in the form of appointments to political posts or gifts of silk. She permitted provincial accusers to ride the horses of the rapid relay system, supplying them with food and lodgings fit for fifth grade officials. Finally, her cruel clerks compiled the *Entrapment Canon*. That text, in several thousand words, provided detailed instructions on methods for informing and creating frame-ups. So armed, the empress's agents fabricated charges on their own or persuaded others to do so. Many innocent victims suffered unjust punishments. In one instance an agent of the empress beheaded a man without investigating the case, then fabricated a charge against him post-humously.

In most cases the officials responsible for conducting trials in the first instance were the county or market commandants. County commandants in particular were busy men charged with all governmental affairs in their districts—tax collection, famine relief, military defense, and public works, to name a few. Most of them probably spent little time on legal matters, delegating most of those duties to subordinates: the marshals and provosts of law as well as to constables, bailiffs, jailers, detectives, and court reporters. Few of those men, including the commandant, had any specialized legal training. There were no lawyers, prosecutors, or judges in the modern sense. The presiding officer, the magistrate, could, however, avail himself of manuals that contained hypothetical judgments.

Investigation of a crime involved examining evidence, and interrogating accusers or suspects. The evidence might be physical. While out carousing with his staff one night, an official noticed something false in the cry of a woman who was wailing in mourning for her deceased husband. The next day he sent a detective to bring the widow in for interrogation. Despite two days of questioning she would not confess. The detective, fearing that his superior would blame him for failing to resolve the matter, stood watch over the corpse. Suddenly he noticed that large black flies were swarming around its head. He parted the hair of the dead man and found the end of a nail protruding from the skull. It turned out that the wife got her husband drunk and killed him by pounding the spike into his brain. She wanted to get rid of him so she could continue an adulterous affair.

Evidence might also take the form of documents. In the late seventh century one of Governor Pei's subordinates cut up a memorandum written by his superior and pasted the pieces together to form a new document containing seditious remarks. He then submitted the forgery to the authorities as proof for his accusation that the governor had plotted rebellion. Although Pei conceded that the handwriting was his, he denied having written the document. After three investigations failed to resolve the matter, Empress Wu sent a clever official to try his hand at it. While the official was reclining on a couch and sunlight from a window struck the back of the paper, he discovered the seams between the pieces. He summoned Pei's accuser and dropped the forgery into a basin of water. The water dissolved the glue and the pieces came apart. The culprit then confessed, and was beheaded.

Nearly all trials included a confrontation between the magistrate and the defendant. Except in cases of murder, robbery by force, flight, and rape of a good woman, the law required magistrates to conduct those hearings on three different days. During the first he took the suspect's statement. That document served as the basis for the judge's oral questions during the second and third sessions. There were five ancient principles for conducting such interrogations. Judges were to examine the accused's statement to discover complications or inconsistencies in it; observe his face to find any signs of blushing; watch his respiration to detect irregularities in his breathing; test his ears to ascertain if he could hear the questions addressed to him; and look into his eyes to see if they were clear. The first three were techniques for detecting lies, and the last two methods for determining the competence of accusers or suspects to stand trial.

Interrogation was an essential element of trials, though it did not always yield the expected results. Four years after the assassination of Chief Minister Wu, an official discovered a document among the papers of Governor Li after his troops assassinated him. According to it, Li had rewarded sixteen of his men for killing Wu. The emperor had the sixteen hauled to the capital and ordered an investigation into the matter. Although all of the prisoners confessed, an interrogator uncovered inconsistencies in their testimony. When confronted with the discrepancies, one of the suspects revealed that both Governor Wang and Governor Li had sent assassins into the capital to murder the chief minister. Before Li's men could carry out their orders, they learned that Governor Wang's agents had already murdered Wu. Undaunted, they returned to Li and falsely claimed credit for the homicide so that they could reap the rewards for the deed. Despite that fact that the true murderers had already been executed, the emperor had all of the innocent men executed.

If, when a magistrate completed his investigation, the facts of the case were in doubt and the defendant refused to admit his crime, he could, with the approval of his superior or colleagues, apply judicial torture to extract a confession. Under those circumstances a conviction required an acknowledgment of guilt from the accused, not only as evidence of his wrongdoing but also as a sign of his contrition and willingness to reform. The only legitimate form of torture was scourging with the interrogation rod, and the law code imposed limitations on its use. It prohibited more than three thrashings and a total of no more than 200 blows. It also stipulated that the three beatings had to be administered at least twenty days apart. Furthermore, the code prohibited the thrashing of dwarfs, mutes, morons, the disabled, and relatives of high-ranking officials who were over sixty-nine years of age or younger than fourteen. If the suspect still did not confess, then the magistrate had to release him. In all cases that did not involve grave offenses, the judge then subjected the accuser to judicial torture. If he confessed, the magistrate sentenced him to the punishment prescribed for the crime that he had alleged. If he endured all 200 blows without admitting guilt, the judge had to release him without punishing him.

During the Tang there were officials, known as "cruel clerks," who flagrantly violated regulations by applying illegal forms of torture. Again the most notorious era for such abuses was the reign of terror under Empress Wu's regime. Her agents established a special prison inside the southwest gate of Luoyang, a jail so infamous that the capital's citizens said anyone who entered it would not leave alive. There her minions applied subtle forms of psychological torture to elicit confessions by denying suspects food or sleep, interrogating them night after night, tossing manure into their cells, and confining them in underground pits. When prisoners were obstinate and refused to admit guilt, they resorted to more brutal methods: suspending them upside down with a rock tied to their heads, filling their ears with mud, hanging them by their hair, singing their ears, pouring vinegar into their nostrils, and jamming bamboo slivers under their fingernails. One particularly fiendish brute devised an iron cage that fit over a victim's head. Once it was in place, he drove wedges into the sides of the cage that cracked the skull and caused the brains to burst out.

Most of Empress Wu's "cruel clerks" met ignominious ends. In one case someone accused one of them, Zhou, of plotting rebellion, and the empress assigned the investigation of his case to another, Lai. While Lai and Zhou were dining, Lai asked Zhou, "What means should be employed when a prisoner continually refuses to confess?" Zhou replied, "That is quite simple. Take a large vat, place burning charcoal all around it and order the prisoner to climb into the pot. How could he not confess?!" Lai obtained a great tub and surrounded it with fire. Then he said to Zhou, "I have a decree from the palace ordering me to investigate your case. Older brother, please climb into the kettle." Terrified, Zhou kowtowed and admitted his guilt. Although his offense warranted death, the empress exiled him to the far south. Someone who bore a grudge against him for an injustice murdered Zhou while he was on the road to the place of his banishment.

Once the defendant had been convicted, the magistrate passed sentence on him. The law required him to assign punishments in accordance with provisions in the code or other collections of statutes. To ensure that all officials were well versed in the laws, the throne ordered that the laws be inscribed on walls of offices so that officials could study them while taking breaks from their duties.

## PUNISHMENT

In its first chapter the Tang law code listed five major forms of punishment. The first was thrashing with the thin rod and had five degrees:

ten, twenty, thirty, forty, and fifty blows. Magistrates who failed to pass sentences according to the laws were subject to thirty blows. Failure to report a fire or assist in putting it out was punishable by twenty blows, and illegal entry into a home during the night, by forty blows. The law prescribed forty blows for masters of mad dogs that they did not kill, as well as for owners of domestic animals and dogs that gored, kicked or bit people. Furthermore, the code required that the owners cut off the horns, hobble the legs, and cut off the ears, respectively, of the offending creatures.

In 630, while examining an anatomical illustration, Emperor Taizong noticed that the internal organs of humans were located just under the skin of the back. To spare his subjects suffering, he ordered that magistrates apply thrashings only to the buttocks and thighs when punishing criminals.

The second was scourging with the thick rod and had five degrees: sixty, seventy, eighty, ninety, and a hundred blows. Shooting arrows toward a city, home, or road was punishable by sixty blows. The maximum penalty for debtors who failed to repay loans worth one foot of cloth within 100 days after the date stipulated in a contract was sixty blows. Eighty blows was the punishment for sticking objects into another person's ears, nostrils or other orifices when the objects obstructed the passage, and for pulling out a square inch or more of an adversary's hair during a fight. Gambling on games of chance was punishable by 100 blows except in cases when the wager was food and drink, or the contest involved archery and other martial arts.

The law set the lengths of all rods, cut from bushes, at three and a half feet and required the removal of all knots. The sizes of the switches differed only in the diameters of the sticks, the thin rod being the smallest and the interrogation rod being the largest. Unlike thrashings, the law permitted magistrates to apply the blows to the back as well as the buttocks and thighs. County and market commandants could impose sentences prescribing thrashings and scourging without review by higher authorities.

The third was penal servitude and had five degrees: one, one and a half, two, two and a half, and three years. One year of penal servitude was the punishment for destroying tombstones and for peering into an imperial palace from a high place. Possession of armor and crossbows was punishable by one and a half years, and possession of military treatises by two years. Artisans who failed to paint or embellish imperial boats were subject to two years. Three years was the sentence for persons who burned coffins while attempting to smoke foxes out of tombs. (The folklore of traditional China depicted foxes as evil creatures.)

In the capitals, magistrates sent men sentenced to penal servitude to labor on the construction of buildings, and women to toil at sewing for the court. In the provinces, judges set criminals to work on city walls, moats, granaries, and warehouses, or employed them for miscellaneous tasks in their offices. In either case the convicts were confined at the offices of the agency involved. The law required that prefects review all sentences to penal servitude that county or market commandants imposed.

The fourth was exile and had three degrees: 666, 833, and 1,000 miles, with compulsory labor added in some cases. Those who submitted anonymous accusations or lodged them under false names were subject to banishment at a place 833 miles from their homes, as were thieves who stole armor or crossbows and Chinese men who married aliens (Persians, Indians, and the like). In 680 the throne sentenced a man to exile in the farthest reaches of the empire for compiling a book of jokes. When the heir apparent was deposed for treason, a friend of his went to retrieve the collection of jests that he had given to the prince. The emperor was angry when he learned of this, and banished the author to Hainan Island. In the early eighth century the wife of a general died, leaving him with five children, so he remarried. His new wife was very cruel and flogged her stepchildren daily. Unable to bear the pain, they went to the grave of their mother and wept bitterly. Suddenly her ghost rose from the tomb to comfort her offspring. Then she wrote a poem on silk to her husband, complaining about the abuses of the stepmother. The children took the poem to their father, who informed his superior about the crimes of his wife. That official submitted a report to the throne. The emperor sentenced the stepmother to 100 blows of the thick rod and banished her to Lingnan.

The most forbidding destination for an exile was Lingnan, the southernmost region of the empire that included Hainan Island and northern Vietnam. Imperial decrees referred to it as that "distant, evil place." Although Chinese had largely settled the region by Tang times, the aborigines remained a constant threat, and frequently attacked the immigrants. The climate of the area was intolerably hot, and periodically suffered devastating typhoons. It was a poisonous land, home of serpent eagles whose flesh was lethal because it ate venomous snakes, and of toxic plants that caused instant death if consumed. The food of the natives did not sit well on the stomachs of the exiles. But the worst of all were Lingnan's noxious miasmas that killed many a northerner condemned there. It was not, of course, the fogs of the damp region that caused men to sicken and die, but the mosquitoes carrying malarial protozoa that thrived in the swamps. One poet declared it unfit for human habitation.

The evil reputation of Lingnan instilled great fear in many northerners. One man had long harbored an obsession that he would suffer exile, could not bear to hear the names of cities in Lingnan, and would close his eyes whenever he came upon a map of southern China. When he became chief minister, he found a chart on the wall of his office that he could not bring himself to look at for several weeks. When he finally glanced at it, he discovered that it was a map of Yai on Hainan Island. His worst fears came to pass in 805, when the throne demoted him to a minor post at Yai, where he soon died, at slightly more than forty years of age.

In exceptional cases, usually political crimes, the condemned might be transported to their places of exile in prisoner vans. Those vehicles probably evolved from mobile cages used for transporting dangerous animals such as tigers, bears, and panthers. Unlike the creature cages, which had bars, the convict carts were crates on wheels, entirely enclosed by planks. The boards were glued or lacquered so that no one could see into them— no doubt to conceal the identity of the prisoner, so that his sympathizers or relatives could not attempt to free him. A hole in the top, as depicted in a seventeenth-century illustration, or perhaps a door, was provided so that food could be given to the prisoner and waste could be removed. Whatever the case, transport by this means was not pleasant. Two Tang princes sent out in prisoner vans did not long survive their journeys. Occasionally, a rebel in the provinces was sent to the capital for execution in such a vehicle. One of them spent thirty-seven days in a convict cart, traveling from Chengdu to the capital in 806.

The objectives of exile were to send offenders far from the capital and the imperial court, to separate them from their clans and hometowns, and to prevent them from performing their sacrificial duties to their ancestors. Both prefectures and the Department of Punition in the capital had to review sentences of exile that county and market commandants imposed.

The gravest of punishments in the Tang was, of course, execution. There were two forms, strangulation and decapitation. According to the law code there were 144 crimes punishable by the former and 89 by the latter. The emperor had to personally approve all executions.

Strangulation was the punishment for lodging an accusation against grandparents or parents with a magistrate, scheming to kidnap and sell a person into slavery, and opening a coffin while desecrating a tomb. Executioners throttled the condemned by placing a noose around the convict's neck and twisting the rope until he suffocated. In Tang China hanging was a means of committing suicide, not a form of capital punishment.

Although strangulation entailed more prolonged pain and suffering, it was preferable to decapitation for most Chinese. They believed that their bodies were gifts from their parents and that it was most disrespectful to their ancestors to die without returning the gift to the grave intact. The behavior of Emperor Daizong perhaps best illustrates that

**Strangulation**

point. While he was heir apparent, the power of the eunuch Li at court appalled him. When he came to the throne, however, he could not publicly execute the eunuch because Li had been instrumental in his accession. So Daizong secretly sent an assassin to slay him. The agent entered the eunuch's home at night and chopped off his head. After he left the mansion, the murderer dropped the head in a privy. Even though the emperor had engineered the death of Li, he retained a sense of propriety. Since the whereabouts of the eunuch's head were unknown, Daizong had a wooden head carved and placed in Li's coffin.

In the capitals most executions took place at the western market because in Chinese cosmology, metal, the executioner's sword, was the element of the west. However, on occasion authorities used the eastern market, post road stations, palace halls, ball fields, and various other sites for that purpose. Nearly all executions were public, in order to warn citizens of the dire consequences that would befall them if they should contemplate committing capital crimes. It is not unlikely that they were also a form of entertainment, spectacles that titillated thrill seekers. After decapitations, the heads were displayed on poles or spears and the bodies thrown on the ground beneath. When local authorities beheaded criminals, they boxed the heads and sent them to the capital to confirm the identity and death of the culprit.

By and large men sentenced to death met their fates silently. However, when the injustice of a judgment was particularly egregious, the convict might create an uproar. In 688 an official in the heir apparent's household was found guilty of plotting rebellion on the basis of a false accusation lodged by one of his slaves. When he arrived in the market, he loudly excoriated Empress Wu and divulged secret evils that had taken place in the palace. Then he seized sticks of firewood from a vendor to assault his executioners. Soldiers of the Gold Bird Guard attacked en masse and slew him. Thereafter, to prevent such embarrassing outbursts, judicial officials stuffed wood balls in the mouths of men about to be executed. The custom persisted until 705.

As always, rank had its privileges. When a high-ranking minister, fifth grade and above, received a death sentence, the throne might grant him a special dispensation by bestowing suicide on him in lieu of imposing strangulation or decapitation. The strong-willed accepted such "gifts" gracefully by bathing, composing themselves, and writing a last state-ment before killing themselves. The weak-willed could not bring them-selves to take their own lives. In 777 a chief minister imprisoned in a county jail at Changan begged the warden to kill him. The man com-plied, taking off his filthy socks and stuffing them down the minister's throat to asphyxiate him. When the emperor did not confer that boon, officials of those ranks still enjoyed some privileges that men of humbler status did not. The law required that their keepers provide them with food and ale (a last meal?) and transport them to the execution grounds in carts.

When the state sentenced a convict to decapitation for rebellion or sedition, it also imposed punishments on his relatives—whether they were guilty or innocent of participating in the crime—by reason of as-sociation. Fathers under the age of seventy-nine and sons over the age of fifteen were strangled. Sons under the age of fifteen, mothers, daugh-ters, wives, concubines, grandfathers, grandsons, brothers, and sisters were enslaved. The women were imprisoned in the Flank Close, and the sons were sent to the Service of the Provost of Agriculture. Uncles and nephews were banished to the farthest reaches of the empire. Finally, the government confiscated all slaves, personal retainers, fields, homes, and movable property owned by the condemned. On occasion the throne also ordered the tombs of their ancestors leveled, and had their coffins destroyed and their bones scattered.

The number of people condemned to strangulation, exile, or slavery by virtue of association with a relative convicted of rebellion could be quite large. In 688 judicial authorities sentenced 5,000 persons in a single district to those punishments because they were related to a Tang prince who revolted against Empress Wu. Only the intervention of a humane governor, who informed the empress that the verdicts were erroneous, saved them.

In early 747 Emperor Illustrious August, who had a strong regard for life, abolished the death penalty. He ordered his officials to refer to the nearest regulation by analogy when sentencing those guilty of crimes calling for execution. Thus, severe scourgings with the thick rod and exile to Lingnan took the place of capital punishment. However, some officials, who apparently did not share the emperor's humane sentiments, resorted to executing criminals by beating them to death. The throne restored the death penalty in the summer of 759 in the wake of the An Lushan rebellion.

There were other forms of punishment besides the five listed at the beginning of the Tang code. The law demanded restitution when the crime involved the destruction of property. Reckless drivers who injured or killed domestic animals, and arsonists had to compensate the injured parties for their losses. For minor infractions the law required mandarins to resign their posts for one year. For more severe offenses the state revoked all of the officials' titles for six years. Some forms of punishment were extralegal. The government fined officials by docking their salaries when fires broke out in their agencies. The throne often demoted mandarins to posts outside the capital, generally for political rather than criminal transgressions. Demotion was actually a mild form of exile, for it did not entail dismissal from all offices. Occasionally the demoted sneaked back into the capital, dressed as women to avoid detection, and restored themselves to the good graces of the throne.

At least two types of capital punishment were extralegal. Throughout the Tang, scourging to death with the thick rod was a common form of execution applied especially in cases of gross corruption. On occasion the throne also employed it to make an example. In the spring of 716 the emperor ordered his brother-in-law beaten to death in front of all his officials for having ambushed and assaulted a man in the lane of a ward at the capital. In that instance the emperor imposed the sentence to serve as an apology to the bureaucratic corps for the misbehavior of his relative. By far the most brutal sort of execution was truncation, cutting in two at the waist with a fodder knife. The condemned, who had committed some crime considered to be particularly treacherous or repugnant, slowly and painfully bled to death.

## CLEMENCY

By modern standards the legal system of the Tang may seem to have been inhumane and discriminatory, but it was also incredibly merciful. Status played a role in the granting of leniency. Except in cases involving the Ten Abominations or the death penalty, the code established an automatic reduction of one degree in the punishment for crimes committed by relatives of the emperor; men of great talent, virtue, and achievement; and mandarins ranked seventh grade or higher. Criminals under fifteen or over sixty-eight years of age and the impaired were exempt from all punishments except the death penalty; those under seven or over eighty-eight were exempt even from the death penalty. The impaired included the mentally ill. Those exclusions did not, however, apply to those sentenced by reason of association with convicts condemned to decapitation. The law also conferred on all of those groups immunity from judicial torture and the right to redeem their punishments by payments of copper.

Common criminals who did not enjoy such privileges could expect to have their sentences nullified or commuted by one of the numerous pardons that emperors bestowed as acts of benevolence. The throne absolved individuals; groups of individuals, such as officials forced against their will to serve rebels, defeated barbarians, or soldiers serving on military campaigns; classes of convicts such as exiles; and all offenders in a specific district. Emperors also regularly reduced the sentences of criminals, commuting the death penalty to exile and exile to penal servitude.

The most generous of such indulgences were the Great Acts of Grace that the throne bestowed on special occasions, such as the emperor's performance of rites, the conferral of imperial titles, the installation of heirs apparent, and the celebration of military victories. At those times the emperor ascended to a hall atop a southern gate of the palace early in the morning. In the street below, a grand assembly of officials attired in their court vestments stood in orderly rows, the civil to the left and the military to the right. Beyond them waited a throng of the capital's citizenry, their carriages and horses choking the roads that led to the gate.

After the emperor arrived, an official led shackled prisoners from jails in the capital, often more than a thousand, into the square before the gate. As soon as a drummer caught sight of them, he beat a tattoo of 1,000 strokes on his drum, tossing his drumstick with each stroke. When the prisoners reached their appointed stations, they turned to face the emperor, setting the stage for the climatic event of the day.

A tall pole, some sixty-seven feet high, rose in front of the gate. Affixed to the top of it was a small platform from which hung scarlet ropes that fell to the ground. The Gold Chicken, a statue five feet tall with a head made of gold and a silk banner fluttering from its beak, perched on the platform. With all eyes fixed on them, young men from the Instruction Ward, a court school for training acrobats and other entertainers, seized the scarlet ropes trailing from the platform and shinnied upward. The first lad to reach the platform seized the banner and brought it down. He received a reward called "chicken feed," an increase in his monthly salary by three piculs (more than one and a half bushels) of grain.

Afterward an official stepped forward and proclaimed the Great Act of Grace, reading the text aloud to the assembled multitude. The main clause of the amnesty probably read something like the following:

All those who have committed offenses prior to dawn of the twenty-third day in the month of January in the year seven-hundred and five—whether their crimes are heavy or light, whether they are subject to capital punishment or lesser forms of punition, whether they have already been revealed or remain as yet concealed, whether they have been adjudicated or not—convicts incarcerated and prisoners present, are forthwith amnestied and pardoned.

As the last words of the edict resounded in the square, wardens undid the fetters binding their prisoners and released them to go their separate ways. In the provinces governors also had the Great Acts of Grace read and liberated inmates in their jails—without, however, the pole-climbing spectacle.

In principle the amnesties pardoned and freed all convicts, emptying all prisons throughout the empire and nullifying the sentences of all criminals from murderers to petty thieves. They also forgave offenders whose cases had not yet come to trial or whose crimes had not yet come to the attention of the authorities before the hour of the day stipulated in the decree. In the latter event the perpetrators had 100 days to turn themselves in and confess if they wished to receive absolution.

In reality provisions in the Great Acts of Grace often excluded convicts guilty of committing one of the Ten Abominations and political criminals. Occasionally they also denied clemency to murderers, exiles, corrupt officials, robbers, and others. Furthermore, there were articles in the law code that circumscribed the sweeping pardons of the amnesties. For example, sorcerers who employed *gu* poison did not enjoy full exonerations. They received a reduction in their punishments from death to exile. Finally, although the Tang issued a Great Act of Grace every twenty-two months, on the average, the distribution was uneven. One emperor bestowed three in one year, and another granted none for ten years. A convict's chances of being fully pardoned depended on the inclination of the sovereign on the throne at the time.

Nevertheless, the vast majority of criminals, those who had not committed a heinous or political crime, could expect some modification of their sentences, either by pardon or by commutation. The convicts who benefited most from imperial indulgences in the Tang were those condemned to penal servitude or exile, because their sentences were the longest. The extent of clemency in the Tang was far greater than that in modern times.

## VENGEANCE

In a society where false accusations were common, nobles or mandarins abused their power to subvert the law, and the courts failed to apprehend culprits, injustices occurred. Since the victims of such inequities or their relatives could find no remedies in public courts, they occasionally resorted to private vengeance. In the early seventh century, a man named Wang got in a brawl with a fellow villager name Li. In the course of the struggle, Li killed Wang. Wang's wife reported the crime to the county court, but Li had fled his home and could not be found or arrested. Some twenty years later, after the founding of the Tang, Li no longer feared punishment because times had changed, and therefore the new officials would not be interested in the legal matters of the previous regime. Furthermore, he believed that Wang's son, who had been five years old at the time of his father's death, was too humble to exact revenge. So he went to the prefecture to confess. The son waylaid the murderer. He pulled a knife from his sleeve and stabbed Li. Then Wang cut open his stomach, excised the liver and heart, and ate them. Afterward he went to the governor of the prefecture and turned himself in. Mandarins there sentenced him to death, but the emperor issued a special decree pardoning him because of his filial devotion to his father. Vengeance based on one's duty to avenge one's father, a principle much esteemed in ancient China, did not always spare the murderers from execution, however. When the sons of a provincial governor slew the official responsible for his execution in 735, the emperor would not exonerate them, and had them executed. In Tang times there were also men, knights-errant, who murdered to settle scores for others—not for money, but because their sense of justice compelled them to right wrongs.

# 10

# Sickness and Health

## ILLNESS

In the early seventh century the mother of Wei, a wealthy man, suddenly lost her sight. The son consulted a fortune-teller, who told him, "Next year someone wearing black garb will come from the east on the first day of the third moon. His therapy is guaranteed to heal your mother." On the appointed day a stranger wearing a short robe woven from coarse, black thread approached Wei's home. Wei invited the man in and spread a lavish feast for him. The man clad in black said, "Your humble servant knows nothing of medicine, but I do know how to make plows. I will make one for you." He took an ax and wandered around the dwelling, looking for wood to fashion the plow shaft. He found a crooked branch on a mulberry tree that had grown over a well, so he cut it down to make the plow. At that moment the mother's vision suddenly returned. Her blindness was caused by the mulberry's crooked branches and leaves covering the mouth of the well.

According to ancient Chinese thought, the causes of diseases were supernatural, natural, or a combination of both. They were also internal, external, or neither (overindulgence). In general, folklore and religion were the sources for beliefs in supernatural agents. Observations of the environment and human beings were the bases for theories that pathogens originated in nature. The story above is a curious combination of the two. Supernatural agents that caused maladies included gods, ghosts, demons, and magic.

**Gods**

Merchant Wang, who accumulated a fortune of 10 million coppers, had a daughter thirteen or fourteen years of age. She was beautiful and clever, but two polyps (swollen tissue) more than an inch long hung down from each of her nostrils. They resembled bath beans, and had roots that were as fine as hemp thread. Whenever she bumped them, excruciating pain shot through her heart and marrow. Her father spent millions of cash to cure his daughter, but nothing worked.

One day an Indian monk came to his gate begging for food, and said to Wang, "I know your daughter has a strange illness. I can cure it. Will you let me have a look at her?" The merchant let the monk in to examine his girl. The monk took out a pure white herbal powder and blew it into the daughter's nostrils. A moment later he plucked off the polyps. They exuded a small amount of yellow fluid, but the girl suffered no pain whatsoever. The merchant tried to give the Indian 100 ounces of gold as a reward for his services, but the monk refused, saying, "I'm a man who practices the faith, and cannot possibly accept your munificent gift. I only wish to ask for the flesh I removed." He left after receiving the polyps, departing with such speed that he seemed to fly.

When the monk was five or six wards away, a handsome young man rode up on a white steed and knocked on Wang's gate. The visitor asked, "Did a western monk come here just now?" The merchant quickly invited the youth in and told him all about his encounter with the mendicant. The lad sighed unhappily and said, "My horse stumbled a little. Consequently, I arrived after the monk left." Wang, bewildered, asked what the reason for the sigh was. The young man replied, "God on High lost two of his divine physicians. He recently learned that they were hiding in your daughter's nose. I am a celestial, and came here to apprehend the doctors in obedience to the god's command. I will receive a reprimand because the monk seized the physicians [the polyps] first."

Disease-causing deities need not be external. According to the Taoists three internal gods, literally "the Three Corpses," reside in the body: one in the head, one in the chest, and one in the abdomen. They record the sins that the individual commits. Once every sixty days they ascend to heaven during the night and present scrolls listing the transgressions to celestial officials. The heavenly mandarins then prescribe appropriate punishments in the form of illnesses that the three deities inflict when they return to the person's body. The head god caused heaviness of the head, dim vision, deafness, loss of teeth, and the like. The chest god produced burning in the heart, a muddled mind, constant forgetfulness, and so on. The abdominal god caused hundreds of diseases. One could avoid contracting the illnesses inflicted by the Three Corpses by staying awake the entire night of their departure. They could leave and report only when the person was asleep. If one dared to ingest cinnabar (mer-

| Head | Chest | Abdomen |

**The Three Corpses**

curic sulfide) and magic mushrooms, the action of the drugs would destroy the three gods. The Buddhists also had a notion that bad behavior was the source of disease. They believed that illness was caused by evil karma, sin. However, according to their tenets, the transgressions that produced ailments could have been committed in previous incarnations. The afflicted was not conscious of such misdeeds, but was punished for them anyway. That doctrine explained why infants were born with congenital deformities and why the upright suffered even though they had done no wrong.

One morning courtier Zhou was making his way to his office in the palace. On the way a physician saw a ghost, who had **Ghosts** pinched the courtier's head between its fingers, drag the man through a gate. Two ghosts carrying staves followed the pair. The doctor reported the matter to Empress Wu, who ordered a servitor to look into the matter. He reported that since there was no business requiring his attention at his office, Zhou had returned to his room after eating lunch. During the afternoon he had gone to the privy. In a while his chief assistant began to wonder what was taking him so long, so he went to see what was the matter. He discovered that his superior had fallen flat on his face in the outhouse. The man's eyes stared straight ahead, he could not speak, and spittle dribbled from his mouth. The empress consulted her physicians about the case. She asked, "How long can this go on?" They replied, "If the progress of the disease is slow, he will live three days. If it is fast, he will die in one day." She provided a brocade quilt to cover the courtier and a litter to carry him home. He died in the middle of the night.

One of the oldest characters for disease depicts a man lying on a bed with an arrow at his side. The notion that contracting a disease was akin to receiving a wound from a weapon was obviously very old in China, dating from the second millennium B.C.E. There is no answer to the question of who fired the missile in that period, but the identity of the malefactor is quiet clear in the folklore of the Tang, if not earlier. Hong claimed that he could see ghosts and converse with them. When he was in the south, he saw a huge spirit carrying a lance. A retinue of subordinate specters followed in his trail. The ghost seer was terrified, so he left the road. After the large ghost passed by, Hong accosted one of the minor spirits and asked about the spear that the large ghost was carrying. It replied, "He uses the lance to kill people. Everyone dies when the spear pierces his belly." Hong asked, "Is there no remedy for the ailment?" "Rub the blood of a black chicken on the stomach, and it will cure the disease," said the specter. The ghost seer then inquired, "Where are you going?" "We're on our way to Jingzhou and Yangzhou," replied the ghost. Soon afterward an epidemic of stomach ailments spread throughout the two districts, and everyone died except those whom Hong had taught. He instructed people to kill black chickens and rub the blood on their abdomens. Eight or nine out of ten that he taught, survived.

Ghosts could also heal the sick, according to Chinese folk beliefs. Mr. Liu's wife was seriously ill. One night before Liu fell asleep, a white-haired woman three feet tall stepped from the shadows, into the light under his lantern. She said to him, "I am the only one who can cure your wife's illness. Why haven't you prayed to me?" Liu had always been very proper, so he cursed her. The ghost folded her hands and exclaimed, "He won't repent! He won't repent!" Then she vanished. Liu's wife was suddenly struck with heart pains and appeared to be on the verge of dying. Her husband had no choice but to pray to the old woman. When he finished speaking, she appeared again. Liu saluted her and invited her to sit. She asked for a cup of tea, then faced the sun, as if praying, turned her head and ordered Liu to pour the tea down his wife's throat. As soon as the tea flowed into her mouth, his wife's pain subsided. Thereafter the ghost often visited Liu's house, so his family no longer feared her.

**Demons**   Taoists saw the world as a space besieged by homicidal demons, most of whom dispatched their victims by propagating diseases. The devils came in all shapes and sizes. There were monsters with two, three, or twelve heads; three legs; vertically arranged eyes; red noses; and three faces with one eye. The fiends executed their murderous missions in a variety of ways. Grass demons hid in the fields to poison people who came to gather vegetables. Drowning devils, three feet, two inches tall, slew men in rivers. Female, "red rope" monsters killed male children in the spring, female children in the autumn, the young in the winter, and the old in the summer. White-headed giants who had black faces and white hair, and stood thirty feet tall, spread ninety types of disease. Black-footed titans, thirty-six feet tall, changed themselves into birds that flew onto the roofs of people's homes and infected them with acute illnesses. The fiends often wielded red staves, striking their victims, who then sickened and died. They attacked only evil men who were unbelievers, the godless, slanderers of Taoist priests, and maligners of scriptures. Buddhists also had their demons. They imported the *yaksa*, flying Hindu deities, from India. The *yaksa* were eaters of the living and inflicted all sorts of injuries on humans.

Madam Su was married to Mr. Li, who was more interested in one of his maidservants than in her. The servant maliciously **Magic** asked a sorcerer to bewitch Su. The wizard buried a talisman in a pile of manure on Li's property. He then hid seven effigies of the wife, each a foot long and made from multicolored cloth, inside a cavity that he dug in the eastern wall of the home and covered with clay. Sometime later, after the maid had passed away, and Madam Su was a widow living alone in the house, the effigies appeared and haunted the dwelling. As a result she became extremely ill. For a year she invited exorcists to expel the evil spirits, but to no avail. Nevertheless, the wizards persisted, and managed to capture one of the effigies. It squirmed in their hands. They struck it with their swords, and it gushed blood on the ground. Then the wizards burned it on a pile of firewood. As the thing went up in smoke, the other effigies appeared and wailed. Some stood on the ground, and others flew above. In half a year the sorcerers caught all but one of the remaining effigies. The last one escaped and dived into the manure pile. Madam Su then directed more than 100 men to excavate the heap, and at a depth of seven or eight feet they unearthed the talisman. It provided a clue that led the men to the hiding place of the last effigy. After they disposed of it, Madam Su recovered her health and nothing untoward happened to her again.

Proponents of the theory that illness sprang from natural causes contended that the internal state of the mind **Natural Causes** and the body was the critical factor in bad health, and that environmental forces, not spirits, were the external agents that attacked the body. They saw the body as a repository of vital energies and essences. Good health depended on preserving and nurturing those life forces. If a person was moderate in his lifestyle and took measures to conserve inner resources, then his skin became an impenetrable husk that prevented energy and essence from leaking out, and an impregnable bulwark that thwarted attacks from external disease-causing agents. They contended that anyone could expect to live for 120 years in good health if he followed the proper practices. Otherwise, people would suffer from ailments, decrepitude, or senility. They would die prematurely.

According to the advocates of the naturalistic conception of disease, the "nurturing of life" and promotion of longevity required the conservation of at least three things. The most important was *qi*, the life force within the body. The original meaning of the word was vapor, steam rising from a cooking pot. At some point it assumed an enormous importance in the thinking of the ancient Chinese. It became a cosmic force that controlled the environment as well as the body. In man it was breath (also thought of as energy). It was the first thing given to a human being at conception and the last thing to depart from him at death. Between those two poles *qi* circulated throughout the body, and good health depended on its uninterrupted flow. It also manifested itself as yin and yang, as well as the five elements (wood, fire, metal, water, and earth). The second was saliva. The Taoists thought of it as the "jade liquor." It was the sweet dew that watered the internal organs, moistened the torso and limbs, and enabled *qi* and blood to circulate through the various conduits of the body. Therefore, one should not spit, to prevent expending it. The last was essence, blood and semen. Blood circulated through the body in the vascular system and, of course, had to be preserved lest death result. Semen (menstrual discharge in women) was a nourishing fluid particularly important for vitalizing the brain. Ideally, an adept striving to prolong his life should not eject it.

Diseases resulted when those resources were depleted or obstructed. Depletion, a disease in itself, resulted from overindulgence. On the one hand, excessive manual labor caused perspiration, drained away yang energy, and therefore led to an excess of yin. It also caused fluid retention by obstructing the body's orifices. On the other hand, reading too many books and immoderate preoccupation with deep thoughts muddled the brain, caused tumors, and induced melancholy. Those conditions might ultimately lead to the complete loss of the mind and a shortening of the life span. Loss of eyesight resulted from playing board games and gambling incessantly, or from inordinate sexual intercourse. A Tang writer recommended that people thirty-nine years or older should keep their eyes shut unless they had some urgent matter requiring their attention. Unrestrained sexual intercourse exhausted the body, weakening the joints so that one could not lift his limbs to his head. It could even cause death.

The notion of excess causing deficiency and disease in the body also had a psychological basis in traditional Chinese thought. Medical authorities contended that strong emotions, five in number, were the roots of ill health. They specified the maladies that resulted from such immoderate passions:

1. Joy: rapid heartbeat, insomnia, and mental bewilderment
2. Anger: flushed face, stuffiness in the chest, hypochondria, headache, dizziness, and coma
3. Grief or sadness: difficulty in swallowing, emaciation, weakness, restlessness, and shortness of breath
4. Anxiety: poor appetite, anorexia, indigestion, flatulence, and loose stools or diarrhea
5. Fear or terror: irritability, incontinence of urination or bowel movements, and nocturnal emissions.

Inordinate desire, linked to the senses in traditional medicine, also caused outflow of energy and essence, resulting in disease. Clearly, a tranquil mind was the foundation for nurturing life. It sealed the skin, forming a means of defense against external threats.

When depletion and imbalance enfeebled the body, they weakened its armor, permitting external forces to attack, invade, and wreak havoc. The naturalists established six categories of external pathogens, based on climate, seasons, and geography, that created imbalances of yin and yang.

1. Wind (yang that damages internal yin): dizziness, fainting, convulsions, tremors, and numbness
2. Cold (yin that injures internal yang): chills, headaches, and general aching (winter, north)
3. Heat (yang that harms internal yin): fevers, thirst, and sweating (summer, south)
4. Damp (yin that damages internal yang): swellings, lassitude, heaviness in limbs, and joint pains (spring, east)
5. Dry (yang that injures internal yin): dry throat and skin, coughing, sore throat, and constipation (autumn, west)
6. Fire (yang that harms internal yin): flushed face, bloodshot eyes, and inflammations.

The notion here was that unseasonable cold in the summer, excessive rains in the autumn, and so forth had catastrophic effects on one whose body was vulnerable. Similarly, the consumption of foods associated with the spring in the autumn, the wearing of heavy clothes in the summer, and other habits of unprepared people invited disease.

The concept of depletion and imbalance had its limitations. It was difficult to prove that a man could make himself invulnerable to external diseases when he took ill even though he was prudent in his lifestyle and took measures to strengthen his internal resources. Furthermore, the naturalists themselves recognized pathogens that attacked the body without regard to the state of its health. Parasites were one of them.

Chinese of the medieval epoch had no knowledge of bacteria or viruses, having no microscope to observe them. They were familiar, however, with parasites living in the human body. One of their conceptions of pests was partially supernatural, or at least imaginary, and partially natural. It was the belief in the "Nine Vermin."

The "ambush worm" was azure and four inches long. It had whiskers and teeth. The pest gnawed on human blood and was fond of eating flesh. It made men feeble and short of breath, caused excessive urination, and inflicted pain in the viscera. It traveled up and down the torso, agitating the chest and ribs. If the affliction from this parasite reached a critical state, the victim would die unless he ingested a mixture of alum and cinnabar (mercuric sulfide).

"Revolving (screw) worms" were black and one foot long. They came in pairs, male and female, and resided above and below the heart, where they drank its blood. Screwworms caused heart pains, rapid breathing, heaviness in the limbs, and difficulty in urination. If they penetrated the heart or spleen, the victim would experience unbearable pain, and die. To kill them required writing a talisman with cinnabar ink and swallowing it with mercury in two gulps.

"White inchworms" were one to five inches long. They caused men to be fond of eating raw grains, tea, fish, and fruit, as well as charred meat. The vermin drained the viscera, emaciated the body, induced excessive discharges of phlegm and mucus, and imparted a yellow tinge to the face. They gnawed into the stomach, inflicting unbearable pain, engendered dysentery, and displaced the rectum. A mixture of mercury and cinnabar would exterminate them.

"Flesh pests" were black and looked like rotten plums. They fed on human blood and exhausted men's *qi*. The bugs weakened the muscles and back, caused intense itching on the skin, and dried out the flesh. They induced a lust for women and a hunger for bloody meat. Swallowing cinnabar in two gulps would annihilate them.

"Lung bugs" were azure and resembled silkworms or red ants. They fed on human semen and energy, causing excessive phlegm and coughing, loss of hair, a lackluster complexion, and weak respiration. One would die prematurely from a deficiency of breath if one did not take a powder of toxic minerals to kill them.

"Stomach worms" look like earthworms. They consume the food ingested by people and so make them famished. The vermin empty the viscera, reduce the skeleton, parch the lips, block nasal passages, produce sores in the mouth, and induce vomiting when drinking ale. Absorb the energies of the sun and moon through visualization during meditation to dissolve the worms.

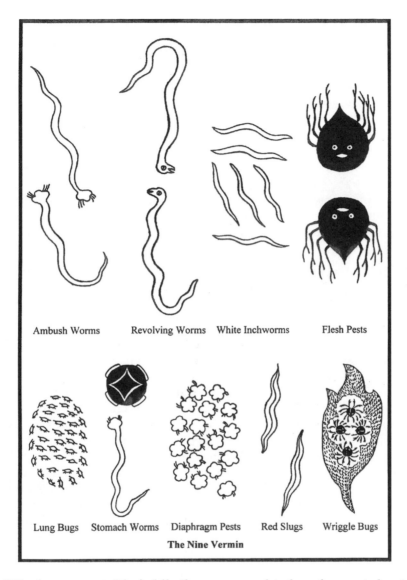

Ambush Worms Revolving Worms White Inchworms Flesh Pests

Lung Bugs Stomach Worms Diaphragm Pests Red Slugs Wriggle Bugs

**The Nine Vermin**

"Diaphragm pests" befuddle the senses and induce frequent sleeping with nightmares of traveling to distant places on boats that sink or falling from peaks while climbing mountains. This is a case of yin disturbing yang. Obtain some black sulfide of mercury and take it. Rub blood on your flesh and you will live.

"Red slugs" sapped men's energy. They darkened vision and deafened the ears with ringing. The pests caused itching in the genitals as well as sores, swellings, paralysis, ulcers, skeletal pain, and rumbling in the gut. The Drug for Soothing the Soul would melt the slugs.

"Wriggle bugs" were black and had countless small mites crawling around them. The pests caused sores, itching, ringworm, ulcers, hemorrhoids, and rheumatism. They fed on the teeth, which then fell out, and they caused madness.

Only three of the nine parasites can be identified with actual worms that infest human beings: the revolving worms, white inchworms, and wriggle bugs. The most familiar are the first two: the roundworm and the tapeworm, respectively. The illustrations shown here apparently were first drawn in the Tang dynasty.

Another type of worm hid in the teeth and caused toothaches. To extract it, Tang physicians placed the seeds of black henbane, leeks, or onions in a bottle with red-hot copper coins. When the seeds smoked, they withdrew the smoke with a bamboo tube and blew it on the infected tooth. The pain ceased immediately.

## HEALERS AND HEALTH CARE

There were several kinds of healers in Tang times. The oldest were the shamans, medicine men or women. They were exorcists who had been practicing their occult arts since the dawn of Chinese civilization. They possessed magical powers that they wielded to cure illnesses as well as to make or stop rain and purge palaces of noxious vapors, serpents, and other pests. The character for shaman, a pictograph depicting a dancer with feathers or some other ornaments attached beneath his or her arms, appears in the most ancient Chinese script, found on the shoulder bones of cattle or the shells of tortoises. Dancing was an essential element of the shaman's art throughout the ages, perhaps because it enabled the exorcist to put himself or herself into a trance.

A class of true physicians emerged by 600 B.C.E. Unlike their predecessors they were distinctly secular doctors who thought of diseases as springing from natural causes, not from demonic possession, and whose treatment of maladies normally did not entail much in the way of ritual or magic. In the Tang there were two sorts, the public (employed by the state) and the private. The public practiced their healing arts in the capitals and the provinces. The Office of Supreme Medicine in Changan and Luoyang had twenty doctors with a staff of 100 medics and forty students. It also had ten practitioners of acupuncture, four master masseurs, and sixteen practitioners of massage. The agency kept records of the number of cures effected by physicians and medics. How well they performed determined how many merits they acquired. The sum of the merits that a man earned was the basis for promoting him if it was high enough. The service also had masters of apothecary gardens, who were in charge of planting and collecting herbs according to the proper seasons. The state set aside forty-two acres of the best land in the capital for such gardens. Young men between the ages of fifteen and nineteen cultivated them. There were 656 officially recognized medicinal substances, which included minerals and animal products. In addition to the resources close at hand in the capitals, the prefectures also annually sent medical materials from their districts as tribute. The best of them went to the Office of Supreme Medicine.

The Office of Supreme Medicine was also a college that offered instruction in four areas, for each of which there was one professor and one assistant professor. The first department was general medicine, that covered the materia medica, acupuncture, and diagnosis by taking pulse. The instructor divided his students into groups for learning five specializations: eleven students concentrated on the healing of the body; three on the treatment of tumors and abscesses; three on children's ailments (pediatrics); two on the care of eyes, ears, mouth and teeth; and one on an unidentified subject. The course of study for the first specialization was seven years, five years each for the second and third, and two years each for the last two. The second department was acupuncture. The professor taught students about the conduits of *qi*, arteries, body orifices, and acupuncture points. Students had to master three texts and take an eight-part examination on them. The third field was massage/ exercise, and had fifteen students. The instructor trained students in the art of "guiding and stretching," a Taoist form of self-massage combined with exercises. According to the wisdom of the time, it was capable of healing eight types of illnesses by eliminating excessive accumulations of *qi* in internal organs and the extremities. The fourth was the department of exorcism, literally "incantations and interdictions." Its professor taught five methods of exorcism, including visualizations, the Pace of Yu, and mudras (hand gestures).

Early in its history the throne took a keen interest in the health of its subjects. In 629 the emperor established medical schools at the seats of all prefectures. By 723 the system had fallen apart in remote districts, and people of the lower classes who took ill had no one to turn to for help. Therefore, Emperor Illustrious August reestablished positions for professors of medicine in each of the empire's prefectures and ordered all of the governors to keep copies of the materia medica and *The Collection of One-Hundred and One Certified Prescriptions on Hand*. In 739 he ordered the governors of prefectures with more than 100,000 households to admit twenty students to their schools, and those with less than 100,000 to admit twelve. He directed all of the students to tour their districts and treat the ill. At some point in that period Illustrious August also instituted positions for assistant professors of medicine in prefectures. He charged them with conducting examinations of the students and explaining the procedures for touring and curing to them. The system apparently suffered greatly during and after the rebellion of An

Lushan. In 796 the throne ordered governors of prefectures to select the best qualified physicians to fill vacant district medical professorships. The emperor, however, took no action with regard to finding personnel to fill the assistant professorships.

The contents of medical examinations during the first half of the Tang are not clear. However, in 759 they included questions on the materia medica, diagnosis by taking the pulse, treatment of diseases involving fevers, and miscellaneous medical procedures for curing ailments. Acceptable answers to seven out of ten questions was a passing mark. Those who successfully answered the required number of queries entered the national medical system, and those who failed were sent home.

Emperor Illustrious August also strove to supply his subjects with the proper remedies for their ailments. In 723 he disseminated throughout the empire a five-chapter collection, *Prescriptions for the Comprehensive Relief of Sufferers*, which he purportedly compiled himself. In 746 he ordered senior officials in counties and prefectures to select the most important formulas in the text and record them on large boards. After completing the task, the officials were to erect the boards on main roads of villages and urban wards so that the people had access to the prescriptions. The emperor sent out inspectors to ensure that the local mandarins carried out his command and made no errors. In 796 one of his successors published another edition of the book, also in five chapters.

There was a set of ethical precepts, set forth in a great medical compendium of the seventh century, that served as a guide for the conduct of secular physicians in the Tang. First and foremost, a doctor must be compassionate. He should dedicate himself to relieving the suffering of all mankind by curing illnesses. The doctor should not reject a patient on the grounds that he was noble or base, poor or rich, old or young, Chinese or outlander, intelligent or simple. Second, a physician should be single-minded in his determination to cure the sick. He should be on call at all times of the night or day, in cold weather or hot, on good roads or bad, when hungry, thirsty, or tired. Third, the doctor must maintain proper decorum. He should talk little, criticize even less, never jest or gossip, refrain from flaunting his reputation, and never disparage the skills of other doctors. Fourth, a doctor should not strive for material rewards to the detriment of his humane service. Fifth, he should be learned. He must master not only medical works but also the Confucian classics, histories, and works of philosophers. Sixth, he should be precise and accurate in his judgments.

Taoists also played an important role in medicine, especially preventive medicine. From 300 to 700 they made great contributions to compiling and editing the materia medica, as well as to assembling collections of formulas for prescriptions. They were the chief theoreticians and practitioners of massage/aerobics, visualization, and dances

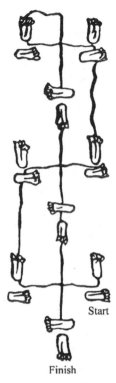

Start

Finish

**The Pace of Yu**

such as the Pace of Yu, which were among the fields incorporated into the curriculum of the Office of Supreme Medicine. Visualization was a kind of meditation in which the adept conjured up the images of the deities residing in his viscera in order to fix them in place, seal the body to prevent the escape of vital resources, and circulate *qi*. The Pace of Yu was a dance that could expel all demonic and noxious entities that caused diseases within the body. Some of the Taoists' exorcistic techniques evolved from the arts of shamanism. However, their particular forte was preventive medicine: breathing exercises, aerobics, dietetic regimens, and sexual therapies.

The Buddhist clergy does not appear to have played much of a role as physicians during the Tang. They were, however, caregivers. Impelled by their devotion to the rule of compassion, they operated Fields of Compassion that not only offered treatment and medicines to the sick, but also cared for the orphaned, aged, and destitute. They used the income from monastic estates to fund those institutions. In the early years of the eighth century, Empress Wu appointed secular officials to take charge of the foundations. The men who served in those posts were unscrupulous.

They took advantage of their positions to make a profit for themselves. Furthermore, under their leadership the Fields of Compassion became havens for outlaws. Later, one of Emperor Illustrious August's officials recommended that he abolish the institutions, then reconsidered and suggested placing the Buddhist clergy in control of them again. The emperor declined to accept either proposal, and apparently government commissioners continued to manage them for some time.

During the persecution of Buddhism in 845, the defrocking of the clergy and the confiscation of monastic estates left the Fields of Compassion without managers or funds to maintain their charitable work. A prominent minister, fearing that the poor and sick would have no one to appeal to for assistance, proposed that the state take them over. He suggested that their names be changed to Wards for Nurturing the Sick, and that officials of the capitals and prefectures select men of reputable conduct and absolute honesty to take charge of the foundations. He also recommended that the state allocate the income from lands it had seized from the church to the wards: 140 acres for those in the two capitals, 98 acres for large prefectures, and 70 acres for smaller districts. The emperor approved the proposal, and the state assumed full control of the charitable institutions.

There were also medical missionaries among the Buddhist monks. One of them, who died in 654, took up residence in the Lepers' Ward at a city on the Yangtze River. There he tended the sick, sucking the pus from their abscesses and bathing them. He also preached to them. Compassion and spreading the doctrine went hand in hand.

Occasionally, a faith healer appears in Tang literature. In the late seventh century a young man named Yang, who was more than nineteen years of age, was working as a hired laborer at the Mount Wen Abbey. He had a daydream in which a Taoist deity appeared to him and said, "My sanctuary is in ruins. If you rebuild it for me, I will endow you with the power to heal all illnesses." When Yang woke, he was delighted. He tested his therapeutic powers, and found that there was no malady that he could not cure. A village chief had a swelling on his back the size of a fist. The laborer cut it with a knife, and the chief recovered in a few days. Yang's cures brought in 10,000 coppers a day and enabled him to reconstruct the deity's hall at the abbey. When it was completed, his therapeutic powers gradually faded.

Finally, there were quacks who deluded the masses with trickery. In the seventh century Liu the Dragon's Son made a gold dragon head to which he attached a sheep's intestine full of honeyed water. He tucked the dragon head up his sleeve. Whenever Liu gathered a crowd, he would pull out the dragon head and declare, "The holy dragon head spews water that will cure all the illnesses of those who drink it." Then he twisted the sheep's gut hidden beneath his clothes, and the honeyed water flowed out of the dragon's mouth for the credulous to drink. After he dispensed his miraculous elixir, some of his henchmen would falsely claim that they had been cured. Subsequently, Liu committed sedition, and fled when his crime came to light. After a long time, arresting officers finally caught him, and executed him in the market along with more than ten of his cohorts.

## TREATMENT

To determine what sort of treatment he would use for an ailing patient, a Chinese physician made a diagnosis on the basis of four methods. First he conducted a visual inspection of the sufferer's physical appearance—face, tongue, lips, and teeth—to find signs of disease. Besides looking for obvious manifestations of a pathological condition, such as ulcers, tumors, rashes, swellings, and the like, he watched for abnormal skin colorations that indicated problems in an organ. For example, a bluish tinge indicated a dysfunction in the liver and a red tinge, in the heart. He checked facial expressions that reflected suffering. In the early seventh century a disease that caused swellings struck a preeminent official, so the emperor called in a physician to make a diagnosis. After looking the patient over, the doctor declared that he would die at noon eleven days later. The minister expired precisely on schedule. A diagnosis was sometimes a prognosis as well.

Second, the doctor carried out an auditory and olfactory examination. He listened to the patient's breathing and voice. The physician was interested in detecting coughing, panting, or wheezing, which were symptoms of lung diseases. A feeble voice or delirious speech indicated debilitating illness or madness, respectively. He also took notice of foul body odor, bad breath, and malodorous feces. Some amateurs went to repulsive extremes with regard to the latter examination. In 692 Guo Ba, a sycophantic subordinate of Censor Wei, who was abed with an illness, paid a visit to inquire after his superior's health. Distressed and alarmed by Wei's appearance, Guo asked to see his stools. After tasting them, Guo declared, "If your excrement had been sweet, then you would probably have had no chance for a cure. However, its flavor is bitter, so you will certainly recover."

Third, the doctor interrogated the patient about his symptoms. Aside from questions about pains and other problems, there were inquiries about dreams because they were supposed to reflect the state of internal organs. When yin was at its peak of power, one had terrifying dreams of wading through water. Conversely, when yang was at its strongest, the patient had visions of conflagrations.

Last, he took the patient's pulse. The Chinese system of palpation was far more complex than that of the West. There were three points on each wrist that the physician felt simultaneously with three of his fingers to make a diagnosis. From the throb—superficial or deep, fast or slow—at each of the six points the doctor could determine the state of internal organs, ascertain what the illness was, and judge whether the ailment was life-threatening or not. Medical authorities considered pulse-taking to be the most important tool for detecting illness. All others were subordinate to it.

Taoist Wang was skilled at making diagnoses on the basis of pulse, and was able to determine the time of a man's death as well as his length of life. When called in to examine the son of a government minister who had suddenly taken ill, he spent a long time taking the young man's pulse. Afterward Wang declared that the patient was not suffering from any affliction, boiled some powdered drugs, and gave them to the son, who recovered. The father asked about the ailment, and the physician replied that it was a case of food poisoning from eating a carp that had no gills. The father did not believe that, so he ordered his retainers to eat a hash made from carp without gills. They all became sick.

Healers had many options open to them for treating ailments. With the exception of Indian methods introduced by the Buddhists, all of them were indigenous and had developed in China over many centuries.

**Acupuncture**   According to the theory of acupuncture, the body contains a network of invisible conduits, analogous to arteries or the nervous system, through which *qi* flows continuously. The system consists of twelve major channels that run under the surface of the skin from the extremities to the head or chest, and a web of minor branches connecting neighboring channels. Along the course of the channels there are minute cavities or pores that serve as regulators of the *qi*'s current. Initially, the medical canon identified 365 points, but by the Tang the number had grown to 670.

The major theory of acupuncture's salutary effects is that it keeps *qi* circulating in the body's network of conduits. Ill health occurs when the energy encounters impediments, and death results when it stops flowing completely. Ailments arise when an agent, such as cold, enters the tracts and obstructs or retards the current. That causes an imbalance in the system, part of which then has a surplus of *qi* and part of which has a deficit of it. A physician can restore the normal rate of flow and redress imbalances in the network by inserting needles into the cavities or points situated along the ducts. In the Tang there were nine varieties of needles that served different purposes:

1. The chisel (1.6 inches long): for soothing fevers in the head or body
2. The round (1.6 inches): for dissipating *qi* in joints and tissue
3. The spearhead (3.5 inches): for expelling noxious *qi*

**Acupuncture Needles**

4. The lance point (1.6 inches): for treating abscesses, fever, or bleeding

5. The probe (2.5 inches): for ministering to large carbuncles exuding pus

6. The round and sharp (1.6 inches): for attending to carbuncles or acute paralysis

7. The hair (3.6 inches): for alleviating chills, aches, or paralysis in the arms

8. The long (7 inches): for contracting deep-seated *qi* or persistent paralysis

9. The large or fire (4 inches): for reducing excess *qi* in the joints.

Actually, the uses of the needles were far more numerous than indicated here. When the physician applied his needle, he might heat it before insertion, preferably over the flame of a candle so it would not leave a black scar. No doubt that precaution also prevented infections.

Traditional medical authorities attributed a host of therapeutic benefits to the use of acupuncture. Its advantages included the healing of diseases and disabilities, relief of pain, alleviation of symptoms, and mitigation of emotional disturbances. A list of maladies that it was supposed to be effective in treating during the Tang would include the following (asterisks mark those that modern Chinese physicians still apply their needles to):

1. *Malaria, *epilepsy, *apoplexy (strokes), *tuberculosis, *paralysis, gonorrhea, blindness, beriberi, *insanity

2. *Nearsightedness; glaucoma; *deafness; loss of smell, voice, taste, and *appetite

3. Pain in the *head, *teeth, *shoulder, *back, or *knee

4. *Dizziness, *nausea, *fever, *coughing, wheezing, *shortness of breath

5. *Jaundice, *diarrhea, *constipation, *difficult urination, thundering noises in the bowels

6. Melancholy, depression, irritability, morbid grief, fear, uncontrollable laughter, rage

7. *Inability to raise arms, spasms, *muscle cramps

8. *Hemorrhoids, *goiters, tumors, carbuncles, swellings, hernias

9. *Impotence, infertility in women

10. *Nocturnal emissions, bed-wetting, runny noses, spitting blood, *vomiting

11. Intoxication, insomnia, *indigestion

12. Yawning, *belching, flatulence, bad breath, violent death, many dreams

This list represents a small fraction of the ailments that Tang physicians claimed they could cure with their needles. Acupuncture was a sovereign treatment, perhaps second only to drugs as the most popular remedy in ancient China.

Some medical works in premodern times made exaggerated claims about acupuncture's efficacy. When Taizong's empress reached term, she was unable to give birth for several days. The emperor summoned a physician, who took her pulse and declared, "The infant has seized his mother's heart with his hand, and therefore she cannot give birth." When Taizong asked what should be done, the doctor said that if he saved the child, the mother would not survive. If he saved the mother, the child would die. The empress chose to save her unborn infant because he would perpetuate the glory of the dynasty. So the physician inserted his needle into her chest until it penetrated her heart and reached the child's hand. The procedure killed the empress, and her son, who became Emperor Gaozong, was born with a scar on his left hand. The story is a complete fabrication, for Gaozong was born in 628, and his mother passed away in 638.

Nevertheless, the story illustrates the point that deep penetration of the body with a needle could have disastrous consequences. The canons of the profession warned that a patient would die within a day if the needle penetrated the heart, within a day and a half if it penetrated the bladder, three days if the lungs or kidneys, five days if the liver, and fifteen days if the spleen. He would also expire if the physician punctured a major blood vessel in the ankle or groin. Less serious disabilities would occur when the needle penetrated less vital points. Piercing the kneecap improperly, so that fluid flowed from it, caused lameness. If a needle penetrated too far under the tongue and broke blood vessels, the patient would lose his voice. If it reached the bone marrow in the vertebrae of the spine, he would become a hunchback.

Sometimes doctors inserted acupuncture needles to draw blood from a patient. In late 683 Emperor Gaozong was gravely ill, perhaps from a

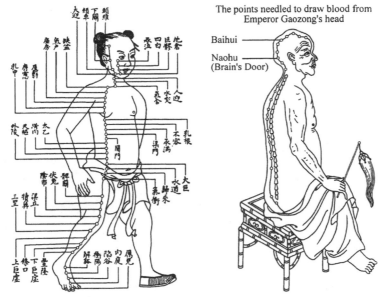

The points needled to draw blood from
Emperor Gaozong's head

Baihui

Naohu
(Brain's Door)

**Acupuncture Points and Tracts**

stroke. He was suffering from a heaviness in the head and could not see. He summoned his attending physician, Chin, to make a diagnosis. After conducting his examination, Chin said he could cure the malady if the monarch granted him permission to needle his head. That angered Empress Wu, who was sitting behind a curtain in the hall. She interrupted, "You should be beheaded for seeking to draw blood from the sovereign's head by needling!" The physician kowtowed and begged for his life. Gaozong, however, agreed to undergo the procedure. Chin pierced the emperor at two acupuncture points on the back of his head. Afterward Gaozong said, "My eyes seem to have cleared." The empress declared, "This a gift from Heaven." Then she bestowed 100 lengths of polychrome silk on the physician. Empress Wu had, however, just cause for concern about the dangers of the procedure. Instantaneous death would have resulted if Chin had pushed his needle too far into the Brain's Door, a point at the base of the skull. The physician could have penetrated the brain when he needled that spot.

Moxabustion was a therapy that called for burning cones of dry, powdered mugwort—a shrub with strong-smelling leaves—on acupuncture points. The area   **Moxabustion**
scorched could not exceed three-tenths of an inch. When it was used to relieve pain, the physician repeated the process until the discomfort ceased. That meant using as many as 50, 100, or more cones. Moxabustion was often employed after acupuncture to enhance its effects. It was

**Guiding and Stretching Exercises**

thought to facilitate the flow of *qi* throughout the body. However, it also had its particular therapeutic benefits. Doctors burned the cones on boils and carbuncles to burst them so that their pus would flow out. Whenever a snake bit a person, mugwort was burned on the wound. A single burning would cure the victim immediately if he acted quickly. If he did not, he would die at once.

The cauterization left scars that usually disappeared in a short time. When they did not, one could apply the ashes from burned cow dung to remove them. As with acupuncture, there were certain dangers to employing the procedure. If the physician burned the cones on a point along the hairline of the head, he might cause blindness. If he placed them improperly behind the kneecap, the patient might suffer loss of mobility at all joints of his limbs. If he positioned them at an acupuncture point located on the foot below the ankle, loss of voice and speech could result.

**Massage/Exercise**     There were at least two forms of massage in the Tang, one Indian and the other native. The latter was a Taoist technique and named after its sage, Lao Tzu. Massage had the same effects as exercise, that is, it resolved congestion and improved the circulation of *qi* within the body. It differed from exercise in that a therapist performed it on a patient. The leading authorities on exercise were the Taoists, who practiced "guiding and stretching." It was a series of movements involving the stretching of limbs that was performed in a closed room. The person exercising stood, sat, or reclined. Of the three, sitting (on a mat or, better yet, on a couch) was the most common. As an element of regimes for "nourishing life," it was intimately linked to breathing exercises. When practiced daily, it prevented illness and prolonged life. As a therapy it was a temporary cure for deafness, muscle tension, rheumatism, dizziness, paralysis, epileptic seizures, digestive problems, and back pain.

Unquestionably the most prevalent remedy for treating illnesses in traditional times was drugs and prescriptions. In 657 the Tang court published the first official materia medica in Chinese history. When the emperor commis- **Drugs and Prescriptions** sioned the project, he ordered local officials to have pictures of curative substances in their districts drawn and sent to the capital. The drawings became illustrations for the compilation. The new materia medica contained descriptions of 833 substances, of which, however, 175 had no known medicinal value. There were eight sections to the text:

1. Stones, minerals, and metals, as well as the dirt from the top of an eastern wall and the dust on house beams (83 items)
2. Plants, as well as the soles of old hemp slippers and the ash of straps for wooden clogs (256 items)
3. Trees and shrubs, including bamboo (100 items)
4. Animals and birds, including human beings (56 items).
5. Reptiles, insects, and fish (72 items)
6. Fruits and nuts, as well as honey and cane sugar (25 items)
7. Vegetables (36 items)
8. Cereals, seeds, and beans, as well as malt sugar, ale, vinegar, and sauces (28 items).

Each class was subdivided into three grades: the superior, which nourished (prolonged) life; the mediocre, which remedied depletions; and the inferior, which cured diseases. For each entry the compilers characterized the substance's taste as sweet, sour, bitter, salty, or pungent; specified whether its effect was to heat or to cool; and rated its toxicity. Then they described its therapeutic benefits and indicated the locations where it could be found. To give some idea of traditional concepts in the Tang materia medica, an account of some substances is provided below.

*Stones, minerals, and metals.* Mica cleared the eyes, stopped dysentery, lightened the body, and prolonged life. Coral removed the film from eyes. Powdered coral blown into the nostrils stopped nosebleeds. Bronze from a crossbow trigger enabled a woman who was having trouble giving birth to deliver, and dislodged menstrual discharge that would not flow.

A physician ordered a man who had fallen off his horse and broken his leg to mix copper dust with ale and drink the liquor. The victim took the potion, his leg healed, and he was as good as new. Some ten years later he died. When his family exhumed his remains for reburial, they examined the fracture on his shinbone, and discovered that the copper filings had knitted the broken bones together.

**Plants.** Seaweed was the sovereign treatment for goiter because it contained high levels of iodine. Ginseng cured cold in the stomach and bowels, as well as throbbing pain in the heart and belly. Apothecaries recommended Chinese rhubarb for fevers, and blood congestion in the vagina and womb. Aconite, one of the most poisonous plants in the Chinese materia medica, was used to abort pregnancies. Crossbow strings were effective in treating difficult childbirth: Wrap them around the woman's waist, heat the trigger of the crossbow until red-hot, place it in a cup of ale, and have the woman drink the brew. Drinking the liquid in which the soles of old hemp slippers had been boiled counteracted poisons acquired from eating beef and horse meat. It also took care of flatulence.

**Trees and shrubs.** Medieval Chinese esteemed the pine over all other trees because it was evergreen, and therefore represented long life. Legend had it that a man who ate only pine nuts could live to be 200 or 300 years old. It was, however, the resin that physicians found useful for treating maladies. They plastered it onto sores exuding bloody pus and packed dental cavities with it to kill the bacteria eating the teeth. The bark of the Chinese cinnamon tree (cassia) yielded an oil that was beneficial to the liver and lungs. It was also effective for treating headaches, coughs and nasal congestion. It could also abort fetuses. Thunder balls were a parasitic growth on trees, small nodules less than an ounce in weight. They were beneficial to men but not to women. Made into an ointment, they could cure all kinds of children's ailments.

**Animals and birds.** Human milk made one fat and fair. A man who subsisted on it lived for more than 100 years, and was as fat and fair as a gourd. Rhinoceros horns were an antidote for poisons and relieved headaches. Ingesting the velvet from the horns of the sika deer grew teeth and eased the pain of arthritis. One authority recommended eating the flesh and blood of the gibbon to cure hemorrhoids, and suggested that sitting for a long time on its hide offered relief to sufferers of that affliction.

Taken internally, bat brains cured forgetfulness. The blood and bile of the bat dripped into the eyes kept one awake and enabled one to see in the dark. Eating dried, pure white bats that fed on stalactites made a person fat and robust, and prolonged his life for 1,000 years.

**Reptiles, insects, and fish.** Southerners administered dried and roasted sea horses to women who were having difficulty in childbirth. Physicians administered sharkskin to patients for heart problems and for overcoming infections. The venom from toads was mixed with cinnabar and musk, formed into pills, and given to infants for malnutrition. Fireflies cured night blindness. A roasted and pulverized dung beetle applied to the skin with vinegar was effective against eczema that resulted from consuming too much honey.

Lu contracted leprosy. The base of his nose was the only part of his body that did not rot. As the fifth day of the fifth moon approached, the medical officer of the prefecture in which he was living wanted to give him the gallbladder of a python. Some people said the flesh of the snake could cure leprosy. The physician fed him a slice of python meat. Within three to five days, Lu began to show signs of gradual improvement, and 100 days later he recovered completely from the illness. There was also a man in Shangzhou who contracted leprosy. His kinsmen built a thatched hut for him in the mountains because his appearance nauseated them. A black snake fell into his vat of ale. Unaware of the fact, the afflicted man drank the brew, and gradually recovered. Only when the level of the ale dropped to the bottom of the barrel did he notice the snake's skeleton, and understand the reason for his cure.

*Fruits and nuts.* Sour pomegranates cured red and white dysentery. Eating cherries gave one a fine complexion. Pistachios dispelled cold *qi* and made the body fat and robust. Betel nuts slew the Three Corpses. Indian pepper warmed the innards and eliminated phlegm. A compound of walnut and lead applied to the head cured baldness. One expert recommended almonds for curing beriberi, a disease caused by vitamin B deficiency.

*Vegetables.* Winter melons were a tonic that prevented hunger, prolonged life, and made the body light. Leeks stopped vomiting. Garlic had a particular power over the kidneys, spleen, and stomach. It was effective in eliminating rheumatism. It could not, however, be eaten too often because it could injure the health.

*Cereals.* Sesame filled depletion, improved vision and hearing, strengthened bones, and prevented aging if consumed for a long time. Barley slaked thirst (cured diabetes?) and dissipated heat. Vinegar dissolved carbuncles and swellings.

In traditional China there were few hard distinctions between what was food and what were drugs. Mercury, for example, was an ingredient in some dishes for the table.

Most of the substances in the materia medica were rarely used alone. An apothecary or physician mixed a number of them together according to formulas provided in readily available manuals. They also combined them with ale for ingestion. Although ale was classified as a toxin, it was thought to activate medicines.

One Tang physician stumbled upon a unique means of determining the proper medicine for curing one of his patient's ailments. There was a scholar in Luoyang who contracted "echo illness." Whenever he spoke, his words reverberated in his throat. He consulted a skilled doctor, who ruminated on the problem overnight before he hit upon a solution. He gave the man a copy of the materia medica and ordered him to read it aloud. The scholar's voice echoed in his throat until he reached a passage that frightened him. At that point his speech ceased to echo. The physician then transcribed the prescription in the passage. He selected the herbs it called for and mixed them to make a pill. Immediately after ingesting it, the man was cured.

**First Aid**     A medical text of the Tang period supplied a host of advice on how to treat injuries, ailments, and other health problems. The following is a short list of examples.

For those who commit suicide by hanging, but who retain signs of life: pulverize soapbeans, place the powder on an onion leaf, and blow it into the nostrils of the victim. Or take the dust lying on a beam, insert it into four bamboo tubes, and have four men blow it into the ears and nostrils of the victim simultaneously.

For those who have drowned: hook their shins over the shoulders of a standing man so that the two are back to back, and pour fine ale in the victim's nostrils. Or stuff soapbeans wrapped in a cloth into the victim's rectum. The objective of the treatments for hanging and drowning was to restore consciousness to the victim.

For snake bites: wash the wound with boiling water or, if that is not available, human urine.

For tiger bites: wash the wound liberally with molten iron. That was a method of cauterizing the puncture to stop bleeding and kill infections.

For hornet stings: make a plaster of a roasted wasp nest and smear it on the sores.

For bites from a rabid dog: roast a dried snake, remove its head, pound the body into a powder, and ingest.

To stanch the flow of blood from a wound inflicted by a metal weapon: sift together the pollen from the cattail and Chinese angelica, mix with ale, and ingest. Or plaster with spiderwebs, or apply human semen, or drink ten pints of urine.

To extract an arrowhead that will not come out: collect a woman's menstrual cloth, burn it to ash, and take the ash with ale.

For poison arrows: extract the water from Chinese foxglove, form the residue into pills, and take them for 100 days. The arrowhead will then push itself out.

For needles broken off during acupuncture treatments: make a powder by scraping elephant ivory, mix it with water, and smear it on the spot where the needle was inserted. The end will then come out by itself.

Other maladies for which the compendium offered treatments included demonic attacks (heart attacks and the like); heat prostration; stings from scorpions, bombardier beetles, and spiders; bruises resulting from fist-fights; injuries from falls off horses and carriages; broken bones; concussions; burns; scalds; and much more.

Surgery was not a common treatment in traditional China.
Autopsies also were rare, because it was a fundamental tenet    **Surgery**
of ancestor worship that the body should return to the grave
in the original, unmutilated state that parents had given it at birth. However, necropsies on criminals were sometimes permissible, on the
grounds that their nefarious acts had disqualified them from humane
and civilized consideration. The first scientific autopsy took place in the
year 16. The emperor dispatched his chief physician, a skilled butcher,
to conduct it on a rebel that had been captured and, presumably, executed. The imperial decree ordered the doctor to dissect the whole body,
remove its organs to weigh and measure them, and to trace the course
of its veins by inserting bamboo probes in them. The emperor believed
that the autopsy would help physicians cure diseases. It is not clear
whether the acquired knowledge was passed down to later ages, but
Tang Taoists and physicians certainly had a fair, if elementary, understanding of human anatomy, especially the shapes, positions and sizes
of the viscera in the chest and abdominal cavities.

Tang physicians did perform some fairly simple surgeries involving
wounds. In 693 or shortly thereafter someone falsely accused Empress
Wu's second son (Emperor Ruizong), whom she had deposed, of secretly
plotting against her. The empress ordered the chief of her dreaded security service to conduct a thorough investigation of the prince's associates. The chief, who had earned a notorious reputation for his cruelty,
interrogated the suspects. Unable to endure the torment of torture, they
readily confessed, all save one. A minor official named An Jinzang refused to betray his friend. When he appeared before the grand inquisitor,
he yelled, "Since Your Lordship will not take my word for it, please cut
out my heart as proof that the prince is not rebellious." He then drew a
dagger from his belt, thrust it into his stomach and ripped open his belly.
His entrails fell out, his flowing blood blanketed the ground, and he
fainted. When the empress learned of this dramatic turn of events, she
sent a litter to fetch the dying man and dispatched a physician to attend
to his wound. The doctor restored the viscera to the abdominal cavity
of the man, sutured the laceration with white mulberry bark thread, and
applied a medicinal plaster that enabled An to recover within a fortnight.
Despite the terrible trauma An survived for decades after the incident,
and subsequently died of old age.

A medical compendium of the Tang recommended the following procedure for cases in which horses bit off men's testicles, undoubtedly a
very rare occurrence: Push the testicles back inside the body and suture
them with fine mulberry bark thread. Cut open a black chicken, remove
its liver, mince it finely, and smear the paste on the wound. Apparently,
there were some instances of reattaching body parts in ancient Chinese
history.

A somewhat more complicated operation involved a war wound. A rebel commander of the early seventh century had an arrowhead embedded in his jaw. He summoned a physician to extract it, but the doctor told him that the arrowhead had penetrated so deep it could not be removed. Enraged, the commander beheaded the man and called for another doctor. The second said that he feared it would be very painful to pull the arrowhead out. The commander decapitated him as well, and summoned yet another physician, who informed him that he could accomplish the task. The doctor drilled into the bone and drove a wedge in the hole. The wedge opened a crack in the jaw more than an inch long, so the physician was finally able to extract the arrowhead. In gratitude the rebel rewarded the doctor with performances of his female singers and feasts of rare fare.

A Tang doctor wrote the oldest Chinese treatise on treating fractures in 841. In it he described how to wash the wound, apply traction, and bind the limb with splints. In cases where bones protruded from the flesh, he advocated surgery to reset the bones. He was not the only physician performing such operations. When a soldier came to a doctor with a broken shinbone, he gave the man some medicinal ale to anesthetize him, cut open his flesh, and removed a bone fragment the size of two fingers. Afterward the doctor sealed the wound with a plaster. The soldier was as good as new in several days. Two years later, however, his shin began to ache, so he returned to the physician and asked him about it. The doctor replied that the bone fragment he had previously removed was cold and causing the pain. They found the splinter underneath a couch, washed it in hot water, and wrapped it in refuse silk. Thereafter the pain in the soldier's shin ceased.

There were several other surgical procedures performed in the Tang. At least one doctor repaired harelips surgically. Another devised a means of curing obstructed urination. He formed a catheter from the tubular leaf of a scallion, inserted it into the urethra, and blew into it. His breath inflated the urethra, permitting the urine to flow out. Physicians in the Tang also performed cataract surgery, a technique imported from India. A Taoist learned it from a western foreigner. The operation involved the use of a metal "sickle," apparently a knife of some sort, to remove a green screen from the eye that was obstructing the vision. The source of that information also mentions the use of needles, instruments more familiar to Chinese doctors.

**Exorcism**            Taoists and Buddhists performed exorcisms during the Tang, but shamans were the oldest experts in its arts. A demon had possessed a village girl and caused her to go mad. During her fits she occasionally inflicted injuries to her body by leaping into fires and throwing herself into rivers. At the same time her belly gradually grew larger, as if she were pregnant. Her parents, who grieved for her, sent for a shaman who claimed that she possessed the power to drive out evil afflictions. After she arrived, she erected an altar in the girl's room and laid the girl beneath it. Then the shaman dug a large fire pit next to the altar and over the fire heated an iron cauldron until it was red-hot. Next she danced to the rhythm of a drum that she beat, and called for her spirit. In an instant he descended into her. She poured a libation for him and intoned an incantation, "Quickly summon the demon forth." When the shaman finished speaking, she stepped into the fire pit and sat. The expression on her face did not change. There were no signs of pain or discomfort. Some time later she adjusted her robes and rose. She took the red-hot cauldron, placed it on her head and danced to the beat of her drum. When she finished her song, the shaman removed the cauldron and ordered the afflicted girl to bind herself. The girl placed her hands behind her as if they were tied. The shaman then ordered the fiend to confess, but at first the girl wept without speaking. That enraged the shaman. She seized her dagger and struck the afflicted girl. The blade passed through her, but her body remained the same as before. The attack, however, unloosened her tongue. She declared, "I submit. I am an old otter. I found the girl delightful when she came to the Huai River, my home, to wash clothes. Now unfortunately I have encountered you, sage priest. I beg you to drive me from here, but it pains me that my children in the maid's womb will not be raised. Is there no hope that you will refrain from slaying them and will return them to me if they are born?" When she finished speaking, the girl cried and, although she was illiterate, she seized a writing brush and wrote an elegant farewell verse to the otter. Afterward she fell asleep. When she awoke the next day, she was free of the demon. She said that when she went to wash clothes at the river, she met a handsome young man who seduced her and slept with her. Ten days after awaking, the maid gave birth to three otters. In accordance with the demon's wishes, someone took the pups and released them in a lake, where a giant otter took them on its back and sank into the waters.

Although the story is far-fetched, it clearly depicts the essential elements of traditional Chinese shamanism: spirit possession, ecstatic dances, trial by fire, incantations, and threatening gestures with a sword.

# 11

# Life Cycle

## MARRIAGE AND DIVORCE

Gaozu, the founder of the Tang, was an extraordinary man in more ways than one. He had a purple birthmark shaped like a dragon, a sure sign of a future emperor, below his left armpit. He was also a superb archer and used his skills to win his wife. The woman's father was so impressed with her that he decided he could not marry her to just anyone. She should have a worthy man for a husband. So he had two peacocks painted on the leaves of his gate and gave suitors two chances to shoot them. He and his wife secretly agreed beforehand that they would be-troth the daughter only to the archer who could place his missiles in the eyes of the birds. Scores of men tried, but failed to hit the mark. Gaozu was the last to arrive. He shot both of his arrows into the peacocks' eyes.

Love matches were nearly as rare as archery contests for betrothals. Marriages were almost always arranged. Two men, usually close friends, might reach an agreement to engage their children when they were in-fants. Sometimes the motive of a father in contracting a marriage was less than honorable. An eminent minister in the seventh century be-trothed a younger daughter to the son of a southern half-breed—a rich chieftain who put down a rebellion of aborigines living along the coast west of Canton in 631—because he would receive a hefty bride-price from the man. In the eyes of high society the union was scandalous. When the minister died in 672, an official suggested that the throne con-fer "Erred" as his posthumous title on him for the indiscretion.

Marriages were very important in China even for the dead. Marshal Wei was responsible for arresting a thief. The thief's uncle, a Buddhist monk, harbored him, but the marshal pardoned him for having committed the crime of concealing a criminal. Wei's superior, governor of the prefecture, reprimanded him for being too lenient and conducted his own interrogation of the monk, who confessed. The governor then had the priest executed. The marshal took ill and died. After they coffined his corpse, his family posthumously married him to his uncle's daughter. Although the account of this marriage comes from a ghost story, it was not at all uncommon for kinsmen to arrange unions between the soul of a dead loved one and that of an outsider. Even the parents of children who died young had posthumous marriages performed for them.

In almost all cases, families relied on outsiders to arrange marriages. The expert at providing such services was a matchmaker, who was always a woman. As such she held an advantage over a man because she had access to the women's apartments in homes. The matchmaker could enter the inner quarters, converse with the mother and examine the prospective bride. Afterward she would convey the information she gleaned there to the intended groom's father. There was also a more compelling reason for employing matchmakers. The Tang code of laws required it. The state did not issue marriage licenses or conduct weddings. Therefore, there was no occasion for it to inquire about the fitness of the union. But it did have an interest in preventing fraud and violations of its laws. Fraud might involve misrepresenting the age of the prospective bride or groom. Legally the marriageable age for males was fourteen, and for females, twelve. Furthermore, a man could not marry a woman who was half his age or younger. The deceit might be a false claim that one of the pair was an adopted child or the child of a concubine instead of the wife's child. Finally, one of the families might conceal their child's disability. As defined in Tang statutes, the impaired included the blind (in one or both eyes), the deaf, the dumb, dwarfs, hunchbacks, the insane, and the dismembered (loss of one or two limbs). A matchmaker could prevent such duplicity because she was able to examine the pair physically and question the family about their status.

The state also undertook to enforce long-standing customs that forbid incest. The definition of incest in traditional China was extremely broad. According to the law, marriages between fourth cousins on the father's side were punishable by 100 blows of the thick rod for both husband and wife; between third cousins, by penal servitude of one year, and between first cousins, by exile to a district 833 miles away. The law also prohibited marriages between men and women who shared the same surname, a crime punishable by two years of penal servitude. The principle was that they might be distantly and unknowingly related. The government annulled all such unions.

Once the matchmaker completed the arrangements, the "marriage master" (normally the father, grandfather, uncle, or older brother of the prospective groom) drew up a contract and sent it to the woman's family. Her senior male relative signed and returned it. If thereafter the woman's family broke the agreement, her marriage master was liable for a punishment of sixty blows with the thick rod. If the man's family canceled it, its marriage master suffered no punishment, but he could not keep betrothal gifts. The prospective groom's family sent betrothal gifts, tokens of good faith, to the prospective bride's home when they received the signed contract or shortly thereafter. In Tang times they included symbolic articles: glue and lacquer for cementing the relationship, a pair of stones for establishing a firm base, silk floss for ensuring meekness, and two mats for assuring that the will would submit. Acceptance of the presents was a legally binding pledge of engagement even when there was no contract established between the two parties.

Marriage was an agreement between families rather than individuals, whom marriage masters apparently did not consult before hand. Generally speaking, children went along with the wishes of their marriage masters. Occasionally, however, they went to extreme lengths to oppose their elders' agreements. In one case a young man who wanted to take vows as a Buddhist monk and take up a life of celibacy cut off his penis. Naturally that put an end to his parents' plans. One official did not marry because he feared that bringing a woman from another family into his would alienate his two younger brothers, to whom he was deeply devoted. His parents no doubt were dead, for he was the head of the household. Therefore, they were unable to interfere in his life. Sometimes daughters could also defy the wishes of their elders. One young woman whose father died when she was seven years old, cut off her hair and swore an oath to remain single when she reached womanhood and her mother wanted to marry her. She got away with her disobedience because she devoted herself to looking after her mother for the rest of her life.

The male's marriage master selected an auspicious day for the wedding. On the eve of the wedding, the parents of the bride visited the home of the groom and arranged the furnishings of the bridal chamber: bed, bed curtains, quilts, and the like. For that reason they were called the bedfather and bedmother. The following day the groom arrived at the bride's home to escort her to his house, usually with members of his family or friends. When such processions involved females of the imperial family, they were quite elaborate. In 608, when Princess Anle married for the second time, Emperor Zhongzong granted her the unusual indulgence of allowing her to use the empress's cortege. The train included more than 700 officials, attendants, guards (some bearing swords, bows, and crossbows), and others. That figure did not include palace

women or the fife and drum corps that provided march music for the
procession. The carriage bearing the princess was blue with gold ornaments, and was drawn by a team of four steeds. Five additional coaches,
red and yellow with gold fittings, also rolled down the streets, pulled
by bay horses with black manes and by bullocks. Banners, pennants,
streamers, and canopies fluttered in the breeze as the cortege paraded
through the avenues of Changan. The wedding of Princess Taiping in
681 took place at night, so imperial minions installed torches along the
procession's route. The heat of the flames killed many of the trees along
the boulevards.

Normally a family of means sent the bride to the groom's home in a
carriage. She arrived there veiled and immediately became a member of
his family although she retained her surname. The groom did not see
her face until the evening of the wedding day. To celebrate the occasion,
his father threw a banquet that only men attended. Sometimes he rented
a mansion for the occasion, perhaps because his dwelling was in another
city. For some unknown reason Emperor Gaozong convened the feast
for Princess Taiping's wedding in the compound of a county administration at Changan, even though he had held other banquets in palaces.

Women, but not men, were supposed to remain virgins until their
wedding nights. The reason was quite simple. The husbands wanted to
be absolutely certain that their first male child and heir was theirs. Some
Chinese took curious measures to ensure that their daughters did not
have premarital sex. They fed lizards ten pounds of cinnabar over a
period of time and pulverized the reptiles when they had eaten it all.
Then they smeared the bloody dye on their girl's legs. It would remain
on the body until the daughters had intercourse.

Tang society was monogamous. A man could have only one wife. The
punishment for taking a second was one year of penal servitude and
annulment of the marriage. That did not mean that he could not install
other women in his household. In fact it was customary for patricians to
do so. Since affection was rarely a basis for matrimony and fidelity to a
wife was not one of their virtues, they took concubines, sometimes a
large number of them. Under Tang law the distinction between a wife
and a concubine was that the latter could be bought and sold. Legally,
betrothal presents were pledges that sealed a marriage contract, not a
bride-price.

The Tang law code declared that the union of husband and wife was
unalterable throughout their lives, and that they must dwell together
even in the grave. That was the ideal marital state, but the law also
recognized that divorce was acceptable and even desirable under certain
circumstances. It sanctioned separations on the grounds of mutual in-
compatibility. In all other cases, however, divorce was a male prerogative
only. A woman who left her husband without his consent was subject

to two years of penal servitude if apprehended. The law recognized seven legitimate grounds for such separations. Failure to bear children was the first. That rule applied specifically to sons since they carried on the family line and were in charge of maintaining sacrifices to ancestors. Daughters did not count because they left the family upon marriage. A man could divorce a wife for barrenness only when she reached the age of forty-nine and had failed to produce a son. However, he need not divorce her, since he could legally make the eldest son born to one of his concubines his heir. If he had no male offspring, he could adopt a son, in which case the boy or man had to be related to him by blood.

The second ground was adultery. An extramarital affair was unacceptable because the woman might bear a child that was not of the husband's bloodline. In some instances the state intervened to rectify the problem. In the late eighth century the wife of a villager pretended that she had come down with tuberculosis. She told her husband that a physician had recommended eating dog meat as a cure. Since they had no dogs, she instructed him to kill a neighbor's dog. He complied. After eating some of the flesh, she told the hound's owner to inform the court that her husband had slaughtered the animal. When the husband appeared before the magistrate, he recounted what his wife had said. The judge believed him, conducted a thorough investigation, and discovered that the wife wanted to get rid of her husband because she was having an affair with another man. The punishment for adultery was two years of penal servitude for both the man and the woman.

In ancient China there was a belief that some women were naturally inclined to adultery, a trait that was written on their faces. The concubine of one patrician was a beauty. Once she went to consult a face reader for a prediction about her longevity and destiny. He told her, "Madam, your eyes are long, and they seductively leer at men. According to the manuals, 'pig gaze' is the sign of a lewd nature. Your irises are surrounded by white, so five men will spend the night in your quarters. Madam, debauchery will destroy you. You should be prudent in your conduct." The lady laughed and departed. As predicted, she later had several affairs for which she was enslaved in the Flank Court as punishment.

Some women were paragons of fidelity. When a man named Fang took ill and was on the brink of dying, he told his wife, who was still young, to marry after he passed away. She crawled behind his bed curtains and plucked out one of her eyes, to show him that she could love no one but him.

The third justification for divorce was a wife's refusal to serve her in-laws. Obedience to the will of a husband's parents or grandparents was as important as, if not more important than, obedience to him. It was difficult for a man who detested his wife to divorce her when his parents were fond of her.

The fourth ground was talkativeness. According to a Tang ballad, a young, newly married woman wandered alone in the market, insulting her husband and abusing her in-laws, so he divorced her with her consent. Women were outsiders who might also spread discord in the family by pressing the interests of their husbands against those of his brothers.

The fifth ground was jealousy. It was considered a cause of disharmony. Because men took concubines, contention between those women and his wife could easily develop as they competed for his affection and favor. In the early seventh century Emperor Taizong bestowed two palace women of outstanding beauty on one of his ministers, Ren. Madam Liu, Ren's wife, was a jealous woman and burned the hair off the women's heads. The emperor sent a eunuch to present her with a gold pitcher of ale and tell her, "If you drink this, you will die immediately. Your husband is an official of the third rank, so it is fitting that he should have concubines. If henceforth you cease being jealous, don't drink this. If you do not change your ways, drink it." Liu opted for the latter course and drained the pitcher. Although she lost consciousness, she survived because the ale contained no poison. Taizong then installed the palace women in a separate dwelling for Ren.

The sixth ground was theft, particularly of her in-laws' property. The last was contracting an incurable disease. A woman with such an ailment was not permitted to prepare food for offerings to the dead, and therefore could not carry out her duty with regard to the rites performed for her husband's ancestors.

Even if a husband had legitimate grounds for divorce, there were three instances when he could not renounce his wife: she had observed the twenty-seven-month mourning period for his parents; she had married into the family when its status was humble or poor, and it subsequently acquired higher status or wealth; and she had no family of her own to which she could return. A man who divorced his wife under those circumstances was subject to a beating of 100 blows with the thick rod and was compelled to take her back.

## CHILDBIRTH AND CHILD REARING

The function of marriage was to produce male children who would perpetuate the husband's line. Procreation, therefore, was the paramount duty of husband and wife. To ensure that they would conceive a child, a Tang medical text recommended that they each drink a cup of rainwater before retiring to the bedchamber. Men in traditional China seem to have had a great deal of anxiety about their potency, and that led herbalists to suggest various remedies to treat the problem. One claimed that pistachio nuts were a marvelous treatment for impotence. He recommended extracting the juice by frying, then bathing the genitals in it. The repute of that cure was so great that by the eighth century, men often applied it before bedtime. Whether because of such balms or not, some men in the Tang were amazingly prolific. One Tang prince fathered fifty-five children.

A bride may have received instructions on sex from her mother before her wedding night, but sometimes the groom might also be of service in that regard. There was a sex manual, titled *Canon of the Plain Maid*, that couples read together before retiring to the bedchamber. It had both illustrations showing various positions for performing sex and written directions. The text also contained taboos about copulating during certain times. Children conceived during the day would be prone to vomiting; at midnight, would be mute, deaf or dumb; during a thunderstorm, would be insane; after overeating or intoxication, would suffer from ulcers and hemorrhoids; during a full moon, would become bandits; and so forth.

Conception occurred when the yang *qi* (sperm) of the man united with the yin *qi* (menstrual fluid) of the woman. The coalescing of the two energies generated a third, the original *qi*, that would create the fetus. The Chinese believed that conception took place ten months before birth, and measured age from that time. They rounded off the number so an infant was one year old when delivered. Traditional medical men believed that the behavior of the mother during pregnancy affected the health and character of the newborn. They cautioned women to avoid eating certain meats: mountain goat caused the child to be sickly; rabbit, to have a harelip; chicken eggs or dried carp, to suffer from suppurating sores or ulcers; chicken with sticky rice, to be afflicted with tapeworms; turtle, to have a short neck; and so forth. If a mother wanted offspring that would be loyal, humane, righteous, intelligent, and free of disease, she should burn fine incense, recite poetry, dwell in a quiet place, sit properly, and strum the zither during her pregnancy. That sort of conduct was called "fetal teaching" because it was thought to affect the moral development of the child. The woman went into seclusion the month before the birth and emerged one month after. She did not have any contact with her husband in that period.

Multiple births were acceptable as long as they were twins. Triplets were abnormal, and quadruplets a bad omen reflecting an overabundance of yin or feminine energy in the cosmos. Occasionally, a woman gave birth to Siamese twins. When the wife of a guardsman bore a son and daughter conjoined at the chest in 678, someone attempted to separate them, but both infants died. Medical technology was not sophisticated enough for such a difficult operation. Later the same woman gave birth to another set, both boys, whom she raised without trying to have them parted.

Chinese physicians had a fair idea about the early stages of an infant's development. At sixty days its eyes were fully developed, and it could laugh in response to an adult's voice. At 100 days the child could turn over on its own. At 180 days its pelvis was completely formed, and it could sit by itself. At 210 days the bones in its hands were mature, and the infant could crawl. At 300 days the child's kneecaps were fully developed, and it could stand by itself. At 360 days it could walk.

In most cases mothers were responsible for child care. If a mother died in childbirth or thereafter, a relative might take over the task. An aunt raised Du Fu, China's greatest poet. In his infancy he and her son took ill, so she invited a sorceress to her house for advice on what to do. The woman predicted that only the boy placed in the southeastern corner of her bedroom would survive. The aunt removed her own son from the crib in that corner and placed Du in it. As a result he lived and his cousin died.

In the homes of the well-to-do, wet nurses took over the duty of suckling infants, and in some cases nursed children for years. Physicians warned families to avoid choosing women with obvious maladies: goiters, swellings, eczema, scabies, baldness due to fungal infections, stuffy noses, deafness, and body odor. The connection between a child and his wet nurse was intimate and enduring, especially when his mother did not attend to his upbringing or died when he was young. Both Emperors Zhongzong and Illustrious August ennobled theirs; the first, because his mother, Empress Wu, did not rear him; and the second, because his mother died in his infancy. In 684 Zhongzong attempted to appoint the son of his wet nurse to a government office ranked fifth grade. The wet nurse of Han Yu, the most renowned master of prose in the Tang, refused to leave him after his parents died before he was two years old. He kept her in his household throughout the remainder of her life. On festivals he, his wife, and their children visited her to pay their respects and on bended knees tendered their best wishes. They also attended her funeral at graveside. Sometimes the relationship endured after death. Emperor Yizong had Princess Tongchang's wet nurse buried with her.

Other alternative caretakers were stepmothers. They might be loving substitutes for the natural mothers who had died, but they could also be abusive, unjustly thrashing their stepchildren or even attempting to murder them. They could be cruel because they did not have the maternal affection of a birth mother, but also because they saw the eldest son of the first marriage, the husband's heir, as an impediment to the interests of their own sons. She might even harbor malice against an adult stepson. When legate Lun returned home after a lengthy mission to Tibet, his wife, Madam Li, greeted him dressed in shabby garb. He asked her why, and she replied that Yan, a county marshal and his son by a former wife, had not provided her with food or clothing in his absence. In a towering rage Lun summoned his son. He ordered his servants to drag Yan to the floor and bare his back so he could flog him. The marshal wept, but would say nothing in his own defense. When the legate's younger brother heard that, he rushed over, shielded his nephew, and said, "Every moon Yan has sent his salary to your wife. I know all about it. How can she claim that he has not supplied her with food and clothing!" Lun's temper cooled, and thereafter he paid no attention to his wife's slander. After he died, the marshal was even more attentive in serving his stepmother. Her natural son took out loans and had the lenders draw up contracts that made Yan responsible for their repayment. Yan always made restitution.

Conversely, stepsons could be as vicious as stepmothers. After the demise of his father, a man of means began to behave disrespectfully toward his stepmother. After he paid his respects to her on New Year's Day, she presented him with a goblet of ale. He pretended that the brew contained poison; spilled it on the ground, where it foamed suspiciously; and accused his stepmother of trying to murder him. When the case came to court, the magistrate interrogated the son and discovered that his wife had brought the goblet that the stepmother had presented to him. The judge sentenced the couple to be punished according to the appropriate statute.

Sometimes stepmother and stepson got along a little too well. In the early seventh century charges of committing incest were lodged against a man named Li and his stepmother. Before having the pair brought in for trial, County Marshal Wang ordered one of his underlings to hide under the cloth covering his bench and listen to what was said in the court. Then he called Li and the stepmother in and interrogated them. They would not confess. During the questioning one of his subordinates, acting on his orders, entered and reported, "The Senior Secretary has summoned you." Wang locked the room and left. After he departed, the pair agreed that they would never admit anything and talked about their private secret. When the county marshal returned and opened the door, the underling hiding under the bench rose. Li and the stepmother, surprised, acknowledged their guilt. The judge imposed the death penalty on them. Death by strangulation was also the punishment prescribed for illicit sex with a father's or paternal grandfather's concubine.

After the birth of an heir, the father threw a feast to celebrate his good fortune. According to an ancient and revered classic on rites, the banquet took place on the third day after the birth and was the first time that he held his son in his arms. Emperor Taizong bestowed feasts to celebrate the births of his grandsons in 638 and 643. At some point after the infant's third month, the father selected a given name for it. The choice was never haphazard, for the words affected the future fortune of the child. The given name was taboo, that is, not used by family or outsiders. Children never referred to their parents by their personal names in speech or in writing. A son would have to decline an appointment to a political post whose title contained a character from his father's or paternal grandfather's given name. If he did not, he was subject to one year of penal servitude. The punishment for using the emperor's given name was much greater: three years of penal servitude. To avoid using it, writers used synonyms as substitutes.

By the seventh century birthday celebrations in adulthood, if not childhood, had become commonplace. The tradition apparently originated in the middle of the sixth century when an emperor convened vegetarian feasts and lectures on his birthday. In the Tang many festivities retained their Buddhist flavor. An infamous chief minister held vegetarian feasts for Buddhist monks at his mansion on his birthday. On one occasion he gave a saddle worth 70,000 coppers to a monk in appreciation for his chanting. He presented another who was famous for his voice with a casket containing what appeared to be a rusty nail. When the monk took it to the western market in Changan, a foreign merchant informed him that it was a Buddhist relic worth more than 1 million coppers.

The grandest of all birthday parties were those for the emperor. They began as court feasts at which mandarins offered their wishes for the sovereign's long life. In 729, however, Illustrious August made his birthday a national festival at the suggestion of his ministers. The following year he issued a decree declaring that all villages in the empire were to sacrifice to the White God of the West, who was his patron deity, and afterward sit down to drink to the emperor's health. He also made it a three-day holiday. In Changan the celebration took on the character of a grand carnival. His famed trained horses performed, and female entertainers danced a version of the "Smashing Battle Formations." Illustrious August set the precedent that most of his successors followed. They established festivals for celebrating their own birthdays. The festivities, however, were usually lectures given by Confucians, Taoists, and Buddhists on their doctrines.

The state divided childhood into three periods: infancy (one to two years of age), childhood (three to fourteen), and adolescence (fifteen to nineteen). Some fathers believed that discipline should begin as soon as a child could recognize the facial expressions of adults that expressed approval or disapproval of its behavior. They favored training the infant to be obedient and started using a bamboo rod to instill obedience several years after its birth. Strictness tempered with tenderness led children to be respectful. Other fathers were indulgent, preferring love to

**Pig's Eye**

**Dragon's Eye**

discipline, praise to blame. Children did as they pleased. Moralists contended that sort of upbringing produced arrogant scoundrels.

According to medical experts, one could determine with a good level of probability how long a child would live by examining its disposition between the ages of two and nine. Most of those who were exceptionally intelligent, perceptive, understanding, and clever would die young. Most of those with well-formed bones, impressive dignity, serenity, and polished spirit would live long.

Physicians were not really in the business of fortune-telling. Face readers were. When Emperor Taizong was four years of age, one of them visited his home, saw him, and told his father, "He has about him the air of the dragon and phoenix, and the outward appearance of the sun. When he is about twenty, he will save the *world* and pacify the *people*." Based on the prophecy, Gaozu chose World People for his son's name. Taizong was in his early twenties when he won battles that were instrumental in establishing the Tang dynasty. When Empress Wu was very young, a face reader visited her mansion and told her mother that she had given birth to noble children. After examining her sons, he saw the girl, who was wearing boy's clothing, in the arms of her wet nurse and asked that she be put down and allowed to walk. As she passed his couch, he had her raise her eyes, and said in amazement, "This child has the pupils of a dragon and the neck of a phoenix. She is the epitome of nobility." Then he turned her to her side and declared, "She is most certainly a girl. It is truly unfathomable, but she will later become the ruler of the empire." "Dragon pupil" and "phoenix neck" were terms for the characteristics of body parts (like pig's eyes) in the jargon of face reading. Although these anecdotes smack of political propaganda devised much later to justify usurpations (Taizong seized the throne from his father), they nonetheless reflect a very common practice in the Tang of consulting face readers to make prophecies based on the physical aspects of the individual's body.

Education began during the second period, usually about the age of six, and continued through the third, adolescence. Peasants passed their agricultural knowledge on to their sons orally, and artisans taught their sons their crafts by training them on the job. Some of the latter—brewers, swordsmiths, and the like—whose crafts involved various forms of technology, often swore their progeny to secrecy because disclosure entailed the loss of their monopoly on production and the income derived therefrom when competitors acquired their secrets and sold their goods at market. The child of a patrician learned the rudiments of reading, writing, and arithmetic. A precocious child might learn to write poetry at the age of five or six and master it by nine years of age. Sometimes the instructors were fathers, and many of them had high expectations for their sons. Such was the case for the greatest of the Tang historians. He had trouble with one text that he could not recite or memorize, so his father beat him frequently. Later he discovered an innate bent for history, which he easily mastered and could explain to his older brothers. At the age of twelve he memorized one of the longest chronicles in one year. Some fathers were harsh in their discipline. The son of Fan, the governor of a prefecture, requested permission to return to the family's native village so that he could prepare for the civil service examinations. The governor tested him and found his knowledge of the classics wanting. He summoned his staff, had his son beaten with the thin rod, placed him in the cangue, and forced him to stand at the city's gate as a demonstration of his rectitude in dealing with his kin.

If a father had died or was serving in a post at a distant district, a mother might take over the task of teaching her son. It was common for literate families to educate their daughters. As already noted, palace ladies received instruction in a host of subjects, and patrician families, which often adopted court fashions, probably followed the same practice. Well-to-do families did not have to burden their women with the duty; they hired tutors for their children. There were plenty of learned men who failed to pass the civil service examinations or find employment in the government who needed money. Some families pooled their funds to support private schools for their sons. Finally, a boy could enter the schools run by the state.

Adolescence for boys came to an end with "capping" at the age of nineteen. The father took his son to the ancestral shrine, if he had one, on an auspicious day and placed a cap on him before the spirits of the family's forebears. Capping was a rite of manhood, and for that reason there was no coronation ceremony for emperors. After the ritual concluded, the son took a new name, a style, that he usually used in signing his literary works. In the Tang, most men went by their styles. The end of adolescence came earlier for girls with "pinning" at the age of fourteen. Their mothers did their hair up on top of their head and inserted a hairpin to keep it there. It was a rite of womanhood that signified the girl was eligible for marriage. Females also took styles at age fourteen.

## FORMAL EDUCATION

There were at least two forms of institutional education in Tang China, one religious and the other secular. Written scriptures were the foundations of both Buddhism and Taoism, and the means of perpetuating their doctrines. Their rituals involved oral recitation (chanting) of the texts, and therefore monks and priests had to be literate. Codes of regulations governed life in and the administration of their monasteries. They compiled histories and biographies to establish the continuity of their orders, legitimize their existence, and inspire piety among their members. Consequently, they had to educate novices so that they could qualify for ordination and assume the duties of the priesthood. Usually, a master passed knowledge on to a disciple, and the bond between the two became very close and enduring.

During the Tang heated debates, oral and written, raged among Buddhists, Taoists, and Confucians. The issues were numerous and complex, but they all boiled down to the question of which religion or doctrine was superior. In addition, the imperial court sponsored lectures on the three teachings, especially on the emperor's birthdays. Both debates and lectures required knowledge of the opponent's literature, so monasteries and abbeys amassed large libraries of their own and their rivals' scriptures, and secular texts. The secular texts included not only the Confucian classics but also works on etiquette, divination, medicine, and music; collections of jokes and poetry; short fiction; and dictionaries, almanacs, histories, and biographies. One Taoist abbey in Changan had 50,000 scrolls of secular works, and became a center of intellectual activity frequently visited by renowned scholars in the middle of the eighth century. Because of their libraries, monasteries and abbeys became convenient places for lay students to pursue their learning. One eminent statesman and poet of the late seventh century left his village school in his youth to study in a classroom behind a Taoist abbey on a mountain in southwestern China.

The educational opportunities offered by religious establishments paled in comparison to those provided by the state. Eight days after ascending the throne in 618, Emperor Gaozu established three colleges in Changan for somewhat more than 300 students. Six years later he ordered prefectures and counties to institute schools in their districts. In 738, Emperor Illustrious August issued a Great Act of Grace containing a stipulation that vastly expanded the system. He ordered all prefectures and counties to establish schools in their villages and supply them with qualified teachers. Three years later the emperor founded a network of schools in the capitals and prefectures that offered instruction in the classics of Taoist philosophy. According to the census of 754, the empire had two capitals, 321 prefectures, 1,538 counties, and 16,829 villages. If all local officials carried out Illustrious August's instructions to the letter of the law, there were approximately 19,000 schools (excluding the medical schools already mentioned) throughout the land. In the mid-eighth century the total enrollment of students in the capitals and provinces was around 63,570 (and may not have included pupils in village schools).

The total number of students supported by the government—including specialized schools, and those for imperial guards, militia, and others—came to around 130,000. The number of the empire's subjects at the time was 48,909,800. That means that students constituted 0.25 percent of the population. By modern standards the number is small, but it is enormous for premodern societies.

Originally, Tang statutes restricted admission to the three capital colleges—the Colleges for Sons of State, Grand Learning, and Four Gates—to sons of fathers whose ranks were grades one to three, four to five, and six to seven, respectively. In 733 the emperor added 800 seats in the Four Gates College for sons of officials of eighth and ninth grades, as well as talented commoners recommended by the governors of prefectures. A government agency had to certify the rank of a student's father or, in the case of commoners, give a test to the candidates seeking to matriculate. The colleges accepted young men between the ages of fourteen and nineteen except for commoners, who could register as late as twenty-five. Age, not social status, determined the rank of a student in the student body. On their first day of class, students had to present their teachers with a gift of silk, jerky, and ale. Afterward the state provided a stipend in the form of grain and a place to live. Senior officials in prefectures and counties selected students between the ages of eighteen and twenty-five for admission to their schools. Pupils in prefectures and counties were required to study marriage and funeral rites. When they became proficient in them, they performed the ceremonies for officials and commoners.

Confucian or Taoist classics were the curriculum for government schools in the capitals and provinces. There were two facets to education in the Tang: memorization by the students and lectures by the faculty. Teachers expected students to commit portions of a text to memory before they arrived in the classroom. Professors and assistant professors expounded on the meanings of the assigned passages during class time. In their spare time students practiced calligraphy and composed trial answers to examination questions. Every ten days the masters gave an examination on the materials covered during the week. It consisted of one fill-in question for every 1,000 words of text memorized (students had to supply from memory a passage of which they received only the beginning sentence) and one interpretive question for every 2,000 words of text covered in lectures. A passing mark was satisfactory answers to two out of three questions. The faculty also gave a year-end examination to determine the progress of students. It consisted of ten oral questions. A passing mark was four or more acceptable answers. If a student failed that examination three years in a row or had been in school for nine years without graduating, he was dismissed and sent home.

The government also offered education in specialized fields. Except for medicine, instruction in them was available only in the capitals. The areas of study included law, mathematics, calligraphy, astronomy, calendrical science, divination, and ritual. The texts for the law school were the Tang code, statutes, ordinances, and regulations. There were ten textbooks for mathematics that students were expected to master in fourteen years. Students of calligraphy studied the classics as engraved in three styles of script on stone tablets, as well as two dictionaries. The course of study had to be completed in six years. Instruction in the remaining fields took place in the appropriate bureaus of the central government.

The behavior of students in capital schools was sometimes less than desirable. An imperial decree of 791 notes that some of them hired substitutes to take their examinations. A report to the throne from the dean of capital schools says that some of his students were shiftless. They gambled, drank too much, quarreled, and showed no respect for authority. Perhaps their most outrageous act took place in the early eighth century. A senior officer of capital schools discovered that students had become more and more slack in their class work. He exhorted them to be more diligent in pursuing their studies and applied the whip a little to prod them. The students resented that, and vilified him. Under the cover of darkness they thrashed him in the streets. When the emperor learned of the incident, he had the recalcitrant students beaten to death. Everything settled down after that.

Some directors of the colleges in the capital indulged and protected their charges. When Yang Cheng assumed the post in 795, he told the students that their business was to learn loyalty and family feelings. Then he suggested that those of them who had been away from home for a long while should take leave immediately. When the faculty took attendence the following day, they discovered that twenty or so of the students had departed. Later the throne sent him out of the capital to a post as governor in a remote prefecture because he was caught concealing a student wanted by constables in his home.

## EXAMINATIONS

The aspiration of most young men who received an education was to acquire a government post, civil or military. To achieve that goal, they had to take examinations given by the government. The breadth of Tang examinations was greater than those of any dynasty before or after it. Among other things, it had a test for child prodigies. The state assigned bureaucratic ranks to children nine years or younger who could recite the *Classic of Filial Piety* and the *Discourses of Confucius* from memory and answer ten out of ten questions on the texts. The government did not appoint them to offices at such tender ages. The ranks were presumably entitlements to take posts of those grades when they reached maturity.

The state granted degrees, privileges to take political offices, to students who passed examinations in all of the fields mentioned above. The three most important examinations were the Classical Masters, Advanced Scholars, and Elevated Warriors.

The deans of capital colleges recommended candidates who had passed school examinations to the Department of Rites. The governors of prefectures forwarded worthy aspirants, students in public or private schools, to the same agency in the capital. They conducted preliminary examinations consisting of five essay questions on current political problems and a few questions on the classics. The governors had to take care in their judgments. If a governor recommended an unworthy candidate lacking virtue, he was subject to one year penal servitude. However, if the man failed the examination, the law imposed only a beating of ninety strokes of the thick rod on the governor or dean. After the provincial examinations the governor convened the Village Drinking Ritual in the autumn, to honor the candidates and local elders.

One well-to-do father sent his talented son to the capital for the examinations, his horses and carriages burdened with provisions for a two-year stay. Another sent his son to the capital with more than a score of wagons to carry his baggage, and ten grand horses. Candidates assembled in the capital during the eleventh moon, in the middle of winter. There they registered and submitted credentials to verify their social status so that officials could reject sons of merchants and other undesirables. Next they appeared at the grand levee on New Year's Day, at which the emperor examined the tribute sent from the provinces and foreign states. The candidates were part of the districts' tribute.

During the interval between their arrival in the capital and the examinations, candidates for the Advanced Scholars' examination who did not prowl the Gay Quarters or haunt the taverns spent their time trying to influence the examiners. Except for a short period during Empress Wu's reign when slips of paper were pasted over the candidates' names on test papers, examiners knew whose work they were evaluating. Candidates did not necessarily contact the examiners directly. Instead, they visited the gates of eminent officials and handed scrolls with their own poems and highly flattering letters to the gatekeepers for presentation to their masters. In that manner they sought to establish great reputations for their literary abilities with the leading figures in the government. If they succeeded in attracting favorable attention from the mandarins, their fame would spread throughout high society and the examiners would hear of their superior abilities. A single scroll might do the trick, but a second might have to be submitted. On one occasion a scholar sent forty scrolls to the official in charge of the examinations, in defiance of the latter's order that candidates could not submit more than three. If fortune smiled on the candidates, officials might receive them for an interview. If it did not, they never got beyond the gate. Sometimes the gatekeepers or maids intercepted the scrolls and sold them. Sometimes the master of the house would not invite them in or do anything to help them. One scholar was remarkably persistent, haunting the doorway of a mandarin for ten years without success.

Scroll presentation, as it was known, was not really a form of cheating. After all, the candidate's patron was not likely to recommend to examiners or other officials a man whose poetry was mediocre or worse. He had his own reputation to maintain. However, it might result in a higher ranking in the final results of examinations for talented writers who were otherwise inferior in their abilities. Some scholars were not above resorting to plagiarism. A senior secretary received some scrolls from a student, and upon opening them discovered that they were poems he had circulated just before passing the examinations. When he confronted the student, the man confessed that he had purchased them at a bookstore for 100 cash.

The examinations in the capital took place in the spring. In the early years of the Tang the most prestigious was the Classical Masters. In 740 it had four parts: sixty-five fill-in questions for eight classics, an oral examination, ten questions on the interpretation of the classics, and three essays on contemporary problems. The Advanced Scholars examination had three sections: ten fill-in questions on one large classic with a commentary, five essays, and compositions of poetry and prose poems. The Advanced Scholars became popular after the throne added the poetry section in 681. It eventually surpassed the Classical Masters examination in prestige, probably because it placed considerably less emphasis on memory and considerably more on mastery of prose and verse. Examination poetry, however, never earned a reputation for excellence.

Empress Wu founded the military examination in 702. As with other examinations, both capital and provincial officials recommended candidates, who came to the capital to take it. It had seven parts:

1. Long target archery: shooting at a target 105 paces away, using a bow with a pull of 180 pounds
2. Mounted archery: shooting at a target having two small deer—five inches long and three inches tall—at a gallop
3. Pedestrian archery: shooting at a straw man while walking
4. Lance manipulation on horseback: knocking two-and-a-half-inch-square plates off four wooden figures—two on the right and two on the left—with a twelve-pound lance (eighteen feet long and an inch and a half in circumference), at a gallop
5. Physique: men over six feet ranked first
6. Discourse: speech that reflected leadership abilities

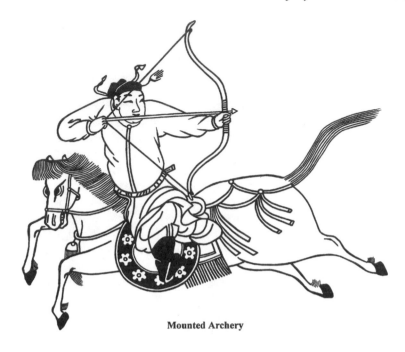

**Mounted Archery**

7. Weight lifting: raising a bar seventeen feet long and three and a half inches in diameter ten times and carrying eight and three-quarter bushels of grain on one's back for twenty paces.

Candidates from the provinces accompanied local officials who went to the capital in the eleventh moon to make their reports to the throne. The Department of the Army was responsible for checking their credentials and conducting the examination.

After the list of the men who had passed the Advanced Scholars appeared, the successful candidates visited the mansion of the examiner and gathered in his garden to express their gratitude to him. They introduced themselves, giving their names, ages, and seat numbers at the examination hall. The meeting established a strong bond between the examiner and the Advanced Scholars he passed, and among the graduates themselves. Later in their careers they would assist one another in times of need. The examiner invited the graduate who scored highest into his house for a reception. The state held a feast of congratulations for the graduates at which the finest food and premium ale were served. The graduates organized feasts for themselves in parks and scenic pavilions of the capital: the Serpentine River, apricot grove, Pavilion of Buddha's Tooth, and others. It was their custom to select two of their number to hunt for the most beautiful flowers in Changan. If someone found a more lovely blossom, the men had to drink a goblet of ale as a penalty. After they dined, the men rode off to admire the flowers that took the prize. Finally, the graduates inscribed their names in one of the city's pagodas.

Successful passage of a national examination in the capital did not by itself guarantee the graduate an office in the government. He had to remain in the capital and take the "selection examination" with candidates from the provinces. In the fifth moon governors of prefectures and commandants of counties submitted the names of men they wished to recommend. In the tenth moon the candidates assembled in the capital, where officials checked their credentials to make sure there were no undesirables, such as merchants, among them. Afterward, the examiners evaluated them on their physique, speech, calligraphy, and judgment. The last part required a written composition and covered all kinds of decisions, not just judicial ones. If all applicants achieved equal ratings, the examiners then ranked them according to their virtue, talent, and merit. Passing that examination might not result in an appointment either. A graduate's chances depended on vacancies in the bureaucracy, and the examination system was not the only avenue to office. In the 680s an official estimated that only 10 percent of qualified candidates received appointments. If there were no openings, the graduate would have to return home and take the examination another year.

The administration of the selection examination in the early eighth century was corrupt. The venality of the official in charge of it was staggering. Once, while candidates were being led to the examination, he noticed that one of the men had 100 coppers tied to his bootstrap. He asked the man why. The candidate replied, "Given the nature of the examination system these days, one cannot get by without cash." The examiner kept his silence.

## OLD AGE

According to Tang statutes, the mandatory age of retirement was fifty-nine. That regulation, however, applied only to peasants, and was the measure that the state used to redistribute land to the younger generation. The law did not apply to merchants and artisans, who could not own land. Furthermore, once the equal fields system broke down after 756, it was meaningless. By law mandarins had to remain in office until the age of sixty-nine. Those ranked fifth grade or higher could then personally submit a request to the throne for release from duty. In special cases the emperor rejected such appeals. The Department of Personnel submitted such requests for lower-ranking bureaucrats. Officials who remained fit could continue to serve in their posts past sixty-nine. The general who conquered northern Korea in 668 was seventy-four at the time. In one case the throne would not accept an eminent minister's resignation until he was eighty. In another, a general who participated in the Korean campaign and later rose to become a chief minister died in office at the age of eighty-three.

In most instances families were responsible for the care of their aged. That was both a traditional obligation and a legal one. According to Tang statutes, everyone seventy-nine to eighty-eight was to be furnished with an attendant; those aged eighty-nine to ninety-eight, with two; and those over ninety-nine, with five. The caretakers were first selected from the elder's adult children or grandchildren. If there were no adults, then adolescents served. If the seniors had neither, then close relatives assumed the burden. If they had no kinsmen at all, then the state appointed an adult or adults from the community to undertake the assignment. The government was reinforcing deeply rooted social mores and conventions with that law. Families inculcated respect for elders, especially parents and grandparents, in their children from a very early age. Men and women procreated in part to provide themselves with social security in their old age.

This is not to say that the state did not provide for the welfare of the aged. Although in theory a farmer lost 80 percent of his fields by his sixtieth birthday, Tang land statutes set aside 40 percent of his land as an allotment for his care until his death. As long as he remained vigorous, he presumably cultivated it. When he was no longer able to work, his sons apparently assumed the task. The law provided for the maintenance of the disabled in the same manner. The regulations also provided for widows, who received 30 percent of their husband's allotment unless they were the head of a household, in which case they received 40 percent.

Sometimes the throne bestowed direct assistance on the old. The occasions for dispensing such philanthropy included imperial progresses and the proclamations of Great Acts of Grace. Usually age was a determining factor in the qualification of the elders so blessed. For example, Emperor Illustrious August once ordered officials to present three lengths of silk cloth (money) and three and a half bushels of grain to caretakers of all men and women seventy-nine to ninety-eight years old, and five lengths of silk cloth and five bushels of grain to those tending seniors ninety-nine years or older. Other gifts included canes, quilted coats, ale, and felt frocks. Sometimes the throne invited the elderly to the palace for a feast. At other times it sent agents to inquire after the health of the old. In rare instances the emperor personally undertook the task himself. In 645 Taizong visited the hut of a man who claimed to have attained the ripe old age of 145 years by ingesting gold. The intent of bestowing the gifts was less to furnish support for the old than to provide an example of the emperor's veneration of the aged and his benevolent concern for them. The court often restricted the recipients to a small number of subjects living in one locality. Even when it presented gifts to "all people of the empire," the number who acquired the gifts must have been very small, given the restrictions on age, usually seventy-nine and older.

**Carving Flesh to Feed an Ailing Elder**

Aging usually involved illness of some sort, and the responsibility for nursing elders fell to their sons, daughters, daughters-in-law, or other family members. Wang was most filial. When his father was critically ill, he looked after him, serving medicine and food. His devotion to his father was so great that he did not change his clothes for more than a month. Later, because he was exhausted from the constant nursing, he dozed off while sitting next to his father's bed. In his sleep Wang dreamed that he heard some ghosts speaking. They were planning to invade his father's stomach. One of them asked, "How are you going to get into his guts?" The other replied, "I will wait until he eats his gruel. Then I will float down into his belly with the porridge." After the ghosts settled on their plan, Wang woke with a start and bored a hole in the bottom of a bowl. When it was time for his father to eat gruel, he plugged the hole with his finger and placed a small jar under it. Then he poured porridge into the bowl and released his finger. The gruel and the ghosts flowed into the flask. Wang sealed the mouth of the jar, placed it in a pot of water, and heated the water to a roaring boil. When he opened the flask to have a look, it was full of flesh. As a result of his quick thinking, his father recovered from his illness. Those who discussed this affair later believed that the cure was effected by Wang's pure filial devotion. The ghost story is unbelievable, but the sentiments expressed in it are not.

The obligation to care for parents in their later years was deeply rooted in the psyche of Tang Chinese. Even Taizong felt compelled to discharge the duty after he usurped the throne from his father. In 630 Gaozu took ill, so the emperor canceled his audiences—that is, he stopped attending to political affairs—in order to personally oversee his medicine and meals, as a good son ought. When his father recovered seventeen days later, Taizong held a feast to celebrate his good fortune.

Some dutiful children went to extremes in preparing medicine for their elders. A pharmacologist in the early eighth century declared that human flesh was a remedy for ailments. At that time and later, sons and daughters were wont to carve muscle from their body to feed their parents. The preferred location was generally the thigh, though sometimes it was the arm. One man sliced off three-quarters of a pound from his hip to prepare a remedy for his mother, who was suffering from tuberculosis. Some intellectuals decried the custom, but the children who sacrificed themselves enjoyed the respect of their contemporaries for their devotion to their parents. The throne bestowed honors and rewards on twenty-nine people for mutilating themselves in that manner.

# 12

# Death and the Afterlife

## DEATH

Since the Chinese believed that breath, *qi*, was the vital energy on which life depended, they took the cessation of breathing as evidence that death had occurred. A family member, friend, or outsider leaned over and placed his face close to the mouth of the unconscious person in order to determine if there was any movement of air coming from the lips. If there was not, he or she assumed that the person had expired, and made funeral arrangements. There was a certain danger in using that method. In some cases the breathing was too slight to detect. In 801 an official awoke after lying in his coffin for thirty days. His, however, was not the worst fate. In 885 a man who was walking past a grave heard someone calling to him from beneath the ground and alerted the family of the entombed. They dug up the grave and found its occupant alive. He died for good more than a year later.

Folklore had a more sinister notion about the cessation of breathing. In the ninth century a general halted for the night at a rapid relay station and took lodgings. In the middle of the night he suddenly awoke because he felt something pressing down on his body. The officer, who was quite strong, rose from his bed and grappled with the ghost. It withdrew under his fierce assault. During the struggle, the general wrested a leather bag from the specter. In the dark the ghost begged for the return of his bag. The officer refused and said, "If you tell me the name of this sack, I will return it to you." The specter hesitated for a long while and then said, "That is the 'harvesting breath bag.' " The general picked up a tile and threw it at the ghost. It ceased speaking immediately. The sack had a capacity of several pints, was green in color, and appeared to be made of thread. When thrust into the sunlight, it cast no shadow.

The Grim Reaper did not always resort to bagging breath. He had other means at his disposal for slaying his victims. Laborer Liu was rooming with a house servant who had been ill for several months and was about to die. One day, while Liu was out and the servant was lying in bed, a man wearing purple robes with broad sleeves and a tall hat suddenly appeared. His face was gaunt; his body, emaciated. He had a large nose and long beard. The stranger came through the door, and from the foot of the servant's bed said, "You are about to rise because your illness has run its course." Then he helped the man to a sitting position with his back against the wall. There was a dining table standing next to the east wall. Several dishes lay on it in orderly rows. The stranger reached into his sleeve and withdrew a handful of something from it. The objects in his hand were shaped like rice kernels, but were black. He placed more than ten of them in the dishes and said, "I am not from the world of the living. In obedience to a command I have come now to summon Liu. He will eat these and die. While he is eating them, you must not reveal a word of what I am telling you. Otherwise, misfortune will befall you." After the ghost finished speaking, it disappeared. When Liu returned that day, he was red in the face and panting. He said, "I've developed a fever from having an empty stomach, and it is almost beyond relief." He picked up the dishes, consumed their contents, and died.

Sometimes the minions of the unseen world were incompetent and summoned souls before their time. Scholar Jia died from a sudden illness. An usher led him to Heaven, where he had an audience with the Provost of Fate. The god checked his records and discovered that the life span allotted the scholar at birth had not yet run out, so he ordered him returned. However, Jia was unable to reach home because he had excruciating pains in his legs and could not walk. This was a source of concern for the underlings in charge of conveying him back. "If Jia cannot return to the world of the living, we will be charged with the crime of having wrongly taken his soul." They went to see the Provost of Fate and explained their dilemma to him. He pondered the problem for quite a while, then said, "Kang Yi, the western barbarian that we just summoned, is outside West Gate right now. That man died at his appointed time, and his legs are quite robust. Swap them for the scholar's. It will do no harm to either of them." The lackeys left to carry out his command. Kang's body was really ugly, and its legs were particularly repulsive. When the officers were about to make the switch, Jia saw the legs and refused to go through with the exchange. The officer in charge told him,

"If you do not swap legs with the western barbarian, you must stay here for eternity." Jia had no choice but to yield. The officer ordered the two men to close their eyes, and the switch took place instantly. An usher then led the scholar back to his home. Jia returned to life suddenly and took a look at his legs. They were indeed the westerner's. Their thick hairs were knotted together, and they stank of barbarian B.O. The scholar was a man of breeding, and admired his hands and feet. He loathed his new legs and hadn't the slightest desire to see them ever again. For the rest of his life he wore double layers of clothing, even in the scorching heat of summer. The legs were never exposed for a moment.

A man might receive a premonition of impending doom from the spirits of his body. When the Director of Personnel was returning to Chang-an from Luoyang, he made a stop at Mount Hua. Five men appeared suddenly and came into the reception hall of the prefecture. The director asked them what they were doing there. They replied, "We are the spirits of your five viscera." He said, "You spirits are supposed to reside in my body. Why have you come out to visit me?" They replied, "We are the guardians of your energies [*qi*], so when they're used up, we disperse." The official inquired, "Judging from what you say, am I about to die?" The spirits confirmed his suspicion. The director hastily pleaded for an extension of his life for a short time so that he could compose some documents. They agreed. After completing his reports, he bathed, donned new clothes, lay down on a bed, and died.

As soon as the family determined that their loved one was dead, they began to wail. After exhausting their grief they undressed the corpse, washed it with perfumed water, placed a piece of jade in its mouth to prevent the body from decaying, clothed it in grave garments, and placed it in a coffin. When a commoner's wife died in childbirth, a black mark was impressed on her face so her spirit could not harm members of her family. A man might purchase his own coffin while alive and store it in his dwelling. Otherwise the family had to purchase one on short notice. Coffins, at least those of the upper classes, were made of sturdy wood and sealed tightly because the family kept the corpse in the home for some time or sent it to a storage area in the city. The reason for the delay in most cases was that burial had to take place on a proper day according to the almanac or that the tomb had not been completed. In one extreme case the coffin containing the corpse of a man was kept in the hall of a house for ten years, probably because the family did not have the money to purchase a burial plot and pay for a funeral. When an official died in a district far from his native place, a family member or the government transported his remains home, an undertaking that could take weeks or months. The government provided ice for bureaucrats ranked third grade and higher who died during the summer, presumably to prevent rapid rotting of the corpse before it was placed in a coffin.

On the day of death or shortly thereafter, the family made a sacrifice to the deceased. For the humble the offering consisted of a simple meal with ale to nourish the soul in the afterlife. For the nobility the sacrifices were opulent. One of the grandest was that rendered to the spirit of Emperor Yizong's eldest and favorite daughter, Princess Tongchang, who died on September 14, 870. The emperor was so overwhelmed with grief that he lost his senses. He had a court physician and more than a score of other men executed for failing to cure her. After her remains were returned to her husband's mansion, the emperor granted civil and military officials the privilege of making sacrifices to her soul. They sent carriages, gowns, and ornaments adorned with gold and jade to his home, where they were burned in the courtyard to send them into the spirit world. When the fires died out, members of his family fought each other to grab the treasures from the ashes.

If the family were devout Buddhists, they arranged services for the departed. The rites were known as Seven-Seven Feasts. Buddhists did not believe in the existence of the soul. After death a person's karma passed into a barely perceptible body and entered a state of suspension during which its ultimate fate was uncertain. Karma was the consequence of the deeds, good and/or bad, that one performed during life. It determined whether a person would be reborn as a god or spirit, human, animal, denizen of hell, or hungry ghost. If after the first seven days the temporary body had not acquired enough merit to be reborn, it would die and come to life again for another seven days. The cycle of dying and reviving continued for seven weeks, at the end of which the karma would automatically pass into a new state of existence. The forty-nine-day interval gave the family of the deceased the opportunity to alter the departed's fate by accumulating merit. Meritorious acts included sponsoring vegetarian feasts at a nearby monastery every seven days. Kinsmen also sent clothing for the deceased on those occasions. In return monks chanted sutras, burned incense, and uttered prayers for the salvation of the dead loved one. If the departed had no family or had not accumulated meritorious deeds during its lifetime, it would be reborn in hell. Taoists also conducted seven-seven memorial services for the dead.

## FUNERALS AND ENTOMBMENTS

There were firms, at least in Changan, that provided exorcists, singers, hearses, and other equipment for funerals when the family had the means to pay for them. If the deceased was a mandarin, the state contributed to his funeral expenses: from 200 lengths of cloth and 350 bushels of millet for those of the first grade to ten lengths of cloth for those

**Hearses**

of the ninth. Those who could afford to pay received nothing, however. Furthermore, if a bureaucrat died in the course of a military campaign, while serving as a member of the imperial entourage when the court traveled, or when carrying out public business on a commission, the government supplied a coffin for him and paid for shipping his remains back to his home. When the man was not an official, his family bore the entire burden of the funeral expenses. According to Tang statutes, if a man died without family (male heirs), his daughter or nearest relative had to sell his slaves, shops, homes, and other property to pay for his funeral and burial. If he had neither a daughter nor close kinsman, then an official undertook the task, presumably drawing the money from government funds.

A funeral required a cortege made up of several elements. Chief among them was a hearse. In the Tang hearses were carts with bamboo poles affixed to their beds. An oiled cloth covered the bamboo framework like a tent. Oiling the fabric made it waterproof and protected the coffin from rain damage. Paintings of dragons adorned the side panels of hearses for mandarins of the third grade and above. Officials of that rank were entitled to an escort of six guides, who walked along the sides of the hearse to prevent it from tipping over; six bearers of wooden standards; six bell ringers; and thirty-six singers, called pall pullers, in six files. In ancient times coffins were dragged along on sledges. That custom disappeared long before the Tang, but the name stuck to the dirges and the singers of them in later times. Poets and even emperors wrote lyrics for the songs. Wooden standards were poles that had square plaques with cloud designs on their tops. Square-faced exorcists accompanied the funeral processions of mandarins fifth grade and above. They wore square masks with four golden eyes. Clad in black tunics and vermilion skirts they carried lances and shields, weapons they wielded to threaten and drive away demons. Mandarins of fifth grade and above were also permitted to have banners on poles nine feet tall in their cor-

**Square-Faced Exorcist**

teges. If the deceased had been well-to-do, his funeral train also had carts for carrying grave goods.

In the early Tang funerals were fairly spartan affairs except in the imperial clan. During the prosperous times of Emperor Illustrious August, they became more lavish. People began to erect tents along city streets where corteges passed. Inside they placed artificial flowers and fruit, as well as human figures made from dough, as offerings to the dead. The tents never exceeded ten square feet in area or several feet in height. After the rebellion of An Lushan the arrangements became extremely extravagant displays, especially among the regional military governors. The tents soared to eighty or ninety feet high and contained 200 to 300 shelves for holding platters of offerings. When one of the governors died in 775, his subordinates erected such sacrificial stations every sixth of a mile for more than seven miles. When another died in 768, one of his associates added a clever innovation to the array of platters. He had automated puppets installed that portrayed a great battle between a heroic Tang general of the seventh century and the Turks. A mechanism, perhaps powered by water, drove the wooden figures, which were completely lifelike in their movements. After the sacrifice finished, the cortege was on the verge of leaving when a subaltern requested that it wait because the show was not over. The mourners dried their tears and watched another drama. New puppets acted out a famous incident when a retainer of the first emperor of the Han saved him from assassination during a sword dance at a banquet.

Funeral processions could be quite large. Even a humble one in a village could attract more than a thousand mourners. One of the grandest of them, organized for the pampered Princess Tongchang, carried her to her last resting place in the eastern suburb of Changan on February 7, 871. It included 120 carts, one for each item of grave goods. The escort's standards, banners, and umbrellas filled the streets, blocking out the sun. The splendor of the train stretched out for seven miles on its way to the tomb. The emperor bestowed 6,342 quarts of ale and thirty camel loads of pastry to feed the men in charge of moving grave goods and other vehicles.

Graves were almost always in the countryside rather than in cities. According to the religious beliefs of premodern Chinese, the land beneath ground level belonged to the gods, and digging into it to construct tombs offended them unless the family of the deceased purchased the site from the deities. Consequently, the deceased's kinsmen drew up a contract to buy the plot. They deposited the document in the sepulcher to resolve any legal problems that might arise for the departed in the afterlife. The agreement contained the dead person's name, titles, and date of death; the exact dimensions of the plot; the price paid for the land—usually 99,999,000 coppers—and signatures of witnesses. Figures with multiples of nine were auspicious because nine was the number of yang, the life-sustaining force. The ideal age for dying, for example, was eighty-one, nine multiplied by nine.

Of course the money referred to in the contract was not genuine. No one, except perhaps the emperor, had access to such huge sums of coppers. By the Tang the belief had emerged that human money could not circulate among the spirits. The gods and souls of the dead required cash, silver, gold, and silk made from paper for their needs. So it became the custom to substitute phony money for the real thing. A man could purchase 100 sheets of paper at the market for sixty cash and cut from them 1,000 cash with scissors. By themselves artificial coppers were as useless as metal money. Souls could use them only if they were burned. Incinerating the paper transformed it into ethereal matter that the dead could employ in the afterlife, especially to reduce their suffering by bribing officials in the underworld. Sometimes the soul of a man who died had to buy off the functionaries of hell to obtain his release even though the mandarin in charge of the place had already authorized his return to life. Since paper coppers were cheap, mountains of them were shipped to and burned at tombs during the Tang.

Some categories of mandarins received government assistance in constructing their tombs. The state provided the labor for building the tombs of mandarins: 100 men for grade one, eighty for grade two, sixty for grade three, forty for grade four, and twenty for grade five. In all cases the grave diggers had ten days to complete the work. Tang statutes regulated the size of plots for mandarins, permitting the highest-ranking to secure parcels ninety paces square, and the lowest, parcels twenty paces square. The tombs were earthen tumuli resembling overturned bowls. The law also imposed limits on their heights. By law those of the highest-ranking officials could not exceed eighteen feet, and the lowest-ranking, eight feet.

The tombs of aristocrats and patricians had paths leading to their tumuli along which stone figures of men and animals stood. Tang statutes permitted mandarins of the third grade or higher to erect six statues, and those of the fourth and fifth grades, four statues. The tombstone was located at the end of the paths, in front of the grave. Tang statutes specified that statues for bureaucrats fifth grade and higher were not to exceed nine feet in height, and those for officials of the sixth and seventh ranks, four feet. They also permitted the former to have stelae with hornless dragons engraved at the top, and bases of carved tortoises. The latter had to settle for rounded tops and square bases. The epitaph on the tombstone was the biography of the deceased, often quite lengthy. According to law their authors, many of whom were authors of note, were to relate the facts of the person's life without excessive praise or embellishment.

Chambers within the tumuli provided space for the coffin and grave goods. Grave goods included not only such everyday items as clothing, but also figurines and models. According to Tang statutes the families of mandarins third grade and above could install ninety of the latter; those of the fourth and fifth ranks, sixty; and those of the sixth or lower grades, forty. The figurines and models included the following:

1. The four divine beasts (azure dragon, red bird, white tiger, and black tortoise), camels, horses, and men, not to exceed one foot in height
2. Entertainers and escorts, not to exceed seven inches in height
3. Houses and gardens, not to exceed five square feet in area
4. Slaves, not to exceed twenty in number and four inches in height.

During the Tang the figurines were ceramic statuettes done in a style called tricolor. As might be expected, the grave goods for Princess

Tongchang's tomb were exceedingly extravagant. Her father withdrew camels, phoenixes, and unicorns, all made of gold and several feet high, from the imperial treasury to provide her with a guard of honor in the grave. He had several model palaces—replete with countless dragons, phoenixes, flowers, trees, people, and domestic animals—carved from wood and placed in her tomb. Its fixtures also included drapes of fine embroidered silk into which gold, pearls and lapis lazuli had been sewn. The grave goods in all tombs were for the use of the deceased in the afterlife.

In the event that the remains of the deceased were missing—for example, when a general died in battle and the enemy disposed of his corpse—his relatives could perform or have performed the rite of "summoning the soul." Around 680 the court had the consort of Emperor Zhongzong, then a mere prince, deposed and imprisoned in the agency for eunuchs. When she died there in solitary confinement, the eunuchs or other palace attendants buried her corpse. After Zhongzong died in 710, Ruizong decided that she should join her husband in his tomb. However, no one could find her remains. A professor in a bureau for supervising rites recommended performing the ritual of summoning the soul for her with the ceremonial robes appropriate for a queen. It was an ancient rite performed at funerals. The individual in charge of it called out to the soul of the deceased, asking it to return. He had garments that the departed had worn in life at hand so that the wandering spirit would recognize and reenter them. In the case of Zhongzong's consort, officiants at the rite placed the garments in a soul cart after the ceremony, performed a triple sacrifice to the dead, and transported the gowns to the emperor's tomb. There they installed the garments to the right of the pedestal on which the emperor's coffin rested and covered them with a quilt. The robes took the place of the corpse.

Given the fact that tombs were prominent landmarks and that they contained valuable grave goods, it is not surprising that they often attracted grave robbers. In 740 more than twenty men, all junior members of noble families and totally lacking moral character, constructed a sham crypt a hundred paces or so from the tomb of imperial consort Hua at Changan. From inside their vault they dug a tunnel straight to the consort's grave. After breaking in, they ripped open her coffin. Discovering that the lady's face looked as it had in life and that her limbs were still flexible, they gave rein to their depraved passions and cruelly defiled her corpse. Then the robbers chopped her hands off at the wrists to remove her gold bracelets. They also cut out her tongue, fearing that her ghost would otherwise talk to the living in dreams. Afterward the thieves fled with the treasures that they found in Hua's tumulus, transporting them down the tunnel to their sham tomb. They spent an entire night loading their booty into empty coffins on hearses and other funeral wagons. Then they returned to the capital. Meanwhile the ghost of Consort Hua, naked and disheveled, appeared to her son in a dream. She informed him that grave robbers had opened her tomb, butchered her corpse, and raped her. Then she gave him a complete description of the thieves. The next morning the prince reported the matter to the throne. The emperor summoned the mayor of the capital and the county commandants. He ordered them to conduct a search for the culprits with utmost haste. When the thieves tried to enter one of the capital's gates, its keeper searched their wagons, found the grave goods, and took the entire band into custody. The authorities tortured them, and they all confessed. The prince requested that five of the leaders be turned over to him so that he could exact private vengeance. The emperor agreed. The consort's son ripped the guts from their bodies while they were still alive, cooked the offal, and offered the innards to the soul of his departed mother. Executioners beat the remaining robbers to death outside one of the city's gates.

## MOURNING

A family's mourning began at the moment of death, and sometimes the grief was overwhelming. After his mother passed away, one man cried without restraint until he went blind. Another's anguish over the loss of his father was so great that he coughed up blood. When the parents of a third died while he was away on a military campaign, he did not speak for thirty years. When his relatives made inquiries of him, he wrote out his replies. As a sign of filial devotion some sons erected mounds over their parents' graves themselves.

Mourning continued after the burial of the dead, its length determined by the relationship of the mourner to the deceased. According to ritual regulations, a man was supposed to mourn for his brother's son for one year, and his uncle's grandson for five months. The longest period, "three years," was that for parents and grandparents, except in the case of army officers, when it was 100 days. The three-year mourning period was actually only twenty-seven months, but imposed great hardships nonetheless. All mandarins had to resign from their posts the moment they learned of their parent's or grandparent's death, don mourning dress, and remain in retirement for the duration of the period. The official lost his salary and had to find other means of supporting himself and his family in the interim. At the end of twenty-seven months he could return to government service at the same rank that he held before. Failure to inform one's superior or to mourn was an offense punishable by exile to a place 666 miles from his place of residence.

Custom and the law demanded that the son or grandson adopt an austere lifestyle during the twenty-seven months. Removing mourning clothes and donning ordinary garments was punishable by three years of penal servitude. So was listening to or performing music. The Tang law code defined music as playing instruments, singing, and dancing, but the proscription undoubtedly applied to other forms of amusement, such as the variety acts of the independent entertainers. That regulation, of course, effectively prohibited all convivial gatherings with friends and kinsmen. Those convicted of playing board games could receive one year of penal servitude. If a son or grandson encountered a performance of music or other form of amusement by chance, he would receive a beating of 100 blows with the thick rod if caught and found guilty. The law banned marriages during the mourning period, imposing a punishment of three years of penal servitude on violators. Mourners had to abstain from sex for twenty-seven months as well. The law specified a sentence of one year of penal servitude for those who conceived or gave birth to a child during that time. The regulation did not apply to children conceived before, but delivered during, the mourning period. There was an escape clause to that article of the code. If the offender confessed before his crime came to light, he was not subject to punishment. Most of the rules also pertained to women. The objective of all of them was to ensure that mourners maintained a proper state of grief and refrained from enjoying any pleasure. There were also Days of National Mourning for deceased Tang emperors and empresses. Tang statutes forbade all subjects from indulging in entertainment on those anniversaries.

In 817 the authorities learned that an imperial son-in-law, the son of his father's concubine, had indulged himself with a nocturnal feast during the mourning period for his father's principal wife. The court stripped him of all official and noble titles, had him beaten forty strokes with the thin rod, and settled him in (banished him to) a prefecture away from the capital. A guest at the festivities received the same beating and exile to a distant prefecture.

Some mourners went to extremes in their expression of grief. One withdrew from public life for more than ten years. Several took to dwelling in huts they built next to the graves of their parents. After the death of his mother, a man erected such a hut, stopped bathing, ceased combing his hair, gave up eating meat, and drank only water. Another planted more than 1,000 cypress and pine trees on the site of his mother's grave.

After the three-year mourning period concluded, a man—or occasionally a woman in cases when no male descendants survived—had to maintain reverence for forebears. That obligation, best known as ancestor worship in the West, consisted of sharing food. The eldest son performed the ritual that took place on the anniversary of his father's death. The government granted one day of leave to mandarins so they could attend to it. The rite embraced all male forebears of the son to the seventh generation, from his great-great-great-great-great grandfather to his father. If he had the means, he erected an ancestral shrine where he displayed the spirit tablets for all of those ancestors. Otherwise, he arrayed them at an altar in his home. Spirit tablets were oblong wooden boards, square at the bottom and round at the top, on which the name of the deceased appeared, written or engraved. During the sacrifice, the eldest son invited the soul of the deceased to descend into the spirit tablet by burning incense. He then presented the offering of cooked food, usually pork, fish, and chicken along with ale. The ancestor partook of the victuals' essence. The family would eat its physical substance.

In the early seventh century a senior secretary from the world of the dead informed a medium that souls needed but one meal a year. In the Tang, descendants usually provided two: one in the home on the anniversary of the ancestor's death and the other on April 5, during the Cold Food Festival. If the spirits did not receive it, they would steal food or perhaps beg for it. The number of ghosts for whom no one provided sustenance was enormous. Once two officials spent the night at an inn. The hostelry provided them with food and ale. The men sat facing one another and ate well into the night. Suddenly they saw a pair of hairy black hands appear beneath their lantern. The hands made a gesture as if asking for something to eat, so each man placed a piece of roasted meat in one of the hands. A moment later the hands reappeared. They made a gesture as if cupping something, so each of the officials poured a goblet of ale and gave it to one of the hands. The hands did not appear again. When they finished eating, the men turned their backs to the lantern and went to sleep. In the second night watch (9 P.M. to 11 P.M.) they heard a voice calling from the street. "A villager twenty miles due east of here has spread a feast for the gods, and the food and brew are abundant. Can you come?" A voice speaking from under the lantern replied, "I am already drunk with ale and stuffed with food." The spirit outside then departed.

## THE AFTERLIFE: SOULS

Ancient Chinese believed that a multiplicity of souls inhabited the human body. A time-honored medical canon contended that each of the five viscera—liver, lungs, heart, spleen, and kidneys—had its own spirit. Religious Taoists went to extremes in their beliefs about the residents of the body. They claimed that it was the abode of 36,000 gods. The consensus, however, was that there were only two. They represented, and were produced by, the cosmological forces of yin and yang.

**The Po**  The *po* soul was a manifestation of yin—earth, water, and the dark. It was the governor of the physical nature of man and gave form to the fetus in the womb. The *po* was the animal nature of man, instincts and urges that first became apparent after birth, when the behavior of an infant was clearly centered on the fulfillment of its self-centered needs. Later in life the soul expressed itself as emotions: joy, anger, sorrow, sadness, glee, love, and hate. The *po* was fixed to the body, and after death returned to earth, where it moldered in the soil and lodged in the bones at the grave.

That belief led to some strange notions about the behavior of the dead among Tang Chinese. The wife of a village headman had just died. One evening at dusk, before her family had coffined her, the sound of music entered the room where her body lay, and her corpse rose to dance. When the music departed, the dead woman followed. After her husband returned home that evening and heard about his wife, he fortified himself with some ale, broke a branch from a mulberry tree, and went looking for her. He found her in a grove of cypress in a graveyard, where she was still dancing to the music beneath the trees. The headman struck the corpse with his stick. The body fell to the ground, and the music ceased. He carried the body of his wife home on his back. In this story the music animates the cadaver by exciting its passions, its *po*.

When it did not receive a proper burial, the *po* might resort to clever ruses to remedy its predicament. During the night the skeleton of a young child paid a call on a family of brothers who were teachers. It entered their hall, cried out, "Mother, suckle me!" and romped about as nimbly as a monkey. The brothers struck the thing with staves. Each time a staff struck home, the spirit's bones scattered like falling stars. The bones then gathered themselves, put the skeleton back together, and shrieked, "Mother, suckle me!" So the men caught the thing, stuffed it into a linen bag, and tossed the sack in a dry well. The next night the skeleton returned with the linen bag in its hand. The brothers stuffed it into the bag again, tied a rock to the bag with a rope, and heaved it into a river. While they were disposing of it, the spirit spoke: "I will return to be your guest, as I was last night." True to its word, the skeleton arrived at the house once more, with the bag in its left hand and the rope in its right. The family was better prepared for it the third time. They had chiseled out the core of a large log to make a canister into which they stuffed the thing. Then they capped both ends of the log with iron plates and nailed the plates to the wood. They attached an iron lock and tied a huge rock to the log. As the brothers were rushing off to set it adrift in a large river, the ghost spoke. "Many thanks for providing the coffin for my send-off." The tale clearly attests to the importance that ancient Chinese attached to interring the bones of the dead, even if they were not those of your own kinsmen.

The Chinese of medieval times had a peculiar obsession with the eyes, which they believed lived on after death. Physician Wang was a skilled acupuncturist. In 831 he died, but revived the following day to tell his tale. In his coma he had traveled to a place where he treated an abscess on a man's shoulder, extracting more than a pint of pus. The patient directed a subordinate dressed in yellow robes to escort the physician to a courtyard. When the doctor entered it, he saw several thousand human eyes stacked to form a mountain. They were sparkling and twinkling. The yellow-clad officer said, "These are 'ends.' " Presently two men of imposing stature appeared. They took positions to the right and left of the mountain, then swung giant fans. The fans stirred a breeze that wafted over the eyes. Some of them flew away on the currents of air. Others rolled away on the ground. All of them vanished in an instant. The physician asked the reason for that. The officer replied, "All living things become 'ends' just after they die." Eyeballs, *po*, survived after death. It is not clear what the source of that belief was, but there were several tales about the strange behavior of eyes.

**The Hun**
The *hun* soul was a manifestation of yang—heaven, fire, and light. It governed the intelligence of man. At birth it was weak, but evolved and strengthened as the child's reason developed, especially after the age of six, when education began. It reached full maturity at the age of twenty, but did not fully perfect itself until the age of fifty. The *hun* governed the character of man: his benevolence, righteousness, decorum, knowledge, and trustworthiness. In the Chinese mind, all of those attributes were distinctly Chinese. The *hun* was *qi*, breath, and therefore not attached to the body. It was free to roam, in life as well as in death. Some of its wanderings occurred during sleep when a person had dreams. At death it returned to heaven but, when summoned, visited its family for sacrifices at the home or its grave.

Some people had a good idea of what the *hun* looked like. Several spirits came to haunt the home of Teacher Yan. After several attempts to exorcise them failed, he fell ill, and his condition took a turn for the worse. In his delirium he had a dream in which a man dressed in vermilion robes and a black bandanna appeared. Standing in midair, the spirit said, "I am returning your soul to you." Then it tossed what appeared to be more than twenty orange robes at the teacher. Yan gathered them up. The next day he recovered from his illness. The notion that the soul resembles clothing may have developed from the pivotal role that the deceased's garments played in the rite of summoning the soul. This ghost story also reveals another ancient Chinese belief about the soul. Some illnesses are occasions when the soul is absent from the body. This was true especially for ailments that involved comas and cataleptic trances. In such cases herbalists concocted a remedy called "soup for returning the soul [to the body]" for administration to the patient.

Intellect and culture were superior to emotions and urges, so the *hun* controlled the *po* while it resided in the body. That belief led the Chinese imagination down some bizarre paths. A judge sentenced a county commandant to death for committing a crime. After the executioner beheaded him, his body did not die, and his family carried it home on a litter. Every time the commandant was hungry, he wrote the word "famished" on the ground. His kin then minced food and stuffed it down the hole in his neck. When he was full, he wrote the word "stop" on the ground. Whenever anyone in the family committed an offense, he wrote a punishment for the person on the ground. Since the passions of the living had not abated in him, he slept with his wife, who bore him another son. Things went on like that for three or four years. One day he wrote, "I will die tomorrow [i.e., my *hun* will depart], so prepare the funeral paraphernalia." His family did as they were told.

Sometimes the body that the *hun* animated was not its own, but a borrowed corpse. Marshal Guo and Liu were good friends, so they made a compact. Whoever died first would return to tell the other about the world of the shades. Several months after Liu died, the marshal heard the sound of his friend's voice speaking outside his door during the night, and invited him to enter. Liu asked Guo to put out the candles, which he did. Guo ushered his friend in, the two sat together on a couch and chatted about the otherworld. After midnight the marshal suddenly smelled a putrid odor all around him. The stench quickly became so strong that he could not stand it. His suspicions aroused, the marshal felt the body of the ghost with his hands and discovered that the corpse was very large, unlike Liu's body. Guo pulled the specter to the ground and lay on it with his hand covering his nose. When the sun was about to rise, the spirit became quite agitated and asked for permission to depart. Guo would not give it. After dawn broke, Guo saw that he was lying on the corpse of a western barbarian. The body was over seven feet tall and appeared to have been dead for several days.

Ghosts had the same needs, appetites, and passions as the living. Seventh Daughter, a courtesan, had had an affair with General Wang. He took ill and died, but six months later she still did not know that he had passed away. At the beginning of autumn he suddenly appeared at her brothel and lingered there until dusk. In the twilight the general asked her to accompany him to his house. The courtesan was reluctant to leave, and asked him to stay at her bordello, but he insisted that they go. He set her behind him on his horse, and the pair rode off. After they arrived at his mansion, they joined in pleasure as they had when he was alive. The next morning a maidservant discovered Seventh Daughter among the blankets on the general's coffin trestle, and rushed off to inform the Wangs. His sons went to have a look for themselves, and asked the courtesan how she had come to be there. After she explained, they sent her back to the brothel. The *hun* was supposed to be the rational force that controlled urges like sex, but popular religious beliefs were often paradoxical.

Vengeance was as strong a passion as sex in traditional China. The

**Bath Powder Dissolves Bones**

soul of a murder victim might, like Consort Hua, appear in a magistrate's dream to reveal the killer who had escaped justice. On occasion a ghost might exact retribution on its own for an offense committed against it. When Marshal Li was in the capital, he tried to take a concubine, but the mother of the women he desired would not grant her permission. So he told her, "I vow never to marry." She then relented. Several years later the concubine died. A year after she passed away, the marshal arranged a marriage with the daughter of Commandant Shen. On his wedding day, while he was bathing in the bath house, Li saw the dead woman march straight forward to his tub with herbs in her hand. She told him, "You promised me that you would never marry. Today you will become the Shen's bridegroom. I have no wedding present for you, but I will give you these herbs to perfume your bathwater." She scattered the powdered herbs in the bathtub and, after stirring the water with her hair pin, vanished. Li felt very uneasy. He became so bloated that he could not drag himself from the bath, and died there. When they found his corpse, its limbs and torso were as soft as silk floss because the bath powder had dissolved his tendons and bones. This was a cautionary tale for people, who gave their solemn word, that they would suffer dire consequences if they broke it.

Sometimes retribution for murder was very swift, effected by a magician without the aid of the spirits. Du saw a Buddhist monk pass by with a trunk. Thinking the chest contained valuable silk, Du devised a plot with his wife to steal it, and they beat the priest to death. Before the monk expired, the couple heard him mutter a magic spell or two. Afterward a fly flew up Du's nostril and plugged his nose for a long time. Du's eyes and nose turned down. His hair and eyebrows fell out. In a daze, he lost his bearings. His vitality ebbed and faded away. In a short while he came down with a demonic disease and died before a year passed. As he approached his end, the fly flew out of his nose and into his wife's. She took ill and passed away a little more than a year later.

Where does the soul go after death? There was a tale written in the Tang about a Ghost Country on an island in the sea, but it was the product of the overactive imagination of its author. It should be quite clear by now that, as far as popular religion went, ghosts and men intermingled and interacted in very intimate ways on the same plane. People of all stripes—emperors, mandarins, intellectuals, merchants, and peasants—saw the spirits of the dead anywhere and everywhere. In one tale the ghost of a merchant meets a monk who was a friend while he was alive. After consuming dumplings in an eatery the pair strolls along a lane in the market and meets a woman selling flowers. The spirit says to the monk, "This woman is a ghost, and the flowers she sells are for the use of specters only. They're invisible to the living." He takes out several coppers, buys some flowers, and gives them to his friend. Then he adds, "All those who smile when they see these flowers, are ghosts," takes leave of the monk, and vanishes. As the monk walks back to his monastery, many people on the road see his flowers and smile. The ghosts are all around, but only ghost seers can detect them.

There were special, invisible cities or bureaus in heaven, beneath holy mountains or at unspecified locations—the unseen world—where the gears of the otherworld's administration ground on inexorably. The government of ghosts was a mirror reflection of the government of the living, at least in the sense of the judicial system. The duty of the Provosts of Fate in heaven and beneath Mount Tai on earth was to examine the dossiers of the dead and determine if the life spans allotted them at birth had expired. They also reviewed the ledgers of the deceased's merits, and sins based on reports submitted by the three corpses and the god of the stove. They deducted 300 days from the soul's birthright for transgressions of great enormity and three days for minor infractions. Resolving lawsuits was the responsibility of judges in the netherworld. The souls of the dead could file complaints against the living who had committed crimes against them while they were alive. Coffin Head Li was a bully who often stole cats and dogs in the eastern market and ate them. One day two men dressed in purple approached him. One of them said, "We have business. Is there someplace we can talk in private?" The three of them walked several paces and halted at a spot away from the crowd.

The man then said to Coffin Head, "The provosts of the unseen world have sent us here to apprehend you. You must go with us at once." At first the bully didn't get it, so he asked, "You are men. Why are you putting me on?" The man replied, "To the contrary, we are ghosts." Then the spirit took an official document from his bosom. The seal on it was still wet, and Coffin Head could clearly make out his name written on it. The paper recounted the details of charges that 460 cats and dogs had lodged against Coffin Head with the magistrates of the shades.

After death a soul might have to appear in court to answer charges lodged against it. Ushers led the spirit of Commandant Yang, a high-ranking minister, into the tribunal of the king of hell. The monarch asked the commandant, "How did you manage to accumulate so many indictments of your sins while you were alive? Since there are so many, how will you be able to redeem yourself?" Yang retorted, "I am truly sinless!" The king ordered the registers brought to him. A moment later a yellow-clad clerk arrived with the books in hand and recited the commandant's sins.

In 692, when the northern prefectures fell to the Turkish khan, the number of troops that the dynasty sent to save the districts was small, so the armies were no match for the invaders. Someone sent a document up to the throne that censured the government for this decision, but Commandant Yang ignored the advice and sent the armies forward anyway. The khan defeated those forces and slew more than 1,000 men.

In 701 locusts ravaged the region north of the Yellow River, and no one had a kernel of grain to eat. Yang would not open the granaries to supply relief to the afflicted population. That caused commoners to leave their homes and migrate. More than 20,000 starved to death.

Yang's statecraft was uneven, and his application of it injured nature's harmony. As a result a great flood struck three prefectures south of the Yellow River, and thousands of people drowned.

There are another sixty-seven indictments of Yang's sins just like these.

The clerk showed the dossier to Commandant Yang, who then acknowledged his transgressions. Suddenly a hand the size of a couch, with frightening bristles, appeared and seized the commandant. With Yang's blood dripping from its fingers, it rose into space and disappeared.

It was the magistrates of the dead who dispatched bailiffs to apprehend the souls of the living whose terms of life had expired. They might charge their minions with the task of gathering in a host of spirits. In that case epidemics broke out in various regions of the empire. A band of them could arrive at a mansion with a wagon full of fire and toss into its flames the soul of a man who had relished delicacies that required roasting jackasses and potting geese alive. Usually, however, the bailiffs confronted a single victim in a conventional setting.

The bailiffs could be flexible in carrying out their duties. Sometimes they spared a man if he could find a substitute who looked like him. Sometimes they were willing to take a bribe. Coffin Head Li begged the spirits that accosted him for a little extra time. After some deliberation they agreed. "If you can manage 400,000 coppers, we will grant you a stay of three years." Coffin Head agreed to this, and the three fixed noon of the following day as the time for the bully to pay. At the appointed hour he prepared the money that he'd pledged, and burned it. As it went up in smoke he saw the two ghosts take the cash and vanish. Three days later he died. Three years in the world of the shades was the equivalent of three days among the living.

After the bailiffs escorted the soul to a court in the unseen world, the spirit might have to endure interminable delays due to the red tape of its bureaucracy. Comely Countenance, whose mistress had murdered her, returned to life and told her tale to a descendant of her mistress's husband. "As soon as I died, two men clad in black led me away to a place with great gates and spacious halls. I paid homage to the king inside, and he made a brief inquiry into the facts of my case. My black-clad escorts muddled their report of the events that led to my death from beginning to end. I did not correct them, however, because I dared not accuse your ancestor's wife of murder. A little later they led me to a bureau where I saw documents and files stacked up to the ceiling. A knot of clerks was bustling about, examining and searching the papers. One of them, with my dossier in hand, was the first to interrogate me. After inspecting my file, he declared that my demise did not agree with the fate that had been assigned me in the document. It was his judgment that eleven years be deducted from my mistress's life and given to me. Another official reviewed my case, and affirmed the decision of the first. However, the second was cashiered as punishment for some reason. As a result my dossier was shelved, and my case remained closed for more than ninety years. Yesterday a celestial mandarin suddenly arrived to search for long-pending cases that the bureaucrats of the unseen world had shelved. He resolved all outstanding cases, including mine. I lost none of the eleven years that the first judge had awarded me."

Comely Countenance was fortunate in one respect. When a soul's case remained unresolved, the ruler of the underworld smeared a potion on its corpse so that it would not decay. Others were not so lucky. The body of Li, whose soul the bailiffs mistakenly seized, had rotted away by the time bureaucrats corrected the bailiffs' error. So the functionaries of the otherworld chose the body of a man who had just died, and compelled Li's soul to enter it. He woke to find himself in a house 300 miles from his own. When he reached home, none of his family recognized him. Only his behavior and voice convinced them of his true identity.

Punishment for sin did not always take place in the world of the shades or involve the dead. A general once asked ghost seer Hong to find out why he had no son to be his heir. Hong encountered the specter of the general's father, who informed him that his son had slept with a maidservant when he was young and vowed to her that he would never marry. Later he broke his word. The maid had died and filed a complaint against him in Heaven. The judgment of the celestial magistrates was that the general should have no sons.

There were some skeptics in the Tang who refused to believe in the existence of specters. They did not fare well in the literature of the times. Li often boastfully told his guests that he did not dread ghosts. One day a red face over one foot in length appeared on the south wall of his dwelling. It had a bent nose, sunken eyes, pointed teeth, and a sharp mouth. All in all, the face was quite repulsive. The sight of it enraged Li, so he struck it with his fist. It vanished the instant that his knuckles hit it, then reappeared immediately on the west wall, now white. Then it showed itself on the east wall in azure. Each time the face disappeared when Li struck it. Finally, a black face popped up on the north wall. It was twice the size of the others and far more terrifying. It aroused greater rage in Li. He dealt it several blows, but it would not vanish. He drew his sword and stabbed it. When his blade struck home, the face left the wall and enveloped him. Li pushed it with his hands, but he could not rid himself of it. The black face then fused itself to his face. Li took on the color of glossy black lacquer, toppled to the ground, and died. When they laid him to rest in a coffin, the inky hue of his face had not changed.

## BUDDHISM

The highest state of spiritual attainment for Buddhists was nirvana, a state of extinction attained by suppressing all desires and delusions in order to terminate suffering, obliterate karma, and escape from the perpetual cycle of rebirth. It was a form of individual salvation that required a monk or nun to live a life of asceticism, self-denial, and meditation in near total isolation from his or her family. The idea did not sit well with most Chinese, but one school of Buddhism offered another, more attractive alternative.

It was Pure Land, a paradise located somewhere to the west of the world. From its gold ground spring jeweled trees that make music when their branches are moved by gentle breezes. Stairs adorned with gold, silver, lapis lazuli, and crystal lead down into bathing pools filled with cool, sweet, thirst-quenching water. In beds of gold dust blue, red, white, and yellow lotus blossoms grow. Four times a day flowers rain down from above, and flocks of birds—peacocks, egrets, and parrots—with elegant plumages sing songs expounding Buddhist tenets. Ethereal music resounds perpetually. It is a paradise of pure bliss in which nothing

unpleasant exists. Dwellers there are free from all suffering, having escaped from the endless cycle of rebirth.

Amitabha, the Buddha of Boundless Light, reigns in Pure Land without a bureaucracy of any sort. That was no doubt an appealing notion
to the Chinese, who had long suffered under the yoke of imperial offi-
cialdom. Out of infinite compassion for all sentient beings, he created
Pure Land, and promises that everyone who truly believes in him will
be reborn in his paradise. His right-hand man is Guanyin, who travels
everywhere to bring the faithful to the paradise. The secret to gaining
admission to Pure Land is uttering the name of Amitabha with true
sincerity. Devotees who have total faith in Pure Land will be reborn
there, sitting cross-legged on open lotus blossoms. Skeptics who utter
the name of Amitabha, but doubt the existence of the paradise, will be
reborn in a closed lotus and spend 500 years there before emerging. In
either case, gods and humans will enjoy bliss eternally in Pure Land until
they attain nirvana. The appeal of Pure Land doctrines was not so much
that they offered an idyllic existence as that they presented an easy
means of acquiring salvation. A believer did not have to practice asceticism and accumulate merit to attain paradise.

Buddhism not only brought to China the belief in a paradise for the
faithful, it also introduced the notion of three woeful modes of existences
for sinners: rebirth as a hungry ghost, as a denizen of hell, or as an
inferior being in a future life. The belief in hungry ghosts was very old
in China, but the notion had no stigma attached to it. The famished
spirits were simply unfortunate souls who had no descendants to supply
them with sustenance. Buddhism saw them in a different light. Starving
specters were suffering as punishment for violating religious ethics.
When Mulian encounters his mother in the beyond, her throat has contracted to the size of a needle's eye, and no water can pass through it.
She sees a clear, cool river in the distance, but, as she approaches it, it
changes into a stream of pus. His mother receives delectable food, but it
immediately transforms itself into fire.

The Buddhist notion of hell was different from that in the West. It was
not an inferno of eternal damnation for sinners. Instead hell was a kind
of purgatory in which the damned suffered torment for limited, albeit
lengthy, terms. When they completed their sentences, they assumed new
forms in another life. King Yama reigned over the netherworld, but ox-
head and horse-head minions actually ran the place. They prodded the
condemned on with pitchforks and truncheons. There were special sectors for the punishment of specific sins. In one people who damaged the
property of monasteries, ate their fruit or stole their firewood had to
climb knife trees that slice off their skin. In another men and women
suffered for having illicit sex on the beds of their parents. The women
were forced down onto beds of iron nails that thrust up through their

bodies while the men were compelled to embrace red hot copper pillars.

Hunters received the worst punishments because the taking of life was an anathema to Buddhists. Archer Li slew enormous numbers of animals with his arrows and caught countless fish. In 645 he died after being ill for several days. A ghost led him to hell, where he entered a walled courtyard full of flying birds and running animals. The creatures pressed closer and closer to the bowman, and demanded his life for having slaughtered them. A bitch whom he had shot dead came straight up to him and bit his face. Then the dog gnawed his body until there was not an inch that was free of wounds. Afterward three large ghosts, more than ten feet tall, appeared. They flayed the archer's skin and flesh. In a moment they had completely butchered Li, leaving only his face, eyes, bones, and innards. The fiends divided the meat and fed it to the birds and beasts. The bowman's skin and flesh grew anew, so the ghosts flayed him again. The butchery continued repeatedly for three days, during which time Li was beyond himself with excruciating pain and misery. When it was over, the specters and the creatures disappeared. The archer climbed over a wall and ran south with no idea of where he was going. Just when he thought he had escaped, another spirit chased him down and slapped an iron cage over him. Inside, innumerable fish nibbled on him. When they finished devouring him, the fiend and the fish vanished. After Li revived, he discovered that he had been dead for six days.

After sinners completed their sentences in hell, officials of the unseen world assigned them new destinies among the living. If their transgressions were minor, they stood a good chance of being reborn as human beings of prominent social standing or as gods. Sometimes their sins were so trivial that they passed straight through hell without suffering any punishment whatsoever. Occasionally, problems developed in the transition from one incarnation to the next. The daughter of a governor had often been ill since infancy. It was as if her spirit lacked strength. The governor asked Recluse Wang, who was a master of Taoist magic, about her condition. Wang said, "This girl is not sick. When she was born, her *hun* soul did not attach itself to her body. The commandant of such-and-such a county has your girl's former body. He should have died several years ago. Since he has been a good man throughout his life, the powers of the unseen world have allowed him to live beyond his allotted time as a reward for his merit. He is now over ninety years of age. On the day of his death your daughter will recover." A month later the governor's daughter suddenly woke, as if from a drunken stupor, and her illness was cured. The governor sent an agent to check on the commandant. He had died without suffering an illness on the same day that the girl recovered.

If the transgressions were grave, the mandarins in the netherworld might consign the sinner to an animal's body. During a journey, monk Lingyin saw a bamboo sedan chair moving ahead of him. A maidservant dressed in the hemp sackcloth of mourning was following it. He followed the palanquin for several days, but never saw its occupant. So he went up to the litter, quickly drew the curtain aside and peaked in. The monk saw a very imposing woman who had a human head and a snake's body. That shocked him. The woman told him, "Because the karmic retribution for my sins was so heavy, my body changed into that of a serpent. Why did you have to look at me?"

A person reincarnated as an animal could accumulate merit and earn a promotion to a higher state of existence in its next life. The aunt of Governor Lu had a dog named Blossom of which she was very fond. One day someone killed it. Several months later the woman died suddenly and had an audience with Judge Li in the world of the shades. He told her, "Madam, when the life span that heaven accorded you was about to expire, someone spoke up for you forcefully. So you will live for another twenty years." The woman thanked him and left. As she was walking along a boulevard, she passed a mansion. A beautiful woman with more than ten maidservants sauntered out from behind the spirit screen in front of its gate. The woman asked the aunt if she recognized her. "No, I don't remember you," she replied. "I am Blossom. I am indebted to you for not treating me cruelly, like a domestic beast, when I was alive, and for constantly nurturing me. I am now the concubine of Judge Li. I was the one who spoke on your behalf yesterday. The provosts of the unseen world did not want to grant all the years I requested for you. They would give you only one degree, but I altered the numbers in the records from twelve to twenty, in order to repay you for your kindness." When the women parted, Blossom said to the aunt, "Please gather up my bones and bury them for me. My remains lie beneath a wall on a street in such-and-such a ward. Someone threw them on a dung heap." After the lady recovered consciousness, she found the dog's bones just where Blossom said they'd be. She buried them with the same rites that she would have used for her own children. Blossom then appeared in her dreams to thank her. Blossom had apparently acquired great merit in her existence as a dog, enough to warrant rebirth as a god.

Regardless of whether one was reborn as an animal in this world or as a deity in the netherworld, reincarnation was always something of an unwelcome event because it did not liberate one from suffering.

## TAOISM

Taoism emerged in the second century as an outgrowth of China's indigenous religions. It adopted and reordered popular beliefs in the afterlife, the courts and justice of the unseen world. Its innovations con-

sisted of vastly expanding the bureaucracy of the dead by populating it
with the souls of its deceased adherents, creating a priesthood that could
intervene with spirit officials on the behalf of the dead and devising
rituals for the salvation of the departed. Taoism also assimilated Buddhist doctrines. It embraced the notions of a subterranean hell and reincarnation. One of its priests' duties was to pray and accumulate merit
for the salvation of ancestors. In their rituals they kowtowed, beat their
brows, and begged the gods to release souls from hell, liberate them from
the consequences of their karma and the endless cycle of reincarnation,
and permit them to ascend to the chamber of bliss in heaven.

Taoism differed from popular Chinese religion and Buddhism in its
belief that both *po*, the body, and *hun*, the spirit, survive after death. For
the vast majority of its adherents, salvation meant resurrection of the
body and the soul. After death the corpse underwent refining in a realm
at the northern reaches of the universe. The process destroyed all of its
corruptible substances, the agents of aging and dying, and transformed
it into imperishable matter. The person then became an immortal, and
therefore qualified to hold office in the bureaucracy of the otherworld.
Those who did not perform good deeds during their life time passed
into a netherworld, where they perished.

The Taoists also restructured the geography of the unseen world, creating complexes of subterranean realms in addition to celestial kingdoms
for the immortals. The grandest were the thirty-six grotto paradises located beneath holy mountains. Taoist notions about those imaginary cav-
erns sometimes stimulated authors to write tales about journeys to them
by ordinary mortals.

In 705 a rich man had a well dug on his property. His workers spent
two years on it and dug more than 1,000 feet without striking water.
One day they heard the sound of barking dogs coming from the well,
so they cut a lateral tunnel and broke through the roof of a cavern beneath which was a mountain peak. One of the diggers lowered himself
onto the peak and found himself in an extraordinary world illuminated
by its own sun and moon. It had mountain ranges and rivers that
stretched out for miles. Gold and silver palaces nestled in the mountains.
Butterflies the size of fans fluttered about giant trees with purple blossoms. The worker climbed down the mountain and came to a gate with
a sign reading Celestial Cassia Mountain Palace. Two men rushed out
of the guardhouses on either side of the portal to confront him. They
were over five feet tall and had jadelike faces with red lips, pearly teeth,
and blue hair like silk threads. They wore gold hats and robes so light
and fine that they seemed to have been woven from white fog and green
smoke. The gatekeepers asked the digger how he came to be there. As
he was explaining, more than a score of men came out of the gate, complained about the foul order emanating from the worker, and scolded

the guards. Terrified, they were giving their explanation of events when a mandarin dressed in dark red robes appeared with a decree ordering the men to treat the stranger kindly.

The gatekeepers suggested that they take the digger for a stroll. They led him to a spring, where he bathed and washed his clothes to get rid of his stench. The water was as sweet as milk. Afterward they toured the realm and came to the capital of the land, where all of the palaces were made of gold, silver, and jade. There the guards informed him that the grotto paradise, Celestial Cassia, was a way station. Immortals dwelt there for 1,918 years before they ascended to a celestial domain. They then led him to a gate through which he passed into the world above ground. When he returned to his village, the worker discovered that the year was 791. His brief stay of less than a day in the grotto paradise was equivalent to eighty-six years among the living.

The cavern realms were fit abodes for lesser immortals who evaded death by good living and rituals. There was also a very small elite of Taoist holy men who transformed their bodies into imperishable matter while still living. They accomplished the feat through a variety of methods. Some abstained from eating cereals, meat, and ale. They consumed only cypress or pine seeds, conifer resins, and mica. Occasionally, the adepts actually mummified themselves, and their corpses did not decay after they died. However, that was not the objective—an immortal did not leave his body behind—nor were dietary regimes the preferred techniques for refining the body. In medieval times Taoists relied on elixirs to convert mortal flesh and bones into immortal matter.

Elixirs, which adepts concocted through the elaborate processes of alchemy, were extraordinarily toxic mineral compounds. One formula called for eight ounces of gold, eight ounces of mercury, one pound of arsenic disulfide, and one pound of arsenic trisulfide. The allure of immortality was so powerful that even emperors were willing to take the risk of ingesting them anyway. At least five of the twenty-one Tang emperors died from swallowing those potent potions. Taoists were well aware that elixirs were deadly poisons. In one prominent case a young man received a summons to take an office in the bureaucracy governing a grotto paradise beneath a mountain. In accordance with instructions given him in a vision by two emissaries from the unseen world, he took an elixir made of mercury sulfide and committed suicide. After the death and burial of a Taoist adept, the corpse would disappear from the coffin. Sometimes disciples or kinsmen would find only a sword or slipper when they opened the casket. In some cases, however, after transforming their body into light matter on earth, the immortals might ascend directly to heaven in broad daylight.

# Epilogue: The Fall

With the assistance of the Turks, imperial forces recovered Changan on May 18, 883. Huang Chao's retreating rebels and the government's invading troops laid waste to the capital. Between 60 and 70 percent of its palaces, office buildings, and the dwellings in its markets and wards went up in flames during the pillaging. Since there were no quarters for him to occupy, Emperor Xizong ordered the mayor of the city to rebuild the metropolis. There was a shortage of labor and funds, so he was able to restore only 10 to 20 percent of the destroyed structures in the twenty-two months before the emperor returned to Changan in 885. While Xizong moved into a domicile befitting his dignity, his officials had to take up residence in abodes unbefitting theirs. Fires had consumed many of the mandarins' mansions. Consequently, high-ranking officials resorted to living in the bordellos of North Hamlet, the courtesan district.

Xizong's sojourn in Changan was short-lived. Although he brought with him the Army of Divine Strategy—some 50,000 troops—it was no match for the forces of military governors in the vicinity of the capital. The emperor directly controlled only two prefectures and the capital itself. Independent military governors ruled the provinces, as they had after the rebellion of An Lushan, and he could count on very few of those warlords for support. Nearly all regions of the empire had ceased forwarding taxes to the court, so he had few funds to raise and maintain armies. Eleven months later the dynasty's Turkish ally—offended by the court's failure to support him against a rival—swept down on the capital and Xizong fled again. When the emperor returned to Changan in 888, he found the palaces and gates in ruins. He died fourteen days later.

His successors fared no better than he. Zhaozong abandoned the capital in late summer of 895 after he narrowly escaped being shot with an arrow during a battle between rival factions of his own armies. He headed for the mountains to the south with more than 20,000 citizens—patricians and commoners—in his train. One-third of the people following him died from thirst. When he reentered Changan a couple of months later, the emperor had to move into an office building because none of his palaces survived. During his second flight the following year, pillaging soldiers demolished all of the reconstruction undertaken from 883 to 885.

The fate of the Tang dynasty was sealed in 903 when Zhu Wen, a powerful warlord, seized control of the region around Changan and the imperial court. He had his troops herd all of Zhaozong's senior eunuchs, perhaps as many as 700, into their headquarters and behead them. On February 10, 904, Zhu ordered the evacuation of the capital and changed the registration of its citizenry from that city to Luoyang. The next day his soldiers drove the people out of Changan and down the road to the east. It took more than a month for the procession to travel the 285 miles to Luoyang. The imperial cortege departed on February 16. After it left, the warlord ordered his army to dismantle all the palaces, office buildings, and homes of commoners—whatever had been rebuilt since 896—and float their timbers down the Wei and Yellow rivers to Luoyang. He sent more than 20,000 carpenters to reassemble the structures in the eastern capital. Because the emperor's quarters were not ready, his entourage had to halt along the way for several months. Just before entering Luoyang, Zhu Wen invited more than 200 of Zhaozong's young eunuchs and child polo players to a feast in a tent, then had them all strangled. Then he replaced them with his own people.

Zhu Wen reduced Changan, probably the greatest city of its time, to a wasteland. In a final act of destruction one of his subordinates razed its outer wall. Then a great windstorm, which blew for several days, struck the Serpentine Park. The gale caused great waves to form, and the lake vanished in a single night. The demise of the dynasty soon followed the ruin of its capital. Zhu Wen had Zhaozong put to the sword on September 22, 904, and placed the emperor's ninth son on the throne. Three years later, on June 1, 907, the last Tang sovereign abdicated. Zhu, who assumed the throne and founded his own dynasty, had him poisoned on March 25, 908, and bestowed the posthumous title Pitiful Sovereign on him.

The demise of the Tang was also the death of a way of life. Its aristocracy and its military ethos passed away. The rulers of the Song dynasty (960–1279) took deliberate steps to reduce the power of warriors so that they could not pose a threat to civilian authority, as the separatist governors had from 750 to 961. As a result the Song never recovered Chinese territory south of the Great Wall that the Khitan had seized nor the northwest territories that the Tibetan Tanguts had occupied. Although it maintained a huge standing army, it preferred to bribe the pastoral peoples with more than half a million ounces of gold and 400,000 lengths of silk annually. The dynasty came to depend more heavily on its navy than its army for defense. It was the first Chinese dynasty to become a great naval power. It had inherited gunpowder from the Tang and developed an arsenal of new weapons—bombs, flame throwers, and guns—that assumed an important role in its efforts to fend off its northern enemies.

Since the Song lost control of the Silk Route, merchants in the southeast developed maritime commerce and challenged Arab dominance of sea trade as far west as the east coast of India. Shipbuilding boomed in China and fortunes were made on sea trading. Anyone, even poor peasants, could invest in such trading argosies. Internal markets and commerce also enjoyed unprecedented prosperity. To facilitate trade, governments began issuing the world's first paper currency.

Under the Song dynasty the population doubled from 50 million or 60 million to 110 million by 1200. By the same year 20 percent of the empire's subjects were residing in cities, in contrast to 5 percent during the Tang. The vacant lands cultivated in Tang cities disappeared completely, and large suburbs grew outside city ramparts. Half of the capital's citizenry in the early thirteenth century—some 2 million people— lived in the metropolis's suburbs. Internally, walled wards and markets gave way to roads lined with shops. The curfew survived, but watchmen patrolled the streets to ensure that no one was burning lamps at night as a fire prevention measure, not as a means to prevent people from traveling. The capital had seventeen amusement quarters where performers entertained into the wee hours of the morning. The Gay Quarters survived, but catered to a more diverse clientele, including merchants and anyone else who could afford the pleasure.

Population pressures led to the construction of new forms of housing. Multistoried tenements appeared in which single families lived on one floor. With the exception of some streets, the broad avenues of Tang Changan vanished, and the spacing of apartment buildings was so close that their eaves touched. As a result, huge conflagrations devastated cities. A fire in Hangzhou that burned for four days during 1208 consumed 58,000 dwellings and blackened more than three square miles of the city. To avoid such destruction, merchants, empresses, and eunuchs built warehouses that had moats surrounding them. The breakdown of walled markets changed the character of the *hang*. They were not simply lanes devoted to a single commodity or service within the bazaars, but guilds that had patron deities and heads who looked after the interests of the members.

The center of the empire shifted eastward permanently. Changan, which had served as its capital off and on for nearly two millennia, would never do so again. Buddhism lost the vigor that it had had in the Tang, and Taoism experienced a burst of creativity that produced new sects and scriptures. Taoists, however, ceased to be a major factor in medicine, yielding their position to secular physicians, the "Confucian doctors." Cremation, formerly confined to Buddhists, became a popular means of disposing of the dead for all sorts of people. Women (at least aristocratic women), who had enjoyed a modicum of independence in the Tang, lost it in the Song when binding the feet—a deformation of the feet that made walking difficult—became fashionable. There was an explosion of printing that led to a wide diffusion of learning. The ease of reproducing books lowered their cost, facilitated the exchange of ideas, and stimulated interest in technologies of all sorts. It also contributed to a certain amount of social leveling, permitting men of low standing the opportunity for social advancement and acquisition of wealth.

These changes and many more created a new culture in China that was more "modern," though not in the sense that the term has been applied to Europe and the rest of the world in recent centuries, than that of the Tang. The fall of the Tang in 907 marked the end of the medieval period in Chinese history.

# Suggested Readings

## GENERAL

Benn, Charles, trans. *All My Days at Court and in the Country* (forthcoming).

Chan, Marie. *Kao Shih*. Boston, 1978.

Ch'en, Kenneth. *Buddhism in China*. Princeton, N.J., 1964.

———. *The Chinese Transformation of Buddhism*. Princeton, N.J., 1973.

Chou I-liang. "Tantrism in China." *Harvard Journal of Asiatic Studies* 8 (1945): 241–332.

Eberhard, Wolfram. *The Local Cultures of South and East China*. Leiden, 1968.

Edwards, E. D. *Chinese Prose Literature of the T'ang Period*. 2 vols. London, 1937–1938.

Hucker, Charles. *China's Imperial Past*. Stanford, Calif., 1975.

The Institute of the History of Natural Sciences, Chinese Academy of Sciences. *Ancient China's Technology and Science*. Beijing, 1983.

Kieschnick, John. *The Eminent Monk*. Honolulu, 1997.

Levy, Howard, trans. *The Dwelling of the Playful Goddess*. Tokyo, 1965.

Needham, Joseph, et al. *Science and Civilization in China*. 21 vols. Cambridge, 1962–1998.

Nienhauser, William. *Liu Tsung-yuan*. Boston, 1973.

———, ed. *The Indiana Companion to Traditional Chinese Literature*. Bloomington, Ind., 1986.

Palandri, Angela. *Yüan Chen*. Boston, 1977.

Schafer, Edward. "The Conservation of Nature Under the T'ang Dynasty." *Journal of the Economic and Social History of the Orient* 5 (1962): 279–308.

———. *The Vermilion Bird*. Berkeley, Calif., 1967.

Soper, Alexander, trans. *Kuo Jo-hsü's Experiences in Painting*. Washington, D.C., 1951.

*T'ang Studies* (1982–).

Waley, Arthur. *The Poetry and Career of Li Po.* London, 1950.

———. *The Real Tripitaka and Other Pieces.* London, 1962.

———. *The Secret History of the Mongols and Other Pieces.* London, 1963.

Wechsler, Howard. *Mirror to the Son of Heaven.* Princeton, N.J., 1974.

———. *Offerings of Jade and Silk.* New Haven, Conn., 1985.

Weins, H. J. *China's March Toward the Tropics.* Hamden, Conn., 1954.

Weinstein, Albert. *Buddhism Under the Tang.* New York, 1987.

Wilkinson, Endymion. *Chinese History, a Manual.* Cambridge, Mass., 1988.

Wright, Arthur, ed. *Perspectives on the T'ang.* New Haven, Conn., 1973.

## THE TANG DYNASTY: HISTORY AND SOCIETY

Backus, Charles. *The Nan-chao Kingdom.* Cambridge, 1981.

Chiu-Duke, Josephine. *To Rebuild the Empire.* New York, 2000.

Fitzgerald, C. P. *The Empress Wu.* Melbourne, 1955.

———. *Son of Heaven.* Melbourne, 1933.

Frankel, Hans. "T'ang Literati." In *Confucian Personalities*, ed. Arthur Wright, 64–83. Stanford, Calif., 1962.

Guisso, R.W.L. *Wu Tse-t'ien and the Politics of Legitimation in T'ang China.* Bellingham, Wash., 1978.

Levy, Howard. "The Career of Yang Kuei-fei." *T'oung Pao* 45 (1957): 451–489.

———, trans. *Biography of Huang Ch'ao.* Berkeley, Calif., 1961.

Mackerras, C., trans. *The Uighur Empire.* Canberra, 1972.

Pan Yihong. *Son of Heaven and Heavenly Qachang: Sui-Tang China and Its Neighbors.* Bellingham, Wash., 1997.

Pulleyblank, Edwin. *The Background of the Rebellion of An Lu-shan.* London, 1955.

Rideout, J. K. "The Rise of the Eunuchs During the T'ang Dynasty." *Asia Major* 1 (1949–1950): 53–72; 3 (1952): 42–58.

Rotours, Robert des. *Le Traité des fonctionnaires et Traité de l'armée* 2 vols. Paris, 1947–1948.

———. *Histoire de Ngan Lou-chan.* Paris, 1962.

Twitchett, Denis. *Financial Administration Under the T'ang Dynasty.* Cambridge, 1963.

———. "Merchant, Trade and Government in Late Tang." *Asia Major* 14 (1968): 63–95.

———. "The Tang Royal Family." *Asia Major* 7 (new series) (1994): 1–62.

———, ed. *The Cambridge History of China*, vol. 3, *Sui and T'ang China, 589–906*, part 1. London, 1979.

Wang Zhenping. "T'ang Maritime Trade Administration." *Asia Major* 38 (new series) (1991): 7–38.

Wright, Arthur, ed. *Perspectives on the T'ang.* New Haven, Conn., 1973.

Yang Lien-sheng. "Buddhist Monasteries and Four Money-Raising Institutions in Chinese History." *Harvard Journal of Asiatic Studies* 13 (1950): 174–191.

## CITIES AND URBAN LIFE

Balazs, Etienne. "Chinese Towns." In *Chinese Civilization and Bureaucracy*, 66–78. Stanford, Calif., 1954.

Dudbridge, Glen, trans. *The Tale of Li Wa*. London, 1983.
Hansen, Valerie. "Gods on Walls." In *Religion and Society in T'ang and Sung China*, ed. by Patricia Ebery, 75–114. Honolulu, 1993.
Katô Shigeshi. "On the Hang or Association of Merchants in China." *Memoirs of the Tôyô Bunka* 8 (1936): 45–83.
Leslie, Donald. "Persian Temples in T'ang China." *Monumenta Serica* 35 (1981–1983): 275–303.
Levy, Howard. "The Gay Quarters of Ch'ang-an." *Oriens/West* 7 (1962): 93–105.
———, trans. "The Original Incidents of Poems." *Sinologica* 10 (1962): 1–54.
———. "Records of the Gay Quarters." *Oriens/West* 8 (1963): 121–128; 8: 115–122; 9: 103–110.
Ma Dezhi. "The Tang Capital of Changan." In *Ancient China's Technology and Science*, 461–470. Beijing, 1983.
Rotours, Robert des, trans. *Courtesanes chinoises a la fin des T'ang*. Paris, 1968.
Schafer, Edward. "Iranian Merchants in T'ang Dynasty Tales." In *Semitic and Oriental Studies Presented to William Popper*, 403–422. Berkeley, Calif., 1951.
———. *The Golden Peaches of Samakand*. Berkeley, Calif., 1963.
———. "The Last Years of Ch'ang-an." *Oriens Extremus* 10 (1963): 93–105.
Soper, Alexander, trans. "A Vacation Glimpse of the T'ang Temples of Ch'ang-an." *Artibus Asiae* 23 (1960): 15–40.
Twitchett, Denis. "The T'ang Market System." *Asia Major* n.s. 12 (1963): 202–248.
Yang Lien-sheng. *Money and Credit in China*. Cambridge, 1952.

## HOUSE AND GARDEN

Acker, William, trans. *Some T'ang and Pre-T'ang Texts on Chinese Painting*. 2 vols. Leiden, 1954; 1974.
Beurdeley, Michel. *Chinese Furniture*. New York, 1979.
Boyd, Andrew. *Chinese Architecture and Town Planning*. Chicago, 1962.
Fitzgerald, C. P. *Barbarian Bed: The Origin of the Chair in China*. London, 1965.
Golany, Gideon. *Chinese Earth-Sheltered Dwellings*. Honolulu, 1992.
Knapp, Ronald. *China's Traditional Rural Architecture*. Honolulu, 1986.
Needham, Joseph. *Science and Civilization in China*, vol. 4, *Physics and Physical Technology*, part 3, *Civil Engineering and Nautics*. Cambridge, 1971.
———. *Science and Civilization in China*, vol. 6, *Biology and Biological Technology*, part 1, *Botany*. Cambridge, 1986.
Schafer, Edward. "Notes on T'ang Culture (1)." *Monumenta Serica* 21 (1962): 194–221.
———. "Li Te-yü and the Azalea." *Asiatische Studien* 18/19 (1965): 105–114.
———. "Notes on T'ang Culture (3)." *Monumenta Serica* 30 (1972–1973): 100–116.
Schafer, Edward, trans. *Tu Wan's Stone Catalogue of Cloudy Forest*. Berkeley, Calif., 1961.
Stein, Rolf. *The World in Miniature*, trans. by Phyllis Brooks. Stanford, Calif., 1990.
Steinhardt, Nancy, ed. *Chinese Traditional Architecture*. New York, 1984.

## CLOTHES AND HYGIENE

Kuhn, Dieter. *Science and Civilization in China*, vol. 5, part 9, *Textile Technology: Spinning and Reeling*. Cambridge, 1988.

Laufer, Berthold. *Jade: A Study in Chinese Archaeology and Religion*. New York, 1912.

———. *Felt*. Chicago, 1937.

Needham, Joseph. "Hygiene and Preventive Medicine in Ancient China." In *Clerks and Craftsmen in China and the West*, 340–378. Cambridge, 1970.

Schafer, Edward. "The Development of Bathing Customs in Ancient and Medieval China and the History of the Floriate Clear Palace." *Journal of the American Oriental Society* 76 (1956): 57–82.

———. "The Early History of Lead Pigments and Cosmetics in China." *T'oung Pao* 44 (1956): 413–438.

Schafer, Edward, and Benjamin Wallacker. "Local Tribute Products of the T'ang Dynasty." *Journal of Oriental Studies* 4 (1958): 213–248.

## FOOD AND FEASTS

Anderson, N. E. *The Food of China*. New Haven, 1988.

Benn, C. *Food and Feasts in Tang China* (in progress).

Chi Han. *Nan-fang ts'ao-mu chuang*, trans. by Li Hui-lin. Hong Kong, 1979.

Chong Key Ray. *Cannibalism in China*. Wakefield, N.H., 1990.

Graff, David. "Meritorious Cannibal." *Asia Major* 8 (1995): 1–18.

Harper, Donald. "The *Analects* Jade Calendar." *T'ang Studies* 4 (1986): 69–89.

Huang Tzu-ch'ing and Chao Yü-ts'ung. "The Preparation of Ferments and Wines." *Harvard Journal of Asiatic Studies* 9 (1945–1947): 24–44.

Laufer, Berthold. *Sino-Iranica*. Chicago, 1919.

———. *Geophagy*. Chicago, 1930.

Li Yu. *The Classic of Tea*, trans. by Francis Carpenter. New York, 1974.

Owens, Stephen. *The Poetry of the Early Tang*. New Haven, Conn., 1977.

Rotours, Robert des. "Quelques notes sur l'anthropophagie en Chine." *T'oung Pao* 50 (1963): 386–427.

———. "Encore quelques notes sur l'anthropophagie en Chine." *T'oung Pao* 54 (1968): 1–49.

Schafer, Edward. "Eating Turtles in Ancient China." *Journal of the American Oriental Society* 82 (1962): 73–74.

———. "T'ang." In *Food in Chinese Culture*, ed. by K. C. Chang, 87–140. New Haven, Conn., 1977.

Shih Shenghan. *A Preliminary Survey of the Book Ch'i Min Yao Shu*. Peking, 1962.

Ukers, William. *All About Tea*. 2 vols. New York, 1935.

## LEISURE AND ENTERTAINMENT

Benn, C. *Carnivals in the Early Tang Dynasty* (in progress).

Cutter, Robert. *The Brush and the Spur: Chinese Culture and the Cockfight*. Hong Kong, 1989.

Dolby, William. "The Origins of Chinese Puppetry." *Bulletin of the School of Oriental and African Studies* 41 (1978): 97–120.

Fu Qifeng. *Chinese Acrobatics Throughout the Ages*. Beijing, 1985.

Gulik, Robert van. *The Lore of the Chinese Lute*. Tokyo, 1969.

Kroll, Paul. "The Dancing Horses of Tang." *T'oung Pao* 67 (1981): 240–269.

Levy, Howard. "T'ang Women of Pleasure." *Sinologica* 8 (1964): 89–113.

Liang Mingyue. *Music of the Billion.* New York, 1985.

Liu, James. "Polo and Cultural Change: From T'ang to Sung China." *Harvard Journal of Asiatic Studies* 45 (1985): 203–224.

Mair, Victor, trans. *Tun-huang Popular Narratives.* Cambridge, 1983.

———. *T'ang Transformation Texts.* Cambridge, 1989.

Picken, Laurence. "Tang Music and Musical Instruments." *T'oung Pao* 55 (1969): 74–122.

———. *Music from the Tang Court.* 6 vols. Oxford and Cambridge, 1985–1997.

Rudolph, Richard. "The Antiquity of T'ou Hu." *Antiquity* 24 (1950): 175–178.

Schafer, Edward. "Notes on T'ang culture (2)." *Monumenta Serica* 24 (1965): 130–154.

———. "Hunting Parks and Animal Enclosures in Ancient China." *Journal of the Economic and Social History of the Orient* 11 (1968): 318–343.

———. *Pacing the Void.* Berkeley, Calif., 1977.

Yang Lien-sheng. "Schedules of Work and Rest in Imperial China." In *Studies in Chinese Institutional History.* Cambridge, 1961.

Yu Ta-kang. "Chinese Acrobatics, Part 2." *Echo* 6, 1 (nd): 26–32.

## TRAVEL AND TRANSPORTATION

Beal, Samuel, trans. *Si-yu-ki, Buddhist Records of the Western World.* London, 1885.

Hargett, James, trans. *On the Road in Twelfth Century China.* Stuttgart, 1989.

Needham, Joseph. *Science and Civilization in China,* vol. 4, *Physics and Physical Technology,* part 3, *Civil Engineering and Nautics.* Cambridge, 1971.

Needham, Joseph, et al. *Science and Civilization in China,* vol. 4, *Physics and Physical Technology,* part 2, *Mechanical Engineering.* Cambridge, 1965.

Reischauer, Edwin. *Ennin's Travels in T'ang China.* New York, 1955.

———. "Notes on T'ang Dynasty Sea Routes." *Harvard Journal of Asiatic Studies* 5 (1940): 142–164.

———, trans. *Ennin's Diary.* New York, 1955.

Schafer, Edward. "The Camel in China Down to the Mongol Dynasty." *Sinologica* 2 (1950): 165–194, 263–290.

Strassberg, Richard, trans. *Inscribed Landscapes.* Berkeley, Calif., 1994.

## CRIME AND PUNISHMENT

Bünger, Karl. "The Punishment of Lunatics and Negligents According to Classical Chinese Law." *Studia Sinica* 9 (1950): 1–16.

Cahill, Suzanne. "The Real Judge Dee." *Phi Theta Papers* 14 (1977): 3–19.

Ch'ü T'ung-tsu. *Law and Society in Traditional China.* Paris, 1961.

Feifel, Eugene, trans. *Po Chü-I as a Censor.* Paris, 1961.

Feng Han-yi and John Shrylock. "The Black Magic in China Known as Ku." *Journal of the American Oriental Society* 55 (1935): 1–30.

Goodrich, Chauncey. "The Ancient Chinese Prisoner's Van." *T'oung Pao* 61 (1975): 215–231.

Gulik, Robert van, trans. *T'ang-yin-pi-shih, Parallel Cases from Under the Pear-Tree.* Leiden, 1956.

Ho, Richard. *Ch'en Tzu-ang, Innovator in T'ang Poetry.* Hong Kong, 1993.

Johnson, Wallace, trans. *The T'ang Code,* vol. 1, *General Principles.* Princeton, N.J., 1979.

——. *The T'ang Code,* vol. 2, *Specific Articles.* Princeton, N.J., 1997.

Johnson, Wallace, and Denis Twitchett. "Criminal Procedure in T'ang China." *Asia Major* 3rd ser. 6 (1993): 113–146.

Lin Yutang. *Lady Wu, a Novel.* New York, 1965.

Liu, James. *The Chinese Knight-Errant,* Chicago, 1967.

MacCormack, Geoffrey. *Traditional Chinese Penal Law.* Edinburgh, 1990.

McKnight, Brian. *The Quality of Mercy.* Honolulu, 1981.

Schafer, Edward. *Shores of Pearls.* Berkeley, Calif., 1969.

Twitchett, Denis. "The Implementation of Law in Early T'ang China." *Civiltà Veneziana: Studi* 34 (1978): 57–84.

——. "The Seamy Side of Late T'ang Political Life." *Asia Major* 3rd ser. 1 (1988): 29–63.

Wallacker, Benjamin. "The Poet as Jurist: Po Chü-I and a Case of Conjugal Homicide." *Harvard Journal of Asiatic Studies* 41 (1981): 507–526.

## SICKNESS AND HEALING

Chen, Ronald. *The History and Methods of Physical Diagnosis in Classical Chinese Medicine.* New York, 1969.

Cooper, William, and Nathan Sivin. "Man as Medicine." In *Chinese Science,* ed. by Shigeru Nakayama, 203–272. Cambridge, 1973.

Despeux, Catherine. "Gymnastics: The Ancient Tradition." In *Taoist Meditation and Longevity Techniques,* ed. by Livia Kohn, 225–267. Ann Arbor, Mich., 1989.

Englehardt, Ute. "*Qi* for Life: Longevity in the Tang." In *Taoist Meditation and Longevity Techniques,* ed. by Livia Kohn, 268–296. Ann Arbor, Mich., 1989.

Hoeppli, Reinhard. *Parasites and Parasitic Infections in Early Medicine and Science.* Singapore, 1959.

Hsia, Emil, et al., trans. *The Essentials of Medicine in Ancient China and Japan.* Leiden, 1986.

Leung, Angela. "Diseases of the Premodern Period in China." In *The Cambridge World History of Human Diseases,* ed. by Kenneth Kiple, 354–361. Cambridge, 1993.

Lu Gwei-djen. *Celestial Lancets.* Cambridge, 1980.

Needham, Joseph. "China and the Origin of the Qualifying Examinations in Medicine." In *Clerks and Craftsmen in China and the West,* 379–395. Cambridge, 1970.

——. "Medicine and Chinese Culture." In *Clerks and Craftsmen in China and the West,* 263–293. Cambridge, 1970.

——. "Proto-Endocrinology in Medieval China." In *Clerks and Craftsmen in China and the West,* 294–315. Cambridge, 1970.

Read, Bernard. *A Compendium of Minerals and Stones.* Peking, 1936.

——, trans. *Chinese Materia Medica: Animal Drugs.* Peking, 1931.

——. *Chinese Materia Medica: Avian Drugs.* Peking, 1932.

———. *Chinese Materia Medica: Dragon and Snake Drugs.* Peking, 1934.

———. *Chinese Materia Medica: Turtle and Shellfish Drugs.* Peking, 1937.

———. *Chinese Materia Medica: Fish Drugs.* Peking, 1939.

———. *Chinese Materia Medica: Insect Drugs.* Peking, 1941.

Stuart, G. A. *Chinese Materia Medica.* Shanghai, 1911.

Unschuld, Paul. *Medical Ethics in Imperial China.* Berkeley, Calif., 1979.

———. *Medicine in China: A History of Ideas.* Berkeley, Calif., 1985.

———. *Medicine in China: A History of Pharmaceutics.* Berkeley, Calif., 1986.

Veith, Elza, trans. *The Yellow Emperor's Classic of Internal Medicine.* Berkeley, Calif., 1972.

Wu Jing-nuan, trans. *Ling Shu or the Spiritual Pivot.* Washington, D.C., 1993.


## LIFE CYCLE

Beurdeley, Michel. *Chinese Erotic Art.* Rutland, Vt., 1969.

Galt, H. S. *A History of Chinese Educational Institutions,* vol. 1. London, 1951.

Gulik, Robert van. *Sexual Life in Ancient China.* Leiden, 1961.

Furth, Charlotte. "From Birth to Birth." In *Chinese Views of Childhood,* ed. by Anne Kinney, 157–192. Honolulu, 1995.

Hinsch, Bret. *Passions of the Cut Sleeve: The Male Homosexual Tradition in China.* Berkeley, Calif., 1990.

Hung, William. *Tu Fu, China's Greatest Poet.* Cambridge, 1952.

Kinney, Anne. "Dyed Silk." In *Chinese Views of Childhood,* ed. by Anne Kinney, 17–56. Honolulu, 1995.

Lessa, William. *Chinese Body Divination.* Los Angeles, 1968.

Mair, Victor. "Scroll Presentation in the T'ang Dynasty." *Harvard Journal of Asiatic Studies* 38 (1978): 35–60.

Miyazaki Ichisada. *China's Examination Hell.* New Haven, Conn., 1976.

Rotours, Robert des, trans. *Le Traité des examen.* Paris, 1932.

Teng Ssu-yü, trans. *Family Instructions of the Yen Clan.* Leiden, 1968.

Waley, Arthur. *The Life and Times of Po Chü-i.* London, 1949.

Wile, Douglas, trans. *The Chinese Sexual Yoga Classics.* New York, 1992.

Wu Pei-yi. "Childhood Remembered." In *Chinese Views of Childhood,* edited by Anne Kinney, 129–156. Honolulu, 1995.

Zürcher, Erik. "Buddhism and Education in T'ang Times." In *Neo-Confucianism Education,* ed. by William Theodore de Bary, 19–56. Berkeley, Calif., 1980.


## DEATH AND THE AFTERLIFE

Bauer, Wolfgang. *China and the Search for Happiness.* New York, 1976.

Benn, Charles. *Tiger Testicles: Strange Chinese Tales of Gods, Ghosts and Goblins* (in progress).

Bokenkamp, Stephen. "Death and Ascent in *Ling-pao* Taoism." *Taoist Resources* 1 (1989): 1–20.

Cedzich, Angelika. "Ghosts and Demons, Law and Order." In *Taoist Resources* 4 (1993): 23–36.

Gjertson, Donald, trans. *Miraculous Retribution.* Berkeley, Calif., 1989.

Gómez, Luis. *Land and Bliss*. Honolulu, 1996.

Groot, J.J.M. de. *The Religious Systems of China*. 6 vols. Leiden, 1892–1910.

Hansen, Valerie. *Negotiating Daily Life in Traditional China*. New Haven, Conn., 1995.

Hou Ching-lang. *Monnaies d'offrande*. Paris, 1975.

Maspero, Henri. *Taoism and Chinese Religion*, trans. by Frank Kierman. Amherst, Mass., 1981.

Needham, Joseph. "Elixir Poisoning in Medieval China." In *Clerks and Craftsmen in China and the West*, 316–339. Cambridge, 1970.

———. *Science and Civilization in China*, vol. 5, *Chemistry and Chemical Technology*, part 2, *Spagyrical Discovery and Invention: Magisteries of Gold and Immortality*. Cambridge, 1974.

———. *Science and Civilization in China*, vol. 5, *Chemistry and Chemical Technology*, part 3, *Spagyrical Discovery and Invention: Historical Survey, from Cinnabar Elixirs to Synthetic Insulin*. Cambridge, 1976.

Seidel, Anna. "Post-Mortem Immortality: Or the Taoists' Resurrection of the Body." In *Gilgul*, ed. by S. Shakal, 223–237. Leiden, 1987.

Sivin, Nathan, trans. *Chinese Alchemy*. Cambridge, 1968.

Strickmann, Michel. "On the Alchemy of T'ao Hung-ching." In *Facets of Taoism*, ed. by Holmes Welch and Anna Seidel, 123–191. New Haven, Conn., 1979.

Teiser, Stephen. *The Ghost Festival in Medieval China*. Princeton, N.J., 1988.

———. "The Growth of Purgatory." In *Religion and Society in T'ang and Sung China*, ed. by Patricia Ebery, 115–146. Honolulu, 1993.

———. *The Scripture of the Ten Kings*. Honolulu, 1994.

# Index

**About the Author**

CHARLES BENN is an independent scholar and an adjunct professor at The University of Hawai'i.